THE WORLD'S GREATEST
AIRCRAFT

THE WORLD'S GREATEST
AIRCRAFT

Christopher Chant

CHARTWELL
BOOKS, INC.

This edition published in 2011 by
CHARTWELL BOOKS, INC.
A division of BOOK SALES, INC.
276 Fifth Avenue Suite 206
New York, NY 10001
USA

Reprinted 2011, 2013, 2014

Copyright © 2011, 2013 Regency House Publishing Limited.
The Manor House
High Street
Buntingford
Hertfordshire
SG9 9AB
United Kingdom

www.regencyhousepublishing.com

ISBN-13: 978-0-7858-2851-8

Printed in China

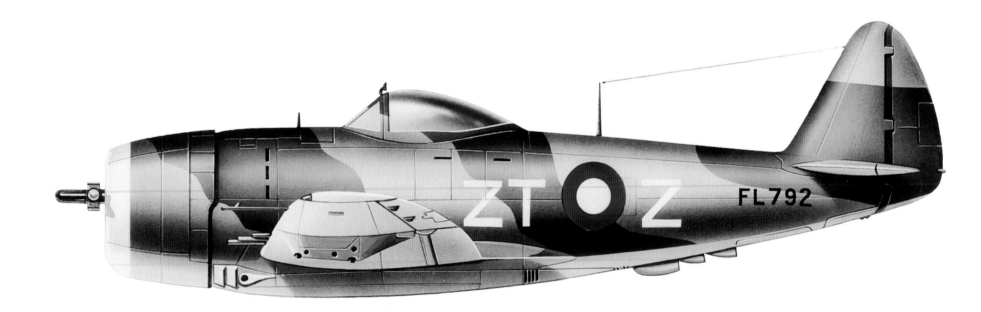

CONTENTS

EARLY
FIGHTERS

PISTON-ENGINED FIGHTERS

Tremendous pioneering achievements in the field of aeroplane development during the first decade of the 20th century meant that it took under six years from the first flight of the Wright Flyer to put a military aeroplane into service with the U.S. Army, in the form of a Wright Model A in 1909. Just two years later, reconnaissance and light bombing using aeroplanes had been extensively practised within America and by others abroad, and in the same year Italy flew the world's first operational missions against Turkish forces, observing positions and dropping explosives. With land warfare conducted by vast ground armies, aeroplanes were seen as convenient 'eyes in the sky', of greater worth than tethered observation balloons but not so vital that they should be allowed to 'frighten the horses'.

Meanwhile, in 1910 a rifle had been fired from a U.S. Army Curtiss biplane. Little significance was drawn from the event and no immediate thought was given to the possibility of arming aeroplanes with guns. Reconnaissance, light bombing and artillery spotting, therefore, continued to be the official roles for aeroplanes up to and beyond the outbreak of World War I. Similarly, when in Britain in 1911 Major Brooke-Popham of the Air Battalion, Royal Engineers, attempted to fix a gun to a Blériot monoplane, he was ordered to remove it in no uncertain terms. Apathy also

attended experiments in America in June 1912, when the newly-invented Lewis machine-gun was fired from an Army Signal Corps Wright Model B by Captain Charles de Forest Chandler. However, the day of the fighting aeroplane was drawing close.

The British Admiralty became an early driving force for arming offensive aeroplanes, and in November 1912 contracted Vickers to design and produce an experimental fighting biplane. The Vickers EFB1 Destroyer, as it became, was put on display at the February 1913 Olympia Aero Show, featuring a rear-mounted pusher engine/propeller and a

nose-mounted Vickers-Maxim machine-gun with a 60° angle of vertical/horizontal movement. Also appearing at the Show was Claude Grahame-White's Type 6 Military Biplane, which offered a wider field of fire for its Colt gun. It was, however, the Destroyer that is best remembered, leading eventually to the development of the famed wartime FB5 Gun Bus fighter which joined British forces in France in early 1915.

Both British fighters at Olympia in 1913 featured pusher engines and propellers, allowing the nose gun in each to be fired forwards without the worry of

hitting the propeller. Other countries later adopted combat aircraft of similar layout, notably the French Voisin that, in early form in October 1914, claimed the first-ever air-to-air victory by gunfire, shooting down a German two-seater.

Since 1913 several countries had produced 'scouting' aeroplanes, front-engined biplanes and monoplanes of more modern streamlined design than the pusher types, often single-seaters and intended mainly for high-speed unarmed reconnaissance but also capable of other uses including 'nuisance' raids and light bombing. Because of their front-turning propellers, fitting them with forward-firing guns had not appeared possible. But, if this could be done, a deadly new weapon would emerge, capable of catching and destroying enemy reconnaissance aircraft and even scouts before they reported back to base. The problem to be faced, however, looked daunting; how to fire a machine-gun through the arc of a turning propeller without damaging the blades and thereby destroying the aircraft.

Raymond Saulnier of the Morane-Saulnier company in France and Franz Schneider of LVG in Germany worked separately on the problem and in 1913/14 devised systems, but for various technical reasons neither was adopted. Instead, with war declared, Morane-Saulnier came up with a simple alternative and fitted

deflector plates (wedges to divert striking bullets) to the propeller of a Morane-Saulnier monoplane, providing a solution of sorts without technical difficulty. Given an early machine, Frenchman Roland Garros shot down his first enemy aircraft on April 1 1915, the first-ever air victory by a fighter firing a gun through the propeller arc.

Unfortunately, he made an emergency landing behind enemy lines on the 19th, thereby passing the secret to the Germans.

Though Germany viewed the deflector system with interest, Fokker returned to the better synchronized 'interrupter' gear method of timing bullets to fire between the turning blades and quickly convinced the authorities that he had a workable system. First combat tested on a converted Fokker M5K reconnaissance monoplane with great success, it lead to the production of the world's first operational fighter with a synchronized gun, the single-seat Fokker E series Eindecker. Though not fast, the small number of Eindeckers soon widened their role from merely offering defence for German reconnaissance two-seaters to searching the skies for vulnerable Allied aircraft. For ten months from the summer of 1915 Eindeckers dominated the Western Front, a period that became known to the Allies as the 'Fokker Scourge' due to extremely heavy losses. The true fighter had exploded onto the scene.

The Type 11 was the fighter largely instrumental for the defeat of the 'Fokker Scourge' in 1916. Planned as a

competition sesquiplane to take part in the Gordon Bennett Trophy race of 1914, the first Type 11 was designed and built in a mere four months. The outbreak of World War I led to the race's cancellation, but the Type 11 was nonetheless recognized as possessing the performance and flight characteristics to make it a useful military aircraft. Early Type 11 aircraft were powered by the 60-kW (80-hp) Le Rhône rotary engine, and were used by the French and British as scouts from 1915. The aircraft's apparent daintiness led to the nickname Bébé (Baby). The Type 11 was then turned into a fighter by the addition of a machine-gun on the upper-wing centre section to fire over the propeller's swept disc.

Many more aircraft were built under licence in Italy by Macchi with the designation Nieuport 1100. The Type 16 was a version with the 82-kW (110-hp) Le Rhône rotary for better performance. The Type 17 was a further expansion of the same design concept with a strengthened airframe but the same 82-kW (110-hp) Le Rhône. The new model retained its predecessors' excellent agility but offered superior performance, including a sparkling rate of climb. The fighter's 7.7-mm (0.303-in) Lewis gun was located on a sliding mount that allowed the pilot to pull the weapon's rear down, allowing oblique upward fire and also making for easier reloading.

The slightly later Type 17bis

introduced the 97-kW (130-hp) Clerget rotary and a synchronized machine-gun on the upper fuselage. Still later models were the Type 21 with the 60-kW (80-hp), later the 82-kW (110-hp), Le Rhône and larger ailerons, and the slightly heavier Type 23 with 60- or 89-kW (120-hp) Le Rhône engines.

OPPOSITE: Fokker E.III, the improved and most produced version of the famous Eindecker fighter of World War I

ABOVE: Nieuport 11 Bébé

NIEUPORT 11 BÉBÉ & 17 (France)

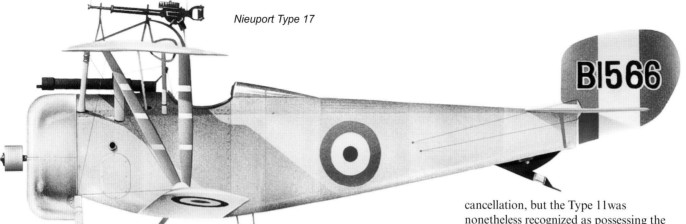

Nieuport Type 17

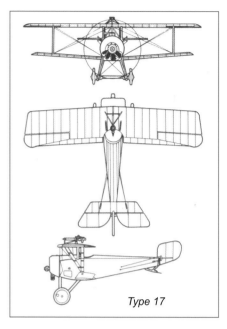

Type 17

Nieuport Type 11

The Type 11 was the fighter largely instrumental for the defeat of the 'Fokker Scourge' in 1916. Planned as a competition sesquiplane to take part in the Gordon Bennett Trophy race of 1914, the first Type 11 was designed and built in a mere four months. The outbreak of World War I led to the race's cancellation, but the Type 11 was nonetheless recognized as possessing the performance and flight characteristics to make it a useful military aircraft. Early Type 11 aircraft were powered by the 60-kW (80-hp) Le Rhône rotary engine, and were used by the French and British as scouts from 1915. The aircraft's apparent daintiness led to the nickname Bébé (Baby). The Type 11 was then turned into a fighter by the addition of a machine-gun on the upper-wing centre section to fire over the propeller's swept disc.

Many more aircraft were built under licence in Italy by Macchi with the designation Nieuport 1100. The Type 16 was a version with the 82-kW (110-hp) Le Rhône rotary for better performance. The Type 17 was a further expansion of the same design concept with a strengthened airframe but the same 82-kW (110-hp) Le Rhône. The new model retained its predecessors' excellent agility but offered superior performance, including a sparkling rate of climb. The fighter's 7.7-mm (0.303-in) Lewis gun was located on a sliding mount that allowed the pilot to pull the weapon's rear down, allowing oblique upward fire and also making for easier reloading.

The slightly later Type 17bis introduced the 97-kW (130-hp) Clerget rotary and a synchronized machine-gun on the upper fuselage. Still later models were the Type 21 with the 60-kW (80-hp), later the 82-kW (110-hp), Le Rhône and larger ailerons, and the slightly heavier Type 23 with 60- or 89-kW (120-hp) Le Rhône engines.

NIEUPORT TYPE 11
Role: Fighter
Crew/Accommodation: One
Power Plant: One 80 hp Gnôme or Le Rhône 9C air-cooled rotary
Dimensions: Span 7.55 m (24.77 ft); length 5.8 m (19.03 ft); wing area 13 m² (140 sq ft)
Weights: Empty 344 kg (759 lb); MTOW 550 kg (1,213 lb)
Performance: Maximum speed 156 km/h (97 mph) at sea level; operational ceiling 4,600 m (15,090 ft); range 330 km (205 miles) with full bombload
Load: One .303-inch machine gun

SPAD S.7 & S.13 (France)

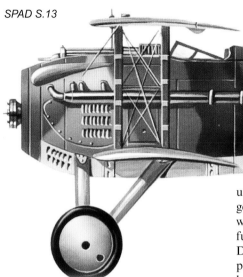

SPAD S.13

cylinder banks of which nestled a 37-mm moteur canon. Further development produced the S.13 that first flew in April 1917 for service from May of the same year. This has two guns rather than one, more power, slightly greater span and a number of aerodynamic refinements. Production of this superb fighter totalled 8,472 aircraft.

SPAD S.13
Role: Fighter
Crew/Accommodation: One
Power Plant: One 220-hp Hispano-Suiza 8 BEC water-cooled inline
Dimensions: Span 8 m (26.3 ft); length 6.2 m (20.33 ft); wing area 21.1 m² (227.1 sq ft)
Weights: Empty 565 kg (1,245 lb); MTOW 820 kg (1,807 lb)
Performance: Maximum speed 222 km/h (138 mph) at sea level; operational ceiling 5,400 m (17,717 ft); range 402 km (250 miles)
Load: Two .303-in machine guns

These two closely related aircraft were France's best fighters of World War I, combining high performance and structural strength without too great a sacrifice of agility. The result was an excellent gun platform comparable with the S.E.5a in British service. After experience with the A1 to A5 aircraft, designer Louis Béchereau turned to the conventional tractor biplane layout for the S.5 that first flew in the closing stages of 1915 and became in effect the prototype for the S.7, which was the first genuinely successful warplane developed by the Société Pour l'Avions et Ses Dérives which is what the original but bankrupt Société Pour les Appareils Deperdussin became after its purchase by Louis Blériot.

The first S.7 flew early in 1916 with a 112-kW (150-hp) Hispano-Suiza 8Aa inline and a single synchronized 7.7-mm (0.303-in) Vickers machine-gun, and was a sturdy two-bay biplane with

unstaggered wings, fixed tail skid landing gear, and a wooden structure covered with fabric except over the forward fuselage, which was skinned in light alloy. Delivery of the essentially similar first production series of about 500 aircraft began in September 1916, being followed by some 6,000 examples of an improved

model with the 134-kW (180-hp) HS 8Ac engine and wings of slightly increased span. In 1917 the company flew two development aircraft, and the S.12 with the 149-kW (200-hp) HS 8Bc paved the way for a production series of some 300 aircraft, including some with the 164-kW (220-hp) HS 8 Bec engine between the

SPAD S.13

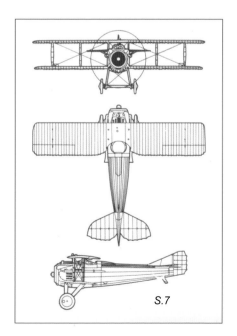

S.7

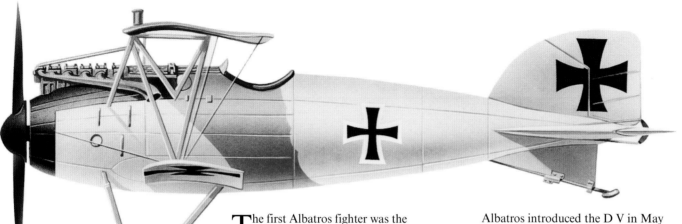

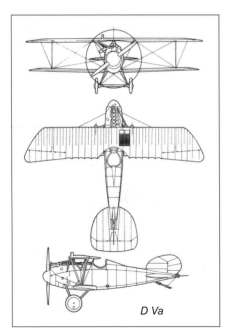

D Va

was then placed on this model and its D Va derivative with the upper wing and aileron control system of the D III. In fact the D V and D Va were outclassed by Allied fighters, and their lower wings were structurally deficient in the dive.

The first Albatros fighter was the excellent D I with virtually identical but staggered upper and lower wings connected toward their outboard ends by parallel interplane struts. The D II was basically similar, apart from the lowering of the upper wing to provide the pilot with improved forward and upward fields of vision. In an effort to improve manoeuvrability, designer Robert Thelen then moved to the D III with a revised and unstaggered wing cellule in which an increased-span upper wing was connected to the smaller and narrower-chord lower wing by V-section interplane struts.

The D III entered service in spring 1917 and proved most successful until the Allies introduced types such as the Royal Aircraft Factory S.E.5, Sopwith Camel and Spad S.13 in the late summer of the same year. During the course of the fighter's production, engine power was raised from 127- to 130-kW (170- to 175-hp) by increasing the compression ratio, and the radiator was shifted from the upper-wing centre section into the starboard upper wing so that the pilot would not be scalded if the radiator was punctured.

Albatros introduced the D V in May 1917 with features such as a still further lowered upper wing, a modified rudder, a revised aileron control system, and a larger spinner providing nose entry for a deeper elliptical rather than flat-sided plywood fuselage to reduce drag and so boost performance. Greater emphasis

ALBATROS D III
Role: Fighter
Crew/Accommodation: One
Power Plant: One 175-hp Mercedes D IIIa water-cooled inline
Dimensions: Span 9.05 m (29.76 ft); length 7.33 m (24 ft); wing area 20.5 m² (220.7 sq ft)
Weights: Empty 680 kg (1,499 lb); MTOW 886 kg (1,953 lb)
Performance: Maximum speed 175 km/h (109 mph) at 1,000 m (3,280 ft); operational ceiling 5,500 m (18,045 ft); endurance 2 hours
Load: Two 7.92-mm machine guns

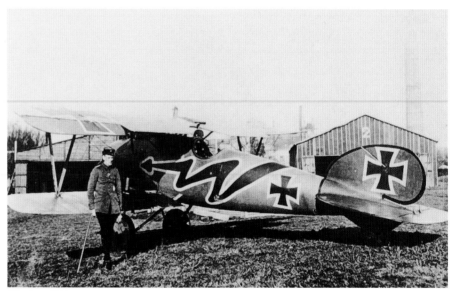

Albatros D Va

BRISTOL F.2 FIGHTER Series (United Kingdom)

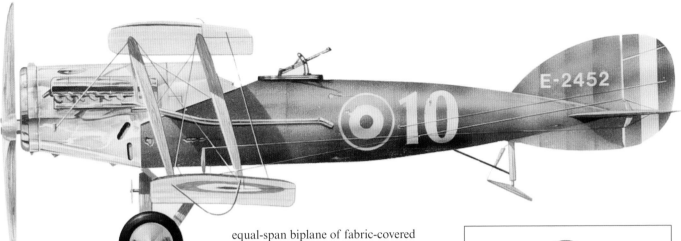

The F.2 Fighter was the best two-seat combat aircraft of World War I, even though it was designed in 1916 as a reconnaissance type. The design was an equal-span biplane of fabric-covered wooden construction, and in its original R.2A form it was planned round an 89-kW (120-hp) Beardmore engine. The availability of the 112-kW (150-hp) Hispano-Suiza engine resulted in the concept's revision as the slightly smaller R.2B sesquiplane, and further revision

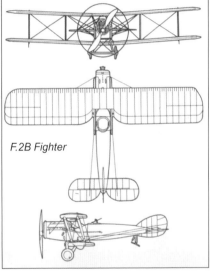

F.2B Fighter

F.2A entered service in February 1917.

The type's combat debut was disastrous, four out of six aircraft being lost to an equal number of Albatros D III fighters. But as soon as pilots learned to fly their F.2As as if they were single-seaters, with additional firepower provided by the gunner, the type became highly successful. The rest of the Fighter's 5,308-aircraft production run was of the F.2B variant with successively more powerful engines and modifications to improve fields of vision and combat-worthiness. Other designations were F.2C for a number of experimental re-enginings, F.2B Mk II for 435 new and reconditioned and tropicalized machines for army co-operation duties in the Middle East and India, Fighter Mk III for 80 strengthened aircraft delivered in 1926 and 1927, and Fighter Mk IV for Mk III conversions with strengthened structure and landing gear as well as a balanced rudder and automatic leading-edges slots. The RAF retired its last Fighters in 1932.

Bristol F.2B

was then made so that the R.2B could also be fitted with the 142-kW (190-hp) Rolls-Royce Falcon engine. In August 1916, two prototypes and 50 production aircraft were ordered. Before the first prototypes flew in September 1916 the type had been reclassified as the F.2A fighter. All 50 aircraft were delivered together with the Falcon engine, and the

BRISTOL F.2B
Role: Fighter
Crew/Accommodation: Two
Power Plant: One 275-hp Rolls-Royce Falcon III water-cooled inline
Dimensions: Span 11.96 m (39.25 ft); length 7.87 m (25.83 ft); wing area 37.6 m² (405 sq ft)
Weights: Empty 875 kg (1,930 lb); MTOW 1,270 kg (2,800 lb)
Performance: Maximum speed 201 km/h (125 mph) at sea level; operational ceiling 6,096 m (20,000 ft); endurance 3 hours
Load: Two or three .303-inch machine guns plus up to 54.4 kg (120 lb) of bombs

ROYAL AIRCRAFT FACTORY S.E.5 (United Kingdom)

Royal Aircraft Factory S.E.5a

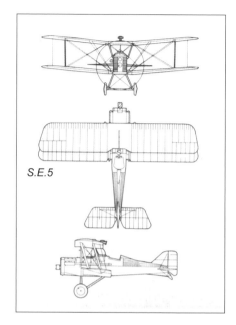

S.E.5

The best aircraft to be designed by the Royal Aircraft Factory, and also the mount of several celebrated British aces of World War I, the S.E.5 was designed by H.P. Folland. Given the minimal levels of training received by pilots before their posting to the front, Folland decided to make his new aircraft easy to fly; thus a static inline engine was preferred to a rotary engine with all its torque problems, and a fair measure of inherent stability was built into the design. At the same time, Folland opted for an extremely strong airframe that was also easy to manufacture. Construction was entirely orthodox for the period, with fabric covering over a wooden primary structure. The result was a fighter that was an exceptionally good gun platform but, without sacrifice of structural strength, possessed good performance

and adequate agility. The armament was an unusual variant on the standard pair of 7.7-mm (0.303-in) machine guns; one was a synchronized Vickers gun located in the forward fuselage and firing through the disc swept by the propeller, while the other was a Lewis located on a rail over the centre section and firing over the propeller. The Lewis gun could be pulled back and down along a quadrant rear extension of its rear so that the pilot could change ammunition drums. The S.E.5 was powered by a 112-kW (150-hp) Hispano-Suiza 8 inline and began to

enter service in April 1917.

From the summer of the same year it was complemented and then supplanted by the S.E.5a version with a 149-kW (200-hp) engine. There were at first a number of teething problems with the engine and the Constantinesco synchronizer gear, but once these had been overcome the S.E.5a matured as a quite superlative fighter that could also

double in the ground-attack role with light bombs carried under the wings. Total production was 5,205 aircraft.

ROYAL AIRCRAFT FACTORY S.E.5a
Role: Fighter
Crew/Accommodation: One
Power Plant: One 200-hp Wolseley W.4A Viper water-cooled inline
Dimensions: Span 8.12 m (26.63 ft); length 6.38 m (20.92 ft); wing area 22.84 m^2 (245.8 sq ft)
Weights: Empty 635 kg (1,399 lb); MTOW 880 kg (1,940 lb)
Performance: Maximum speed 222 km/h (138 mph) at sea level; operational ceiling 5,182 m (17,000 ft); endurance 2.5 hours
Load: Two .303-inch machine guns, plus up to 45 kg (100 lb) of bombs

The Royal Aircraft Factory S.E.5a was an outstanding fighter

SOPWITH CAMEL (United Kingdom)

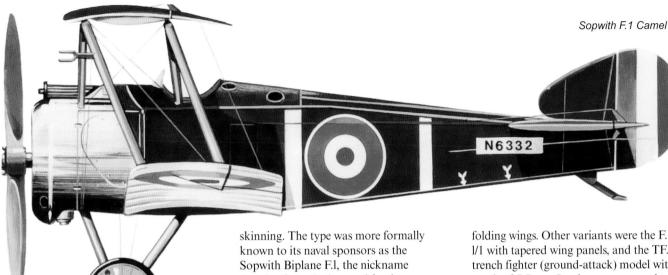

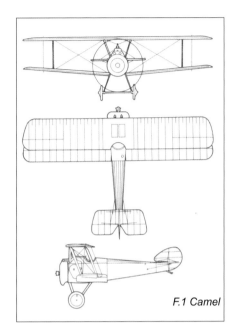

Sopwith F.1 Camel

F.1 Camel

The Camel was clearly an evolution of the Pup's design concept and was in fact designed to supplant this type, but had all its major masses (engine, fuel/lubricant, guns/ammunition and pilot) located in the forward 2.1 m (7 ft) of the fuselage, on and around the centre of gravity to offer the least inertial resistance to agility. The type was therefore supremely manoeuvrable; the torque of the powerful rotary meant that a three-quarter turn to the right could be achieved as swiftly as a quarter turn to the left, but this also meant that the type could easily stall and enter a tight spin if it was not flown with adequate care.

In configuration Camel was a typical single-bay braced biplane with fixed tailwheel landing gear, and was built of wood with fabric covering except over the forward fuselage, which had light alloy

skinning. The type was more formally known to its naval sponsors as the Sopwith Biplane F.l, the nickname deriving from the humped fuselage over the breeches of the two synchronized 7.7-mm (0.303-in) Vickers machine guns that comprised the armament. Production of 5,490 aircraft made this the most important British fighter of late 1917 and 1918. The type was powered in its production forms by a number of Bentley, Clerget, Gnôme and Le Rhône rotary engines in the power class between 75 and 112 kW (100 and 150 hp), though some experimental variants had engines of up to 134-kW (180-hp) rating. Some F.ls were operated from ships, but a specialized derivative for this role was the 2F. 1 with

folding wings. Other variants were the F. l/1 with tapered wing panels, and the TF. 1 trench fighter (ground-attack) model with a pair of 7.7-mm Lewis guns arranged to fire obliquely downward and forward through the cockpit floor, but neither of these entered production.

SOPWITH F.1 CAMEL

Role: Fighter
Crew/Accommodation: One
Power Plant: One 130-hp Clerget 9B air-cooled rotary
Dimensions: Span 8.53 m (28 ft); length 5.71 m (18.75 ft): wing area 21.5 m² (231 sq ft)
Weights: Empty 436 kg (962 lb); MTOW 672 kg (1,482 lb)
Performance: Maximum speed 168 km/h (104.5 mph) at 3,048 (10,000 ft); operational ceiling 5,486 m (18,000 ft); endurance 2.5 hours
Load: Two .303-inch machine guns

Sopwith F.1 Camel

FOKKER Dr. I (Germany)

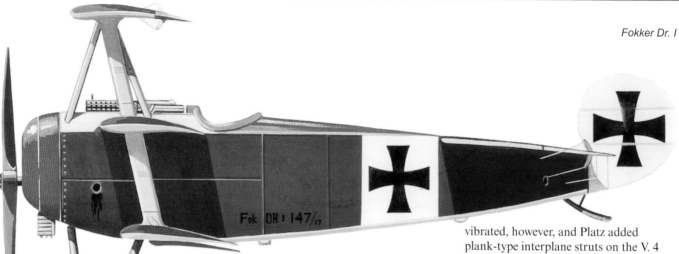

Fokker Dr. I

capabilities, which were modest in the extreme, but of the fact that it was flown by a number of aces who had the skills to exploit the Dr. I's superb agility in the defensive air combat waged by Germany over the Western Front. The type was grounded late in 1917 because of structural failures in the wing cellule, but with this defect remedied, the type was swiftly restored to service. Production ended in May 1918 after the delivery of about 300 aircraft.

FOKKER Dr. I
Role: Fighter
Crew/Accommodation: One
Power Plant: One 110-hp Oberursel U.R. II air-cooled rotary
Dimensions: Span 7.17 m (23.52 ft); length 5.77 m (18.93 ft); wing area 16 m² (172.2 sq ft)
Weights: Empty 405 kg (893 lb); MTOW 585 kg (1,289 lb)
Performance: Maximum speed 185 km/h (115 mph) at sea level; operational ceiling 5,975 m (19,603 ft); range 210 km (130 miles)
Load: Two 7.92-mm machine guns

in fabric) added triplane wings. These were of thick section and wooden construction, with plywood covering as far aft as the spar, and were cantilever units that did not require bracing wires or interplane struts. In flight the wings vibrated, however, and Platz added plank-type interplane struts on the V. 4 second prototype that also incorporated a number of aerodynamic refinements. The type was put into production during the summer of 1917 as the F. I, though this designation was soon altered to Dr. I. The new triplane soon built up a phenomenal reputation, though this was the result not of the type's real

When the Sopwith Triplane entered British service in the spring of 1917, German pilots were quick to notice and appreciate this novel type's high climb rate and excellent manoeuvrability. When this information filtered back to aircraft manufacturers in Germany, there appeared an almost literal plague of triplane fighter prototypes. One of these manufacturers was Fokker, whose V. 3 prototype was designed by Reinhold Platz, who had become Fokker's chief designer after the death of Martin Kreutzer in a flying accident during June 1916.

Platz decided on a rotary-engined fighter of light weight for maximum agility rather than high performance, and to the typical Fokker fuselage and tail unit (welded steel tube structures covered

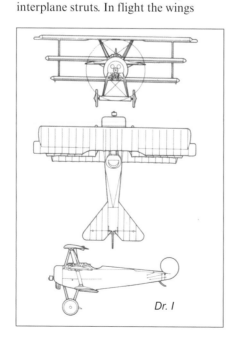

Dr. I

Replica of Baron Manfred Von Richthofen's Fokker Dr. I

FOKKER D. VII (Germany)

Fokker D. VII

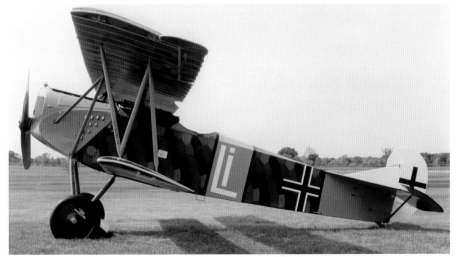

The Fokker D. VII was perhaps the best fighter of World War I

The D. VII was arguably the finest fighter of World War I, for it was a package that featured great structural strength, considerable agility, good firepower and a combination of those intangible qualities that go to making a 'pilot's aircraft'. The type was developed for Germany's first single-seat fighter competition, and the VII prototype made its initial flight just before this during January 1918. This machine had many similarities to the Dr. I triplane in its fuselage, tail unit and landing gear. Reinhold Platz, designer of the D. VII, intended his new fighter to offer considerably higher performance than that of the Dr. I, and for this reason a more powerful inline engine, the 119-kW (160-hp) Mercedes D.III, was installed. This dictated the use of larger biplane wings. Despite the N-type interplane struts, these were cantilever units of Platz's favourite thick aerofoil section and wooden construction with plywood-covered leading edges.

As a result of its success in the competition, the type was ordered into immediate production as the D. VII. Within three months, the type was in operational service, and some 700 had been delivered by the time of the Armistice. The type proved a great success in the type of defensive air fighting forced on the Germans at this stage of World War I.

It was particularly impressive in the high-altitude role as it possessed a good ceiling and also the ability to 'hang on its propeller' and fire upward at higher aircraft. Later examples were powered by the 138-kW (185-hp) BMW III inline for still better performance at altitude, and a number of experimental variants were built. Fokker returned to his native Netherlands at the end of the war, in the process smuggling back components for a number of D. VIIs as a prelude to resumed construction.

FOKKER D. VII
Role: Fighter
Crew/Accommodation: One
Power Plant: One 160-hp Mercedes D.III water-cooled inline
Dimensions: Span 8.9 m (29.2 ft); length 6.95 m (22.8 ft); wing area 20.25 m² (218 sq ft)
Weights: Empty 700 kg (1,543 lb); MTOW 878 kg (1,936 lb)
Performance: Maximum speed 188 km/h (117 mph) at 1,000 m (3,281 ft); operational ceiling 6,100 m (20,013 ft); range 215 km (134 miles)
Load: Two 7.9-mm machine guns

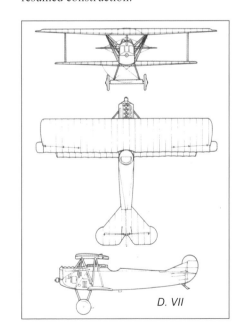

D. VII

ARMSTRONG WHITWORTH SISKIN (United Kingdom)

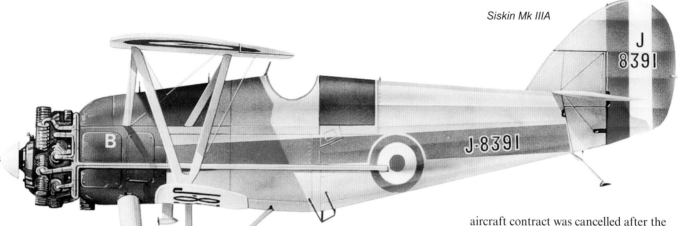

Siskin Mk IIIA

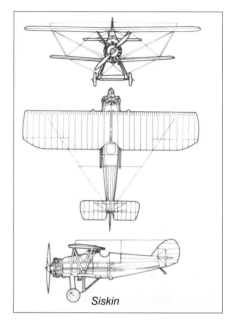

Siskin

The Siskin was the mainstay of the Royal Air Force's fighter arm in the mid-1920s, and originated from the Siddeley Deasy S.R.2 of 1919. This was designed to use the 224-kW (300-hp) Royal Aircraft Factory 8 radial engine, a promising type whose final development was later passed to Siddeley Deasy but then put to one side so that the company could concentrate its efforts on the Puma.

The type first flew with the 239-kW (320-hp) A.B.C. Dragonfly radial and then as the Armstrong Siddeley Siskin with the definitive 242-kW (325-hp) Armstrong Siddeley Jaguar radial in 1921. The Siskin offered promising capabilities but, because the Air Ministry now demanded a primary structure of metal to avoid the possibility of wood shortages in the event of a protracted

war, had to be recast as the Siskin Mk III of 1923 with a fabric-covered structure of aluminium alloy.

The 64 examples of the Siskin Mk began to enter service in May 1924 with the 242-kW (325-hp) Jaguar III. These were later supplemented by 348 examples of the Siskin Mk IIIA, together with the supercharged Jaguar IV and 53 examples of the Siskin Mk IIIDC dual-control trainer variant. The Siskin Mk IIIB, Mk IV and Mk V were experimental and racing machines. In October 1924 Romania placed an order for the Siskin, but unfortunately the balance of the 65-

aircraft contract was cancelled after the fatal crash of one of the first seven aircraft to be delivered. In British service, the Siskin was replaced by the Bristol Bulldog from October 1932, but in Canadian service the type was not replaced by the Hawker Hurricane until as late as 1939.

ARMSTRONG WHITWORTH SISKIN Mk IIIA
Role: Fighter
Crew/Accommodation: One
Power Plant: One 400-hp Armstrong Siddeley Jaguar IVS
Dimensions: Span 10.11 m (33.16 ft); length 7.72 m (25.33 ft); wing area 27.22 m² (293 sq ft)
Weights: Empty 997 kg (2,198 lb); MTOW, 1,260 kg (2,777 lb)
Performance: Maximum speed 227 km/h (141 mph) at sea level; operational ceiling 6,401 m (21,600 ft); endurance 2.75 hours
Load: Two .303-inch machine guns

Armstrong Whitworth Siskin Mk IIIA

BOEING PW-9 & FB (U.S.A.)

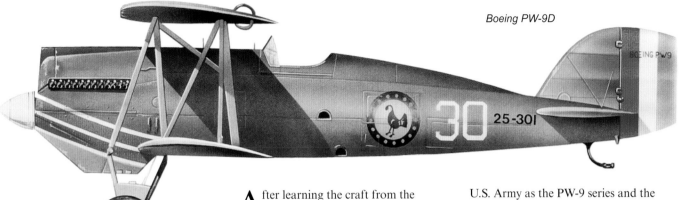

Boeing PW-9D

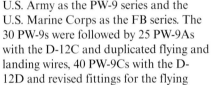

After learning the craft from the manufacture of another company's designs, most notably the Thomas-Morse MB-3A, Boeing entered the fighter market with the Model 15 that first flew in June 1923 as an unequal-span biplane with a massive 324-kW (435-hp) Curtiss D-12 inline engine. The fixed landing gear was of the through-axle type, and while the flying surfaces were of wooden construction the fuselage was of welded steel tube; most of the airframe was covered in fabric. Performance was impressive, and after the type had been evaluated by the U.S. Army as the XPW-9, two more XPW-9s were ordered.

The second of these aircraft had divided landing gear, and it was this type that was ordered into production for the U.S. Army as the PW-9 series and the U.S. Marine Corps as the FB series. The 30 PW-9s were followed by 25 PW-9As with the D-12C and duplicated flying and landing wires, 40 PW-9Cs with the D-12D and revised fittings for the flying and landing wires, and 16 PW-9Ds with a balanced rudder that was retrofitted to earlier aircraft. A total of 14 FB-ls was ordered for the U.S. Marines, this model being virtually identical to the PW-9. Only 10 were delivered as such, the last four being used for experimental purposes with different engines (the Packard 1 A-1500 inline in the first three and the Wright P-l then Pratt & Whitney Wasp radial in the last) and designations in the sequence from FB-2 to FB-6 except FB-5. This was reserved for 27 aircraft with the Packard 2A-1500 engine, revised landing gear and in addition to this increased wing stagger.

BOEING PW-9
Role: Fighter
Crew/Accommodation: One
Power Plant: One 435-hp Curtiss D-12 water-cooled inline
Dimensions: Span 9.75 m (32 ft); length 7.14 m (23.42 ft); wing area 24.15 m² (260 sq ft)
Weights: Empty 878 kg (1,936 lb); MTOW 1,415 kg (3,120 lb)
Performance: Maximum speed 256 km/h (159.1 mph) at sea level; operational ceiling 5,768 m (18,925 ft); range 628 km (390 miles)
Load: One .5-inch and one .303-inch machine guns

PW-9D

Boeing PW-9D

Curtiss F6C Hawk

Curtiss F6C-3 Hawk

With its Model L-18-1, Curtiss began the private-venture development of an advanced fighter that was to prove one of the decisive designs of the 1920s. The type first flew late in 1922 but was followed by only 25 PW-8 production fighters for the U.S. Army. The XPW-8B experimental variant with the 328-kW (440-hp) Curtiss D-12 engine introduced tapered wings and other alterations, resulting in an order for 10 examples of the P-l production variant. This was then produced in a bewildering number of developed variants, of which the most significant were the 25 P-lAs with detail improvements, the 25 P-lBs with the 324-kW (435-hp) Curtiss V-1150-3 engine and larger-diameter wheels, and the 33 P-ICs with the V-1150-5 wheel brakes and provision for alternative ski landing gear. The type was also developed as the AT-4 advanced trainer. The type was based on the P-lA but engined with the 134-kW (180-hp) Wright-Hispano E, and of the 40 aircraft ordered, 35 became P-lDs when re-engined with the V-1150, and the other five became AT-5s with the 164-kW (220-hp) Wright Whirlwind J-5 radial; they were later converted to P-lEs with the V-1150 engine. Some 31 AT-5As with a longer fuselage were ordered, but soon became P-1F fighters with the V-1150 engine.

The army's P-l series was also attractive to the U.S. Navy, which ordered the type with the designation F6C. The F6C-1 was intended for land-based use by the U.S. Marine Corps and was all but identical with the P-l, but only five were delivered as such, while the four others were delivered as F6C-2s with carrier landing equipment including an arrester hook. The F6C-3 was a modified F6C-2, and these 35 aircraft were followed by 31 of the F6C-4 that introduced the 313-kW (420-hp) Pratt & Whitney R-1340 Wasp radial in place of the original D-12 inline.

CURTISS F6C-3 HAWK
Role: Naval carrierborne fighter
Crew/Accommodation: One
Power Plant: One 400-hp Curtiss D.12 Conqueror water-cooled inline
Dimensions: Span 9.63 m (31.6 ft); length6. 96 m (22.83 ft); wing area 23.41 m² (252 sq ft)
Weights: Empty 980 kg (2,161 lb); MTOW 1,519 kg (3,349 lb)
Performance: Maximum speed 248 km/h (154 mph) at sea level; operational ceiling 6,187 m (20,300 ft); range 565 km (351 miles)
Load: Two .303-inch machine guns

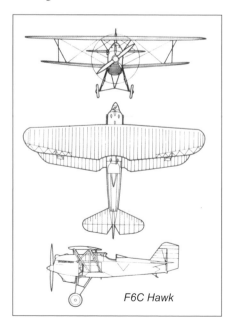

F6C Hawk

BRISTOL BULLDOG (United Kingdom)

Bristol Bulldog Mk IIA

By the mid-1920s, the performance of light day bombers, such as the Fairey Fox, was outstripping the defensive capabilities of fighters such as the Armstrong Whitworth Siskin, and in an effort to provide the British fighter arm with a considerably improved fighter, the Air Ministry in 1926 issued a fairly taxing specification for a high-performance day/night fighter armed with two fixed machine guns and powered by an air-cooled radial engine. Several companies tendered designs, and the Type 105 proposal from Bristol narrowly beat the Hawfinch from Hawker. The Type 105 was a conventional biplane of its period, with a fabric-covered metal structure, unequal-span wings and fixed landing gear of the spreader-bar type. The Bulldog Mk I prototype first flew in May1927, and was later fitted with larger wings for attempts on the world altitude and time-to-height records. A second prototype introduced the lengthened fuselage of the Bulldog Mk II production model, which was powered by the 328-kW (440-hp) Bristol Jupiter VII radial, and had a number of modern features such as an oxygen system and shortwave radio.

The Bulldog Mk II entered service in June 1929, and the Bulldog became the U.K.'s most important fighter of the late 1920s and early 1930s. Total production was 312, including 92 basic Bulldog Mk IIs, 268 Bulldog Mk IIAs of the major production type with a strengthened structure and the 365-kW (490-hp) Jupiter VIIF engine, four Bulldog MK IIIs for Denmark with the Jupiter VIFH, two interim Bulldog MK IIIAs with the 418-kW (560-hp) Bristol Mercury IVS.2, 18 Bulldog Mk IVAs for Finland with strengthened ailerons and the 477-kW (640-hp) Mercury VIS.2, and 59 Bulldog TM trainers with a second cockpit in a rear fuselage section that could be replaced by that of the standard fighters in times of crisis.

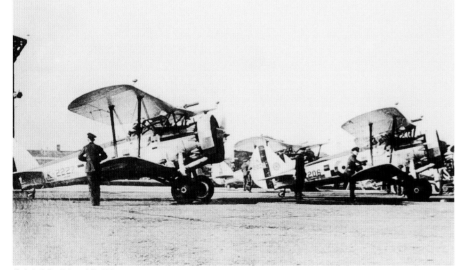

Bristol Bulldog Mk IIA

BRISTOL BULLDOG Mk IVA
Role: Fighter
Crew/Accommodation: One
Power Plant: One 640-hp Bristol Mercury VIS.2 air-cooled radial
Dimensions: Span 10.26 m (33.66 ft); length 7.72 m (25.33 ft); wing area 27.31 m² (294 sq ft)
Weights: Empty 1,220 kg (2,690 lb); MTOW 1,820 kg (4,010 lb)
Performance: Maximum speed 360 km/h (224 mph) at sea level; operational ceiling 10,180 m (33,400 ft); endurance 2.25 hours
Load: Two .303-inch machine guns, plus up to 36 kg (80 lb) of bombs

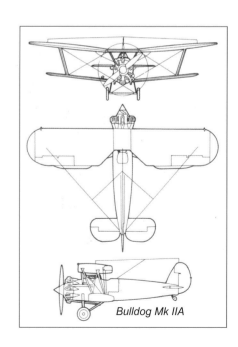

Bulldog Mk IIA

BOEING F4B & P-12 (U.S.A.)

Boeing F4B-4

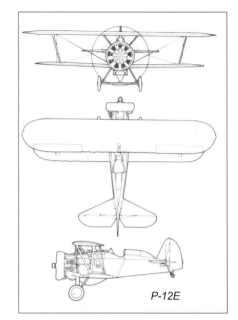

P-12E

I n an effort to produce replacements for the PW-9 and F2B/F3B series, Boeing developed its Models 83 and 89; the former had through-axle landing gear and an arrester hook, while the latter had divided main landing gear units and an attachment under the fuselage for a bomb. Both types were evaluated in 1928, and a hybrid variant with divided main units and an arrester hook was ordered for the U.S. Navy as the F4B-1 with tail skid landing gear. These 27 aircraft were followed by 46 F4B-2s with a drag-reducing cowling ring and through-axle landing gear with a tailwheel, 21 F4B-3s with a semi-monocoque fuselage and 92 F4B-4s with a larger fin and, to be found in the last 45 aircraft, a life raft in the pilot's headrest.

The U.S. Army ordered the type as the P-12, the first 10 aircraft being generally similar to the Model 89; later aircraft were 90 P-12Bs with revised ailerons and elevators, 95 P-12Cs similar to the F4B-2, 36 improved P-12Ds, 110 P-12Es with a semi-monocoque fuselage, and 25 P-12Fs with the Pratt & Whitney SR-1340 engine for improved altitude performance. There were also several experimental and even civil models, and also a number of export variants in a total production run of 586 aircraft. The aircraft began to enter American service in 1929, and were the mainstay of the U.S. Army's and U.S. Navy's fighter arms into the mid-1930s, and at that time they were replaced by more modern aircraft. Many aircraft were then used as trainers, mainly by the U.S. Navy, right up to the eve of the entry of the U.S.A. into World War II.

BOEING F4B-4

Role: Naval carrierborne fighter bomber
Crew/Accommodation: One
Power Plant: One 500-hp Pratt & Whitney R-1340-D Wasp air-cooled radial
Dimensions: Span 9.14 m (30 ft); length 7.75 m (25.42 ft); wing area 21.18 m² (228 sq ft)
Weights: Empty 1,049 kg (2,312 lb); MTOW 1,596 kg (3,519 lb)
Performance: Maximum speed 301 km/h (187 mph) at sea level; operational ceiling 8,382 m (27,500 ft); range 941 km (585 miles)
Load: One .5-inch and one .303-inch machine guns, plus one 227-kg (500-lb) bomb

Boeing P-12E

CURTISS P-6 HAWK and F11C Series (U.S.A.)

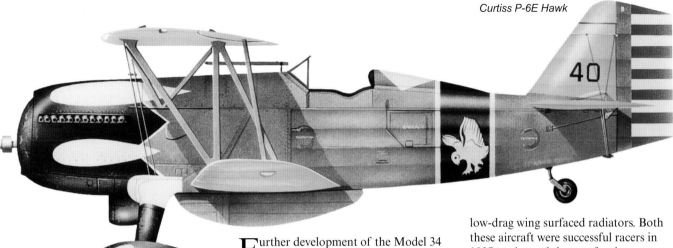

Curtiss P-6E Hawk

Further development of the Model 34 (P-l and F6C series) led to the P-6 series with the Curtiss V-1570 Conqueror engine. The development was pioneered in two P-l conversions, namely the XP-6 with tapered wings and the XP-6A with the uptapered wings of the PW-8 and low-drag wing surfaced radiators. Both these aircraft were successful racers in 1927, and paved the way for the production series later on.

The main variants were the original P-6 of which nine were delivered with refined fuselage lines, the nine P-6As with Prestone-cooled engines, and the P-6E of which 46 were delivered in the winter of 1931-32 with the 522-kW (700-hp) V-1570C Conqueror. This was the finest of the army's Hawk fighters, and was the Curtiss Model 35.

There were many experimental variants including the radial-engined P-3 and P-21, and the turbocharged P-5 and P-23.

The type also secured comparatively large export orders under the generic designation Hawk. The Hawk I was sold to the Netherlands East Indies (eight aircraft), Cuba (three) and Japan (one), while the same basic type with a Wright Cyclone radial was sold with the name Hawk II to Bolivia (nine), Chile (four plus licensed production), China (50), Colombia (26 float-equipped aircraft), Cuba (four), Germany (two), Norway (one), Siam (12) and Turkey (19).

In addition, the U.S. Navy ordered a version of the Hawk II with the 522-kW (700-hp) Wright R-1820-78 Cyclone radial and the designations F11C-2 (28 aircraft), and with manually-operated landing gear that retracted into a bulged lower fuselage, another type, the BF2C-1 (27 aircraft).

Curtiss P-6E Hawk

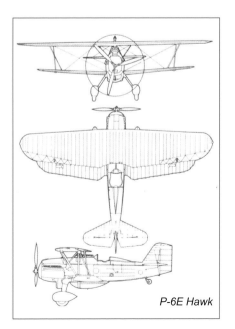

P-6E Hawk

CURTISS P-6E HAWK
Role: Fighter
Crew/Accommodation: One
Power Plant: One 700-hp Curtiss V-1570C Conqueror water-cooled inline
Dimensions: Span 9.6 m (31.5 ft); length 6.88 m (22.58 ft); wing area 23.4 m^2 (252 sq ft)
Weights: Empty 1,231 kg (2,715 lb); MTOW 1,558 kg (3,436 lb)
Performance: Maximum speed 311 km/h (193 mph) at sea level; operational ceiling 7,285 m (23,900 ft); range 393 km (244 miles)
Load: Two .303-inch machine guns

HAWKER FURY I & II biplanes (United Kingdom)

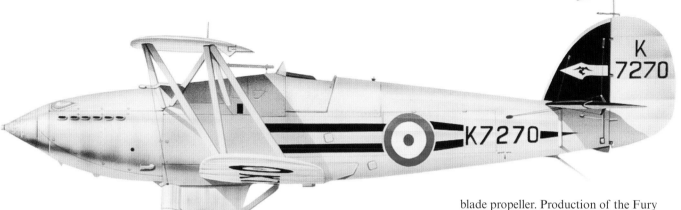

This entered service in 1937, and the 98 aircraft were used as interim fighters pending large-scale deliveries of the Hawker Hurricane monoplane fighter. The Fury II was exported to Yugoslavia, which took 10 aircraft. The Nimrod was a naval equivalent; 100 were produced for British and Danish service.

HAWKER FURY Mk II

Role: Interceptor
Crew/Accommodation: One
Power Plant: One 525-hp Rolls-Royce Kestrel IIS water-cooled inline
Dimensions: Span 9.15 m (30 ft); length 8.13 m (26.67 ft); wing area 23.4 m² (251.8 sq ft)
Weights: Empty 1,190 kg (2,623 lb); MTOW 1,583 kg (3,490 lb)
Performance: Maximum speed 309 km/h (192 mph) at 1,525 m (5,000 ft); operational ceiling 8,534 m (28,000 ft); range 491 km (305 miles)
Load: Two .303-inch machine guns

This single-seat fighter resulted from a 1927 requirement that led to the construction of a prototype that first flew with the 336-kW (450-hp) Bristol Jupiter radial specified by the Air Ministry. The aircraft failed to win a production contract, but its experience with this prototype stood the company in good stead. After its Hart high-speed day bomber had entered service as a pioneer of a new breed of high-performance warplanes, Hawker developed as a private venture fighter prototype. Sydney Camm decided not to follow current Air Ministry preference for radial engines, but instead opted for the Rolls-Royce F.XIX inline engine in an elegantly streamlined nose entry. The whole prototype was of very clean lines, and after purchase by the Air Ministry was renamed Fury.

Trials confirmed the type's capabilities as the first British fighter capable of exceeding 200 mph (322 km/h) in level flight, and the type was placed in production for service from May 1931. The fighter was of metal construction covered with panels of light alloy and with fabric, and the powerplant was a single 391-kW (525-hp) Rolls-Royce Kestrel IIS engine driving a large two-blade propeller. Production of the Fury (later the Fury I) for the RAF totalled 118, though another 42 were built for export with a number of other engine types. Hawker developed the basic concept further in the Intermediate Fury and High-Speed Fury prototypes that led to the definitive Fury II with the 477-kW (640-hp) Kestrel VI and spatted wheels.

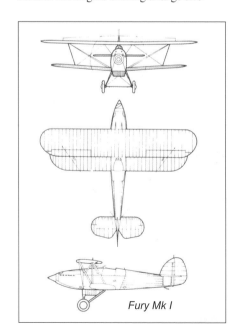

Fury Mk I

The Fury was always notable for the elegance of its lines

BOEING P-26 'PEASHOOTER' (U.S.A.)

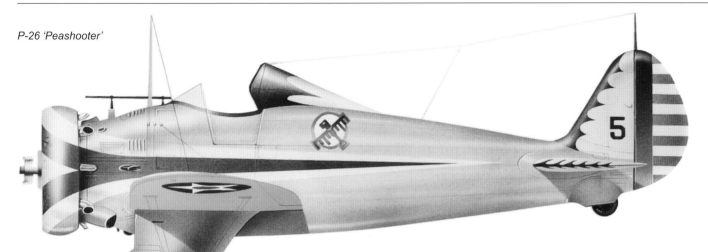

P-26 'Peashooter'

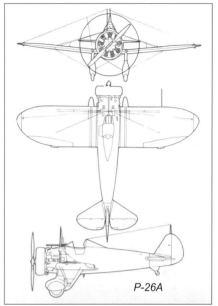

P-26A

The Model 266 was a step, but only an interim step, towards the 'modern' monoplane fighter of all-metal construction that appeared in definitive form during the mid-1930s. The Model 266 was indeed a monoplane fighter, but the wing was not a cantilever structure and had, therefore, to be braced by flying and landing wires. This bracing was in itself an obsolescent feature, and so too were the open cockpit and fixed landing gear, though the latter's main units were well-faired. Boeing began work on its Model 248 private-venture prototype during September 1931, and the first example flew in March 1932. The U.S. Army Air Corps evaluated three examples with the designation XP-936, and then ordered 111 examples of the Model 266 production version with a revised structure, flotation equipment and radio. The P-26As were often known

as 'Peashooters', and were delivered between January 1934 and June 1934.

Later aircraft had a taller headrest for improved pilot protection in the event of a roll-over landing accident, and were produced with the trailing-edge split flaps that had been developed to reduce landing speed; in-service aircraft were retrofitted with the flaps. Other variants were two P-26Bs with the fuel-injected R-1340-33 radial, and 23 P-26Cs with modified fuel systems.

Some 11 aircraft were also exported to China, and surplus American aircraft were later delivered to Guatemala and

Panama. Ex-American aircraft operated by the Philippine Air Corps saw short but disastrous service in World War II.

BOEING P-26C
Role: Fighter
Crew/Accommodation: One
Power Plant: One 600-hp Pratt & Whitney R-1340-33 Wasp air-cooled radial
Dimensions: Span 8.52 m (27.96 ft); length 7.24 m (23.75 ft); wing area 13.89 m² (149 sq ft)
Weights: Empty 1,058 kg (2,333 lb); MTOW 1,395 kg (3,075 lb)
Performance: Maximum speed 378 km/h (235 mph) at sea level; operational ceiling 8,230 m (27,000 ft); range 1,022 km (635 miles)
Load: Two .5-inch machine guns, plus 90.8 kg (200 lb) of bombs

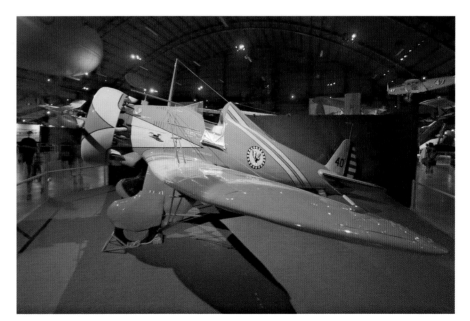

Boeing P-26 'Peashooter'

FIAT CR.32 and CR.42 FALCO (Italy)

Fiat CR.32

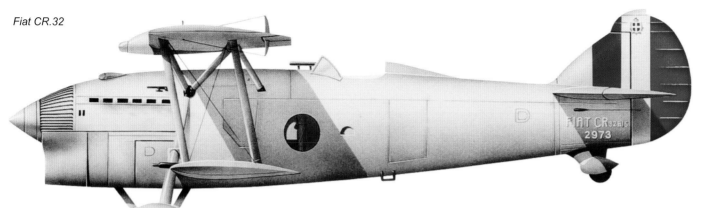

The CR.32 was Italy's finest fighter of the late 1930s, and marks one of the high points in biplane fighter design. The type was planned as successor to the CR.30 with smaller dimensions and reduced weight so that the type would have a comparably high level of agility but better overall performance on the same power. The prototype first flew in April 1933 with the 447-kW (600-hp) Fiat

A.30 RAbis inline engine, and the successful evaluation of this machine led to production of slightly more than 1,300 aircraft in four series. These were about 350 CR.32 fighters with two 7.7-mm (0.303-in) machine guns, 283 CR.32bis close-support fighters with two 12.7-mm (0.5-in) and two 7.7-mm guns as well as

provision for two 50-kg (110-lb) bombs, 150 CR.32ter fighters with two 12.7-mm (0.5-in) guns and improved equipment, and 337 CR.32quater fighters with radio and reduced weight. Another 100 or more of this last type were built in Spain as Hispano HA-132-L 'Chirri' fighters.

The Spanish Civil War led to the CR.42 Falco (Falcon) that first flew in prototype form during May 1938. This could be regarded as an aerodynamically refined version of the CR.32 with cantilever main landing gear units and more power in the form of a 626-kW (840-hp) Fiat A.74 R1C radial. More than 1,780 aircraft in five series were produced. The original CR.42 was armed with one 12.7-mm and one 7.7-mm machine guns. The CR.42AS was a close-support fighter with two 12.7-mm guns and two 10-kg (220-lb) bombs. The CR.42bis fighter was produced for Sweden with two 12.7-mm guns. The CR.42CN night fighter had two searchlights in underwing fairings. And the CR.42ter was a version of the CR.42bis with two 7.7-mm guns in underwing fairings.

FIAT CR.32bis
Role: Fighter
Crew/Accommodation: One
Power Plant: One 600-hp Fiat A30 RAbis water-cooled inline
Dimensions: Span 9.5 m (31.17 ft); length 7.47 m (24.51 ft): wing area 22.1 m² (237.9 sq ft)
Weights: Empty 1.455 kg (3.210 lb): MTOW 1,975 kg (4.350 lb)
Performance: Maximum speed 360 km/h (224 mph) at 3,000 m (9.840 ft): operational ceiling 7,700 m (25,256 ft): range 750 km (446 miles)
Load: Two 12.7-mm and two 7.7-mm machine guns, plus provision to carry up to 100 kg (220 lb) of bombs

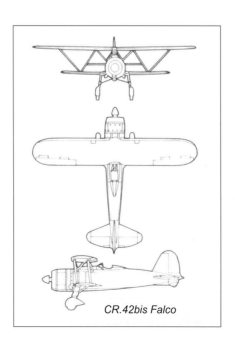

CR.42bis Falco

Fiat CR.42 Falco

POLIKARPOV I-16 (U.S.S.R.)

The I-16 was the first low-wing monoplane fighter to enter full service with retractable landing gear. The aircraft had a cantilever wing of metal construction married to a monocoque fuselage of wooden construction and, in addition to the manually retracted main landing gear unit, the type had long-span split ailerons that doubled as flaps. The type first flew in 1933 as the TsKB-12 with the 358-kW (480-hp) M-22 radial. The TsKB-12bis flew two months later with an imported 529-kW (710-hp) Wright SR-1820-F3 Cyclone radial and offered better performance. The handling qualities of both variants were tricky, because the short and very portly fuselage reduced longitudinal stability to virtually nothing, but its speed and rate of climb ensured that the machine was ordered into production, initially as an evaluation batch of 10 I-16 Type 1 fighters with the M-22.

Total production was 7,005 in variants with progressively more power and armament: the I-16 Type 4 used the imported Cyclone engine, the I-16 Type 5 had the 522-kW (700-hp) M-25 licensed version of the Cyclone and improved armour protection, the I-16 Type 6 was the first major production model and had the 544-kW (730-hp) M-25A, the I-16 Type 10 had the 559-kW (750-hp) M-25V and four rather than two 7.62-mm (0.3-in) machine-guns, the I-16 Type 17 was strengthened and had 20-mm cannon in place of the two wing machine guns plus provision for six 82-mm (3.2-in) rockets carried under the wings, the I-16 Type 18 had the 686-kW (920-hp) M-62 radial and four machine guns, the I-16 Type 24 had the 746-kW (1,000-hp) M-62 or 820-kW (1,100-hp) M-63 radial, strengthened wings and four machine guns, and the I-16 Types 28 and 30 that were reinstated in production during the dismal days of 1941 and 1942 had the M-63 radial. There were also SPB dive-bomber and I-16 UTI dual-control trainer variants.

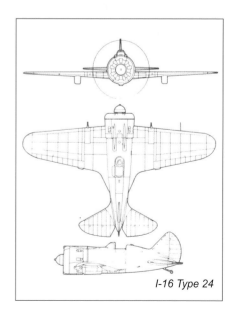

I-16 Type 24

POLIKARPOV I-16 TYPE 24
Role: Fighter
Crew/Accommodation: One
Power Plant: One 1,000-hp Shvetsov M-62 air-cooled radial
Dimensions: Span 9 m (29.53 ft); length 6.13 m (20.11 ft); wing area 14.54 m² (156.5 sq ft)
Weights: Empty 1,475 kg (3,313 lb); MTOW 2,050 kg (4,519 lb)
Performance: Maximum speed 525 km/h (326 mph) at sea level; operational ceiling 9,000 m (29,528 ft); range 700 km (435 miles)
Load: Two 20-mm cannon and two 7.62=mm machine guns, plus six rocket projectiles

Polikarpov I-16 Type 24

31

DEWOITINE D.500 and D.510 Series (France)

Dewoitine D.510

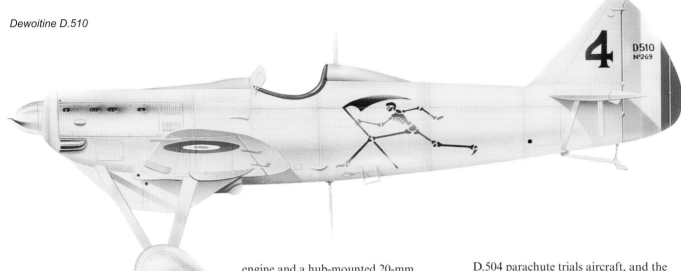

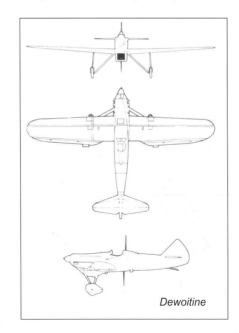

Dewoitine

The ungainly but impressive D.500 spanned the technological gap between the fabric-covered biplanes of the 1920s and the all-metal monoplane fighters of the mid-1930s. Designed as a successor to the Nieuport 62 and 622, the D.500 was of all-metal construction with a low-set cantilever wing, but these modern features were compromised by obsolescent items such as an open cockpit and fixed tailwheel landing gear the main legs of which carried large fairings. The D.500.01 prototype first flew in June 1932 with the 492-kW (660-hp) Hispano-Suiza 12Xbrs inline engine, and the type was ordered into production. The initial D.500 was produced to the extent of 101 aircraft, later aircraft with 7.5-mm (0.295-in) Darne machine guns in place of the original 7.7-mm (0.303-in) Vickers guns. There followed 157 D.501s with the 515-kW (690-hp) Hispano-Suiza 12Xcrs

engine and a hub-mounted 20-mm cannon in addition to the two machine guns.

Projected variants were the D.502 catapult-launched floatplane fighter, the

D.504 parachute trials aircraft, and the D.505 to D.509 with different engines. The main variant in service at the beginning of World War II was the D.510 based on the D.501 but powered by the 641-kW (860-hp) Hispano-Suiza 12Ycrs inline in a longer nose and featuring a number of refinements such as modified landing gear, greater fuel capacity and, in late aircraft, 7.5-mm MAC 1934 machine

guns in place of the Darne weapons. Production of the D.510 totalled 120 aircraft in all.

An interesting experimental derivative was the D.511 of 1934: this had a smaller wing, cantilever main landing gear units, and the HS 12Ycrs engine. The type was never flown; it was modified as the D.503 with the HS 12Xcrs, proving inferior to the D.501 aircraft.

DEWOITINE D.510

Role: Fighter
Crew/Accommodation: One
Power Plant: One 860-hp Hispano-Suiza 12Ycrs water-cooled inline
Dimensions: Span 12.09 m (39.67 ft); length 7.94 m (26.05 ft); wing area 16.5 m² (177.6 sq ft)
Weights: Empty 1,427 kg (3,145 lb); MTOW 1,915 kg (4,222 lb)
Performance: Maximum speed 402 km/h (250 mph) at 4,850 m (15,912 ft); operational ceiling 8,350 m (27,395 ft); range 985 km (612 miles)
Load: One 20-mm cannon and two 7.5-mm machine guns

Dewoitine D.500

MESSERSCHMITT Bf 109 (Germany)

Bf 109F

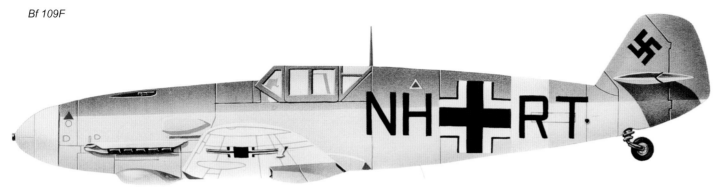

The Bf 109 was Germany's most important fighter of World War II in numerical terms, and bore the brunt of the air war until supplemented by the Focke-Wulf Fw 190 from 1941. The type went through a large number of production variants, and in common with other German aircraft was developed within these basic variants into a number of subvariants with factory- or field-installed modification packages.

The Bf 109 was designed from 1934 to provide the German Air Force with its first 'modern' fighter of all-metal stressed-skin construction with a low-set

MESSERSCHMITT Bf 109G-6
Role: Fighter
Crew/Accommodation: One
Power Plant: One 1,475-hp Daimler-Benz DB605A water-cooled inline
Dimensions: Span 9.92 m (32.55 ft); length 9.02 m (29.59 ft); wing area 16.5 m² (172.75 sq ft)
Weights: Empty 2,700 kg (5.953 lb): MTOW 3.150 kg (6,945 lb)
Performance: Maximum speed 623 km/h (387 mph) at 7,000 m (22,967 ft): operational ceiling 11,750 m (38,551 ft): range 725 km (450 miles)
Load: One 30-mm cannon, two 20-mm cannon and two 13-mm machine guns, plus a 500-kg (1,102-lb) bomb

Messerschmitt Bf 109

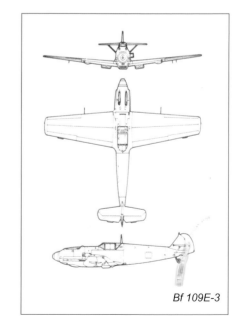

Bf 109E-3

33

34

OPPOSITE & BELOW: Messerschmitt Bf 109

cantilever wing, retractable landing gear and enclosed cockpit. The first prototype flew in May 1935 with a 518-kW (695-hp) Rolls-Royce Kestrel inline, but the second had the 455-kW (610-hp) Junkers Jumo 210A for which the aircraft had been designed. The overall production figure has not survived, but it is thought that at least 30,500 aircraft were produced, excluding foreign production. The limited-number Bf 109A, B and C variants can be regarded mostly as pre-production and development models with differing Jumo 210s and armament fits.

The Daimler-Benz DB 600A inline was introduced on the Bf 109D, paving the way for the first large-scale production variant, the Bf 109E produced in variants up to the E-9 with the 820-kW (1,100-hp) DB 601A. The Bf 109F introduced a more refined fuselage with reduced armament, and in addition was powered by the DB 601E or N in variants up to the F-6.

The most important production model was the Bf 109G with the DB 605 inline and provision for cockpit pressurization in variants up to the G-16. Later in the war there appeared comparatively small numbers of the Bf 109H high-altitude fighter with increased span in variants up to the H-1, and the Bf 109K improved version of the Bf 109G with the DB 605 inline in variants up to the K-14.

HAWKER HURRICANE (United Kingdom)

Hurricane Mk I

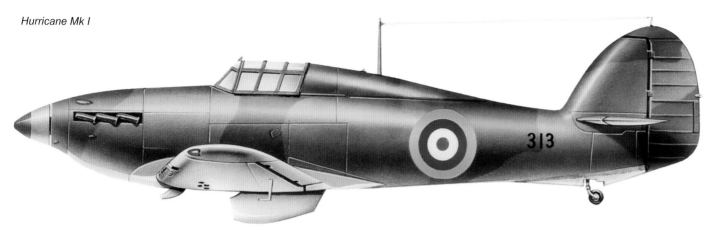

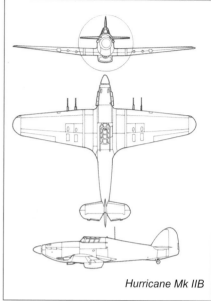

Hurricane Mk IIB

The Hurricane was the first British example of the 'modern' monoplane fighter, even though it lacked the stressed-skin construction of later machines such as the Supermarine Spitfire. The initial design was created as a private venture, and offered such advantages over current biplane fighters that a 1934 specification was written around it. The prototype first flew in November 1935 and revealed itself as a

mix of advanced features (retractable landing gear, flaps and an enclosed cockpit) and an obsolescent structure of light alloy tube covered in fabric. This last did facilitate construction and repair, but limited the Hurricane's longer-term development potential despite an overall production total of 14,232 aircraft.

The Hurricane Mk I entered service in December 1937 with an armament of eight 7.7-mm (0.303-in) machine guns

and the 768-kW (1,030-hp) Rolls-Royce Merlin II inline driving a two-blade propeller, and in the Battle of Britain was the RAF's most important and successful fighter with the 767-kW (1,029-hp) Merlin III driving a three-blade propeller. British production of 3,164 Mk Is was complemented by 140 Canadian-built Hurricane Mk Xs and a few Belgian- and Yugoslav-produced machines. Adoption of the 954-kW (1,280-hp) Merlin XX resulted in the Hurricane Mk II, of which 6,656 were produced in the U.K. in variants such as the Mk IIA with eight 7.7-mm machine guns, the Mk IIB with

12 such guns and provision for underwing bombs, the Mk IIC based on the Mk IIB but with four 20-mm cannon, and the Mk IID with two 40-mm cannon in the anti-tank role; Canadian production amounted to 937 similar Hurricane Mks X, XI and XII aircraft. The final version was the Hurricane Mk IV, of which 2,575 were built with the 1208-kW (1,620-hp) Merlin 24 or 27 and a universal wing allowing the use of any of the standard armament combinations. About 825 aircraft were converted into Sea Hurricane Mks I and II.

HAWKER HURRICANE Mk IIB
Role: Fighter bomber
Crew/Accommodation: One
Power Plant: One 1,280-hp Rolls-Royce Merlin XX water-cooled inline
Dimensions: Span 12.19 m (40 ft); length 9.75 m (32 ft); wing area 23.9 m² (257.5 sq ft)
Weights: Empty 2.495 kg (5,500 lb); MTOW 3,311 kg (7,300 lb)
Performance: Maximum speed 722 km/h (342 mph) at 6,706 m (22,000 ft); operational ceiling 10,973 m (36,000 ft); range 772.5 km (480 miles) on internal fuel only
Load: Twelve .303-inch machine guns, plus up to 454-kg (1,000-lb) bombload

The Hawker Hurricane was the RAF's first 'modern' monoplane fighter

OPPOSITE: Hurricane Mk I

NAKAJIMA Ki-27 'NATE' (Japan)

Ki-27 'Nate'

The production programme lasted from 1937 to 1942 and totalled 3,384 aircraft in the original Ki-27a and modestly improved Ki-27b variants. The Ki-27a had an uprated Ha-Ib (Army Type 97) engine and a metal-faired canopy, while the Ki-27b reverted to the clear-vision canopy and featured light ground-attack capability in the form of the four 25-kg (55-lb) bombs that could be carried under the wings. A number of the fighters were converted as two-seat armed trainers, and two experimental lightweight fighters were produced with the designation Ki-27 KAI. The Ki-27 was used operationally up to 1942, when its light structure and poor armament forced its relegation to second-line duties. The type was initially known to the Allies in the China-Burma-India theatre as the 'Abdul', but 'Nate' later became the standard reporting name.

The Ki-27 was the Imperial Japanese Army Air Force's equivalent of the Navy's Mitsubishi A5M, and though it was an interim 'modern' fighter with fixed landing gear (selected because of its light weight) it had more advanced features such as flaps and an enclosed cockpit. The type was evolved from the company's private-venture Type PE design, and the first of two prototypes flew in October 1936 with the 485-kW (650-hp) Nakajima Ha-Ia radial. Flight trials with the prototypes confirmed the Ki-27's superiority to competing fighters, and 10 examples of the type with a modified clear-vision canopy were ordered for evaluation. These aircraft proved highly effective, and the first full-production type was ordered with the company designation Ki-27a and the service designation Army Type 97 Fighter Model A.

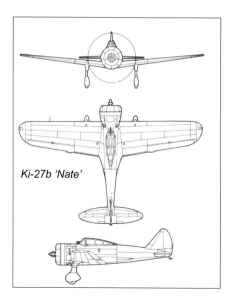

Ki-27b 'Nate'

Nakajima Ki-27

NAKAJIMA Ki-27 'NATE'
Role: Fighter
Crew/Accommodation: One
Power Plant: One 710-hp Nakajima Ha-Ib air-cooled radial
Dimensions: Span 11.3 m (37.07 ft); length 7.53 m (24.7 ft); wing area 18.6 m² (199.7 sq ft)
Weights: Empty 1,110 kg (2.447 lb); MTOW 1,650 kg (3,638 lb)
Performance: Maximum speed 460 km/h (286 mph) at 3,500 m (11,480 ft); operational ceiling 8,600 m (28,215 ft); range 1,710 km (1,050 miles)
Load: Two 7.7-mm machine guns, plus up to 100 kg (220 lb) of bombs

CURTISS P-36 MOHAWK and HAWK 75 (U.S.A.)

P-36C

In 1934 Curtiss decided on the private-venture design of a modern fighter that might interest the U.S. Army Air Corps as a successor to the Boeing P-26 and would also have considerable export attractions.

The Model 75 prototype first flew in May 1935 as a low-wing monoplane of all-metal construction with an enclosed

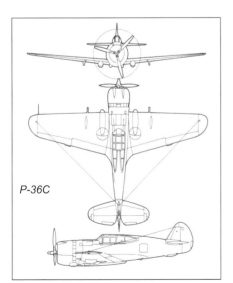

P-36C

cockpit, retractable landing gear and a 671-kW (900-hp) Wright XR-1670-5 radial. The type was evaluated by the USAAC as the Model 75B with the 634-kW (750-hp) Wright R-1820 radial, but was initially beaten by a production order for the Seversky prototype that became the P-35.

The Curtiss machine was reworked into the Model 75E with the 783-kW (1,050-hp) Pratt & Whitney R-1830-13 derated to 708 kW (950 hp) and then re-evaluated as the Y1P-36. This was clearly a superior fighter, and in July 1937 the type was ordered into production as the

CURTISS P-36C (RAF MOHAWK)
Role: Fighter
Crew/Accommodation: One
Power Plant: One 1,200-hp Pratt & Whitney R-1830-17 Twin Wasp air-cooled radial
Dimensions: Span 11.35 m (37.33 ft); length 8.72 m (28.6 ft); wing area 21.92 m² (236 sq ft)
Weights: Empty 2,095 kg (4,619 lb); MTOW 2,790 kg (6,150 lb)
Performance: Maximum speed 501 km/h (311 mph) at 3,048 m (10,000 ft); operational ceiing 10,272 m (33,700 ft); range 1,320 km (820 miles) at 322 km/h (200 mph) cruise
Load: Four .303-inch machine guns

P-36A with the fully rated version of the R-1830-13 driving a constant-speed propeller. Some 210 of the type were ordered, but only 31 were completed to P-36C standard with the 895-kW

(1,200-hp) R-1830-17 engine and the two fuselage-mounted guns (one of 12.7-mm/0.5-in and the other of 7.62-mm/0.3-in calibre) complemented by two wing-mounted 7.62-mm guns.

The type was exported in fairly large numbers as the H75A, principally to France and the United Kingdom but in smaller numbers to other countries. British aircraft were named Mohawk and comprised four main variants. Some 30 repossessed Norwegian aircraft were taken in charge by the Americans with the designation P-36G. In addition to this, Curtiss developed a less advanced version as the Hawk 75, in the main similar to the pre-production Y1P-36 but with a lower-powered 652-kW (875-hp) Wright GR-1820 radial and fixed landing gear.

Curtiss P-36A

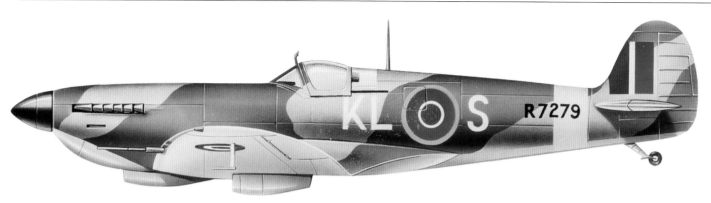

the two-stage Merlin 61, 64 or 71, the LF, F and HF.Mk VIII with the two-stage Merlin 61, 63, 66 or 70 but an unpressurized cockpit, the LF, F and HF.Mk IX using the Mk V airframe with the two-stage Merlin 61, 63 or 70, the LF and F.Mk XVI using the Mk IX airframe with a cutdown rear fuselage, bubble canopy and Packard-built Merlin 226.

The Spitfire was also developed in its basic fighter form with the larger and more powerful Rolls-Royce Griffon

The Spitfire was the most important British fighter of World War II and remained in production right through the conflict for a total of 20,334 aircraft bolstered by 2,556 new-build Seafire naval fighters. The prototype first flew in March 1936 with a 738-kW (900-hp) Rolls-Royce Merlin C engine, and was soon ordered into production as the Spitfire Mk I with the 768-kW (1,030-hp) Merlin II and eight 7.7-mm (0.303-in)

machine guns or, in the Mk IB variant, four machine guns and two 20-mm cannon; the suffix A indicated eight 7.7-mm machine-guns, B four such machine-guns and two 20-mm cannon, C four cannon, and E two cannon and two 12.7-mm (0.5-in) machine guns.

Major fighter variants with the Merlin engine were the initial Mk I, the Mk II with the 876-kW (1,175-hp) Merlin XII, the Mks VA, VB and VC in F medium- and LF low-altitiude forms with the 1974-kW (1,440-hp) Merlin 45 or 1096-kW (1,470-hp) Merlin 50, the HF.Mk VI high-altitude interceptor with the 1055-kW (1,415-hp) Merlin 47 and a pressurized cockpit, the HF.Mk VII with

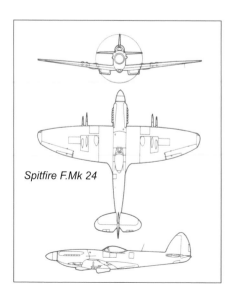

Spitfire F.Mk 24

SUPERMARINE SPITFIRE F.Mk XIV E
Role: Fighter
Crew/Accommodation: One
Power Plant: One 2,050-hp Rolls-Royce Griffon 65 water-cooled inline
Dimensions: Span 11.23 m (36.83 ft); length 9.96 m (32.66 ft); wing area 22.48 m² (242 sq ft)
Weights: Empty 2,994 kg (6,600 lb); MTOW 3,856 kg (8,500 lb)
Performance: Maximum speed 721 km/h (448 mph) at 7,925 m (26,000 ft); operational ceiling 13,106 m (43,000 ft); range 740 km (460 miles) on internal fuel only
Load: Two 20-mm cannon and two .303-machine guns, plus up to 454 kg (1,000 lb) of bombs

This Mk II Supermarine Spitfire is the oldest still flying

inline, and the major variants of this sequence were the LF.Mk XI with the 1294-kW (1,735-hp) Griffon II or IV, the LF and F.Mk XIV with the 1529-kW (2,050-hp) Griffon 65 or 66 and often with a bubble canopy, the F.Mk XVIII

with the two-stage Griffon and a bubble canopy, the F. Mk 21 with the Griffon 61 or 64, the F.Mk 22 with the 1771-kW (2,373-hp) Griffon 85 driving a contra-rotating propeller unit, and the improved F.Mk 24.

The Spitfire was also used as a unarmed reconnaissance type, the major Merlin-engined types being the Mks IV, X, XI and XIII, and the Griffon-engined type being the Mk XIX. The Seafire was the naval counterpart to the Spitfire, the

main Merlin-engined versions being the Mks IB, IIC and III, and the Griffon-engined versions being the Mks XV, XVII, 45, 46 and 47.

Supermarine Spitfire Mk XVI

DEWOITINE D.520 (France)

Dewoitine D. 520

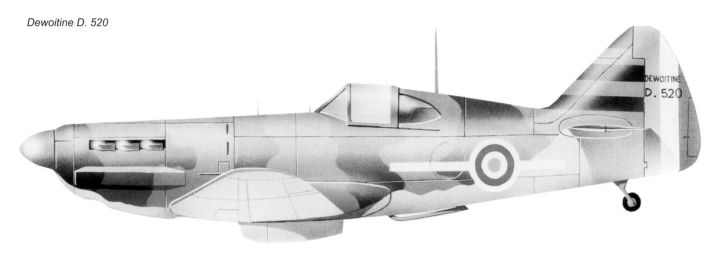

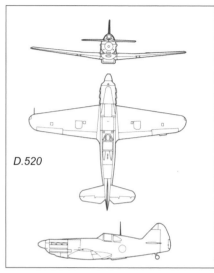

D.520

Dewoitine D. 520

Dewoitine's first 'modern' low-wing monoplane fighter was the D.513 that first flew in January 1936 with a 641-kW (860-hp) Hispano-Suiza 12Ycrs inline. The type introduced advanced features such as an enclosed cockpit and retractable landing gear, but its low performance and severe instability problems proved very disappointing. The type was extensively revised but still had problems, so it was abandoned.

The company used the lessons learned from the D.513 fiasco in the creation of the D.520, which proved a far more satisfactory type and was ordered in substantial numbers. One of the most advanced fighters to serve with the French Air Force in the disastrous early campaign of 1940, the D.520 was a modern fighter of considerably trimmer and more pleasing lines than the D.513. It embodied an enclosed cockpit, trailing-edge flaps, retractable tailwheel landing gear and a variable-pitch propeller for the engine located in a much cleaner nose installation.

DEWOITINE D.520
Role: Fighter
Crew/Accommodation: One
Power Plant: One 920-hp Hispano-Suiza 12Y-45 water-cooled inline
Dimensions: Span 10.2 m (33 ft); length 8.76 m (28 ft); wing area 15.95 m² (171.7 sq ft)
Weights: Empty 2,092 kg (4,612 lb); MTOW 2,783 kg (6,134 lb)
Performance: Maximum speed 535 km/h (332 mph) at 6,000 m (19,685 ft); operational ceiling 11,000 m (36,090 ft); range 900 km (553 miles)
Load: One 20-mm cannon and four 7.5-mm machine guns

The D520.01 prototype first flew in October 1938 with the 664-kW (890-hp) Hispano-Suiza 12Y-21 inline, though the two following prototypes had wing, vertical tail and cockpit canopy modifications as well as the 746-kW (1,000-hp) HS 12Y-51 and 619-kW (830-hp) HS 12Y-31 engines respectively. Substantial orders were placed for the D.520 with the 686-kW (920-hp) HS 12Y-45 or -49, but only 403 aircraft had been delivered before the fall of France in June 1940. The in-service fighters did well in combat with German aircraft, and 478 aircraft were built for the Vichy French Air Force. Surviving aircraft remained up to the early 1950s. There were several experimental variants including the very promising D.524 with the 895-kW (1,200-hp) HS 12Y-89.

BLOCH M.B. 151 and M.B. 152 (France)

M.B. 152 C1

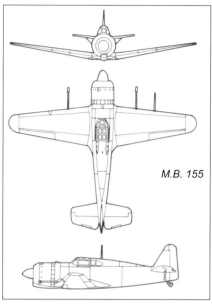

M.B. 155

The M.B. 151 was one of France's first 'modern' monoplane fighters and resulted from the unsuccessful M.B. 150 prototype produced to meet a 1934 requirement. The M.B. 150 could not at first be persuaded to fly, but after it had been fitted with a larger wing, revised landing gear and a 701-kW (940-hp)

Gnôme-Rhône 14N radial, the type first flew in October 1937. In 1938 further improvement in flight performance was achieved with a slightly larger wing and the Gnôme-Rhône 14N-7 engine, and a pre-production batch of 25 M.B. 151 fighters was ordered with slightly reduced wing span and the 695-kW (920-hp)

Gnôme-Rhône 14N-11 radial. The first of these flew in August 1938, and there followed 115 production aircraft with the identically rated Gnôme-Rhône 14N-35 radial.

The type was deemed to lack the performance required of a first-line fighter and was generally used as a fighter trainer. An improved version was developed as the M.B. 152 with the more powerful 768-kW (1,030-hp) Gnôme-Rhône 14N-25 or 790-kW (1,060-hp)

Gnôme-Rhône 14N-49. Production was slow, and only a few M.B. 152s were combat-ready in time for the German invasion of May 1940; more than 30 aircraft had been delivered by January 1940, but most lacked the right propeller. The airworthy examples served with success during the German invasion of mid-1940, and then remained operational with the Vichy French air force. Some aircraft were used by the Luftwaffe as trainers, and 20 were passed to Romania.

BLOCH M.B. 152
Role: Fighter
Crew/Accommodation: One
Power Plant: One 1,000-hp Gnôme-Rhône 14N-25 air-cooled radial
Dimensions: Span 10.54 m (34.58 ft); length 9.1 m (29.86 ft); wing area 17.32 m² (186.4 sq ft)
Weights: Empty 2,158 kg (4,758 lb); MTOW 2,800 kg (6,173 lb)
Performance: Maximum speed 509 km/h (316 mph) at 4,500 m (14,765 ft); operational ceiling 10,000 m (32,808 ft); range 540 km (335 miles)
Load: Two 20-mm cannon and two 7.5-mm machine guns

Bloch M.B. 151

BOULTON PAUL DEFIANT (United Kingdom)

Defiant Mk II

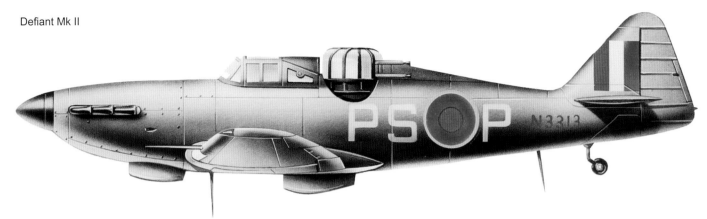

Defiant TT.Mk I target-tugs and another 140 were built as such; similarly converted Mk Is became Defiant TT.Mk IIIs. Total production was 1,075.

BOULTON PAUL DEFIANT Mk II

Role: Night fighter
Crew/Accommodation: Two
Power Plant: One 1,280-hp Rolls-Royce Merlin XX water-cooled inline
Dimensions: Span 11.99 m (39.33 ft); length 10.77 m (35.33 ft); wing area 23.23 m² (250 sq ft)
Weights: Empty 2,850 kg (6,282 lb); MTOW 3,773 kg (8,318 lb)
Performance: Maximum speed 507 km/h (315 mph) at 5,029 m (16,500 ft); operational ceiling 9,251 m (30,350 ft); range 748 km (465 miles)
Load: Four .303-inch machine guns in power-operated turret.
Note: The Defiant Mk III was retrofitted to embody AIMk4 radar.

In the mid-1930s there was considerable enthusiasm among Royal Air Force planners for the two-seat fighter in which all the armament would be concentrated in a power-operated turret. Such a fighter, its protagonists claimed, would be able to penetrate into enemy bomber streams and wreak havoc. A first expression of this concept was found in the Hawker Demon, of which 59 were manufactured in 1934 by Boulton Paul with a Frazer-Nash turret. The company was therefore well placed to respond to a 1935 requirement for a more advanced two-seat turret fighter. The P.82 design was for a trim fighter of the 'modern' monoplane type, little larger than current single-seaters and fitted with a four-gun turret immediately aft of the cockpit. The first of two Defiant prototypes flew in August 1937 with a 768-kW (1,030-hp) Rolls-Royce Merlin I inline engine, and the Defiant Mk I fighter began to enter service in December 1939.

After early encounters with German warplanes, in which the Defiant scored some success because of the novelty of its layout, operations soon revealed the inadequacy of a type in which the turret's weight and drag imposed severe performance and handling limitations and also left the pilot without fixed forward-firing armament. It was decided to convert existing fighters to Defiant NF.Mk IA night fighter standard with primitive AI.Mk IV or VI radar. Mk I production totalled 723, and another 210 night fighters were built as Defiant NF.Mk IIs with the more powerful Merlin XX engine and larger vertical tail surfaces. Many were later converted to

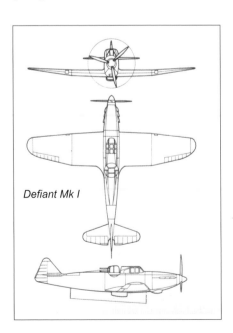

Defiant Mk I

Boulton Paul Defiant Mk I

GRUMMAN F4F WILDCAT (U.S.A.)

F4F-4 Wildcat

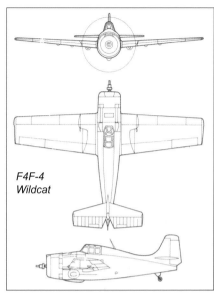

F4F-4 Wildcat

The F4F designation was first used for the G-16 biplane ordered as the XF4F-1 in competition to the Brewster monoplane prototype that was accepted for service as the F2A Buffalo carrierborne fighter. Grumman did not build the biplane prototype, but instead reworked the design as the G-18 monoplane. Re-evaluation of Grumman's proposal led the U.S. Navy to call for an XF4F-2 monoplane prototype, and this first flew in September 1937 with a 783-kW (1,050-hp) Pratt & Whitney R-1830-66 Twin Wasp radial. This initial model was judged slightly inferior to the Buffalo, but was revised as the G-36 with a redesigned tail, a larger wing and the XR-1830-76 engine.

This XF4F-3 first flew in March 1939, and its performance and handling were so improved that the type was ordered as the F4F-3, the British taking a similar version as the Martlet Mk I; the armament was four 12.7-mm (0.5-in) machine guns and production totalled 369 excluding 95 F4F-3As with the R-1830-90 engine. The

F4F/Martlet was the first Allied carrierborne fighter able to meet land-based opponents on anything like equal terms, and proved invaluable during the early war years up to 1943 in variants such as the 1,169 examples of the F4F-4

A Grumman XF4F-3 Wildcat during a test flight

(Martlet Mks II, III and IV) with wing-folding, armour, self-sealing tanks and six rather than four machine guns, and the 21 examples of the F4F-7 unarmed long-range reconnaissance version. The Eastern Aircraft Division of General Motors built

1,060 of the FM-1 (Martlet Mk V) equivalent to the F4F-4 with the R-1830-86 engine, four wing guns, and provision for underwing stores, and 4,127 of the FM-2 (Martlet Mk V) based on Grumman's XF4F-8 prototype with the 1007-kW (1,350-hp) Wright R-1820-56 Cyclone, taller vertical tail surfaces and, on the last 826 aircraft, provision for six 127-mm (5-in) rockets under the wings.

GRUMMAN F4F-4 WILDCAT
Role: Naval carrierborne fighter
Crew/Accommodation: One
Power Plant: One 1,200-hp Pratt & Whitney R-1830-86 Twin Wasp air-cooled radial
Dimensions: Span 11.58 m (38 ft); length 8.76 m (28.75 ft); wing area 24.16 m² (260 sq ft)
Weights: Empty 2.624 kg (5.785 lb): MTOW 3,607 kg (7,952 lb)
Performance: Maximum speed 512 km/h (318 mph) at 5,913 m (19,400 ft); operational ceiling 10,638 m (34,900 ft); range 1.239 km (770 miles) on internal fuel only
Load: Six .5-inch machine guns

BRISTOL BEAUFIGHTER (United Kingdom)

2,205 Beaufighter TF.Mk Xs with search radar and an armament of one torpedo plus light bombs or eight rockets. The 163 Beaufighter TF.Mk XIs were similar, while the 364 Beaufighter TF.Mk 21s were the Australian-built equivalents of the TF.Mk X.

BRISTOL BEAUFIGHTER Mk IF

Role: Night fighter
Crew/Accommodation: Two
Power Plant: Two 1,400-hp Bristol Hercules XI air-cooled radials
Dimensions: Span 17.63 m (57.83 ft); length 12.60 m (41.33 ft); wing area 46.7 m² (503 sq ft)
Weights: Empty 6,382 kg (14,069 lb); MTOW 9,525 kg (21,000 lb)
Performance: Maximum speed 520 km/h (323 mph) at 4,572 m (15,000 ft); operational ceiling 8,839 m (29,000 ft); range 2,413 km (1,500 miles) internal fuel only
Load: Four 20-mm cannon and six .303 machine guns (interception guided by AI Mk IV radar)

The Beaufighter was born of the Royal Air Force's shortage of heavy fighters (especially heavily armed night fighters and long-range escort fighters) as perceived at the time of the 'Munich Crisis' late in 1938. The Type 156 was planned round the wings, tail unit and landing gear of the Type 152 Beaufort torpedo bomber married to a new fuselage and two Hercules radials. The first of four prototypes flew in July 1939, and production was authorized with 1119-kW (1,500-hp) Hercules XI engines. Development of the Beaufighter at this time divided into two role-orientated streams. First of these was the night fighter, as exemplified by the 553 BeaufighterMk IFs with Hercules XIs, nose radar and an armament of four 20-mm nose cannon and six 7.7-mm (0.303-in) wing machine guns. This model entered service in July 1940, and further evolution led to the 597 Beaufighter Mk IIFs with 954-kW (1,280-hp) Rolls-Royce Merlin XX inlines, and finally the 879 Beaufighter Mk VIFs with 1245-kW (1,675-hp) Hercules VIs or XVIs and improved radar in a 'thimble' nose.

With its high performance and capacious fuselage, which made the installation of radar a comparatively simple matter, the Beaufighter night fighter provided the RAF with its first truly effective method of combating nocturnal German bombers. More significant in the longer term, however, was the anti-ship version first developed as the 397 Beaufighter Mk ICs and then evolved via the 693 torpedo-carrying Beaufighter Mk VICs and 60 Beaufighter Mk VI (ITF)s with eight 27-kg (60-lb) rockets in place of the wing guns, to the

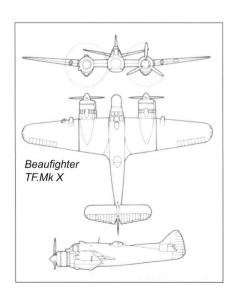

Beaufighter TF.Mk X

Bristol Type 156 Beaufighters

MACCHI MC.200 to MC.205 Series (Italy)

MC.200 Saetta

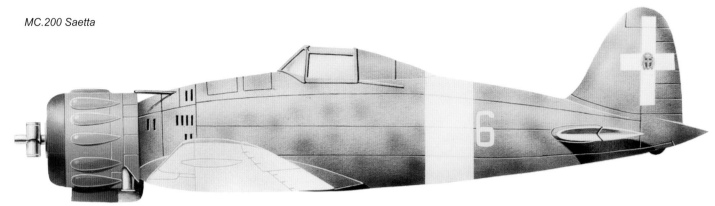

of the MC.202 with the 1100-kW(1,475-hp) DB 605A engine and considerably heavier armament. The MC.205 was first flown in April 1942 but production had then to await availability of the licensed DB 605A, the RA.1050 RC 58 Tifone, so deliveries started only in mid-1943.

Production amounted to 252, and most of these aircraft served with the fascist republic established in northern Italy after the effective division of Italy by the September 1943 armistice with the Allies.

In 1936 the Italian Air Force belatedly realized that the day of the biplane fighter was effectively over, and requested the development of a 'modern' monoplane fighter with stressed-skin metal construction, a low-set cantilever monoplane wing, an enclosed cockpit and retractable landing gear. Macchi's response was the MC.200 Saetta (Lightning) that first flew in December 1937 with the 649-kW (870-hp) Fiat A.74 RC 38 radial engine. The type was declared superior to its competitors during 1938 and ordered into production to a total of 1,153 aircraft in variants

that 'progressed' from an enclosed to an open and eventually a semi-enclosed cockpit.

The MC.200 was a beautiful aircraft to fly, but clearly lacked the performance to deal with the higher-performance British fighters. There was no Italian inline engine that could offer the required

performance, so the MC.202 Folgore (Thunderbolt), that flew in August 1940 with an enclosed cockpit, used an imported Daimler-Benz DB 601A engine. About 1,500 production aircraft followed, initially with imported engines but later with licence-built Alfa-Romeo RA.100 RC 41-I Monsone engines rated at 876-kW (1,175-hp). The MC.205V Veltro (Greyhound) was a development

MACCHI MC.205V VELTRO Series II
Role: Fighter
Crew/Accommodation: One
Power Plant: One 1,475-hp Fiat-built Daimler-Benz DB605A water-cooled inline
Dimensions: Span 10.58 m (34.71 ft): length 8.85 m (29.04 ft); wing area 16.8 m² (180.8 sq ft)
Weights: Empty 2.581 kg (5.690 lb): MTOW 3,224 kg (7.108 lb)
Performance: Maximum speed 642 km/h (399 mph) at 7.200 m (2.620 ft); operational ceiling 1 1,000 m (36,090 ft); range 950 km (590 miles)
Load: Two 200-mm cannon, plus up to 320 kg (706 lb) of bombs

MC.205V Veltro

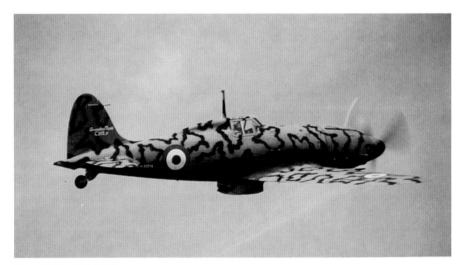

Macchi MC.205V Veltro

CURTISS P-40 WARHAWK Family (U.S.A.)

P-40B Warhawk

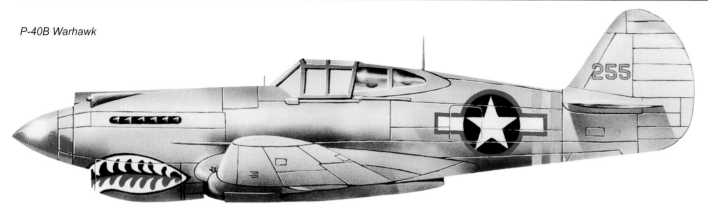

The P-40 series was in no way an exceptional warplane, but nonetheless proved itself a more than adequate fighter-bomber. It was exceeded in numbers by only two other American fighters, the Republic P-47 Thunderbolt and North American P-51 Mustang. The basis for the P-40 series was the Model 75I, a Model 75/XP-37A airframe modified to take the 858-kW (1,150-hp)

Allison V-1710-11 inline engine. This became the first U.S. fighter to exceed 300 mph (483 km/h) in level flight, and the type was ordered by the U.S. Army Air Corps in modified form with the designation P-40 and the less powerful V-1710-33; export versions were the Hawk 81-Al for France and Tomahawk Mk I for the UK.

Improved models were the P-40B (Tomahawk Mk IIA) with self-sealing tanks, armour and better armament, the P-40C (Tomahawk Mk IIB) with improved self-sealing tanks and two more wing guns, the P-40D (Kittyhawk Mk I) with the 858-kW (1,150-hp) V-1710-39 with better supercharging to maintain performance to a higher altitude, and the P-40E with four wing guns plus the similar Kittyhawk Mk IA with six wing guns. The P-40 series had all along been limited by the indifferent supercharging of the V-1710, and this situation was remedied in the P-40F and generally similar P-40L (Kittyhawk Mk II) by the adoption of the 969-kW (1,300-hp) Packard V-1650-1 (licence-built Rolls-Royce Merlin). The type's forte was still the fighter-bomber role at low altitude, and further developments included the P-40K (Kittyhawk Mk III) version of the P-40E with the V-1710-33 engine, the P-40M with the V-1710-71 engine, and the definitive P-40N (Kittyhawk Mk IV) with the V-1710-81/99/115 engine and measures to reduce weight significantly as a means of improving performance.

P-40E Warhawk

P-40 Warhawk Tomahawk / Kittyhawk

CURTISS P-40F WARHAWK
Role: Fighter
Crew/Accommodation: One
Power Plant: One 1,300-hp Packard-built Rolls-Royce V-1650-1 Merlin water-cooled inline
Dimensions: Span 11.38 m (37.33 ft); length 10.16 m (33.33 ft): wing area 21.93 m² (236 sq ft)
Weights: Empty 2,989 kg (6.590 lb); MTOW 4.241 kg (9,350 lb)
Performance: Maximum speed 586 km/h (364 mph) at 6,096 m (20,000 ft); operational ceiling 10,485 m (34,400 ft); range 603 km (375 miles)
Load: Six .5-inch machine guns, plus up to 227 kg (500 lb) of bombs

FOCKE-WULF Fw 190 and Ta 152 (Germany)

Focke-Wulf Fw 190A

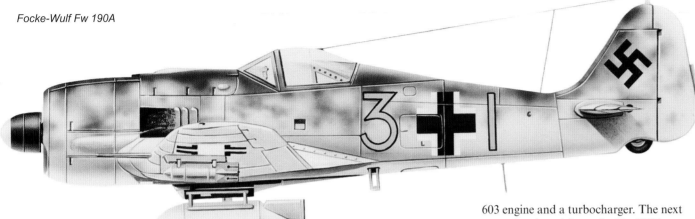

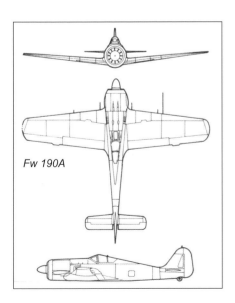

Fw 190A

The Fw 190 was Germany's best fighter of World War II, and resulted from the belief of designer Kurt Tank that careful streamlining could produce a radial-engined fighter with performance equal to that of an inline-engined type without the extra complexity and weight of the latter's water-cooling system. The first of three prototypes flew in June 1939, and an extensive test programme was required to develop the air cooling system and evaluate short- and long-span wings, the latter's additional 1.0 m (3 ft 3.7 in) of span and greater area reducing performance but boosting both agility and climb rate. This wing was selected for the Fw 190A production type in a programme that saw the building of about 19,500 Fw 190s. The Fw 190A was powered by the BMW 801 radial, and was developed in variants up to the Fw 190A-8 with a host of sub-variants optimized for the clear- or all-weather interception, ground-attack, torpedo attack and tactical reconnaissance roles, together with an immensely diverse armament.

The Fw 190B series was used to develop high-altitude capability with longer-span wings and a pressurized cockpit, and then pioneered the 1304-kW (1,750-hp) Daimler-Benz DB 603 inline engine. The Fw 190C was another high-altitude development model with the DB 603 engine and a turbocharger. The next operational model was the Fw 190D, which was developed in role-optimized variants between Fw 190D-9 and Fw 190D-13 with the 1324-kW (1,776-hp) Junkers Jumo 213 inline and an annular radiator in a lengthened fuselage. The Fw 190E was a proposed reconnaissance fighter, and the Fw 190F series, which preceded the Fw 190D model, was a specialized ground-attack type based on the radial-engined Fw 190A-4. Finally in the main sequence came the Fw 190G series of radial-engined fighter-bombers evolved from the Fw 190A-5. An ultra-high-altitude derivative with longer-span wings was developed as the Jumo 213-engined Ta 152, but the only operational variant was the Ta 152H.

FOCKE-WULF Fw 190 A-8
Role: Fighter
Crew/Accommodation: One
Power Plant: 1,600-hp BMW 801C-1 air-cooled radial
Dimensions: Span 10.5 m (34.45 ft); length 8.84m (29 ft); wing area 18.3 m² (196.98 sq ft)
Weights: Empty 3.170 kg (7,000 lb); MTOW 4,900 kg (10.805 lb)
Performance: Maximum speed 654 km/h (408 mph) at 6.000 m (19,686 ft); operational ceiling 11,400 m (37,403 ft); range 805 km (500 miles)
Load: Four 20-mm cannon and two 13-mm machine guns, plus up to 1,000 kg (2,205 lb) of bombs

Captured Fw 190A in replicated Luftwaffe insignia

LOCKHEED P-38 LIGHTNING (U.S.A.)

P-38J Lightning

The Lightning was one of the more important fighters of World War II and, though it was not as nimble as a machine as single-engined types, found its métier in the long-range role with heavy armament and high performance. The machine resulted from a 1937 specification issued by the U.S. Army Air Corps for a high-performance fighter providing such speed, climb rate and range that a single-engined aircraft was

virtually out of the question. Having opted for the twin-engined configuration, the design team then chose an unconventional layout with a central nacelle and twin booms extending as rearward extensions of the engine nacelle to accommodate the turbochargers and

support the wide-span tailplane and oval vertical surfaces.

The XP-38 prototype flew in January 1939 with 716-kW (960-hp) Allison V-1710-11/15 engines driving opposite-rotating propellers. Development was protracted, and the first of 30 P-38s, with

V-1710-27/29 engines, did not enter service until late 1941. Production totalled 10,037 in variants that included 36 P-36Ds with a revised tail unit and self-sealing fuel tanks, 210 P-38Es with the nose armament revised from one 37-mm cannon and four 12.7-mm (0.5-in) machine guns to one 20-mm cannon and four machine guns, 527 P-38Fs for tropical service with V-1710 49/53 engines, 1,082 F-38Gs with V-1710-55/55 engines and provision for 907-kg (2,000-lb) of underwing stores, 601 P-38Gs with 1062-kW (1,425-hp) V-1710-89/91s and greater underwing stores load, 2,970 P-38Js with an improved engine installation and greater fuel capacity, 3,810 P-38Ls with 1193-kW (1,600-hp) V-1710-111/113s, provision for underwing rockets and, in some aircraft, a revised nose accommodating radar or a bomb-aimer for use as a bomber leader, the P-38M conversions of P-38L as two-seat night fighters, and the F-4 and F-5 conversions.

P-38J Lightning

Lockheed P-38J Lightning

LOCKHEED P-38L LIGHTNING
Role: Long-range fighter bomber
Crew/Accommodation: One
Power Plant: Two 1,475-hp Allison V-1710-111 water-cooled inlines
Dimensions: Span 15.85 m (52 ft); length 11.53 m (37.83 ft); wing area 30.47 m² (327 sq ft)
Weights: Empty 5,806 kg (12,800 lb); MTOW 9,798 kg (21,600 lb)
Performance: Maximum speed 666 km/h (414 mph) at 7,620 m (25,000 ft); operational ceiling 13,410 m (44,000 ft); range 725 km (450 miles) with 1,451 kg (3,200 lb) of bombs
Load: One 20-mm cannon and four .5-inch machine guns, plus up to 1,451 kg (3,200 lb) of bombs

OPPOSITE: Lockheed P-38 Lightning

MITSUBISHI A6M REISEN 'ZEKE' (Japan)

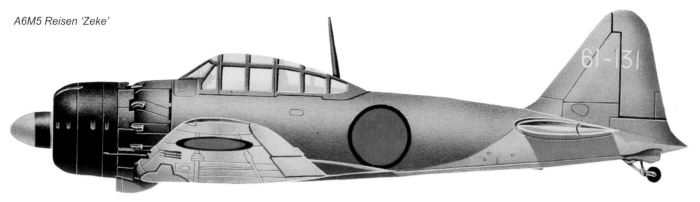

A6M5 Reisen 'Zeke'

31, and the A6M7 dive-bomber and fighter. There were also a number of experimental and development models as well as the A6M2-N floatplane fighter built by Nakajima. The principal Allied reporting name for the type was 'Zeke'.

MITSUBISHI A6M5 'ZEKE'
Role: Naval carrierborne fighter
Crew/Accommodation: One
Power Plant: One 1,130-hp Nakajima Sakae 21 air-cooled radial
Dimensions: Span 11 m (36.09 ft); length 9.09 m (29.82 ft); wing area 21.3 m² (229.3 sq ft)
Weights: Empty 1.894 kg (4,176 lb) MTOW 2,952 kg (6,508 lb)
Performance: Maximum speed 565 km/h (351 mph) at 6,000 m (19,685 ft); operational ceiling 11,740 m (38,517 ft); range 1,570 km (976 miles)
Load: Two 20-mm cannon and two 7.7-mm machine guns

The A6M Reisen (Zero Fighter) will rightly remain Japan's best known aircraft of World War II, and was in its early days, without doubt, the finest carrierborne fighter anywhere in the world. The A6M was the first naval fighter able to deal on equal terms with the best of land-based fighters, and was notable for its heavy firepower combined with good performance, great range and considerable agility. This combination could only be achieved with a lightweight and virtually unprotected airframe. Thus from 1943 the Zero could not be developed effectively to maintain it as a competitive fighter.

The A6M was planned to an Imperial Japanese Navy Air Force requirement for a successor to the Mitsubishi A5M, a low-wing fighter with an open cockpit and fixed landing gear. The first of two A6M1 prototypes flew in April 1939 with a 582-kW (780-hp) Mitsubishi Mk2 Zuisei radial. The new fighter was a cantilever low-wing monoplane with retractable tailwheel landing gear, an enclosed cockpit and powerful armament. Performance and agility were generally excellent, but the type was somewhat slower than anticipated. The sole A6M2 prototype therefore introduced the 690-kW (925-hp) Nakajima NK1C Sakae radial, and this was retained for the first series-built A6M2 aircraft that entered service with the designation Navy Type 0 Carrier Fighter Model 11. Production of the series amounted to 11,283 aircraft to the end of World War II, and major variants after the A6M2 were the A6M3 with the 843-kW (1,130-hp) Sakae 21 and clipped wingtips, the A6M5 with improved armament and armour in three subvariants, the A6M6 with the Sakae

A6M5 Reisen

Mitsubishi A6M3 Zero

BELL P-39 AIRACOBRA (U.S.A.)

P-39 Airacobra Mk I

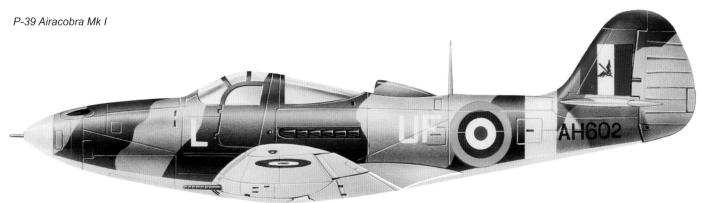

P-39 Airacobra

The P-39 Airacobra was an attempt to create a fighter that possessed greater manoeuvrability and more powerful nose-mounted armament than contemporary fighters. The engine was located behind the cockpit on the aircraft's centre of gravity. It drove the propeller by means of an extension shaft, and the nose volume was left free for the forward unit of the retractable tricycle landing gear and also for heavy fixed armament, including one 37-mm cannon firing through the propeller shaft. The XP-39 prototype flew in April 1938, and was followed by 13 YP-39 pre-production aircraft, including one YP-39A with an unturbocharged Allison V-1710 engine. This last became the prototype for the production version, which was ordered in August 1939 as the P-45. These aircraft were in fact delivered as 20 P-39Cs and 60 P-39Ds with heavier armament and self-sealing tanks. Large-scale production followed. Total P-39 production was 9,590, even though the Airacobra was never more than adequate as a fighter and found its real mileu in the low-level attack role.

The main models were the 229 P-39Fs modelled on the P-39D but with an Aeroproducts propeller, the 210 P-39Ks with the V-1710-63 engine and a Curtiss propeller, 240 P-39Ms with the V-1710-83 engine and a larger propeller, 2,095 P-39Ns with the V-1710-85 engine but less fuel and armour, and 4,905 P-39Qs with two underwing gun gondolas. Large numbers were supplied to the U.S.S.R. in World War II.

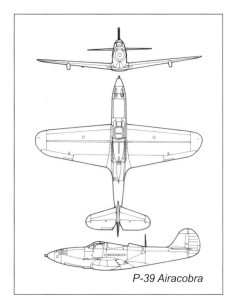

P-39 Airacobra

P-39N of the Italian Air Force

BELL P-39D AIRACOBRA
Role: Fighter
Crew/Accommodation: One
Power Plant: One, 1,150-hp Allison V-1710-35 water-cooled inline
Dimensions: Span 10.36 m (34 ft); length 9.19 m (30.16 ft); wing area 19.79 m² (213 sq ft)
Weights: Empty 2,478 kg (5,462 lb); MTOW 3,720 kg (8,200 lb)
Performance: Maximum speed 592 km/h (368 mph) at 4,206 m (13,800 ft); operational ceiling 9,784 m (32,100 ft); range 1,287 km (800 miles) with 227 kg (500 lb) of bombs
Load: One 37-mm cannon, plus two .5-inch and four .303-inch machine guns, along with 227 kg (500 lb) of bombs

MIKOYAN-GUREVICH MiG-1 and MiG-3 (U.S.S.R.)

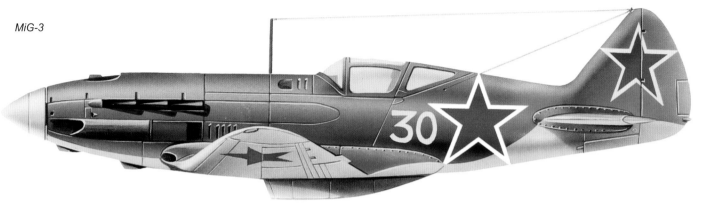

MiG-3

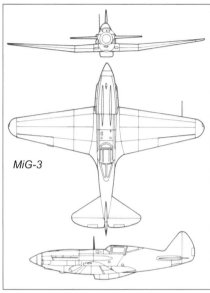

MiG-3

To design the new interceptor fighter requested by the Soviet Air Force in 1938, Artem Mikoyan and Mikhail Gurevich began a collaboration that led eventually to a succession of world-famous fighters. The two men's first effort was not so successful. As the starting point for the new interceptor, the MiG team produced I-65 and I-61 design concepts, the latter in variants with the Mikulin AM-35A and AM-37 inlines. The I-61 was deemed superior and ordered in the form of three I-200 prototypes.

The first of these flew in April 1940, and on the power of the AM-35A the type proved to have the excellent speed of 630 km/h (391 mph), making it the world's fastest interceptor of the period. The type was ordered into production as the MiG-1 with an open cockpit or a side-hinged canopy, and an armament of one 12.7-mm (0.5-in) and two 7.62-mm (0.3-in) machine guns. But range and longitudinal stability were both minimal, and structural integrity was inadequate after battle damage had been suffered, so only 100 were delivered before the MiG-1 was superseded by the strengthened and aerodynamically refined MiG-3. This had a rearward-sliding canopy, increased dihedral on the outer wing panels, greater fuel capacity, better armour protection and provision for weightier armament in the form of 200kg (440lb) of bombs or six 82-mm (3.2-in) rockets carried under the wings. Some 3,322 such aircraft were built, but these saw only limited use; the MiG-3 performed well at altitudes over 5000 m (16,405 ft), but most air combats with the generally better flown German fighters of the period took place at the low and medium altitudes below this height.

Restored Mikoyan-Gurevich MiG-3

MIKOYAN-GUREVICH MiG-3
Role: Fighter
Crew/Accommodation: One
Power Plant: One 1,350-hp Mikulin AM-35A water-cooled inline
Dimensions: Span 10.3 m (33.79 tt); length 8.15 m (26.74 ft); wing area 17.44 m² (187.7 sq ft)
Weights: Empty 2,595 kg (5,720 lb); MTOW 3,285 kg (7,242 lb)
Performance: Maximum speed 640 km/h (398 mph) at 7,000 m (22,965 ft); operational ceiling 12,000 m (39,370 ft) range 820 km/h (510 miles) with full warload
Load: Three 12.7-mm machine guns, plus up to 200 kg (441 lb) of bombs or rockets

VOUGHT F4U CORSAIR (U.S.A.)

A-7P Corsair II

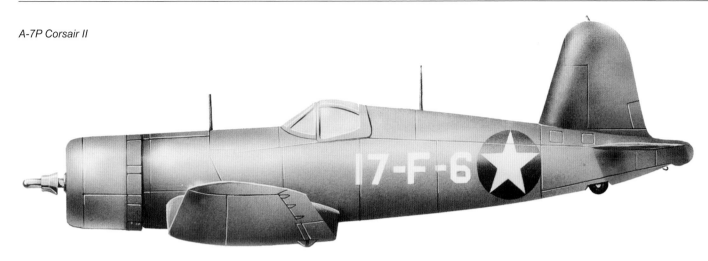

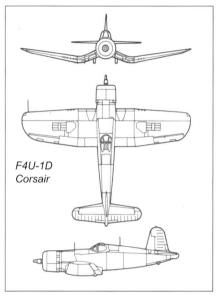

F4U-1D Corsair

One of several fighters with a realistic claim to having been the best fighter of World War II, the Corsair was certainly the war's best fighter-bomber and a truly distinguished type in this exacting role with cannon, bombs and rockets. The type originated as the V.166A design in response to a U.S. Navy requirement of 1938 for a high-performance carrierborne fighter. The design team produced the smallest possible airframe round the most powerful engine available, the 1491-kW (2,000-hp) Pratt & Whitney XR-2800 Double Wasp radial. This engine required a large-diameter propeller, and to provide this with adequate ground clearance without recourse to stalky main landing gear legs, the design team opted for inverted gull wings that allowed short main gear legs and also helped to keep the type's height as low as possible with the wings folded.

The V.166B prototype first flew in May 1940 as the XF4U-1, and after a troubled development in which the U.S. Navy refused to allow carrierborne operations until after the British had achieved these on their smaller carriers, the type entered service as the F4U-1. Total production was 12,571 up to the early 1950s, and the main variants were the baseline F4U-1 (758 aircraft), the F4U-1A (2,066) with a frameless canopy, the F4U-1C (200) with four 20-mm cannon in place of the wing machine guns, the F4U-1D (1,375) fighter-bomber, the F4U-1P photo-reconnaissance conversion of the F4U-1, the FG-1 built by Goodyear in three subvariants (1,704 FG-ls, 2,302 FG-lDs and FG-1E night fighters in the FG-1

total), the F3A built by Brewster in two subvariants (735 F3A-ls and F3A-lDs), the F4U-4 (2,351) with the 1827-kW (2,450-hp) R-2800-18W(C), a few of the F25 Goodyear version of the F4U-4, and several F4U-5, F4U-7 and AU-l postwar models.

Vought F4U Corsair

VOUGHT F4U-1D CORSAIR
Role: Naval carrierborne fighter bomber
Crew/Accommodation: One
Power Plant: One 2,000-hp Pratt & Whitney R-2800-8 Double Wasp air-cooled radial
Dimensions: Span 12.50 m (41 ft); length 1-0.16 m (33.33 ft); wing area 29.17 m² (314 sq ft)
Weights: Empty 4,074 kg (8,982 lb); MTOW 6,350 kg (14,000 lb)
Performance: Maximum speed 578 km/h (359 mph) at sea level; operating ceiling 11,247 m (36,900 ft); range 1,633 km (1,015 miles)
Load: Six .5-inch machine guns plus up to 907 kg (2,000 lb) of bombs

NORTH AMERICAN P-51 MUSTANG (U.S.A.)

P-51D Mustang

totalled 15,469, and the first variant was the Mustang Mk I reconnaissance fighter with an armament of four 12.7-mm (0.5-in) machine-guns; two of these 620 aircraft were evaluated by the U.S. Army Air Corps with the designation XP-51. The next variants were the 93 Mustang Mk IAs and 57 equivalent P-51s with four 20-mm cannon, and the 50 longer-range Mustang Mk IIs and 250 equivalent P-51As with more power and four machine guns. U.S. Army offshoots were the F-6 and F-6A reconnaissance

The Mustang was perhaps the greatest fighter of World War II in terms of all-round performance and capability, and resulted from a British requirement of April 1940 that stipulated a first flight within 120 days of contract signature. The NA-73X flew in October of the same year with an 820-kW (1,100-hp) Allison V-1710-F3R inline. Mustang production

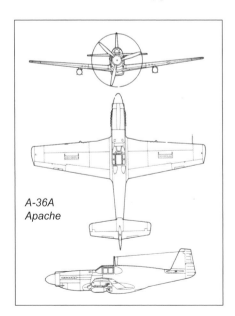

A-36A Apache

North American P-51 Mustang

decisive fighter of the second half of World War II.

Later variants expanded on the theme of the P-51D: the 555 P-51Hs were of a lightened version, the 1,337 P-51Ks were of a similarly lightened variant with an Aeroproducts propeller, and the F-6K was the reconnaissance conversion of the P-51K. The type was also built under licence in Australia with designations running from Mustang Mk 20 to Mustang Mk 24.

aircraft and the A-36A Apache dive-bomber and ground-attack aircraft.

Tactical capability was hampered by the V-1710 engine, so the basic airframe

NORTH AMERICAN P-51D MUSTANG
Role: Day fighter
Crew/Accommodation: One
Power Plant: One 1,450-hp Packard/Rolls Royce Merlin V-1650-7 water-cooled inline
Dimensions: Span 11.28 m (37 ft); length 9.83 m (32.25 ft); wing area 21.83 m² (235 sq ft)
Weights: Empty 3,466 kg (7,635 lb); MTOW 5,493 kg (12,100 lb)
Performance: Maximum speed 703 km/h (437 mph) at 7,625 m (25,000 ft); operational ceiling 12,192 m (40,000 ft); range 2,655 km (1,650 miles) with maximum fuel
Load: Six .5-inch machine guns, plus up to 907 kg (2,000 lb) of externally carried bombs or fuel tanks

was revised to take the Rolls-Royce Merlin built under licence in the United States by Packard as the V-1650. Production versions were the 910 Mustang Mk IIIs with four machine-guns and the equivalent P-51B and P-51C, respectively 1,988 and 1,750 aircraft with original and bubble canopies; there were also F-6C reconnaissance aircraft.

The classic and most extensively built variant was the P-51D (71,966, of which 875 became British Mustang Mk IVs) with a cutdown rear fuselage, a bubble canopy, six machine guns, greater power and more fuel; the F-6D was the reconnaissance version. The P-5ID had the range to escort U.S. bombers on deep raids, and was the

REPUBLIC P-47 THUNDERBOLT

P-47D Thunderbolt

The Thunderbolt was one of a trio of superb American fighters to see extensive service in World War II. The massive fuselage of this heavyweight fighter was dictated by the use of a large turbocharger which was located in the rear fuselage for balance reasons and therefore had to be connected to the engine by extensive lengths of wide-diameter ducting. The type was clearly related to Republic's early portly-fuselage fighters, the P-35 and P-43 Lancer, but was marked by very high performance, high firepower and great structural strength.

The XP-47B prototype flew in May 1941 with the 1380-kW (1,850-hp) XR-2800 radial, later revised to develop 1491 kW (2,000 hp). This formed the basis of the 171 P-47B production aircraft with the R-2800-21 radial, and the 602 P-47Cs with a longer forward fuselage for the same engine or, in later examples, the 1715-kW (2,300-hp) R-2800-59 radial; the type also featured provision for a drop tank or bombs. The P-47D was the main production model, 12,602 being built with the 1715-kW (2,300 hp) R-2800-21W or 1890-kW (2,535-hp) R-2800-59W water-injected radials, as well as a greater load of external stores that could include 1134kg (2,500lb) of bombs or ten 127-mm (5-in) rockets in the fighter-bomber role that became an increasingly important part of the Thunderbolt's repertoire. Early aircraft had the original 'razorback' canopy/rear fuselage, but later machines introduced a 360° vision bubble canopy and a cutdown rear fuselage. P-47G was the designation given to 354 Wright-built P-47Ds. and the only other production models were the 130 P-47M 'sprinters' with the 2088-kW (2,800-hp) R-2800-57(C) radial and the 1,816 P-47N long-range aircraft with a strengthened and longer wing plus the 2088-kW (2,800-hp) R-2800-77 radial. The Thunderbolt was never an effective close-in fighter, but excelled in the high-speed dive-and-zoom attacks useful in long-range escort.

P-47D Thunderbolt

REPUBLIC P-47C THUNDERBOLT
Role: Fighter
Crew/Accommodation: One
Power Plant: One 2,000-hp Pratt & Whitney R-2800-21 Double Wasp air-cooled radial
Dimensions: Span 12.42 m (40.75 ft); length 10.99 m (36,08 ft); wing area 27.87 m² (300 sq ft)
Weights: Empty 4,491 kg (9,900 lb); MTOW 6,770 kg (14,925 lb)
Performance: Maximum speed 697 km/h (433 mph) at 9,144 m (30,000 ft); operational ceiling 12,802 m (42,000 ft); range 722 km (480 miles) with a 227 kg (500 lb) bomb
Load: Eight .5-inch machine guns, plus up to 227 kg (500 lb) of bombs

Republic P-47 Thunderbolt

YAKOVLEV Yak-9 (U.S.S.R.)

Yak-9D

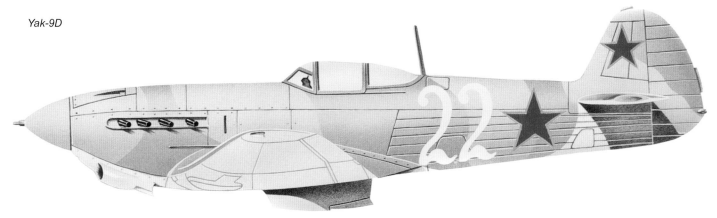

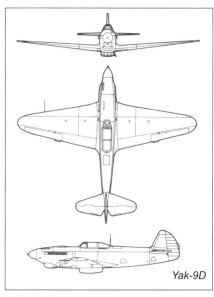

Yak-9D

The Yak-9 was one of the finest fighters of World War II, and was the most prolific culmination of the evolutionary design philosophy that started with the Yak-1. The Yak-9 entered combat during the Battle of Stalingrad late in 1942, and was a development of the Yak-7DI that was notable for its mixed wood and metal primary structure.

Production lasted to 1946 and totalled 16,769 aircraft in several important and some lesser variants. These included the original Yak-9 with the 969-kW (1,300-hp) Klimov VK-105PF-1 or 1014-kW (1,360-hp) VK-105PF-3 inline engine plus an armament of one 20-mm cannon and one or two 12.7-mm (0.5-in) machine guns, the Yak-9M with revised armament, the Yak-9D long-range escort fighter with the VK-105PF-3 engine and greater fuel capacity, the Yak-9T anti-tank variant with one 37- or 45-mm cannon and provision for anti-tank bomblets under the wings, the Yak-9K heavy anti-tank fighter with a 45-mm cannon in the nose, the Yak-9B high-speed light bomber with provision

for four 100-kg (220-lb) bombs carried internally as part of a 600-kg (1,323-lb) total internal and external warload, the Yak-9MPVO night fighter carrying

searchlights for the illumination of its quarry, the Yak-9DD very long-range escort fighter based on the Yak-9D but fitted for drop tanks, the Yak-9U

conversion trainer in three subvariants, the YAK-9P post-war interceptor with the 1230-kW (1,650-hp) Klimov VK-107A inline and two fuselage-mounted 20-mm cannon, and the Yak-9R reconnaissance aircraft.

Yakovlev Yak-9

YAKOVLEV Yak-9D
Role: Fighter
Crew/Accommodation: One
Power Plant: One 1,360-hp Klimov VK-105PF-3
Dimensions: Span 9.74 m (32.03 ft); length 8.55 m (28.05 ft); wing area 17.1 m² (184.05 sq ft)
Weights: Empty 2,770 kg (6,107 lb); MTOW 3,080 kg (6,790 lb)
Performance: Maximum speed 602 km/h (374 mph) at 2,000 m (6,560 ft); operational ceiling 10,600 m (34,775 ft); range 1,410 km (876 miles)
Load: One 20-mm cannon plus one 12.7-mm machine gun

KAWASAKI Ki-61 HIEN and Ki-100 'TONY' (Japan)

Ki-61-I-KAIc Hien 'Tong'

completion of the 272 Ki-61-II airframes as Ki-100-Ia fighters, while new production amounted to 99 Ki-100-Ib aircraft with the cut-down rear fuselage and bubble canopy developed for the proposed Ki-61-III fighter. The designation Ki-100-II was used for three prototypes with the Mitsubishi Ha-112-IIru turbocharged radial for improved high-altitude performance.

The Ki-61 Hien (Swallow) was the only inline-engined Japanese fighter to see substantial use in World War II, and was developed in parallel with the unsuccessful Ki-60 though using the same Kawasaki Ha-40 engine, a licence-built version of the Daimler-Benz DB 601 A. The first Ki-61 prototype flew in December 1941. The Ki-61-I entered combat in April 1943 and soon acquired the Allied reporting name 'Tony'. By the time production ended in January 1945, 2,666 aircraft had been built in variants such as the Ki-61-I with two 7.7-mm (0.303-in) fuselage and two 12.7-mm (0.5-in) wing machine guns, the Ki-61-Ia with two 20-mm wing cannon, the Ki-61-Ib with 12.7-mm (0.5-in) fuselage machine guns, the Ki-61-Ic with a rationalized structure, and the Ki-61-Id with 30-mm wing cannon.

The Ki-61-II had a larger wing and the more powerful Ha-140 engine, but was so delayed in development that only 99 had been produced before United States Air Force bombing destroyed engine production capacity. Variants were the Ki-61-II KAI with the Ki-61-I's wing, the Ki-61-IIa with the Ki-61-Ic's armament, and the Ki-61-IIb with four 20-mm wing cannon. With the Ha-140 engine unavailable for a comparatively large number of completed Ki-61-II airframes, the Japanese army ordered the type adapted to take the Mitsubishi Ha-112-II radial engine, the 1119-kW (1,500-hp) rating of which was identical to that of the Ha-140. The resulting Ki-100 first flew in 1945 and proved an outstanding interceptor, perhaps Japan's best fighter of World War II, also known to the Allies as 'Tony'. The army ordered

Kawasaki Ki-61-1

KAWASAKI KI-100-II ,'TONY'
Role: Fighter
Crew/Accommodation: One
Power Plant: One 1,500-hp Mitsubishi Ha-112-II air-cooled radial
Dimensions: Span 12 m (39.37 ft); length 8.82 m (28.94 ft); wing area 20 m² (215.3 sq ft)
Weights: Empty 2,522 kg (5,567 lb); MTOW 3,495 kg (7,705 lb)
Performance: Maximum speed 590 km/h (367 mph) at 10,000 m (32,808 ft); operational ceiling 11,500 m (37,500 ft); range 1,800 km (1,118 miles)
Load: Two 20-mm cannon and two 12.7-mm machine guns

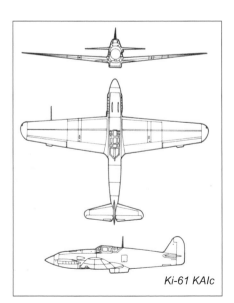

Ki-61 KAIc

FAIREY FIREFLY (United Kingdom)

Firefly AS.Mk 6

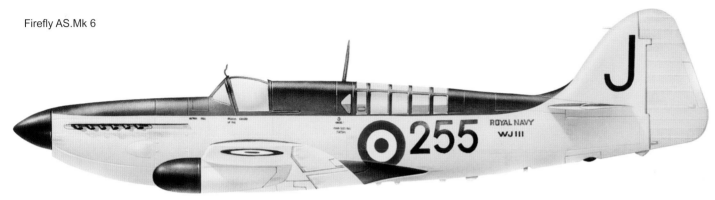

Firefly F.Mk I

Designed to a requirement for a carrierborne two-seat reconnaissance fighter and first flown in December 1941 as the first of four prototypes powered by the 1290-kW (1,730-hp) Rolls-Royce Griffon IIB inline engine, the Firefly was one of the Royal Navy's most successful warplanes of the 1940s. The type had an all-metal construction, low-set cantilever wings, retractable tailwheel landing gear, and naval features such as folding wings and an arrester hook.

The Firefly Mk I initial production series featured wings spanning 13.55 m (44 ft 6 in) and the 1484-kW (1,990-hp) Rolls-Royce Griffon XII with a chin radiator, and was produced in F.Mk I fighter, FR.Mk I fighter reconnaissance, NF.Mk I night-fighter and T.Mk I trainer versions to the extent of 937 aircraft. The 37 Firefly NF.Mk II night fighters had a longer nose and different radar, but were soon converted to Mk I standard.

Post-war conversions of the Mk I were the Firefly T.Mk 1 pilot trainer, T.Mk 2 operational trainer, and T.Mk 3 anti-submarine warfare trainer. The Firefly Mk IV switched to the 1566-kW (2,100-hp) Griffon 61 with root radiators in wings spanning 12.55 m (41 ft 2 in), and was produced in F.Mk IV and FR.Mk 4 versions. The Firefly Mk 5 introduced power-folding wings, and was produced in FR.Mk 5, NF.Mk 5, T.Mk 5 and anti-submarine AS.Mk 5 versions. The AS.Mk 6 was identical to the AS.Mk 5 other than in its use of British rather than American sonobuoys. The last production model, which raised the overall construction total to 1,623 aircraft, was the Firefly AS.Mk 7, which had the original long-span wing and a 1678-kW (2,250-hp) Griffon 59 with a chin radiator. Surplus Fireflies were also converted as remotely controlled target drones for the British surface-to-air missile programme.

FAIREY FIREFLY FR. Mk 5
Role: Fighter reconnaissance
Crew/Accommodation: Two
Power Plant: One 2,250-hp Rolls-Royce Griffon 74 water-cooled inline
Dimensions: Span 12.55 m (41.17 ft); length 11.56 m (37.91 ft); wing area 30.65 m² (330 sq ft)
Weights: Empty 4,389 kg (9,674 lb); MTOW 6,114 kg (13,479 lb)
Performance: Maximum speed 618 km/h (386 mph) at 4,270 m (14,000 ft); operational ceiling 8,660m (28,400 ft); range 2,090 km (1,300 miles) with long-range tankage
Load: Four 20-mm cannon, plus up to 454 kg (1,000 lb) of externally underslung bombs

Fairey Firefly from the Canadian Navy

61

GRUMMAN F6F HELLCAT (U.S.A.)

F6F-3 Hellcat

Cyclone and R-2800 Double Wasp units respectively). In June 1942, the XF6F-1 became the first of these to fly, and the type selected for production was the XF6F-3 powered by the 1491-kW (2,000-hp) R-2800-10 Double Wasp with a two-stage turbocharger. This model entered production as the F6F-3 and reached squadrons in January 1944; the Fleet Air Arm designated the type Gannet Mk I, but later changed the name to Hellcat Mk I. Production lasted to mid-1944, and amounted to 4,423 aircraft including 18 F6F-3E and 205 F6F-3N night fighters with different radar equipments in pods under their starboard wings.

That the Hellcat was in all significant respects 'right' is attested by the relatively

The Hellcat was the logical successor to the Wildcat with more size and power in a generally similar airframe with a low- rather than mid-set wing. A number of operational improvements suggested by Wildcat experience were incorporated in the basic design, and

after evaluating this, the U.S. Navy contracted in June 1941 for a total of four XF6F prototypes. These were built

with different Wright and Pratt & Whitney engine installations (normally aspirated and turbocharged R-2600

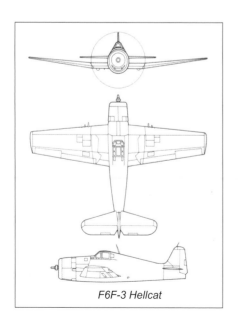

F6F-3 Hellcat

Grumman XF6F-4 Hellcat prototype

few variants emanating from a large production run that saw the delivery of 12,275 aircraft in all. From early 1944, production switched to the F6F-5 (Hellcat Mk II) with aerodynamic refinements including a revised cowling, new ailerons, a strengthened tail unit, and the R-2800-10W radial the suffix of which indicated the water injection system that produced a 10 per cent power boost for take-off and combat. These 6,436 aircraft also featured provision for underwing bombs or rockets. There were also 1,189 examples of the F6F-5N (Hellcat NF.Mk II) night fighter, and some F6F-5 and F6F-5N fighters were also converted as F6F-5P photo-reconnaissance aircraft.

Hellcat pilots claimed 4,947 aircraft shot down in combat, more than 75 per cent of all 'kills' attributed to U.S. Navy pilots in World War II.

GRUMMAN F6F-5 HELLCAT
Role: Naval carrierborne fighter
Crew/Accommodation: One
Power Plant: One 2,000-hp Pratt & Whitney R-2800-10W Double Wasp air-cooled radial
Dimensions: Span 13.06 m (42.83 ft); length 10.31 m (33.83 ft): wing area 31.03 m² (334 sq ft)
Weights: Empty 4,100 kg (9.060 lb): MTOW 5,714 kg (12,598 lb)
Performance: Maximum speed 612 km/h (380 mph) at 7,132 m (23.400 ft): operational ceiling 11,369 m (37,300 ft); range 1.521 km (945 miles)
Load: Two 20-mm cannon and four .5-inch machine guns, plus up to 975 kg (2,150 lb) of weapons, including one torpedo

Grumman F6F Hellcat

63

HAWKER TEMPEST (United Kingdom)

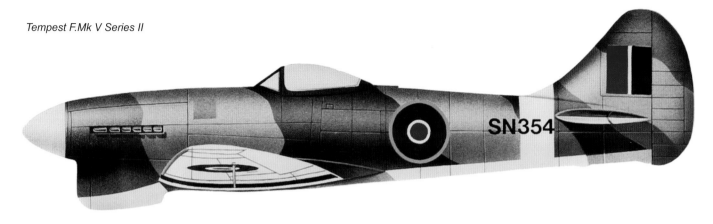

Tempest F.Mk V Series II

The failure of the Hawker Typhoon in its designed interceptor role left the British short of an advanced interceptor; in 1941 it was suggested the Typhoon be revised with a thinner, elliptical wing with low-drag radiators in the leading edges to replace the Typhoon's chin radiator. In

November 1941 two prototypes were ordered with the Napier Sabre inline. Early in 1942, the type was renamed Tempest. The two original prototypes became the Tempest F.Mks I and V with the Sabre IV and II respectively, and another four prototypes were ordered as two Tempest F.Mk IIs with the 1879-kW (2,520-hp) Bristol Centaurus radial and two Tempest F.Mk IIIs with the Rolls-Royce Griffon IIB inline, the latter becoming Tempest F.Mk IVs when fitted with the Griffon 61.

Initial orders were placed for 400 Tempest F.Mk Is, and the first such fighter flew in February 1943. The engine suffered development problems, however,

and the variant was abandoned. The first Tempest to fly had been the Tempest F.Mk V in September 1942, and an eventual 800 were built as 100 Tempest F.Mk V Series I and 700 Series II aircraft with long- and short-barrel cannon respectively, some later being converted as Tempest TT.Mk 5 target tugs. The Tempest Mk II materialized with the Centaurus V radial, and production for postwar service amounted to 136 F.Mk II fighters and 338 FB.Mk II fighter-bombers. The only other production model was the Tempest F.Mk VI, of which 142 were produced for tropical service with the 1745-kW (2,340-hp) Sabre V. Some of these were later adapted as Tempest TT.Mk 6s.

HAWKER TEMPEST Mk V
Role: Strike fighter
Crew/Accommodation: One
Power Plant: One 2,180-hp Napier Sabre IIA water-cooled inline
Dimensions: Span 12.49 m (41 ft); length 10.26 m (33.67 ft); wing area 28.05 m² (302 sq ft)
Weights: Empty 4,196 kg (9,250 lb); MTOW 6,187 kg (13,640 lb)
Performance: Maximum speed 700 km/h (435 mph) at 5,180 m (17,000 ft); operational ceiling 11,125 m (36,500 ft); range 1,191 km (740 miles) on internal fuel only
Load: Four 20-mm cannon, plus up to 907 kg (2,000 lb) of bombs or rockets

Tempest F.Mk V

Hawker Tempest V

DORNIER Do 335 PFEIL (Germany)

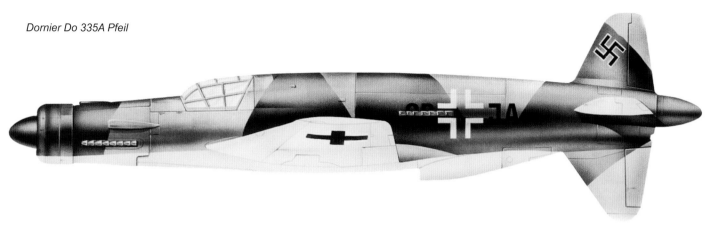

Dornier Do 335A Pfeil

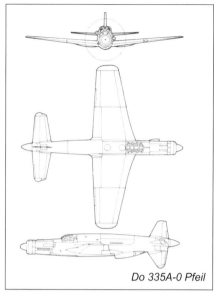

Do 335A-0 Pfeil

The unusual configuration of the Do 335 Pfeil (Arrow) was designed to allow the installation of two powerful engines in a minimum-drag layout that would also present no single-engined asymmetric thrust problems. Dr Claudius Dornier patented the concept in 1937, and the configuration was successfully evaluated in the Goppingen Go 9 research aircraft during 1939. Dornier then developed the basic concept as a high-performance fighter, but the Do P.231 type was adopted by the Reichsluftfahrtministerium (German Air Ministry) as a high-speed bomber. Initial work had reached an advanced stage when the complete project was cancelled. There then emerged a German need for a high-performance interceptor, and the wheel turned full circle as Dornier was instructed to revive its design in this role. The resulting aircraft was of all-metal construction, and in layout was a low-wing monoplane with sturdy retractable tricycle landing gear, cruciform tail surfaces, and two 1342-kW (1,800-hp) Daimler-Benz DB 603 inline engines each driving a three-blade propeller. One engine was mounted in the conventional nose position and the other in the rear fuselage powering a propeller aft of the tail unit by means of an extension shaft. The first of 14 prototypes flew in September 1943. Considerable development flying was undertaken by these one- and two-seater models, and 10 Do 335A-0 pre-production fighter-bombers were evaluated from the late summer of 1944. The first production model was the Do 335A-1, of which 11 were completed. None of these entered full-scale service, though some were allocated to a service test unit in the spring of 1945. The only other aircraft completed were two examples of the Do 335A-12 two-seat trainer. There were also many projected variants.

Dornier Do 335

DORNIER Do 335A-0 PFEIL
Role: Long-range day fighter
Crew/Accommodation: One
Power Plant: Two 2,250-hp Daimler-Benz DB 603E/MW50 liquid-cooled inlines
Dimensions: Span 13.80 m (45.28 ft); length 13.85 m (45.44 ft); wing area 38.50 m^2 (414.41 sq ft)
Weights: Empty 7,400 kg (16,315 lb); MTOW 9,600 kg (21,160 lb)
Performance: Maximum speed 768 km/h (477 mph) at 6,890 m (21,000 ft); operational ceiling 11,400 m (37,400 ft); radius 1,397 km (868 miles) at military power
Load: One 30-mm and two 15-mm cannons, plus a 500-kg (1,103-lb) bomb

KAWANISHI NIK 'REX' and 'GEORGE' (Japan)

N1K2-1 'George'

N1K4-J and N1K5-J prototypes had a longer forward fuselage, the 1491-kW (2,000-hp) Homare 23 engine and the 1641-kW (2,200-hp) Mitsubishi MK9A radial engine respectively.

Designed from 1940 as a fighter able to protect and support amphibious landings, the N1K was schemed as a substantial seaplane with single main/two stabilizing floats and a powerful engine driving contra-rotating propellers that would mitigate torque problems during take-off and landing. The first prototype flew in May 1942 with the 1089-kW (1,460-hp) Mitsubishi MK4D Kasei radial, but problems with the contra-rotating propeller unit led to the use of a conventional propeller unit. The type began to enter service in 1943 as the N1K1 Kyofu (Mighty Wind), but the type's raison d'être had disappeared by this stage of the war and production was terminated with the 97th machine. The Allied reporting name for the N1K1 was 'Rex'.

The N1K2 with a more powerful engine remained only a project, but in 1942 the company began development of a landplane version as the N1K1-J Shiden (Violet Lightning) with retractable tailwheel landing gear and the 1357-kW (1,820-hp) Nakajima NK9H

Homare 11 radial. This suffered a number of teething problems, and its need for a large-diameter propeller dictated the design of telescoping main landing gear legs. The new type flew in prototype form during December 1942,

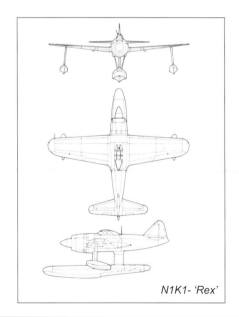

N1K1- 'Rex'

but development difficulties delayed the type's service debut to early 1944. N1K1-J production totalled 1,007 in three subvariants known to the Allies as 'George'. Yet this had been planned as an interim version pending deliveries of the N1K2-J version with a low- rather than mid-set wing, a longer fuselage, a revised tail unit, and less complicated main landing gear units. Only 423 of this version were produced/The N1K3-J,

KAWANISHI N1K1 'REX'

Role: Fighter floatplane
Crew/Accommodation: One
Power Plant: One 1,460-hp Mitsubishi Kasei 14 air-cooled radial
Dimensions: Span 12 m (39.37 ft); length 10.59 m (34.74 ft); wing area 23.5 m² (252.9 sq ft)
Weights: Empty 2,700 kg (5,952 lb); MTOW 3,712 kg (8,184 lb)
Performance: Maximum speed 482 km/h (300 mph) at 5,700 m (18,701 ft); operational ceiling 10,560 m (34,646 ft); range 1,690 km (1,050 miles) with full bombload
Load: Two 20-mm cannon, two 7.7-mm machine guns, plus up to 60 kg (132 lb) of bombs

Kawanishi N1K2-J Shiden KAI

de HAVILLAND D.H.103 HORNET (United Kingdom)

D.H. 103 Hornet F1

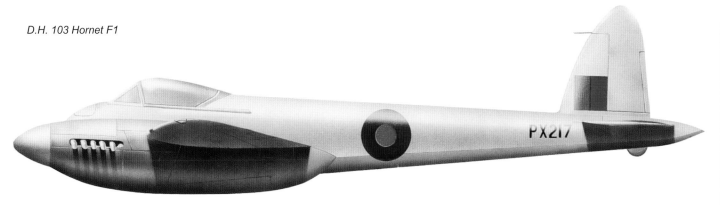

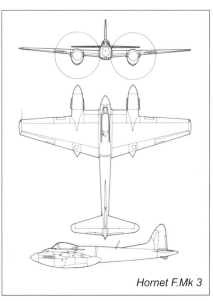

Hornet F.Mk 3

The D.H. 103 was designed to provide the British forces fighting the Japanese with a long-range fighter with the advantages of a twin-engined layout. The type was based on the aerodynamics of the Mosquito multi-role warplane, and so impressive were the estimated performance figures that a specification was written around the type in 1943. The D.H. 103 retained the Mosquito's plywood/balsa/ plywood structure for its single-seat fuselage, but featured new wood and metal wings. Work began in June1943, and the first prototype flew in July 1944 with two Merlin 130/131 inline engines. Performance and handling were excellent, and initial deliveries were made in April 1945. This first model was the Hornet F.Mk1, of which 60 were built, but it was too late for service in World War II.

The major variant of this land-based series was the Hornet F.Mk 3 with a dorsal fillet (retrofitted to earlier aircraft), greater internal fuel capacity, and provision for underwing loads of weapons or drop tanks. The last of 120 aircraft were delivered to Hornet FR.Mk 4 reconnaissance fighter standard with the rear fuselage fuel tank deleted to

provide accommodation for a single camera. The basic design also appealed to the Fleet Air Arm, which ordered the navalized Sea Hornet series. Deliveries included 78 Sea Hornet F.Mk 20 fighters based on the F.Mk 3 and first flown in August 1946 for a final delivery in June 1951, 79 Sea Hornet NF.Mk 21 two-seat night fighters based on the F.Mk 20 but with radar in a revised nose, and 43 Sea Hornet PR.Mk 23 photo-reconnaissance aircraft based on the F.Mk 20 but with one night or two day cameras.The last Sea Hornets were retired in 1955.

D.H. 103 Hornet F1

de HAVILLAND D.H.103 HORNET F.Mk 1
Role: Long-range fighter
Crew/Accommodation: One
Power Plant: Two 2,070-hp Rolls-Royce Merlin 130/131 liquid-cooled inlines
Dimensions: Span 13.72 m (45.00 ft); length 11.18m (36.66 ft); wing area 33.54 m² (361 sq ft)
Weights: Empty 5,671 kg (12,502) lb; MTOW 8,029 kg (17,700 lb)
Performance: Maximum speed 760 km/h (472 mph) at 6,706 m (22,000 ft); operational ceiling 11,430 m (37,500 ft); range 4,023 km (2,500 miles)
Load: Four 20-mm cannon

HAWKER SEA FURY (United Kingdom)

Sea Fury FB.Mk 11

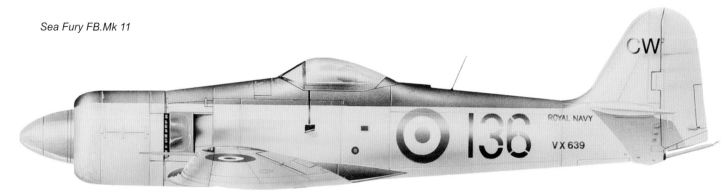

Centaurus XII, and development continued after the war to produce the first fully navalized machine with folding wings and the Centaurus XV. This flew in October 1945, and paved the way for

HAWKER SEA FURY FB.Mk 11
Role: Carrierborne fighter bomber
Crew/Accommodation: One
Power Plant: One 2,480-hp Bristol Centaurus 18 air-cooled radial
Dimensions: Span 11.70 m (38.40 ft); length 10.57 m (34.67 ft); wing area 26.01 m² (280.00 sq ft)
Weights: Empty 4,191 kg (9,240 lb); MTOW 5,670 kg (12,500 lb)
Performance: Maximum speed 740 km/h (460 mph) at 5,486 m (18,000 ft); operational ceiling 10,912 m (35,800 ft); radius 1,127 km (700 miles) without external fuel tanks
Load: Four 20-mm cannon, plus up to 907 kg (2,000 lb) of bombs or twelve 3-inch rocket projectiles

The origins of Hawker's second Fury fighter lay in a 1942 requirement for a smaller and lighter version of the Tempest, and was developed in parallel land-based and naval forms to 1943 specifications. Hawker was responsible for the overall design, with Boulton Paul allocated the task of converting the type for naval use. By December 1943, six prototypes had been ordered, one with the Bristol Centaurus XII radial, two with the Centaurus XXI radial, two with the Rolls-Royce Griffon inline, and one as a test airframe. The first to fly was a Centaurus XII-powered machine that took to the air in September 1944, followed in November by a Griffon-powered machine that was later re-engined with the Napier Sabre inline. Orders were placed for 200 land-based Fury and 100 carrierborne Sea Fury fighters, but the Fury order was cancelled at the end of World War II. The first Sea Fury flew in February 1945 with the

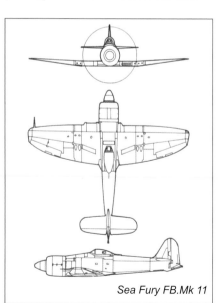

Sea Fury FB.Mk 11

Hawker Sea Fury

the Sea Fury F.Mk X, of which 50 were built.

The first type to enter widespread service was the Sea Fury FB.Mk 11 of which 615 were built including 31 and 35 for the Royal Australian and Royal Canadian Navies respectively. The Fleet Air Arm also took 60 Sea Fury T.Mk 20 trainers, of which 10 were later converted as target tugs for West Germany. Additional operators of new-build aircraft were the Netherlands with 22 Sea Fury F.Mk 50s and FB.Mk 50s, and Pakistan with 93 Sea Fury FB.Mk 60s and five T.Mk 61s. Other buyers were Burma (21 ex-British aircraft), Cuba (17 aircraft) and Iraq (60 aircraft).

Hawker Sea Fury

FIGHTERS & BOMBERS

PAGE 70: McDonnell Douglas
F/A-18 Hornet

PAGE 71: Dassault Mirage III

RIGHT: Grumman F-14A Tomcat

OPPOSITE: Harrier Jump Jet

JET FIGHTERS

Many argue that great progress in combat aircraft performance during World War I came mainly from the development of improved aero engines, with speeds from typically 105 km/h (65 mph) for unarmed reconnaissance aircraft at outbreak of war to over twice that by 1918 for fast fighters and bombers. Yet, by the start of the 1930s, major air forces were taking in new fighters that could only manage 322 km/h (200 mph), although these were followed from 1935 by a new breed of sleek and high-power fighters that raised speed to more than 483 km/h (300 mph). In August 1944 a U.S. Republic XP-47J Thunderbolt proved that a piston-engined fighter could pass the 800 km/h (500 mph) mark. But, by then, RAF and Luftwaffe jets were scoring air victories under combat conditions, proving once again the importance of engine technology in the development of fighters.

To achieve 811 km/h (504 mph) the XP-47J had been specially prepared, even having two guns deleted to save weight. In truth, the fastest operational piston fighters were somewhat slower, making the Luftwaffe's new Me 262 jet the only true over 500-mph fighter in service (with the exception of Germany's equally revolutionary Me 163 Komet rocket-powered interceptor), and thereby a real threat to Allied aircraft involved in continental operations. Fortunately for the Allies, only a small number of the Me 262s built were ever to become fully operational, though if proof was needed

of the menace they posed it came with the achievements of unit JV 44, which in just over one month in 1945 managed to destroy some 45 Allied aircraft while keeping only six or so of its many

accumulated Me 262s flying at a time. Conversely, many Me 262s were lost in operations, often caught in gunfire as they slowed to attack their heavily defended targets.

Simultaneously, the RAF put its own jet fighter into service as the Gloster Meteor. Compared with the Me 262, the first Meteors had less engine thrust and offered a much lower speed. But the

OPPOSITE: McDonnell Douglas F/A-18 Hornet

ABOVE: Avro Vulcan

overall design was very well suited to development and the Mk III version that appeared later in 1944 had more thrust, more fuel and higher performance, while postwar versions approached 965 km/h (600 mph).

Piston fighters generally had their swansong during the Korean War in the early 1950s, the first U.S. air victory coming in June 1950 when a Twin Mustang overcame a North Korean Yak-9, both piston-engined. Five months later a U.S.A.F. Lockheed F-80C Shooting Star jet fighter shot down a Chinese MiG-15, thus recording the first ever victory by one jet over another, seemingly sealing the fate of the piston fighters, although it is worth recording that reworked North American F-51D Mustang piston fighters survived in service with a handful of South American countries for counter-insurgency right through the 1970s. But, by the 1950s, the era of the jet fighter had begun in earnest and there was no looking back. The U.S. North American F-100 Super Sabre jet introduced the ability to sustain supersonic flight; in 1958 a Lockheed F-104 Starfighter greatly exceeded 2,000 km/h, and subsequently the Soviet MiG-25 took the speed of a production fighter well beyond 3,000 km/h. The story continues.

MESSERSCHMITT Me 262 SCHWALBE (Germany)

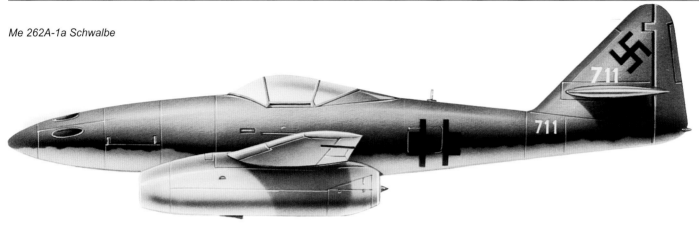

Me 262A-1a Schwalbe

the Schwalbe began in July 1944. Total production of the Me 262 was over 1,400 aircraft, but the majority failed to reach operational status. Variants included the Me 262A-2 Sturmvogel (Stormbird) fighter-bomber, the Me 262A-5 reconnaissance fighter, the Me 262B-1a two-seat conversion trainer and the Me 262B-2 night fighter.

MESSERSCHMITT Me 262A-1a SCHWALBE
Role: Fighter
Crew/Accommodation: One
Power Plant: Two 990-kgp (1,984-lb s.t.) Junkers Jumo-004B turbojets
Dimensions: Span 12.5 m (41.01 ft); length 10.605 m (34.79 ft); wing area 21.68 m² (233.3 sq ft)
Weights: Empty 4,000 kg (8,820 lb); MTOW 6,775 kg (14,938 lb)
Performance: Maximum speed 868 km/h (536 mph) at 7,000 m (22,800 ft) operational ceiling 11,000 m (36,080 ft); range 845 km (524 miles) at 6,000 mm (19,685 ft) cruise altitude
Load: Four 30-mm cannon

The Me 262 Schwalbe (Swallow) was, alongside the British Gloster Meteor, one of the world's first two operational jet fighters. Because of German indecision whether the Luftwaffe most needed a jet fighter or jet fighter-bomber, and difficulties in engine development,

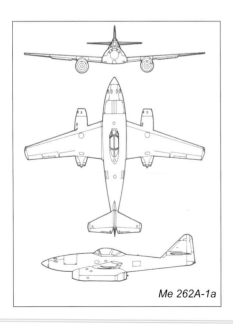

Me 262A-1a

operational deployment was later than might have otherwise been possible; with its clean lines, tricycle landing gear, slightly swept wings and axial-flow turbo jets, it was arguably the most advanced fighter to see service in World War II. Design work was launched in 1938 to meet a specification that called for a fighter powered by two of the new turbojet engines then under development by BMW, and eventually an order was placed for three prototypes powered by the 600-kg (1,323-lb) thrust BMW P-3302 engines. Work on the airframe proceeded more rapidly than development of the engine, so the Me 262 V1 first flew in April 1941 with a single nose-mounted Junkers Jumo 210G piston engine and retractable tailwheel landing gear, a type replaced by tricycle landing gear in later prototypes and all production aircraft. The piston engine was later supplemented by two BMW 003 turbojets, but these proved so unreliable that they were replaced by 840-kg (1852-lb) thrust Junkers 004As in a programme that required some redesign as the Junkers engines were larger and heavier

than the BMW units. The first all-jet flight took place on 18 July 1942. The five prototypes were followed by 23 pre-production Me 262A-0s before the Me 262A-1 entered service as the first production variant: the -1a had four 30-mm cannon and the -1b added 24 air-to-air unguided rockets. Operational use of

Me 262A-1a Schwalbe

GLOSTER METEOR (United Kingdom)

Meteor N F.Mk 11

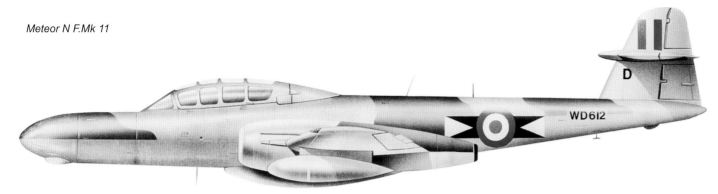

The Meteor was the only Allied jet fighter to see combat in World War II, and just pipped the Germans' Me 262 to the title of becoming the world's first operational jet aircraft. Given its experience with the E.28/39, the research type that had been the first British jet aircraft, Gloster was the logical choice to develop a jet fighter, especially as this would leave 'fighter companies' such as

Hawker and Supermarine free to concentrate on their definitive piston-engined fighters. The G.41 design took shape comparatively quickly. The first of eight prototypes started taxiing trials in July 1942 with 454-kg (1,000-lb) thrust

Rover W.2B engines, but it was March 1943 before the fifth machine became the first Meteor to fly, in this instance with 680-kg (1,500-lb) thrust de Havilland H.l engines.

Trials with a number of engine types

and variants slowed development of a production variant, but the 20 Meteor F.Mk Is finally entered service in July 1944 with 771-kg (1,700-lb) thrust Rolls-Royce W.2B/23C Welland I turbojets. The Meteor remained in RAF service until the late 1950s with the Derwent turbojet that was introduced on the second production variant, the Meteor F.Mk III, of which 280 were built, in most cases with the 907-kg (2,000-lb) thrust Rolls-Royce W.2B/37 Derwent I.

The type underwent considerable development in the postwar period when 3,237 were built. The main streams were the Meteor F.Mks 4 and 8 single-seat fighters of which 657 and 1,183 were built with Derwent I and 1633-kg (3,600-lb) thrust Derwent 8s respectively, the Meteor FR.Mk 9 reconnaissance fighter of which 126 were built, the Meteor NF.Mks 11 to 14 radar-equipped night fighters, the Meteor PR.Mk 10 photo-reconnaissance type of which 58 were built, and the Meteor T.Mk 7 two-seat trainer of which 712 were built. Surplus aircraft were often converted into target tugs or target drones.

Meteor F.Mk 8

A Gloster Meteor NF11 (above) and a Hawker Hunter T7A

GLOSTER METEOR F. Mk 8
Role: Fighter
Crew/Accommodation: One
Power Plant: Two 1,723-kgp (3,800-lb s.t.) Rolls-Royce Derwent 9 turbojets
Dimensions: Span 11,33 m (37.16 tt); length 13.59 m (44.58 ft); wing area 32.5 m² (350 sq ft)
Weights: Empty 4,846 kg (10,684 lb); MTOW 7,121 kg (15,700 lb)
Performance: Maximum speed 962 km/h (598 mph) at 3,048 m (10,000 ft); operational ceiling 13,106 m (43,000 ft); endurance 1.2 hours with ventral and wing fuel tanks
Load: Four 20-mm cannon

LOCKHEED F-80 SHOOTING STAR and T-33 (U.S.A.)

F-80C Shooting Star

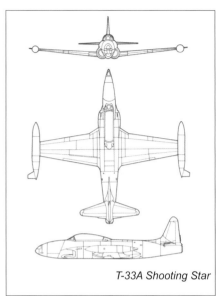

T-33A Shooting Star

The Shooting Star was the best Allied jet fighter to emerge from World War II, though the type was in fact just too late for combat use in that conflict. The design was launched in June 1943 on the basis of a British turbojet, the 1834-kg (2,460-lb) thrust de Havilland (Halford) H. 1B, and the first XP-80 prototype with this engine flew in January 1944 as a sleek, low-wing monoplane with tricycle landing gear and a 360° vision canopy. The two XP-80As switched to the 1746-kg (3,850-lb) thrust General Electric I-40 (later J33) engine, and this powered all subsequent models. The P-80A version began to enter service in January 1945, and just 45 had been delivered before the end of World War II. Production plans for 5,000 aircraft were then savagely cut, but the development of later versions, with markedly improved capabilities, meant that as many as 5,691 of the series were finally built.

The baseline fighter was redesignated in the F- (fighter) series after World War II, and variants were the 917 F-80As with the J33-GE-11 engine, the 240 improved F-80Bs with an ejector seat and provision

for RATO, and the 749 F-80Cs with 2087- or 2449-kg (4,600- or 5,400-lb) thrust J33-GE-23 or -35 engines and provision for underwing rockets in the

ground-attack role. The versatility of the design also resulted in 222 F-14 and later RF-80 photo-reconnaissance aircraft, 5,871 TF-80 (later T-33A) air force and

TO-1/2 (later TV-1/2) navy flying trainers that were in numerical terms the most important types by far, 150 T2V Sea Star advanced naval flying trainers with the 2767-kg (6,100-lb) thrust J33-A-24 and a boundary-layer control system, many AT-33A weapons trainers for the export and defence aid programmes, and many other variants.

P80 Shooting Star

LOCKHEED F-80B SHOOTING STAR
Role: Day fighter
Crew/Accommodation: One
Power Plant: One 2,041-kgp (4,500 lb s.t.) Allison J33-A-21 turbojet
Dimensions: Span 11.81 m (38.75 ft); length 10.49 m (34.42 ft); wing area 22.07 m² (237.6 sq ft)
Weights: Empty 3,709 kg (8,176 lb); MTOW 7,257 kg (16,000 lb)
Performance: Maximum speed 929 km/h (577 mph) at 1,830 m (6,000 ft); operational ceiling 13,870 m (45,500 ft); range 1,270 km (790 miles) without drop tanks
Load: Six .5-inch machine guns

de HAVILLAND D.H.100, 113 and 115 VAMPIRES (United Kingdom)

D.H 115 Vampire T.Mk 11

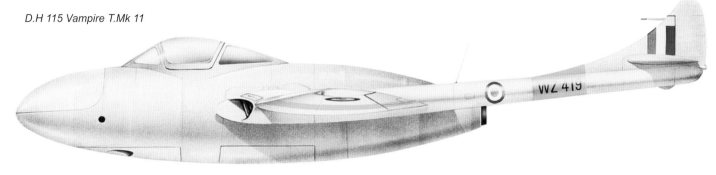

The Vampire, the second turbojet-powered British fighter, was too late for service in World War II. The type, known originally as the Spider Crab, was planned round a portly central nacelle and twin booms to allow the use of a short and therefore less inefficient jetpipe for the de Havilland Goblin engine, which was of the centrifugal-flow type and therefore of greater diameter than axial-flow types. The first prototype flew in September 1943, a mere 16 months after the start of detail design.

The Vampire F.Mk 1 entered service in 1946 with the 1225-kg (2,700-lb) thrust de Havilland Goblin I turbojet, and was followed by the Vampire F.Mk 3 with provision for underwing stores and modifications to improve longitudinal stability. Next came the Vampire FB.Mk 5 fighter-bomber with a wing of reduced span but greater strength for the carriage of underwing stores, and finally in the single-seat stream the Vampire FB.Mk 9 for tropical service with a cockpit air conditioner. British variants on the Vampire FB.Mk 5 theme were the Sea Vampire FB.Mks 20 and 21 for carrierborne use, while export variants included the generally similar Vampire FB.Mk 6 for Switzerland and a number of Vampire FB.Mk 50 variants with Goblin and Rolls-Royce Nene engines, the latter featuring in the licence-built French version, the Sud-Est S.E.535 Mistral. A side-by-side two-seater for night fighting was also produced as the Vampire NF.Mk 10 (exported as the Vampire NF.Mk 54 to France), and a similar accommodation layout was retained in the Vampire T.Mk 11 and Sea Vampire T.Mk 22 trainers. Australia produced the trainer in Vampire T.Mks 33, 34 and 35 variants, and de Havilland exported the type as the Vampire T.Mk 5.

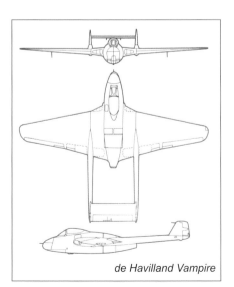

de Havilland Vampire

de HAVILLAND D.H.100 VAMPIRE FB Mk 5
Role: Strike fighter
Crew/Accommodation: One
Power Plant: One 1,420-kgp (3,100-lb s.t.) de Havilland Goblin 2 turbojet
Dimensions: Span 11.6 m (38 ft); length 9.37 m (30.75 ft); wing area 28.7 m² (266 sq ft)
Weights: Empty 3,310 kg (7,253 lb); MTOW 5,600 kg (12,290 lb)
Performance: Maximum speed 861 km/h (535 mph) at 5,791 m (19,000 ft); operational ceiling 12,192 m (40,000 ft); range 1,883 km (1,170 miles) with maximum fuel
Load: Four 20-mm cannon, plus up to 904 kg (2,000 lb) of ordnance

de Havilland Vampire T.Mk 11

F-84F Thunderflash

interesting of these being the GRF-84F (later RF-84K) designed to be carried by the Convair B-36 strategic bomber for aerial launch and recovery.

REPUBLIC F-84B THUNDERJET
Role: Fighter bomber
Crew/Accommodation: One
Power Plant: One 1,814-kgp (4,000-lb s.t.) Allison J35-A-15 turbojet
Dimensions: Span 11.1 m (36.42 ft): length 11.41 m (37.42 ft): wing area 24.15 m² (260 sq ft)
Weights: Empty 4,326 kg (9,538 lb): MTOW 8,931 kg (19,689 lb)
Performance: Maximum speed 945 km/h (587 mph) at 1,219 m (4,000 ft); operational ceiling 12,421 m (40,750 ft); range 2,063 km (1,282 miles)
Load: Six .5-inch machine guns and thirty-two 5-inch rocket projectiles

The Thunderjet was Republic's first jet-powered fighter, a straight-winged successor to the P-47 Thunderbolt that first flew in February 1946 as the first of three XP-84 prototypes with the 1701-kg (3,750-lb) thrust General Electric J35-GE-7 turbojet. The 25 YP-84A service trial aircraft switched to the 1814-kg (4,000-lb) thrust Allison J35-A-15, the type chosen for the 226 P-84B initial production aircraft. The 191 P-84C (later F-84C) aircraft had the similarly rated J35-A-13C but a revised electrical system, while the 154 F-84Ds had the 2268-kg (5,000-lb) thrust J35-A-17D engine, revised landing gear and thicker-skinned wings.

Korean War experience resulted in the F-84E, of which 843 were built with a lengthened fuselage, enlarged cockpit and improved systems. The F-84G was similar but powered by the 2540-kg (5,600-lb) thrust J35-A-29, and the 3,025 of this variant were able to deliver nuclear weapons in the tactical strike role. The basic design was then revised as the Thunderstreak to incorporate swept flying surfaces and the more powerful Wright J65 turbojet for significantly higher performance. Some 2,713 such F-84Fs were built, the first 375 with the J65-W-1 and the others with the more powerful 3275-kg (7,220-lb) thrust J65-W-3.

The final development of this tactically important warplane series was the RF-84F Thunderflash reconnaissance variant with the 3538-kg (7,800-lb) thrust J65-W-7 aspirated via root inlets, a modification that left the nose clear for the camera installation.

There were a number of experimental and development variants, the most

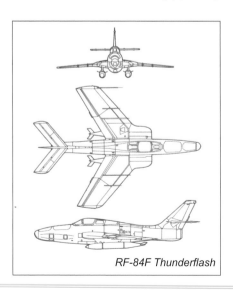

RF-84F Thunderflash

Republic P-84B Thunderjet fighters

MIKOYAN-GUREVICH MiG-15 'FAGOT' Family (U.S.S.R.)

MiG-17 'Fresco'

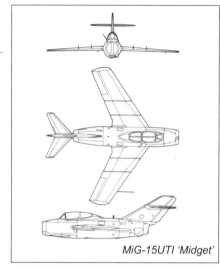

MiG-15UTI 'Midget'

The MiG-15 was the North American F-86 Sabre's main opponent in the Korean War, and was the production version of the 1-310 prototype that first flew in late 1947. The MiG-15 was the U.S.S.R.'s first swept-wing fighter to enter large-scale production. The type was powered by the Soviet version of the Rolls-Royce Nene turbojet, which was initially known as the Klimov RD-45 but then in further developed form as the VK-1.

MIKOYAN-GUREVICH MiG-17PF 'FRESCO-D'
Role: Fighter
Crew/Accommodation: One
Power Plant: One 3,380-kgp (7,452-lb s.t.) Klimov VK/1 FA turbojet with reheat
Dimensions: Span 9.63 m (31.59 ft): length 11.26 m (36.94 ft); wing area 22.6 m² (243.26 sq ft)
Weights: Empty 4,182 kg (9,220 lb); MTOW 6,330 kg (13,955 lb)
Performance: Maximum speed 1.074 km/h (667 mph) at 4,000 m (13,123 ft); operational ceiling 15,850 m (52,001 ft); range 360 km (224 miles) with full warload
Load: Three 23-mm cannon, plus up to 500 kg (1,102 lb) of bombs or unguided rockets

The MiG-15 proved itself a competent fighter, but the type's only major variant, the improved MiG-15bis, could outclimb and out-turn the Sabre in most flight regimes. Many thousands of the series were produced, most of them as standard day fighters, but small numbers as MiG-15P all-weather fighters and MiG-15SB fighter-bombers. The type was given the NATO reporting name 'Fagot', and there was also an important MiG-15UTI tandem-seat advanced and conversion trainer known as the 'Midget'. Licensed production was undertaken in Czechoslovakia and Poland of the S.102 and LIM variants.

The MiG-17 'Fresco' was the production version of the 1-330 prototype developed to eliminate the MiG-15's tendency to snap-roll into an uncontrollable spin during a high-speed turn. A new wing of 45° rather than 35° sweep was introduced, together with a longer fuselage, a revised tail unit and more power. Several thousand aircraft were delivered from 1952 in variants such as the MiG-17 day fighter, MiG-15F

improved day fighter with the VK-1F afterburning engine, MiG-17PF limited all-weather fighter, and MiG-17PFU missile-armed fighter. The type was also built in China, Czechoslovakia, and

Poland with the designations J-5 (or export F-5), S.104 and LIM-5/6 respectively.

MiG-15

NORTH AMERICAN F-86 SABRE (U.S.A.)

F-86F Sabre

OPPOSITE: North American F-86 Sabre

The Sabre was the most important American air combat fighter in the Korean War. In 1944 the U.S. Army Air Forces contracted for three XP-86 prototypes for a day fighter that could also double in the escort and ground-attack roles. When the fruits of German aerodynamic research became available to the Americans after World War II, the type was reworked to incorporate swept flying surfaces, and the first such prototype flew in October 1947 with a 1701-kg (3,750-lb) thrust General Electric TG-180 (later J35-GE-3) axial-flow turbojet. The type was then re-engined with the General Electric J47 turbojet to become the YP-86A, leading to the P-86A (later F-86A) production model with the 2200-kg (4,850-lb) thrust J47-GE-1 engine.

These 554 aircraft with four J47 marks up to a thrust of 2359-kg (5,200-lb) were followed in chronological order by the 456 F-86Es with a slab tailplane and the 3877-kg (5,200-lb) thrust J47-GE-27, the 2,540 F-86Fs with the 2708-kg (5,970-lb) thrust J47-GE-27 and, in later aircraft, the '6-3' wing with extended leading edges, the 2,504 F-86D redesigned night and all-weather fighters with the 2517-kg (5,550-lb) thrust J47-GE-33, the 473 F-86H fighter-bombers with the 4037-kg (8,900-lb) thrust J73-GE-3, greater span and a deeper fuselage, the 341 examples of the F-86K simplified version of the F-86D with the 2461-kg (5,425-lb) J47-GE-17B, and the 981 examples of the F-86L rebuilt version of the F-86D with a larger wing and updated electronics. The Sabre was also built in Australia as the CAC Sabre in Mk 30, 31 and 32 versions with two 30-mm cannon and the Rolls-Royce Avon turbojet, and in Canada as the Canadair Sabre in Mk 2, 4 and 6 versions with the Orenda turbojet.

NORTH AMERICAN F-86F SABRE
Role: Day fighter
Crew/Accommodation: One
Power Plant: One 2,708-kgp (5,970-lb s.t.) General Electric J47-GE-27 turbojet
Dimensions: Span 11.3 m (37.08 ft); length 11.43 m (37.5 ft); wing area 26.76 m² (288 sq ft)
Weights: Empty 4,967 kg (10,950 lb); MTOW 7,711 kg (17,000 lb)
Performance: Maximum speed 1,110 km/h (690 mph) at sea level; operational ceiling 15,240 m (50,000 ft); range 1,263 km (785 miles) without external fuel
Load: Six .5-inch machine guns, plus up to 907 kg (2,000 lb) of bombs or fuel carried externally

F-86E Sabre

TF-86 Transonic Trainer

SAAB 29 (Sweden)

Saab J 29

In 1943 SAAB flew its first fighter, the SAAB 21, an unconventional twin-boom pusher type with an ejection seat for the pilot. In 1947 a jet version was first flown as the SAAB 21R, with a British de Havilland Goblin turbojet replacing the earlier piston engine. Although the jet version was put into production and then operated in fighter and attack versions from 1949 to 1955, SAAB by then had much more advanced projects in hand, of which the SAAB 29 became the company's next production jet fighter and, historically, the first European swept-wing fighter to enter operational service.

The Goblin jet engine, then in production in Sweden, also powered Vampire fighters bought direct from Britain to boost Swedish squadrons, and it was logical therefore to design the SAAB 29 around the Goblin. However, with the appearance of the more-powerful 2,268-kg (5,000-lb thrust) de Havilland Ghost engine, the SAAB 29 was revised to use this (as the RM2).

Initial design work on the SAAB 29 had begun as early as 1945, then known as project R 1001. As a completely new design, SAAB chose a 'straight through' fuselage layout, with a nose air intake to feed the jet engine, the latter which exhausted below the narrowing boomlike rear portion of the fuselage and a conventional tail. However, by far the most important design feature was the eventual adoption of wings with 25° of sweepback, original plans to use straight wings having been reviewed after a SAAB engineer had shown foresight to act upon confiscated wartime German technical research material on advanced wing shapes seen during a visit to Switzerland.

The adoption of swept wings followed considerable wind-tunnel testing plus actual flight testing using scaled wings fitted to a Safir lightplane known for research purposes as the SAAB 201.

Featuring also a pressurized cockpit, the first of four prototype SAAB 29s first flew on 1 September 1948 and proved capable of bettering its designed maximum speed of 1,050 km/h (650

Two SAAB J 29Fs in flight

SAAB J 29F 'Tunnan'
Role: Fighter and attack
Crew/Accommodation: Pilot
Power Plant: One 2,800-kgp (6,170-lb s.t.) SFA-built RM2B turbojet with reheat (de Havilland Ghost 50)
Dimensions: Span 11.0 m (36.09 ft); length 10.23m (33.56 ft); wing area 24 m² (258 sq ft)
Weights: MTOW typically 8,000 kg (17,637 lb), but 8,375 kg (18,464 lb) possible
Performance: Maximum speed 1,060 km/h (658 mph); operational ceiling 15,500 m (50,850 ft); range 1,100 km (683 miles)
Load: Four 20-mm cannon plus rockets or two Sidewinder missiles

J 29F

mph). Production J 29As were delivered from May 1951, initially to F13 day fighter Wing at Norrkoping. Because of its stubby appearance, the fighter gained the nickname Tunnan (Barrel).

After the J 29A came the longer-range SAAB 29B of 1953 appearance, used both as the J 29B fighter and A 29B attack aircraft. The S 29C was a photo reconnaissance variant, which in 1955 established a world closed-circuit speed record of 906 km/h (563 mph). A few J 29Ds followed with Swedish-built afterburners, while the J 29E introduced the 'dog-tooth' wing leading edge to raise the critial Mach number and offer improvements in transonic handling. The final version was the J 29F, with dog-tooth wings, an afterburner to the Ghost 50 (RM2B) engine that raised thrust to 2,800 kg (6,170 lb), and the ability to carry two Sidewinder air-to-air missiles. In total, the Flygvapnet received 661 SAAB 29s, and many Bs were subsequently upgraded to F standard, while Cs later received dog-tooth wings. Austria took in 30 ex-Swedish J 29Fs from 1961. The final flight of a Tunnan was recorded in 1976.

SAAB J 29F 'Tunnan'

HAWKER HUNTER (United Kingdom)

Hunter FGA.Mk 58

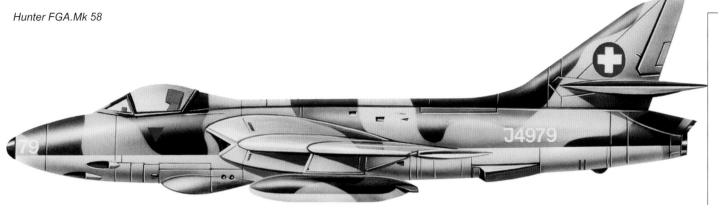

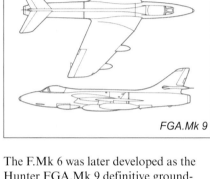

FGA.Mk 9

The Hunter was numerically the most successful of British post-World War II fighters, with 1,972 built including 445 manufactured under licence in Belgium and the Netherlands. The type still serves in modest numbers with a few air forces, though not as a fighter. This superb fighter resulted from a British need to replace the obsolescent Gloster Meteor with a more advanced type offering transonic performance and the P. 1067 prototype first flew in July 1951, and was followed just one month later by the first Hunter F.Mk 1 pre-production aircraft.

The first production article flew in May 1953, and the Hunter F.Mk 1 entered squadron service in July 1954 These aircraft were powered by the Rolls-Royce Avon turbojet, but the Hunter F.Mk 2 used the Armstrong Siddeley Sapphire Mk 101 turbojet. Further evolution led to the similar Hunter F.Mks 4 and 5 with more fuel and underwing armament capability, the former with the Avon Mk 115/121 and the latter with the Sapphire Mk 101. The Hunter F.Mk 6 introduced the Avon Mk 200 series turbojet in its Mk 203/207 forms, greater fuel capacity, along with the underwing armament of the F.Mk 4.

The F.Mk 6 was later developed as the Hunter FGA.Mk 9 definitive ground-attack fighter with the dogtoothed leading edges and Avon Mk 207 engine.

There were also tactical reconnaissance variants based on the FGA.Mk 9 and produced in Hunter FR.Mk 10 and FR.Mk 11 forms for the RAF and Fleet Air Arm respectively. Another variant was the side-by-side two-seat trainer, pioneered in the P.1101 prototype that first flew in mid-1955. This was produced in Hunter T.Mks 7 and 8 forms for the RAF and Fleet Air Arm respectively. Export derivatives of the single- and two-seaters were numerous, and Switzerland continued to acquire large numbers of refurbished Hunters for roles including ground attack.

HAWKER HUNTER F.Mk 6
Role: Day fighter
Crew/Accommodation: One
Power Plant: One 4,605-kgp (10,150-lb s.t.) Rolls-Royce Avon Mk 207 turbojet
Dimensions: Span 10.25 m (33.33 ft); length 13.97 m (45.83 ft); wing area 32.42 m² (349 sq ft)
Weights: Empty 6,505 kg (14,22 lb); MTOW 8,051 kg (17,750 lb)
Performance: Maximum speed 1,002 km/h (623 mph) at 10,975 m (36,000 ft); operational ceiling 14,630 m (48,000 ft); range 789 km (490 miles) on internal fuel only
Load: Four 30-mm cannon

Hawker Hunter T7

OPPOSITE: Hawker Hunter T7A

DASSAULT MYSTERE and SUPER MYSTERE (France)

Mystère IVA

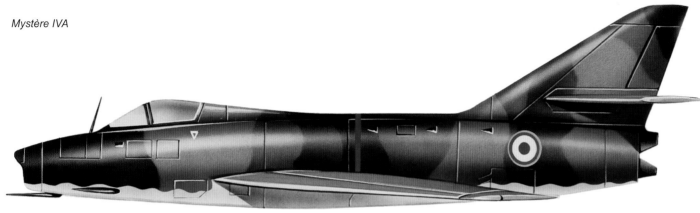

OPPOSITE: Dassault Mystère

At the end of World War II, Marcel Bloch was released from a German concentration camp, promptly changed his named to Dassault, and started to rebuild his original aircraft company as Avions Marcel Dassault, the premier French manufacturer of warplanes. After gaining experience in the design and construction of jet-powered fighters with the straight-winged M.D. 450 Ouragan fighter-bomber, Dassault turned his attention to a swept-wing design, the Mystère (Mystery). This first flew in the form of the M.D. 452 Mystère I

DASSAULT MYSTERE IVA
Role: Strike fighter
Crew/Accommodation: One
Power Plant: One 3,500-kgp (7,716-lb s.t.)
  Hispano-Suiza Verdun 350 turbojet
Dimensions: Span 11.13 m (36.5 ft); length
  12.83 m (42.1 ft); wing area 32 m² (344.5 sq ft)
Weights: Empty 5,875 kg (12,950 lb); MTOW
  9,096 kg (20,050 lb)
Performance: Maximum speed 1,120 km/h(604
  knots) at sea level; operational ceiling 13,716 m
  (45,000 ft); range 460 km (248 naut. miles)
Load: Two 30-mm DEFA cannon, plus to up
  907 kg (2,000 lb) of externally carried bombs

prototype form during February 1951, and was followed by eight more prototypes each with the Rolls-Royce Tay turbojet: two more Mystère Is, two Mystère IIAs and four Mystère IIBs. Then came 11 pre-production Mystère IICs with the 3000-kg (6,614-lb) thrust SNECMA Atar 101 turbojet, and these paved the way for the Mystère IV production prototype that first flew in

September 1952 with the Tay turbojet but thinner and more highly swept wings, a longer oval-section fuselage, and modified tail surfaces. There followed nine Mystère IVA pre-production aircraft and finally more than 480 production fighters, of which the first 50 retained the Tay but the others used the 3500-kg (7,716-lb) thrust Hispano-Suiza Verdun 350 turbojet.

Further development led to the Mystère IVB prototype with a Rolls-Royce Avon turbojet, a thinner and more highly swept wing, and a revised fuselage of lower drag. The resulting Super Mystère B1 production prototype flew in March 1955 with an afterburning turbojet as the first genuinely supersonic aircraft of European design, and was followed by 185 examples of the Super Mystère B2 production model with the 4460-kg (9,833-lb) thrust Atar 101G-2/3 afterburning turbojet. Some aircraft were supplied to Israel, which modified a number with the 4218-kg (9,300-lb) thrust Pratt & Whitney J52-P-8A non-afterburning turbjojet.

Dassault Mystère IVA fighters of the French Air Force's EC 8 wing

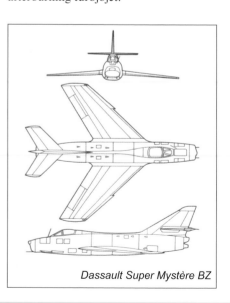

Dassault Super Mystère BZ

CONVAIR F-102 DELTA DAGGER and F-106 DELTA DART (U.S.A.)

F-106A Delta Dart

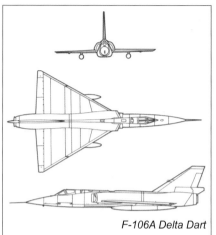

F-106A Delta Dart

These two delta-winged fighters were designed specifically for air defence of the continental United States and were among the first aircraft in the world designed as part of a complete weapon system integrating airframe, sensors and weapons. The YF-102 was developed on the basis of data derived from the experimental programme undertaken with the XF-92A, which itself was derived from American assessment of German research into delta-winged aircraft during World War II. The Model 8 was planned to provide the U.S. Air Force with an 'Ultimate Interceptor' for the defence of North American airspace, and was intended to possess Mach 2+ performance and carry the very advanced MX-1179 Electronic Control System. The resulting Model 8-80 was ordered as a single YF-102 prototype and first flew in October 1952 with a 4400-kg (9,700-lb) thrust Pratt & Whitney J57-P-11 turbojet. This prototype was soon lost in an accident but had already displayed disappointing performance.

The airframe of the succeeding YF-102A was redesigned with Whitcomb area ruling to reduce drag, and this improved performance to a degree that made feasible the introduction of F-102A

Convair F-106A Delta Dart

CONVAIR-F-106A DELTA DART
Role: All-weather interceptor
Crew/Accommodation: One
Power Plant: One 11,115-kgp (24,500-lb s.t.)
 Pratt & Whitney J75-P-17 turbojet with reheat
Dimensions: Span 11.67 m (38.29 ft); length
 21.56 m (70.73 ft); wing area 64.83 m²
 (697.8 sq ft)
Weights: Empty 10,904 kg (24,038 lb); MTOW
 17,779 kg (39,195 lb)
Performance: Maximum speed 2,135 km/h (1,152
 knots) at 10,668 m (35,000 ft); operational
 ceiling 16,063 m (52,700 ft); radius 789 km
 (490 miles) on internal fuel only
Load: One 20-mm multi-barrel cannon, plus
 one long-range and four medium-range air-
 to-air missiles

single-seat fighter and TF-102A two-seat trainer variants. The MX-1179 ECS had proved too difficult for the technology of the time, so the less advanced MG-3 fire-control system was adopted for these models, of which 875 and 111 respectively were built. Greater effort went into the development of the true Mach 2 version, which was developed as the F-102B but then ordered as the F-106 before the first of two YF-106A prototypes flew in December 1956. The F-106A single-seat fighter and F-102B two-seat trainer versions were produced to the extent of 277 and 63 aircraft respectively, and these served into the later 1980s.

F-106 Delta Dart

91

VOUGHT F-8 CRUSADER (U.S.A.)

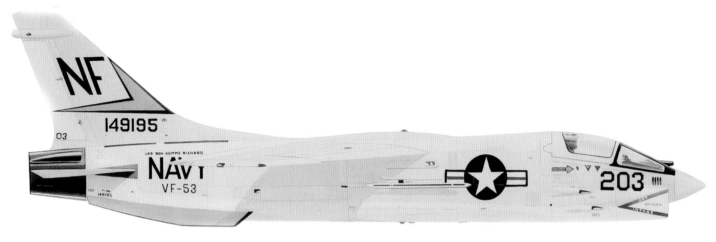

Aslightly later contemporary of the North American F-100 Super Sabre that used practically the same powerplant, the Crusader carrierborne fighter was an altogether more capable machine despite the additional fixed weight of its naval equipment. The design's most interesting feature was a variable-incidence wing that allowed the fuselage to be kept level during take-off and landing, thereby improving the pilot's fields of vision. The type resulted from a 1952 U.S. Navy requirement for an air-superiority fighter with truly supersonic performance, and from eight submissions the Vought design was selected in May 1953.

The first of two XF8U-1 prototypes flew in March 1955 with the 6713-kg (14,800-lb) thrust Pratt & Whitney J57-P- 11 turbojet. Deliveries to operational squadrons began in March 1957 of the F8U-1 with the 7348-kg (16,200-lb) thrust J57-P-4A, four 20-mm cannon, rockets in an underfuselage pack and, as a retrofit, Sidewinder air-to air missiles. Production totalled 318, and from 1962 these aircraft were redesignated F-8A. There followed 30 examples of the F8U- 1E (F-8B) with limited all-weather capability, 187 examples of the F8U-2 (F-8C) with the 7666-kg (16,900-lb) thrust J57-P-16, 152 examples of the F8U-2N (F-8D) with the 8,165-kg (18,000-lb) thrust J57-P-20, extra fuel and four Sidewinder missiles, and 286 examples of the F8U-2NE (F-8E) with the 8165-kg (18,000-lb) thrust J57-P-20A, advanced radar and provision for 1,814 kg (4,000 lb) of external stores on four underwing hardpoints. In addition, 42 F-8E (FN)s were built for the French Navy, the only remaining type in service, to be replaced by Rafales. The F-8H to L were rebuilds of older aircraft to an improved standard with a strengthened airframe and blown flaps, and a reconnaissance variant was the F8U-1P (RF-8A); 73 were later rebuilt to RF-8G standard with the J57-P-20A.

F8U-2 Crusader

The French Navy's version of the Vought Crusader is the F-8E (FN)

VOUGHT F-8E CRUSADER
Role: Naval carrierborne fighter
Crew/Accommodation: One
Power Plant: One 8,165-kgp (18,000-lb s.t.) Pratt & Whitney J57-P-20 turbojet with reheat
Dimensions: Span 10.9 m (35.7 ft); length16.5 m (54.2 ft); wing area 34.8 m² (375 sqft)
Weights: Empty 8,960 kg (19,750 lb); MTOW 15,420 kg (34,000 lb)
Performance: Maximum speed 1,802 km/h (973 knots) Mach 1.7 at 12,192 m (40,000 ft); operational ceiling 17,374 m (57,000 ft); radius 966 km (521 naut. miles)
Load: Four 30-mm cannon, plus up to 2,268 kg (5,000 lb) of externally carried weapons, which can include four short-range air-to-air missiles

SUD-OUEST S.O.4050 VAUTOUR (France)

S.O.4050 Vautour II-N

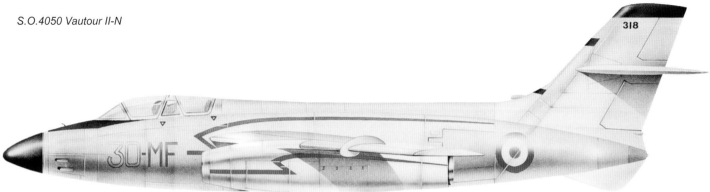

OPPOSITE: Sud-Ouest S.O.4050 Vautour

variants with a powerplant standardized as two 3500-kg (7,716-lb) thrust Atar 101Es. Even so, production totalled just 140 aircraft. These comprised 30 single-seat Vautour II-A ground-attack aircraft, 40 two-seat Vautour II-B bombers, and 70 two-seat Vautour II-N night fighters, with equipment and armament optimized for the three types' specific role. The first of these three types flew in April 1956, July 1957 and October 1956 respectively. Some 18 aircraft were later supplied to Israel, and after retrofit with slab tailplanes, the Vautour II-N became the Vautour II-IN.

In the late 1940s, Sud-Ouest produced two half-scale research aircraft as the S.O.M.I air-launched research glider and its powered version, the S.O.M.2 with a Rolls-Royce Derwent turbojet. The company then evolved the S.O.4000 full-scale prototype with two Rolls-Royce Nene turbojets (licence-built by Hispano-Suiza) in the rear fuselage and the unusual landing gear ot a single nosewheel and four main wheels, the latter arranged in tandem pairs.

The S.O.4000 first flew in March 1951 and paved the way for the S.O.4050 Vautour (Vulture) prototype with swept flying surfaces and a landing gear arrangement comprising two twin-wheel main units in tandem under the fuselage and single-wheel outriggers under the nacelles of the wing-mounted engines. The first of three prototypes was a two-seat night fighter and flew in October 1952 with 2400-kg (5,291-lb) thrust SNECMA Atar 10IB turbojets; the second machine was a single-seat ground-attack type with 2820-kg (6,217-lb) thrust Atar 101Ds; and the third machine was a two-seat bomber with Armstrong Siddeley Sapphire turbojets. There followed six pre-production aircraft before it was decided to procure all three

S.0.4050 Vautour II

SUD S.O. 4050 VAUTOUR II-N
Role: All-weather/night fighter
Crew/Accommodation: Two
Power Plant: Two 3.300-kgp (7,275-lb s.t.) SNECMA Atar 101E-3 turbojets
Dimensions: Span 15.1 m (49.54 tt); length 16.5 m (54.13 ft): wing area 45.3 m² (487.6 sq ft)
Weights: Empty 9,880 kg (21,782 lb); MTOW 17,000 kg (37,479 lb)
Performance: Maximum speed 958 km/h (595 mph) at 12,200 m (40,026 ft); operational ceiling 14,000 m (45, 932 ft); range 2,750 km (1,709 miles) with maximum fuel
Load: Four 20-mm cannon

Sud-Ouest S.O.4050 Vautour

LOCKHEED F-104 STARFIGHTER (U.S.A.)

F-104S Super Starfighter

OPPOSITE: Lockheed F-104 Starfighter

The Starfighter resulted from the U.S. Air Force's experiences in the Korean War, where the need for a fast-climbing interceptor became clear. The type was planned by 'Kelly' Johnson with the smallest airframe that would accommodate the most powerful available axial-flow turbojet. This resulted in a fighter possessing a long and basically cylindrical fuselage with unswept and diminutive wings, plus a large T-tail assembly.

The first of two XF-104 prototypes first flew in March 1954 with an interim engine, the 4627-kg (10,200-lb) thrust Wright XJ65-W-6, and four years of troubled development followed with 17

YF-104As before the F-104A entered service with a longer fuselage accommodating the 6713-kg (14,800-lb) thrust J79-GE-3 engine and an armament of one 20-mm multi-barrel cannon and two AIM-9 Sidewinder air-to-air missiles. The USAF eventually ordered only 296 examples of the Starfighter in variants that included 153 F-104A interceptors, 26 F-104B tandem-seat trainers, 77 F-104C tactical strike fighters with provision for a 907-kg (2,000-lb) external load, and 21 F-104D tandem-seat trainers. The commercial success of the type was then ensured by the adoption of the much-improved F-104G all-weather multi-role type by a NATO consortium. This model had a strengthened airframe, a larger vertical tail, greater power, and more advanced electronics, and itself spawned the F-104J interceptor that was built in Japan. This multi-national programme resulted in the largely licensed production of another 1,986 aircraft up to 1983. The F-104G itself produced TF-104 trainer and RF-104 reconnaissance variants, and Italy developed the special F-104S variant as a dedicated interceptor with better radar and medium-range Sparrow and Aspide air-to-air missiles.

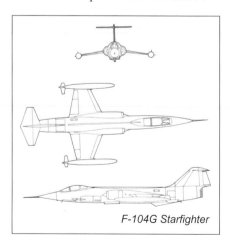

F-104G Starfighter

Lockheed F-104 Starfighter

LOCKHEED F-104A STARFIGHTER
Role: Interceptor
Crew/Accommodation: One
Power Plant: One 6,713-kgp (14,800-lb s.t.) General Electric J79-GE-3B turbojet with reheat
Dimensions: Span 6.63 m (21.75 ft); length 16.66 m (54.66 ft); wing area 18.2 m² (196.1 sq ft)
Weights: Empty 6,071 kg (13,384 lb); MTOW 11,271 kg (25,840 lb)
Performance: Maximum speed 1,669 km/h (1,037 mph) at 15,240 m (50,000 ft) operational ceiling 19,750 m (64,795 ft); range 1,175 km (730 miles) with fullwarload
Load: One 20-mm multi-barrel cannon and two short-range air-to-air missiles

REPUBLIC F-105 THUNDERCHIEF (U.S.A.)

F-105D Thunderchief

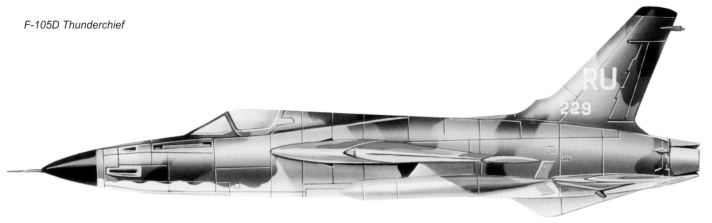

OPPOSITE: *Republic F-105 Thunderchief*

The Thunderchief was the final major type to come from the Republic company before its merger into the Fairchild organization and accorded well with its manufacturer's reputation for massive tactical warplanes. The type was schemed as a successor to the F-84F Thunderstreak and was therefore a strike fighter, but one that offered the advantages of an internal weapons bay able to accommodate 3629-kg (8,000-lb)

of stores and fully supersonic performance. This last was provided by the use of a powerful afterburning turbojet in an advanced airframe incorporating the lessons of the area-rule principle.

Two YF-105A prototypes were ordered, and the first of these flew in

October 1956 with the 6804-kg (15,000-lb) thrust Pratt & Whitney J57-P-25 turbojet and an 'unwaisted' fuselage. No production followed, for the availability of the new J75 engine and the area-rule theory resulted first in another four prototypes designated YF-105B and powered by 7471-kg (16,470-lb) thrust

J75-P-3. Production thus began with 71 F-105B aircraft modelled on the YF-105B and its area-ruled 'waisted' fuselage and forward-swept inlets in the wing roots for the 7802-kg (17,200-lb) thrust J75-P-5 engine. The major variant was the F-105D, of which 610 were built with all-weather avionics, an improved nav/attack system, the 7802-kg (17,200-lb) J75-P-19W turbojet and provision for up to 6350-kg (14,000-lb) of ordnance carried on four underwing hardpoints as well as in the internal load.

The final version was the F-105F tandem two-seat conversion trainer, and of 86 aircraft 60 were later converted to EF-105F (and then F-105G) 'Wild Weasel' defence-suppression aircraft. These were fitted with special radar-detection equipment and anti-radar missiles, and played an important part in American air operations over North Vietnam.

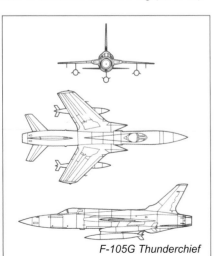

F-105G Thunderchief

Republic F-105 Thunderchief

REPUBLIC F-105D THUNDERCHIEF
Role: Fighter
Crew/Accommodation: One
Power Plant: One 11,113-kgp (24,500-ib s.t.) Pratt & Whitney J75-P-15W turbojet with reheat
Dimensions: Span 10.65 m (34.94 ft); length 19.58 m (64.25 ft); wing area 35.76 m² (385 sq ft)
Weights: Empty 12,474 kg (27,500 lb); MTOW 23,834 kg (52,546 lb)
Performance: Maximum speed 2,369 km/h (1,279 knots) Mach 2.23 at 11,000 m (36,090 ft); operational ceiling 12,802 m (42,000 ft); radius 1,152 km (662 naut. miles)
Load: One 20-mm multi-barrel cannon, plus up to 6,350 kg (14,000 lb) of weapons/fuel

SAAB 35 DRAKEN (Sweden)

F35 Draken

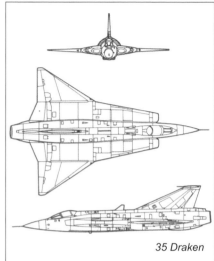

35 Draken

An even more remarkable achievement than the Saab 32, the Saab 35 Draken (Dragon) was designed as an interceptor of transonic bombers. This role demanded supersonic speed, a very high rate of climb, better than average range and endurance, and a sizeable weapon load. The tactical philosophy of the Swedish Air Force also dictated that the new type should have STOL capability so that it could operate from lengths of straight road during dispersed operations. The fighter was therefore designed on the basis of a slender circular-section fuselage and a double-delta wing in a combination that provided large lifting area and fuel capacity at minimum profile drag. To achieve much the same performance as the slightly later English Electric Lightning powered by two Rolls-Royce Avon afterburning turbojets, the design team opted for such a single example of the same engine built under licence in Sweden as the Flygmotor RM6. The layout was evaluated successfully in the Saab 210 research aircraft that was in essence a scaled-down Saab 35 and first flew in February 1952 with the 476-kg (1,050-lb) thrust Armstrong Siddeley Adder turbojet.

The first prototype of the Saab 35 flew in October 1955, and the J 35A initial production variant began to enter service in 1958. Production totalled 525 in variants such as the J 35A fighter with the 7000-kg (14,432-lb) thrust RM6B, the J 35B improved fighter with collision-course radar and a data-link system, the Sk 35C tandem-seat operational trainer, the J35D fighter with the 7830-kg (17,262-lb) thrust RM6C and more advanced electronics, the S 35E tactical reconnaissance aircraft and the J 35F with more advanced radar and Hughes Falcon air-to-air missiles. The type was also exported as the Saab 35X, and surviving J 35Fs have been upgraded to J 35J standard for service into the 1990s.

SAAB 35/J 35 DRAKEN

Role: Interceptor/strike/reconnaissance
Crew/Accommodation: One
Power Plant: One 7,830-kgp (17,262-lb s.t.) Flygmotor-built Rolls-Royce Avon RM6C turbojet with reheat
Dimensions: Span 9.4 m (30.83 ft); length15.4 m (50.33 ft); wing area 50 m² (538sq ft)
Weights: Empty (not available); MTOW 16,000 kg (35,274 lb)
Performance: Maximum/Cruise speed 2,150 km/h (1,160 mph) Mach 2.023 at 11,000 m (36,090 ft); operational ceiling 18,300 m (60,039 ft); range 1,149 km (620 naut. miles) with 2,000 lb warload
Load: Two 30-mm cannon, plus up to 4,082 kg (9,000 lb) of bombs

Saab 35 Draken

DASSAULT MIRAGE III and IAI KFIR (France and Israel)

IAI Kfir C-7

make most Mirage 5 and up-engined Mirage 50 models superior to the baseline Mirage III models.

Israel produced a Mirage 5 variant as the IAI Kfir with a General Electric J79 afterburning turbojet and advanced electronics, and this spawned the impressive Kfir-C2 and later variants with canard foreplanes for much improved field and combat performance.

Many surviving Mirages have been modernized to incorporate aerodynamics, avionics and weapon improvements, with newly-named variants including the Chilian ENAER Pantera, Belgian SABCA Elkan (for Chile), and South African Denel Cheetah.

The Mirage was designed to meet a 1954 French requirement for a small all-weather supersonic interceptor, and emerged as the delta-winged M.D.550 Mirage prototype for a first flight in June 1955 with two 980-kg (2,160-lb) thrust Armstrong Siddeley Viper turbojets. The type was too small for any realistic military use, and a slightly larger Mirage II was planned; this was not built, both these initial concepts being abandoned in favour of the still larger Mirage III that first flew in November 1956 with an Atar 101G-1 afterburning turbojet. Further development led to the Mirage IIIA pre-production type with an Atar 9B of 6,000-kg (13,228-lb) afterburning thrust boosting speed from Mach 1.65 to 2.2 at altitude.

The type went into widespread production for the French forces and for export, and as such was a considerable commercial success for Dassault, especially after Israeli success with the type in the 1967 'Six-Day War'. The basic variants became the Mirage IIIB two-seat trainer, the Mirage IIIC single-seat interceptor, the Mirage HIE single-seat strike fighter and the Mirage IIIR reconnaissance aircraft. The Mirage 5 was produced as a clear-weather type, though the miniaturization of electronics in the 1970s and 1980s have allowed the installation or retrofit of avionics that

DASSAULT MIRAGE HIE
Role: Strike fighter
Crew/Accommodation: One
Power Plant: One 6,200-kgp (13,670-lb s.t.) SNECMA Atar 9C turbojet, plus provision for one 1,500 kgp (3,307 lb s.t.) SEPR 844 rocket engine
Dimensions: Span 8.22 m (27 ft); length15.03 m (49.26 ft); wing area 34.85 m² (375 sq ft)
Weights: Empty 7,050 kg (15,540 lb); MTOW 13,000 kg (29,760 lb)
Performance: Maximum speed 2,350 km/h (1,268 knots) Mach 2.21 at 12,000 m (39,375 ft); operational ceiling 17,000 m (55,775 ft); radius 1,200 km (648 naut. miles)
Load: Two 30-mm DEFA cannon, plus up to 1,362 kg (3,000 lb) of externally carried ordnance

Mirage 5

Dassault Mirage III

101

MIKOYAN-GUREVICH MiG-21 'FISHBED' (U.S.S.R.)

MiG-21 'Fishbed'

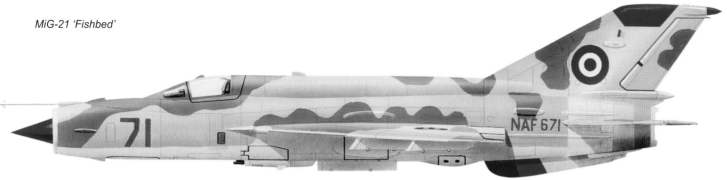

aerodynamically refined version of the MiG-2 IMF with increased fuel and ECM capability and MiG-2 Ibis third-generation multi-role fighter. There have also been three MiG-21U 'Mongol' conversion trainer variants. Currently, upgrades are offered by Russia and others, including the MiG-21-93 as chosen by India.

The MiG-21 (NATO name 'Fishbed') was designed, after the U.S.S.R. had digested the implications of the Korean War, to provide a short-range interceptor. The type was analogous to the Lockheed F-104 Starfighter in rationale, but was a radically different aircraft based on a tailed delta configuration, small overall size, and light weight to ensure adequate performance on just one relatively low-powered afterburning turbojet, the Tumansky R-11, that was only slightly larger and heavier than the RD-9 used

in the preceding MiG-19's twin-engined powerplant.

Differently configured Ye-2A and Ye-5 prototypes were flown in 1956, the latter paving the way for the definitive Ye-6 prototype that flew in May 1958. 10,158 MiG-21s were built in the U.S.S.R. (others in India, China as the J-7, and Czechoslovakia) in variants such as the MiG-21 clear-weather interceptor, MiG 21PF limited all-weather fighter with search and track radar, MiG-21 PFS fighter with blown flaps and provision for

RATO units, MiG-21FL export version of the MiG-21 PFS but without blown flaps or RATO provision, MiG-21PFM improved version of the MiG-21 PFS, MiG-21 S/SM second-generation dual-role fighter with a larger dorsal hump and four rather than two underwing hardpoints, MiG-21M export version of the MiG-2 IS, MiG-21R tactical reconnaissance version, MiG-2 IMF with the more powerful but lighter R-13-30 engine, MiG-21RF reconnaissance version of the MiG-2IMF, MiG-21SMT

MIKOYAN-GUREVICH MiG-21 SMT
FISHBED-K' Role: Strike fighter
Crew/Accommodation: One
Power Plant: One 6,600-kgp (14,550-lb s.t) Tumansky R-13 turbojet with reheat
Dimensions: Span 7.15 m (23.46 ft); length 13.46 m (44.16 ft); wing area 23 m² (247.57 sq ft)
Weights: Empty 5.450 kg (12,015 lb): MTOW 7,750 kg (17,085 lb)
Performance: Maximum speed 2,230 km/h (1.386 mph) Mach 2.1 at 12,000 m (39.370 ft); operational ceiling 18,000 m (59.055 ft); radius 500 km (311 miles) with full warload
Load: Two 23-mm cannon, plus up to 1,000 kg (2.205 lb) of air-to-air missiles or bombs depending upon mission

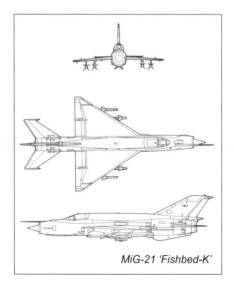

MiG-21 'Fishbed-K'

Mikoyan-Gurevich MiG-21 'Fishbed'

MiG-21 'Fishbed'

ENGLISH ELECTRIC LIGHTNING (United Kingdom)

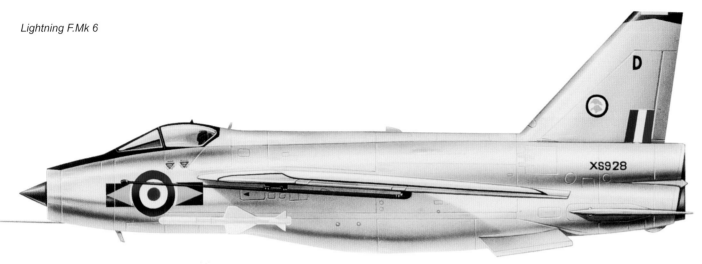

Lightning F.Mk 6

OPPOSITE: English Electric Lightning

The Lightning was the United Kingdom's first supersonic fighter. The type offered superlative speed and climb performance, but was always limited by poor range and indifferent armament. The origins of the type lay in the P.1A, which resulted from a 1947 requirement for a supersonic research aircraft. The first of three prototypes flew in August 1954 and later revealed supersonic performance on two Bristol Siddeley non-afterburning turbojets. It was seen that the type had the makings of an interceptor, and the type was revised as the P.1B that first flew in April 1957 with two superimposed Rolls-Royce Avon turbojets. After a lengthy development with 20 pre-production aircraft, the type began to enter service in 1960 as the Lightning F.Mk 1 with two 30-mm cannon and two Firestreak air-to-air missiles.

Later variants were the Lightning F.Mk 1A with inflight-refuelling capability, the Lightning F.Mk 2 with improved electronics and fully variable afterburners, the Lightning F.Mk 3 with 7420-kg (16,360-lb) thrust Avon Mk 300 series engines, provision for overwing drop tanks, a square-topped vertical tail, improved radar, no guns, and a pair of Red Top air-to-air missiles that offered all-aspect engagement capability in place of the earlier marks' pursuit-course Firestreak missiles.

The final variant was the Lightning F.Mk 6 (originally lightning F.Mk 3A) with a revised wing with cambered and kinked leading edges, and a ventral tank that virtually doubled fuel capacity while also accommodating a pair of 30-mm cannon. There were also two side-by-side trainer models, the Lightning T.Mks 4 and 5; these were based on the F.Mk 1A and F.Mk 3 respectively, and retained full combat capability. For export there was the Lighting Mk 50 series of fighters and trainers.

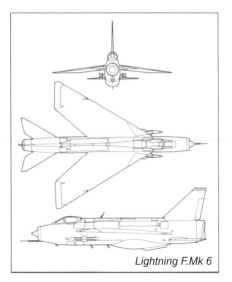

Lightning F.Mk 6

English Electric Lightning

ENGLISH ELECTRIC/BAC LIGHTNING
F.Mk 6 Role: Interceptor fighter
Crew/Accommodation: One
   Power Plant: Two 7,420-kgp (16,360-lb s.t.)
   Rolls-Royce Avon 300 turbojets with reheat
Dimensions: Span 10.61 m (34.9 ft); length
   16.84 m (55.25 ft); wing area 44.08 m²
   (474.5 sq ft)
Weights: Empty 11,340 kg (25,000 lb); MTOW
   18,144 kg (40,000 lb)
Performance: Maximum speed 2,230 km/h (1,203
   knots) Mach 2.1 at 10,975 m (36,000 ft);
   operational ceiling 17,375 m (57,000 ft); radius
   972 km (604 miles)
Load: Two Red Top missiles, plus two 30-mm
   Aden cannon

MCDONNELL DOUGLAS F-4 PHANTOM II (U.S.A.)

IAI F-4 Phantom 2000

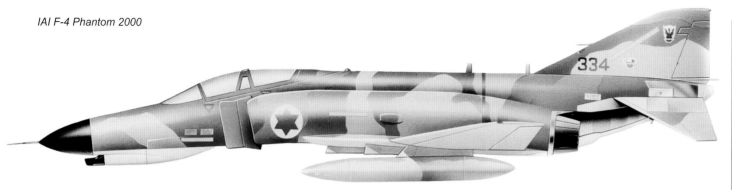

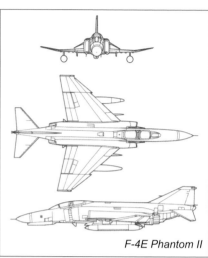

F-4E Phantom II

In October 1979, the 5,057th Phantom II was completed, ending the West's largest warplane production programme since World War II. The programme was devoted to an exceptional type that must be numbered in the five most important warplanes of all time. It was planned initially as an all-weather attack aircraft, but then adapted during design into an all-weather fleet-defence and tactical fighter. The first of two XF4H-1 prototypes flew in May 1958 with early examples of the equally classic J79 afterburning turbojet. The 45 F4H-lFs (later F-4As) were really pre-production types with 7326-kg (16,150-lb) thrust J79-GE-2/2A engines.

True operational capability came with 649 F4H-1 (later F-4B) with 7711-kg (17,000-lb) thrust J79-GE-8 engines, 46 RF-4B reconnaissance aircraft for the U.S. Marine Corps, 635 F-4C (originally F-110A) attack fighters for the U.S. Air Force with 7711-kg (17,000-lb) thrust J79-GE-15 engines, 499 RF-4C USAF tactical reconnaissance aircraft, 773 F-4Ds based on the F-4C but with electronics tailored to USAF rather than U.S. Navy requirements, 1,405 F-4Es for the USAF with 8119-kg (17,900-lb) thrust J79-GE-17 engines, improved radar, leading-edge slats and an internal 20-mm rotary-barrel cannon, 175 F-4F air-superiority fighters for West Germany, 512 F-4Js for the U.S. Navy with 8119-kg (17,900-lb) thrust J79-GE-10 engines, a revised wing and modified tail, 52 F-4Ks based on the F-4J for the Royal Navy with Rolls-Royce Spey turbofans, and 118 F-4Ms based on the F-4K for the Royal Air Force.

There have been several other versions produced by converting older airframes with more advanced electronics as well as other features, such as the similar F-4N and F-4S developments of the F-4B and F-4J for the U.S. Navy, the F-4G for the USAF's 'Wild Weasel' radar-suppression role, and the Super Phantom (or Phantom 2000) rebuild of the F-4E by Israel Aircraft Industries.

MCDONNELL DOUGLAS F-4E PHANTOM II
Role: All-weather strike fighter
Crew/Accommodation: Two
Power Plant: Two 8,119 kgp (17,900 lb s.t.) General Electric J79-GE-17 turbojets with reheat
Dimensions: Span 11.71 m (38.42 ft); length 19.2 m (63 ft); wing area 49.2 m2(530 sq ft)
Weights: Empty 13,397 kg (29,535 lb); MTOW 27,965 kg (61,651 lb)
Performance: Maximum speed 2,390 km/h (1,290 knots) Mach 2.2 at 12,190 m (40,000 ft); operational ceiling 18,975 m (62,250 ft); radius 960 km (518 naut. miles) typical combat mission
Load: One 20 mm multi-barrel cannon and four medium-range air-to-air missiles, plus up to 7,257 kg (16,000 lb) of externally carried weapons or fuel

McDonnell Douglas F-4C Phantom II

OPPOSITE: A McDonnell Douglas F-4E Phantom II in a German museum

NORTHROP F-5 Family (U.S.A.)

F-5E Tiger II

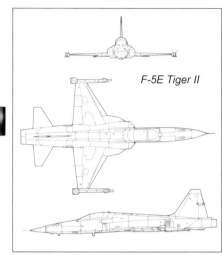

F-5E Tiger II

The F-5 Freedom Fighter was developed, using U.S. Government funding, from Northrop's private-venture N-156 design as a modestly supersonic fighter and attack aircraft with the light weight, compact dimensions and simple avionics that would make it suitable for export under the U.S.'s 'Military Assistance Programs', or for sale to other forces requiring an uncomplicated jet.

The concept's first concrete expression was the N-156T supersonic trainer that first flew in April 1959 as the YT-38 with two 953-kg (2,600-lb) thrust General Electric J85-GE-1 non-afterburning turbojets, though the third to sixth prototypes had the 1,633-kg (3,600-lb) afterburning thrust J85-GE-5 engines that paved the way for the 1,746-kg (3,850-lb) thrust J85-GE-5As used in the T-38A Talon version, of which 1,189 were built (including the two prototypes), most going to USAF training establishments;

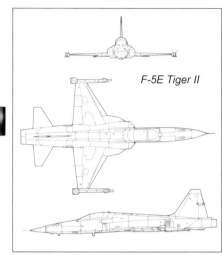

The Northrop F-5F Tiger II became the two-seat version of the F-5E single-seater

NORTHROP F-5E TIGER II
Role: Strike fighter
Crew/Accommodation: One
Power Plant: Two 2,268-kgp (5,000-lb s.t.)
 General Electric J85-GE-21 turbojets with
 reheat
Dimensions: Span 8.13 m (26.66 ft); length
 14.68 m (48.16 ft); wing area 17.3 m²
 (186.2 sq ft)
Weights: Empty 4,392 kg (9,683 lb); MTOW
 11,195 kg (24,680 lb)
Performance: Maximum speed 1,730 km/h
 (934 knots) Mach 1.63 at 11,000 m (36.090 ft);
 operational ceiling 15,790 m (51,800 ft); radius
 222 km (138 miles) with full warload
Load: Two 20-mm cannon, plus up to 3,175 kg
 (7,000 lb) of ordnance, including two short-
 range air-to-air missiles

in 1999 many hundreds remained flying and were undergoing upgrade.

The N-156F fighter was developed in F-5A single-seat and F-5B two-seat variants, and first flew in July 1959 with 1,850-kg (4,850-lb) thrust J85-GE-13 turbojets. Production of the F-5A and F-5B totalled 818 and 290 respectively for various countries in differently designated versions that included the Canadair-built CF-5 for Canada, NF-5 for the Netherlands, F-5G for Norway and the CASA-built SF-5 for Spain. There was also an RF-5A reconnaissance model. The mantle of the Freedom Fighter was then assumed by the more capable Tiger II variant produced in F-5E single-seat and F-5F two-seat forms with an integrated fire-control system as well as 2,268-kg (5,000-lb) thrust J85-GE-21 engines and aerodynamic refinements for much improved payload and performance.

The F-5E first flew in August 1972 and deliveries of Tiger IIs began in 1973. Large-scale production followed in the U.S.A. and abroad (including Switzerland and Taiwan), and by the close of production Tiger IIs had raised the overall F-5 production total to well over 2,600 aircraft, including a small number of RF-5E Tiger Eye reconnaissance aircraft.

Northrop F-5E Tiger II

MIKOYAN MiG-25 'FOXBAT' Series (U.S.S.R.)

MiG-25 'Foxbat'

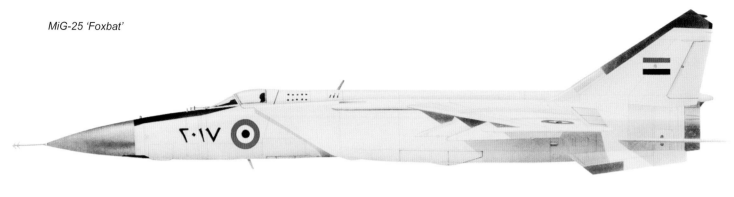

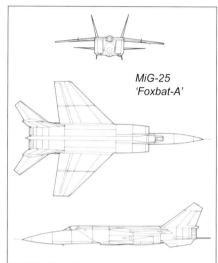

MiG-25 'Foxbat-A'

The MiG-25 was designed to provide the Soviets with an interceptor capable of dealing with the United States' North American B-70 Valkyrie Mach 3 high-altitude strategic bomber. When the B-70 was cancelled, the Soviets continued to develop this very high-performance interceptor which first flew as the Ye-266 in 1964. The type is built largely of stainless steel with titanium leading edges to deal with friction-generated heat at Mach 3, but at such a speed is virtually incapable of manoeuvre.

The type entered service in 1972 with valve-technology radar that lacked the sophistication of then current Western

equipments but offered very high power, and thus the ability to 'burn through' the defences provided by the enemy's

electronic counter-measures. Variants became the 'Foxbat-A' interceptor with four air-to-air missiles, the 'Foxbat-B'

MIKOYAN MIG-25 'FOXBAT-B'
Role: High-speed reconnaissance-bomber
Crew/Accommodation: One
Power Plant: Two 11,200-kgp (24,700-lb s.t.)
  Soyuz/Tumansky R-15B turbojets with reheat
Dimensions: Span 13.38 m (43.9 ft); length
  21.55 m (70.7 ft); wing area 61.4 m²
  (660.9 sq ft)
Weights: MTOW 41,200 kg (90,830 lb)
Performance: Maximum speed 3,006 km/h
  (1,868 mph) at 13,000m (42,630 ft); operational
  ceiling 23,000 m (75,460 ft); range 2,400 km
  (1,491 miles) with 4 bombs and a drop-tank
Load: 5,000 kg (11,023 lb) of bombs

Mikoyan MiG-25 'Foxbat'

operational-level reconnaissance bomber, the 'Foxbat-C' two-seat conversion trainer, and the 'Foxbat-D' improved reconnaissance aircraft.

As 'Foxbat-A' became obsolete, two further combat versions were developed as 'Foxbat-E', with much-improved radar (both newly built and by conversion of 'Foxbat-A's) and 'Foxbat-F' for an air-defence suppression role with a specialized radar-warning suite and AS-11 'Kilter' anti-radar missiles. Russian interceptors were withdrawn by 1994, although others were used abroad, but reconnaissance versions remain operational. The MiG-31 'Foxhound' entered service in 1983 as a development of the MiG-25 with greater power and the combination of electronically-scanned phased array radar with multi-target capability, improved missiles (mainly to protect against cruise missile attack) and longer range/duration. Maximum speed is Mach 2.83.

MiG-25 'Foxbat'

111

MIKOYAN MiG-23 and MiG-27 'FLOGGER' Series

MiG-27 'Flogger'

In 1967 the MiG bureau flew its 23-11 swing-wing fighter prototype for evaluation against the 23-01 tailed-delta prototype powered by a single Tumansky R-27-300 turbojet propulsion engine and given V/STOL capability by the incorporation of two Kolesov RD36-35 lift jets in the centre of the fuselage. The 23-11 proved superior, and as the MiG-23 was produced between 1969 and 1985 for

Soviet use and export, with 5,047 completed. 'Flogger-A' was given one Tumansky R-27 engine and Sapfir-21

radar, but 'Flogger-B' introduced the R-29 engine and Sapfir-23 'High Lark' radar, plus other improvements and

become the standard basic production version. Other versions followed, including 'Flogger-Fard H' as ground-attack variants with Lyulka or Tumansky engines, mainly for export. The final variant was known in the West as 'Flogger-K', an upgrade with vortex generators at the wingroots and nose probe, a radar suited to close-air combat, AA-11 'Archer' missiles and more. The MiG-27 first flew in 1970 as a supersonic dedicated attack derivative of the MiG-23 with a revised forward fuselage offering heavy armour protection and fitted with terrain-avoidance rather than search radar. The MiG-27 also has a less advanced powerplant with fixed inlets and a simple nozzle for its reduced-

MiG-23 'Flogger-B'

Two Indian Air Force MiG-27 'Floggers' with two McDonnell Douglas F-15 Eagles

MIKOYAN MIG-27 'FLOGGER-J'
Role: Ground-attack with variable geometry wing
Crew/Accommodation: One
Power Plant: One 11,500-kgp (25,350-lb s.t.)
  Soyuz R-29B-300 turbofan with reheat
Dimensions: Span 13.97 m (45.8 ft), swept
  7.78 m (25.5 ft); length 17.08 m (56 ft); wing
  area 27.26 m² (293.42 sq ft)
Weights: Empty 12,100 kg (26,676 lb); MTOW
  18,100 kg (39,900 lb)
Performance: Maximum speed 1,350 km/h (839
  mph) Mach 1.1 at sea level; operational ceiling
  13,000+ m (46,650+ ft); radius 540 km (336
  miles) with two missiles and three drop-tanks
Load: One 30-mm cannon, plus up to 3,000 kg
  (6,614 lb) of weapons

performance role at low altitude; special
target-acquisition and weapon guidance
equipment are installed, as are a multi-
barrel cannon and additional hardpoints
for the larger offensive load. Two variants
became the 'Flogger-D' and 'Flogger-J'.

ABOVE: MiG-23 'Flogger'

*LEFT: This 'Flogger-D' was given terrain-
avoidance radar*

SAAB 37 VIGGEN (Sweden)

JA 37 Viggen

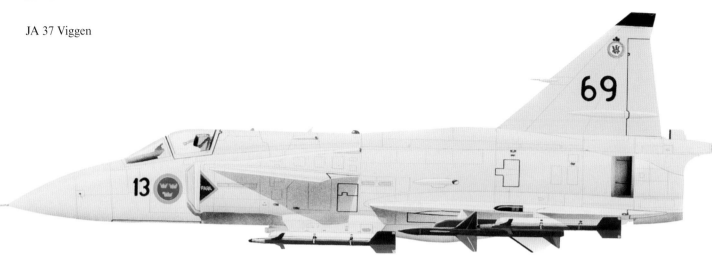

the integrated weapon system concept pioneered in the United States, with power based on a Swedish licence-built version of the Pratt & Whitney JT8D turbofan but fitted in this application with Swedish-designed afterburning and thrust-reversing units. The advanced electronics include pulse-Doppler radar, a head-up display and other items linked by a digital fire-control system to maximize the type's offensive and defensive capabilities with effective weapons and electronic countermeasures.

Production totalled 329, and the variants have been the AJ 37 attack aircraft with the 11,790-kg (25,992-lb) thrust RM8A, the SF 37 overland

With the Saab 37 Viggen (Thunderbolt), first flown in February 1967, Sweden produced a true multi-role fighter with a thrust-reversible afterburning turbofan and a canard layout for true STOL capability using short lengths of road as emergency airstrips. The type was designed around

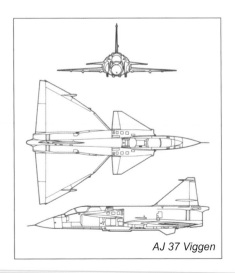

AJ 37 Viggen

Saab 37 Viggen

reconnaissance aircraft with a modified nose accommodating seven cameras and an infra-red sensor, the SH 37 overwater reconnaissance aircraft with search radar, and the SK 35 tandem two-seat operational trainer with a taller vertical tail. A 'Viggen Mk 2' development became the JA 37 interceptor with the 12,750-kg (28,109-lb) thrust RM8B turbofan, a number of airframe modifications, an underfuselage pack housing the extremely potent Oerlikon-Buhrle KCA 30-mm cannon, together with a revised electronic suite with much improved radar. Finally, 75 AJ/SH/SFs were converted between 1993 and 1995 to

SAAB JA 37 VIGGEN
Role: Interceptor
Crew/Accommodation: One
Power Plant: One 12,750-khp (28,109-lb s.t.)
  Volvo Flyg motor RM8B turbofan withreheat
Dimensions: Span 10.6 m (34.78 ft); length
  16.4 m (53.8 ft); wing area 46 m² (495.1sq ft)
Weights: Empty 12,200 kg (26,455 lb); MTOW
  20,000 kg (44,090 lb)
Performance: Maximum speed 2,231 km/h
  (1,386 mph) Mach 2.10 at 11,000 m (36.090 ft);
  operational ceiling 18,000 m (59,050ft); radius
  500 km (311 miles)
Load: One 30-mm cannon, plus up to 6,000 kg
  (13,277 lb) of externally-carried weapons/fuel,
  including two medium-range and four short-
  range air-to-air missiles

AJS 37s, given more modern computers and other avionics, plus new reconnaissance equipment and new weapon choices, allowing any aircraft to perform air defence, attack or reconnaissance roles.

ABOVE: Saab 37 Viggen

LEFT: The SH 37 is the overwater reconnaissance variant of the Saab Viggen family

115

GRUMMAN F-14 TOMCAT (U.S.A.)

F-14 Tomcat

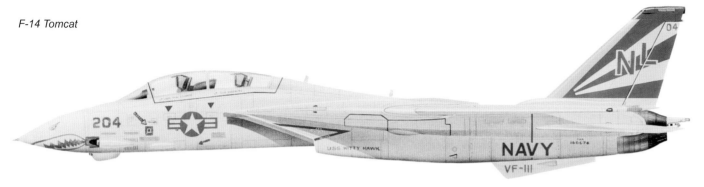

OPPOSITE: A Grumman F-14A taking off from the USS Kitty Hawk

After the cancellation of the F-111B, developed primarily by Grumman as the fleet defence fighter equivalent of the General Dynamics F-111A land-based interdictor, the U.S. Navy issued a requirement for a new fighter. Submissions were received from five companies, but Grumman had a headstart with its G-303 design that made valuable use of the company's experience of variable-geometry wings, and also incorporated the F-11 lB's TF30 engines, AIM-54 Phoenix long-range air-

to-air missiles, and AWG-9 radar fire-control system. In January 1969, the G-303 was selected for development as the F-14, and the first of 12 YF-14A pre-production aircraft flew in December 1970. The Tomcat was aerodynamically more tractable because of its 'glove

vanes', small surfaces extending from the leading-edge roots of the main wings' fixed structure as the outer surfaces swept aft, which regulated movement in the centre of pressure to reduce pitch alterations.

The F-14A initial model entered

service in October 1972 and immediately proved itself a classic fighter of its type in terms of performance, manoeuvrability and weapon system capability. Some aircraft have been adapted for the reconnaissance role as the F-14A/ TARPS with a ventral equipment pod. The only limitation to the F-14's total success was the powerplant of two 9480-kg (20,900-lb) thrust Pratt & Whitney TF30-P-412-A turbofans, which were not designed for fighter use and therefore lack the flexibility required for this role. For F-14As built after 1984, theTF30-P-414A was introduced, while F-14Bs and Ds produced by manufacture and conversion have 12,247-kg (27,000-lb) thrust General Electric F 110-GE-400 turbofans. In addition, many F-14s have been given LANTIRN infra-red pods to permit FAC and strike missions, nicknamed 'Bombats'. Iran also received F-l4s.

F-14A Tomcat

F-14A Tomcats flying over the aircraft carrier USS Dwight D Eisenhower

GRUMMAN F-14A TOMCAT
Role: Carrier fighter, attack and reconnaissance
Crew/Accommodation: Two
Power Plant: Two 9480-kg (20,900-lb) thrust Pratt & Whitney TF30-P-412A turbofans
Dimensions: Span unswept 19.6 m (64.1 ft), swept 11.7 m (38.2 ft); length 19.1 m (62.7 ft); wing area 52.5 m² (565 sq ft)
Weights: Empty 17,650 kg (38,910 lb); MTOW 33,725 kg (74,350 lb)
Performance: Maximum speed 2,498 km/h (1,552 mph), Mach 2.34 at 11.276 m (37,000 ft); operational ceiling 19,500 m (64,000 ft); typical range for air-to-air mission 852 km (530 miles)
Load: Up to 6,577 kg (14,500 lb) with typically 4 AIM-54C Phoenix and 2 AIM-9 Sidewinders, plus an internal 6-barrel 20-mm General Electric M61 Vulcan cannon. F-14D can carry AMRAAM AAMs

DASSAULT MIRAGE F1 (France)

Dassault Mirage F1C

Mirage F1C

The Mirage F1 was developed as a successor to the Mirage III/5 family but is a markedly different aircraft with 'conventional' flying surfaces. The French government originally wanted a two-seat warplane, and such a type was evolved by the company as the Mirage F2, powered by a SNECMA/Pratt & Whitney TF306 turbofan. At the same time the company worked as a private venture on the Mirage F1, a smaller and lighter single-seater sized to the SNECMA Atar turbojet.

The Mirage F2 flew in June 1966, but cost too much for a profitable production contract. The Mirage F1 first flew in December 1966 with the Atar 09K-31 turbojet. After the Mirage F2 programme was cancelled the French government ordered three pre-production examples of the Mirage F1. These displayed excellent performance and overall

DASSAULT MIRAGE F1CT
Role: Strike fighter
Crew/Accommodation: One
Power Plant: One 7,900-kgp (15,873-lb) SNECMA Atar 09K-50 turbojet with reheat
Dimensions: Span 8.4 m (27.55 ft); length 15.3 m (50.2 ft); wing area 25 m² (270 sq ft)
Weights: Empty 7,400 kg (16,315 lb); MTOW 16,200 kg (35,700 lb)
Performance: Maximum speed 2,335 km/h (1,450 mph) Mach 2.2 at 12.000 m (39,370 ft); operational ceiling 20,000 m (65,600 ft) radius of action 425 km (264 miles) with 3,500 kg attack load
Load: Two 30-mm DEFA cannon, plus up to 6,300 kg (13,890 lb) of externally carried weapons

Dassault Mirage F1 of the Spanish Air Force

capabilities as multi-role warplanes, their primary advantages over the Mirage III/5 family being larger warload, easy handling at low altitude, good rate of climb, and 40 per cent greater fuel capacity (through the use of integral rather than bladder tanks) all combined with semi-STOL field performance

thanks to the use of droopable leading edges and large trailing-edge flaps on the sharply swept wing, which is mounted in the shoulder position.

The Mirage F1 was ordered into production with the Atar 09K-50 afterburning turbojet. Like the preceding Mirage HI/5 series, the Mirage F1 has

been a considerable (if not outstanding) commercial success. The main variants have been the Mirage F1A clear-weather ground-attack fighter, the Mirage FIB and D two-seat trainers, the Mirage F1C (and Mirage F1C-200 long-range) multi-role all-weather interceptor with attack capability, the Mirage FIE multi-role

export fighter, and the Mirage F1CR-200 long-range reconnaissance aircraft. Some French F1C-200s have been adapted as Mirage FICTs, basically to F1E standard.

French Air Force Dassault Mirage F-1CR

119

BOEING (McDONNELL DOUGLAS) F-15 EAGLE (U.S.A.)

F-15C Eagle

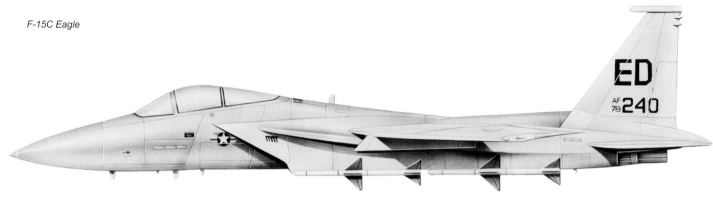

OPPOSITE: Two U.S. Air Force F-15C Eagle fighters taking on fuel from a Boeing KC-1235R Stratotanker

The F-15 was planned as the U.S. Air Force's successor to the F-4 in the air superiority role. After three years of design studies the type was selected for hardware development in December 1969. The first of two YF-15A prototypes emerged for its first flight in July 1972 as a massive aircraft with two 10,809-kg (23,830-lb) thrust Pratt & Whitney F100-P-100 turbofans, sophisticated aerodynamics, advanced electronics, including the APG-63 multi-role radar and a pilot's head-up display, and the world's first production cockpit of the HOTAS (Hands-On-Throttle-And-Stick) type.

The Eagle entered service in November 1974, and has since proved itself a first-class and versatile warplane. Its powerful engines allow the type to carry a large weight of widely assorted weapons in the primary air-to-air and secondary air-to-ground roles, and also generate a thrust-weight ratio in the order of unity for an exceptionally high rate of climb and very good manoeuvrability. The initial F-15A single-seat model was complemented by the F-15B (originally TF-15A) two-seat combat-capable version.

In 1979 production switched to the F-15C and F-15D respectively. These are powered by 10,637-kg (23,450-lb) thrust F100-P-220 engines, and have more advanced systems, including the improved APG-70 radar from 1985 production onward, as well as provision for external carriage of the so-called

FAST (Fuel and Sensor Tactical) packs that provide considerably more fuel and weapons at a negligible increase in drag and weight. The F-15C and D are built under licence in Japan as the F-15J and F-15DJ. In 1988 the USAF received its first example of the F-15E airframe (though strengthened) and offering advanced air-to-air capability combined with ground attack. In 1989 the first flight took place of the F-15 SMTD, an experimental vectored-thrust conversion of an F-15B, with two-dimensional nozzles and foreplanes.

F-15C Eagle

MCDONNELL DOUGLAS F-15E EAGLE
Role: All-weather strike fighter
Crew/Accommodation: Two
Power Plant: Two 10,782-kgp (23,770-lb s.t.) Pratt & Whitney F100-PW-220 turbofans with reheat
Dimensions: Span 13.05 m (42 ft); length19.45 m (63.79 ft); wing area 56.5 m² (608 sq ft)
Weights: Empty 14,515 kg (32,000 lb); MTOW 36,741 kg (81,000 lb)
Performance: Maximum speed 2,698 km/h (1,675 mph); operational ceiling 18,300 m (60,000 ft); radius of action 1,271 km (790 miles)
Load: Up to 11,113 kg (24,500 lb) of weaponry and one 20-mm multi-barrel cannon mounted

Two Republic of Korea Air Force F-15K Slam Eagles

LOCKHEED MARTIN F-16 FIGHTING FALCON (U.S.A.)

F-16A Fighting Falcon

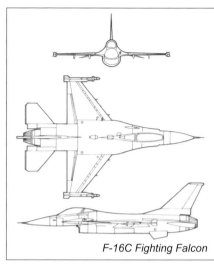

F-16C Fighting Falcon

During the Vietnam War the United States Air Force discovered that its fighters were in general handicapped by their very large size, weight and Mach 2 performance, all of which were liabilities that seriously eroded reliability and combat agility in the type of turning dogfight that became increasingly common at low and medium altitudes. To help find a solution to this problem, in 1971 the U.S. Air Force instituted a Light-Weight Fighter competition for a low cost day fighter, and General Dynamics produced its Model 401 design.

The first of two YF-16 prototypes flew in January 1974, and 12 months later the type was declared winner of the LWF competition. The basic type was adopted as the U.S. Air Force's Air-Combat Fighter, but its role was greatly expanded to include ground attack and, because of provision for radar and upgraded navigation equipment, all-weather operations. In June 1975 it was announced that the same type had been adopted by a four-nation European consortium. The first production models were the single-seat F-16A and two-seat F-16B, which entered service in January 1979 and received the name Fighting Falcon in 1980. Since then, the type has

LOCKHEED MARTIN F-16C FIGHTING FALCON
Role: Air-dominance and ground-attack fighter
Crew/Accommodation: One
Power Plant: One 13,154-kgp (29,000-lb s.t.) General Electric F110-GE-129 or 13,200-kgp (29,100-lb s.t.) Pratt & Whitney F100-PW-229 in current Block 50/52 F-16Cs
Dimensions: Span 10 m (32.79 ft); length 15.02 m (49.3 ft); wing area 17.87 m² (300 sq ft)
Weights: Empty 8,753 kg (18,900 lb); MTOW 19,187 kg (42,300 lb)
Performance: Maximum speed 2,146 km/h (1,335 mph) Mach 2.02 at 12,190 m (40,000 ft); operational ceiling over 15,240 m (50,000 ft); radius of action 1,605 km (997 miles) with four air-to-air missiles and maximum internal fuel and 3,936 litres in drop-tanks
Load: One 20-mm cannon, plus up to 7,071–7,225 kg (15,590–15,930 lb) of other weapons

Lockheed Martin F-16 Fighting Falcons

gone on to become numerically the most important fighter in the Western world, with nearly 4,000 delivered to many countries. The type is based on blended contours and relaxed stability, the latter controlled by a fly-by-wire system. The pilot controls the fighter using a sidestick joystick 'controller', and occupies a 30° reclining ejection seat that assists in helping the pilot withstand high 'g' forces.

Many structural and electronic improvements, including a more capable radar, created the current F-16C single-seat and F-16D two-seat variants, which can again use either General Electric or Pratt & Whitney engines in their most recent and powerful forms. Other variants produced for specific missions or experimental use includes the USAF's F-16HTS (F-16Cs) for SEAD (suppression of enemy air defenses) and F-16CAS for close air support and battlefield interdiction.

F-16 Fighting Falcon

BOEING (McDONNELL DOUGLAS) F/A-18 HORNET Family (U.S.A.)

F/A-18 Hornet

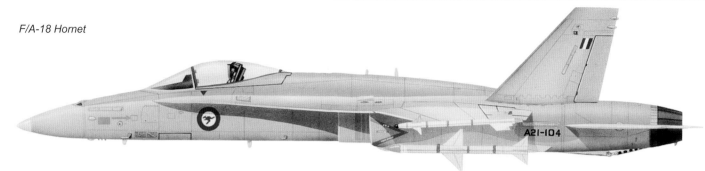

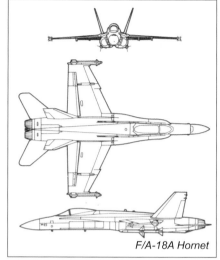

F/A-18A Hornet

Serving with the U.S. Navy and Marine Corps as replacement for the F-4 and A-7 in the fighter and attack roles respectively, the dual-capability F/A-18 is one of the West's most important carrierborne warplanes, and has also secured useful export orders for land-based use. Originally a McDonnell Douglas product (before the company's merger with Boeing in 1997), the type was derived from the Northrop YF-17 (losing contender to the YF-16 in the USAF's Light-Weight Fighter competition) in order to meet the requirements of the Navy Air Combat Fighter requirement.

In the development programme undertaken by Northrop and McDonnell Douglas, the YF-17 was enlarged, aerodynamically refined, re-engined and fitted with advanced mission electronics. The Hornet prototype first flew in November 1978. Initial plans to procure separate F-18 and A-18 fighter and attack variants had been abandoned when it was realized that different software in the mission computers would allow a single type to be optimized in each role. McDonnell Douglas assumed production leadership, and the F/A-18s entered service late in 1983 as the F/A-18A single-seater and its combat-capable

MCDONNELL DOUGLAS F/A-18C HORNET
Role: Naval and land-based strike fighter
Crew/Accommodation: One
Power Plant: Two 7,257 kgp (16,000 lb s.t.) General Electric F404-GE-400 turbofans with reheat, or more powerful GE-402s from 1992
Dimensions: Span 11.4 m (36.5 ft); length 17.1 m (56 ft); wing area 37.16 m2 (400 sq ft)
Weights: Empty 10,810 kg (23,832 lb); MTOW 25,401 kg (56,000 lb)
Performance: Maximum speed over Mach 1.8; operational ceiling 15,240 m (50,000 ft); radius 740 km (461 miles) with missiles and sinternal fuel only
Load: One 20-mm multi-barrel cannon plus up to 7,030 kg (15,500 1b of weapons, including up to 10 AMRAAM and two Sidewinder missiles or a \ mix of AAMS and attack weapons

An F/A-18 Hornet aboard the USS John C. Stennis

two-seat partner, the F/A-18B, originally designated the TF/A-18A.

The F/A-18A was replaced in production by the F/A-18C in 1987 with a number of electronic and system improvements and the ability to carry more advanced weapons. The two-seat equivalent became the F/A-18D. Night-attack capability was added to C/Ds from the 139th aircraft delivered since 1989. Also, 31 USMC F/A-18Ds began entering service as F/A-18D (RC)s in 1999 for reconnaissance. Meanwhile, in November 1995, the F/A-18E Super Hornet prototype first flew, and deliveries to the U.S. Navy have begun of 'E' single-seaters and 'F' two-seaters, offering more power, greater range and payload, improved avionics and more.

A Boeing F/A-18 Hornet taking off from the aircraft carrier USS Kitty Hawk

MAPO 'MiG' MiG-29 'FULCRUM' Family (Russia)

MiG-29 'Fulcrum'

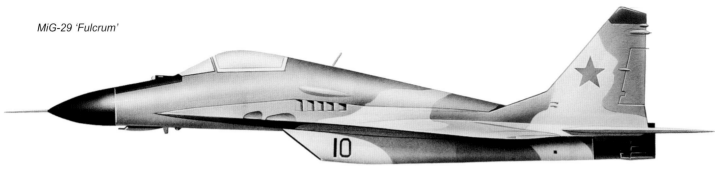

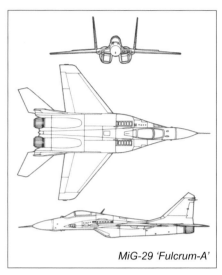

MiG-29 'Fulcrum-A'

First flown in October 1977 and delivered to the Soviet Air Force from 1983, the MiG-29 is also known by the NATO reporting name 'Fulcrum' and is a lightweight close-air fighter optimized for air combat but with a secondary-attack capability. Despite its use of a conventional mechanical control system in an airframe of very advanced but basically conventional configuration, the type possesses great agility. Moreover, a genuine look-down/shoot-down capability is offered by the combination of a radar that can track up to ten targets simultaneously and engage one or two, and use of AA-10 'Alamo' snap-down air-to-air missiles.

The 'Fulcrum-A' has undergone a number of changes since it was first seen, the consensus being that these indicate a number of fixes to bring the design up to the present standard.

The first variant was probably a pre-production model and carried small detachable ventral tail fins reminiscent of those carried by the Sukhoi Su-27 'Flanker'. Later 'Fulcrum-A's introduced extended-chord rudders. The MiG-29UB 'Fulcrum-B' became the two-seat combat-capable conversion and continuation trainer derivative of the 'Fulcrum-A' with the radar removed, though a planned upgrade may restore radar to allow full multi-role capability. The next single-seater became 'Fulcrum-C, distinguishable by its larger dorsal fairing for carriage of an active ECM system and more internal fuel.

An improved version of C introduced better Topaz radar and added new AA-12 'Adder' missiles to the weapon choices. MiG-29M 'Fulcrum-E' has been under trial as a new tactical fighter and ground-attack model with greatly enhanced capabilities, with export versions including the MiG-33, while MiG-29K has undergone trials as a naval version suited to aircraft carrier operations.

OPPOSITE: MiG-29 'Fulcrum'

MAPO 'MiG' MiG-29 'FULCRUM'
Role: Fighter
Crew/Accommodation: One
Power Plant: Two 8,300-kgp (18,300-lb s.t.) Klimov RD-33 turbofans with reheat
Dimensions: Span 11.36 m (37.27 ft); length 17.32 m (56.83 ft); wing area 38.1 m² (410 sq ft)
Weights: Empty 10,900 kg (24,030 lb); MTOW 18,480 kg (40,740 lb)
Performance: Maximum speed 2,440 km/h (1,516 mph Mach 2.3 at 11,000 m (36.090 ft); operational ceiling 17,500 m (57,400 ft); range 2,100 km (1,305 miles) maximum
Load: One 30-mm cannon plus about 4,000 kg (8,818 lb) of external weapons, typically 2 medium-range AA-10s and 4 AA-11 or AA-8 short-range missiles

Mapo MiG-29 'Fulcrum'

SUKHOI Su-27 'FLANKER' Family (Russia)

Su-27 'Flanker-A'

OPPOSITE: Cockpit of the Sukhoi Su-27 'Flanker'

Developed during the 1970s as a long-range air-superiority fighter to match the U.S. Air Force's McDonnell Douglas F-15 Eagle, the Su-27 drew on similar aerodynamic research that assisted the MiG-29, but was designed to be inherently unstable because of the adoption of an analog fly-by-wire control system. First flown in May 1977, initial operational capability was achieved in December 1984. The first version became known to NATO as the 'Flanker-A', though referring to four prototypes and five preproduction aircraft with the vertical tail surfaces located centrally above the engine installations, rounded wingtips and mostly AL-21F3 engines.

The basic full-production version became the 'Flanker-B' with squared-off wingtips, plus a number of refinements such as leading edge slats and vertical tail surfaces located farther outboard. 'Flanker-B' has been built in Su-27S tactical and Su-27P air defence models.

Su-27UB 'Flanker-C' is a tandem two-seat combat trainer variant, first flown in production form in 1986. Although adding a second cockpit forced a reduction in fuel load, it retains full combat capability and has all the necessary radar and weapon systems.

From Su-27 has been developed a wide family of related warplanes. These include the Su-30 two-seat long-range multi-role interceptor that has extra avionics to lead a group of Su-27 fighters; Su-32FN with side-by-side seating for maritime strike and related Su-27IB/Su-34 for tactical interdiction; Su-33/Su-27K carrierborne fighter and anti-ship single-seater, known to NATO as 'Flanker-D' (also two-seat version); and Su-35 and Su-37 (or Su-27M) as fighter and ground-attack aircraft, the Su-37 with thrust-vectoring nozzles.

Su-27 'Flanker-B'

SUKHOI Su-27 'FLANKER B'
Role: Interceptor
Crew/Accommodation: One
Power Plant: Two 12,500-kgp (27,560-lb s.t.)
 Saturn AL-31F turbofans with reheat
Dimensions: Span 14.7 m (48.25 ft); length
 21.94 m (72 ft); wing area 62.04 m² (667.8 sq ft)
Weights: Empty 16,380 kg (36,112 lb); MTOW
 28,300 kg (62,390 lb)
Performance: Maximum speed 2,300 km/h
 (1,429 mph) Mach 2.17; operational ceiling
 18,500 m (60,700 ft); range 2,800 km (1,740
 miles)
Load: One 30-mm multi-barrel cannon plus up to
 8,000 kg (17,636 lb) of weapons, including 10
 air-to-air missiles (up to six AA-10 'Alamos'

Sukhoi Su-27 'Flanker'

DASSAULT MIRAGE 2000 (France)

Mirage 2000C

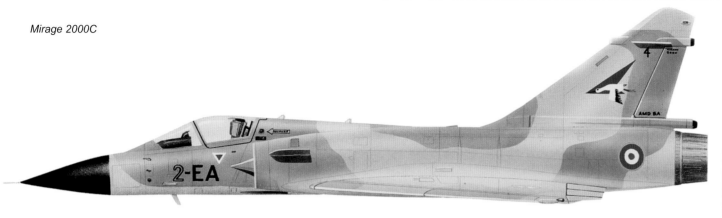

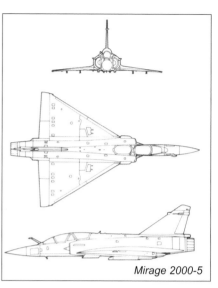

Mirage 2000-5

With the Mirage 2000 the manufacturer reverted to the delta-wing planform but, in this instance, of the relaxed-stability type with an electronic 'fly-by-wire' control system to avoid many of the low-level handling and tactical limitations suffered by the aerodynamically similar Mirage III/5 family. In the early and mid-1970s, Dassault was working on a prototype to meet the French Air Force's ACF (Avion de Combat Futur) requirement, but this was cancelled in 1975 when the service decided that a warplane powered by two

SNECMA M53-3 turbofans was too large. In December 1975, therefore, the French government authorized the design and development of a smaller single-engined machine. This emerged as the Mirage 2000 with the 9,000-kg (19,840-lb) thrust SNECMA M53-5 turbofan in the smallest and lightest possible airframe for a high power/weight ratio.

The first of five prototypes flew during March 1978 and the prototypes soon demonstrated the Mirage 2000's complete superiority to the Mirage III in all flight regimes. The type remains in production, and the primary variants have been the Mirage 2000B two-seat operational trainer with a lengthened fuselage, the Mirage 2000C single-seat

interceptor and multi-role fighter (now with the 9,700-kg (21,384-lb) thrust M53-P2 turbofan and RDI pulse Doppler radar in place of the original RDM multi-mode radar), the Mirage 2000N two-seat nuclear-capable strike fighter based on the airframe of the Mirage 2000B and optimized for low-level penetration, the Mirage 2000D based on 'N' and for all-weather attack, the Mirage 2000R single-seat reconnaissance fighter, the Mirage 2000E single-seat multi-role export derivative of the Mirage 2000C with RDM radar, the Mirage 2000ED training version of 'E' and the Mirage 2000-5 latest advanced multi-role combat aircraft for export and as some modified Mirage 2000Cs for French operation, with RDY radar capable of tracking up to 24 targets.

DASSAULT MIRAGE 2000C
Role: Air-superiority fighter
Crew/Accommodation: One
Power Plant: One 9,700-kgp (21,385-lb s.ts) SNECMA M53-P2 turbofan with reheat
Dimensions: Span 9.13 m (29.95 ft); length 14.36 m (47.1 ft); wing area 41 m² (441.3 sq ft)
Weights: Empty 7,500 kg (16,534 lb); MTOW 17,000 kg (37,480 lb)
Performance: Maximum speed 2,335 kn/h (1,450 mph) Mach 2.2 at 11,000m (36,000 ft); operational ceiling 18,000 m (60,000 ft); range 3,335 km (2,072 miles) with external fuel and four 250 kg bombs
Load: Two 30-mm DEFA cannon plus up to 6,300 kg (13,890 lb) of weapons including two Matra Magic 2 and two Matra Super 530 D missiles

Dassault Mirage 2000

OPPOSITE: French Air Force Dassault Mirage 2000B

JAS 39 Gripen

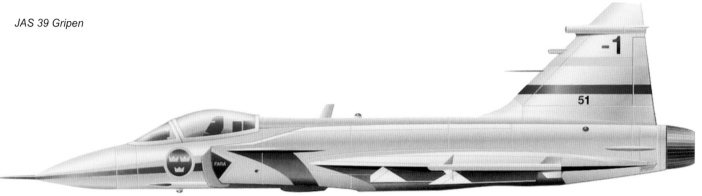

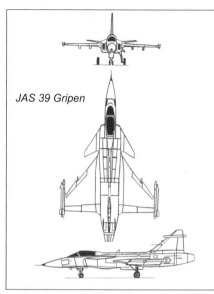

JAS 39 Gripen

The Gripen is Sweden's very latest multi-role warplane, and is generally acknowledged to be the world's first production combat aircraft of the new fourth generation. It was developed and is being built by a Swedish industrial group in which SAAB is the largest partner in terms of programme value. Such is the potential of the aircraft that British Aerospace became a partner for joint marketing, adapting and supporting the Gripen on the export market.

SAAB JAS 39A GRIPEN
Role: Multi-role fighter, attack, maritime attack and reconnaissance
Crew/Accommodation: One
Power Plant: One 8,212-kgp (18.105-lb s.t.) Volvo RM12 with reheat
Dimensions: Span 8.4 m (27.56 ft); length 14.1 m (46.26 ft);
Weights: Empty 6,620 kg (14,600 lb); MTOW 14,000 kg (30,865 lb)
Performance: Supersonic at all heights; radius of action 800 km (497 miles)
Load: One 27-mm Mauser cannon. Pylons on each wingtip (two), under the wings (four), under the air intakes (two) and under the fuselage (one) for a selection of weapons and stores that can include Sidewinder, AMRAAM or operational Mica air-to-air missiles, anti-ship, air-to-surface or other missiles, cluster weapons, rockets or other types.

Although a fairly small nation, Sweden has never compromised on its military aircraft, deciding its needs and building accordingly, even without the backing of export orders, though Gripen may well prove internationally successful. Another Swedish tradition has been to produce a single aircraft capable of fulfilling many roles through the adoption

of specifically-equipped variants, while Swedish aircraft also have the ability to disperse to and operate from short sections of the nation's main road network in an emergency. With Gripen, the concept has been taken a stage further by having advanced computer systems so that each single Gripen can fully perform in any of the required fighter, attack and

A Czech JAS 39 Gripen

reconnaissance roles with the same pilot at any time, merely by selecting the system function and thereby the characteristics required to undertake that mission.

As a lightweight combat aircraft intended to eventually replace Viggens and Drakens in Swedish service, development of Gripen began in 1980 with a project definition phase. Full development started in June 1982, with the signing of a contract for five test aircraft and the first thirty production aircraft (Batch l). The first flight of a test aircraft was achieved on 9 December 1988 and the Gripen joined the Air Force in 1996, first going to F7 Wing. The final Gripen of Batch 1 (30 aircraft) was delivered in December 1996, when deliveries of Batch 2 aircraft (including JAS 39B two-seat operational trainers) began to the Swedish Defence Material Administration. Batch 2 covered 96 single-seaters and 14 two-seaters,

equipped with upgraded avionics software and new flight control system hardware, while in 1997 a third batch was ordered (64 aircraft). Eventually, twelve of the Air Force's thirteen squadrons will operate Gripens.

Gripen has rear-mounted delta wings and close-coupled all-moving canards, and uses a flight-by-wire flight control system. Strong but light carbonfibre has been used in the construction of about a third of the airframe. Remarkably, Gripen can be refuelled, rearmed, and essential servicing and inspections made in a turnaround time of under ten minutes by a technician and five conscripts under combat conditions.

A Swedish Air Force JAS 39 Gripen

LOCKHEED MARTIN F-22 RAPTOR (U.S.A.)

YF-22A Raptor

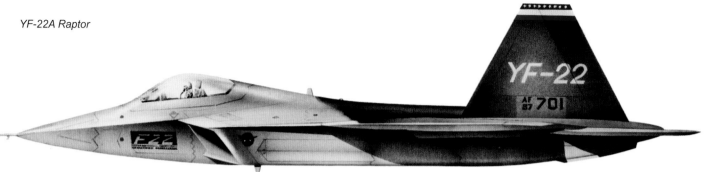

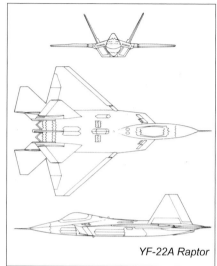

YF-22A Raptor

In late April 1991 the U.S. Air Force Secretary announced the selection of the Lockheed/Boeing/General Dynamics team to develop the Advanced Tactical Fighter (ATF) as the replacement for the F-15 Eagle.

The ATF was conceived in the first year of President Reagan's administration. In June 1981, a specification was issued whilst the F-15 and F-16 were quite new. At the time, however, there was a shortage of low-level, all-weather strike and interdiction aircraft. The Air Force set certain requirements and limits for the project. These subsequently included the ability to fly at supersonic speed without afterburner (known as supercruise), have enough fuel for mission radius, have unrestricted manoeuvrability with the use of two-dimensional engine nozzles, incorporate stealth technology and other systems to provide high survivability, internal weapons carriage in air-superiority role, conform to specific weight and cost requirements, have a cruise speed of Mach 1.5 with a combat radius of 800 miles, and more.

Two prototypes were ordered, one powered by Pratt & Whitney F119 engines, the other with General Electric F-120s. Boeing would build the wings and aft fuselage, General Dynamics the

Lockheed Martin F-22 Raptor

OPPOSITE: Lockheed Martin F-22 Raptors

centre fuselage and empennage and Lockheed the cockpit and nose section.

Boeing provided a 757 for flight-testing the complete avionics system, the first with active matrix liquid crystal displays instead of cathode ray tubes.

In 1987 radical redesign was undertaken because of weight problems; consequently, the contract was extended by six months.

The first YF-22 flew on 29 September 1990 and in 1991 the F-22/F119 engine combination was selected over the rival Northrop/McDonnell Douglas YF-23. A further 9 test aircraft (EMDs) followed, the first flying in September 1997, and it is expected that the USAF will eventually receive 339 F-22As, with deliveries from the year 2002.

LOCKHEED MARTIN F-22A
Role: Advanced Tactical Fighter (ATF)
Crew/Accommodation: One (in 360° teardrop pressurized cockpit)
Power Plant: Two 15,875-kgp(35,000-lb s.t) Pratt & Whitney F119-PW-100 turbofans with reheat
Dimensions: Span 13.56 m (44.5 ft); length 18.92 m (62.08 ft); wing area 78.04 m² (840 sq ft)
Weight: Empty 14,515 kg (32,000 lb); MTOW 24,950 kg (55,000 lb)
Performance: Maximum speed Mach 2+, also quoted as Mach 1.8+; Mach 1.58 supercruise, also quoted as Mach 1.4+; operational ceiling 15,240 m+ (50,000 ft+); range 3,200 km+ (2,000 miles +)
Load: One M61A-2 20-mm cannon; two side bays with AIM-9M Sidewinder air-to-air missiles (one in each) and one main bay with up to six AIM-120C AMRAAM air-to-air missiles. 8 AMRAAMs can be carried under the wings. Attack weapons can be carried under the wings. Attack weapons can be carried in main bay

HEAVY BOMBERS

HEAVY BOMBERS

Strategic bombing began at the very start of World War I, when in November 1914 three tiny Avro 504 biplanes of the Royal Naval Air Service set out to destroy the German Zeppelin sheds at Friedrichshafen. Each aircraft carried just four 20-lb bombs but still managed to damage Zeppelin LZ32 and blow up the adjacent gasworks.

Such tiny aircraft could hardly be termed strategic bombers, despite the nature of their historic mission, but in February 1915 giant four-engined Russian Sikorsky Ilya Mourometzes began their wartime raids with an attack on a target in Poland. It fell to Italy to begin the first sustained strategic bombing offensive when, from August 1915, triple-engined Caproni Ca 32s and other types began striking targets in Austria-Hungary. Ca 32s also recorded the first Italian night bombing raids.

Already, by January 1915, German Navy Zeppelin airships had begun bombing attacks on Great Britain, with London hit for the first time that May. Such attacks lasted until April 1918, the 51 Zeppelin raids on Britain dropping 199 tonnes of bombs and causing 557 fatalities. However, from 1917 Germany put greater faith in new Gotha and other heavy bombing aeroplanes to undertake strategic attacks, with the first mass raid by 21 Gothas recorded on 25 May.

Despite some earlier success in bringing down Zeppelins, the British RFC and RNAS found the bombers a different matter and on that first raid no contacts with the enemy were made during 77 defence sorties. Night attacks by Gothas started in September 1917, the same month that Germany introduced even larger Zeppelin Staaken RVI bombers capable of dropping 1,000-kg bombs, the largest of the war.

In retaliation for German bombing of civilians, and to meet public outcry, in 1916 Britain fielded the Handley Page O/l 00, a twin-engined heavy bomber built to the Admiralty's call for a 'bloody paralyzer'. It was followed by the high-powered O/400, but other heavy bombers such as the Vickers Vimy had hardly reached service status by the Armistice and so saw most service post-war. Indeed, the Vimy will always be remembered in the annals of aviation for carrying Alcock and Brown on the first-ever non-stop flight across the Atlantic in 1919.

The heavy bomber was, by the start of the 1920s, standard equipment for all major air forces and by the 1930s huge monoplanes began the slow process of superseding biplanes, with the Soviet Union establishing the world's most potent heavy bomber force with its Tupolev TB series of metal low-wing monoplanes. The stage was set for the development of the bombers used in World War II, as detailed in the following pages.

PAGE 136: Avro Vulcan bomber

PAGE 137: Northrop Grumman B-2A Spirit

BELOW: Zeppelin Staaken R VI represented Germany's largest bomber of World War I, some versions having six engines

BOEING B-17 FLYING FORTRESS (U.S.A.)

B-17G Flying Fortress

The Flying Fortress was one of the United States' most important warplanes of World War II and resulted from a 1934 requirement for a multi-engined bomber with the ability to carry a 907-kg (2,000-lb) bomb load over minimum and maximum ranges of 1640 and 3540 km (1,020 and 2,200 miles) at speeds between 322 and 402 km/h (200 and 250 mph). Boeing began work on its Model 299 design in June 1934, and the prototype flew in July 1935 with four

599-kW (750-hp) Pratt & Whitney R-1680-E Radials.

Although it crashed during a takeoff in October 1935 as a result of locked controls, the prototype had demonstrated sufficiently impressive

performance for the U.S. Army Air Corps to order 14 YB-17 (later Y1B-17) pre-production aircraft including the static test airframe brought up to flight standard. Twelve of these aircraft were powered by 694-kW (930-hp) Wright

GR-1820-39 radials, while the thirteenth was completed as the Y1B-17A with 746-kW (1,000-hp) GR-1820-51 radials, each fitted with a turbocharger for improved high-altitude performance. The early production models were development variants and included 39 B-17Bs, 38 B-17Cs with 895-kW (1,200-hp) R-1820-65 engines, and 42 B-17Ds with self-sealing tanks and better armour. The tail was redesigned with a large dorsal fillet, which led to the first of the definitive Fortresses, the B-17E and B-17F, of which 512 and 3,405 were built, the latter with improved defensive armament.

The ultimate bomber variant was the B-17G with a chin turret and improved turbochargers for better ceiling, and this accounted for 8,680 of the 12,731 Flying Fortresses built. The type was discarded almost immediately after World War II, only a few special-purpose variants remaining in service. In addition, there were a number of experimental and navy models.

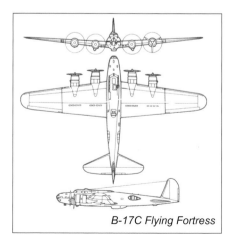

B-17C Flying Fortress

Boeing B-17G Flying Fortress 'Shoo Shoo Baby'

BOEING B-17G FLYING FORTRESS
Role: Long-range day bomber
Crew/Accommodation: Ten
Power Plant: Four 1,200-hp Wright R-1820-97 Cyclone air-cooled radials
Dimensions: Span 31.62 m (103.75 ft); length 22.66 m (74.33 ft); wing area 131.92 m² (1,420 sq ft)
Weights: Empty 16,391 kg (36,135 lb); MTOW 29,484 kg (65,000 lb)
Performance: Maximum speed 462 km/h (287 mph) at 7,620 m (25,000 ft); operational ceiling 10,851 m (35,600 ft); range 5,472 km (3,400 miles)
Load: Twelve .5-inch machine guns, plus up to 2,722 kg (6,000 lb) of bombs

CONSOLIDATED B-24 LIBERATOR (U.S.A.)

B-24H Liberator

OPPOSITE: U.S.A.F. Consolidated B-24D Liberator

The Liberator was a remarkably versatile aircraft, and was built in greater numbers than any other U.S. warplane of World War II. The Model 32 was designed to a U.S. Army Air Corps request of January 1939 for a successor to machines such as the Boeing XB-15 and Douglas XB-19, neither of which entered production, and offering higher performance than the Boeing B-17. The design was based on the exceptional wing of the Model 31 flying boat, the high aspect ratio of which offered low drag and thus the possibility of high speed and great range. The XB-24 prototype flew in December 1939 with 895-kW (1,200-hp) R-1830-33 radial engines, and the seven YB-24 pre-production machines were followed by nine B-24As with two 7.62-mm (0.3-in) tail guns and six 12.7-mm (0.5-in) guns in nose, ventral, dorsal and waist positions, and nine B-24Cs with turbocharged R-1830-41 engines and eight 12.7-mm guns in single-gun nose, ventral, and twin waist positions, and twin-gun dorsal and tail turrets. These paved the way for the first major model, the B-24D based on the B-24C but with R-1830-43 engines, self-sealing tanks and, in later aircraft, a ventral ball turret together with two 12.7-mm guns.

These 2,381 aircraft were followed by 801 B-24Es with modified propellers. Then came 430 B-24Gs with R-l830-43 engines and a power-operated nose turret carrying twin 12.7-mm guns, and 3,100 improved B-24Hs with a longer nose. The most important variant was the slightly modified B-24J, of which 6,678 were built with R-1830-65 engines, an autopilot and an improved bombsight. The 1,667 B-24Ls were similar to the B-24Js but had hand-operated tail guns, as did the 2,593 B-24Ms in a lighter mounting. There were also a number of experimental bomber variants, while other roles included transport (LB-30, air force C-87 and navy RY variants), fuel tanking (C-109), photographic reconnaissance (F-7), patrol bombing (PB4Y-1 and specially developed PB4Y-2 with a single vertical tail surface) and maritime reconnaissance (British Liberator GR models).

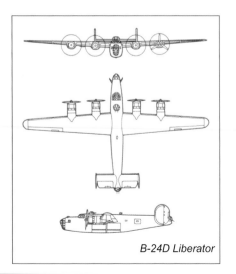

B-24D Liberator

A Consolidated B-24D Liberator in U.S.A.F. markings

CONSOLIDATED B-24J LIBERATOR
Role: Long-range day bomber
Crew/Accommodation: Ten
Power Plant: Four 1,200-hp Pratt & Whitney R. 1830-65 Twin Wasp air-cooled radials
Dimensions: Span 33.53 m (110 ft); length 20.47 m (67.16 ft); wing area 97.36 m² (1,048 sq ft)
Weights: Empty 16,556 kg (36,500 lb); MTOW 29,484 kg (65,000 lb)
Performance: Maximum speed 467 km/h (290 mph) at 7,620 m (25,000 ft); operational ceiling 8,534 m (28,000 ft); range 3,379 km (2,100 miles) with full bombload
Load: Ten .5-inch machine guns, plus up to 3,992 kg (8,800 lb) of internally carried bombs

HANDLEY PAGE HALIFAX (United Kingdom)

Halifax B.Mk II

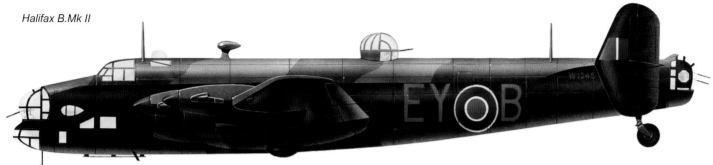

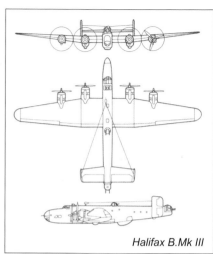

Halifax B.Mk III

The Halifax was one of the RAF's trio of four-engined night bombers in World War II, and while not as important in this role as the Lancaster, it was more important in secondary roles such as maritime reconnaissance transport and airborne forces' support. The type originated from a 1936 requirement for a medium/heavy bomber powered by two Rolls-Royce Vulture inline engines, and the resulting H.P.56 design was ordered in prototype form. The company had doubts about the Vulture, and began to plan an alternative

H.P.57 with four Rolls-Royce Merlin inlines. In September 1937, two H.P.57 prototypes were ordered. The first flew in October 1939.

The type entered service as the

Halifax B.Mk I with 954-kW (1,280-hp) Merlin Xs, and these 84 aircraft were produced in three series as the initial Series I, the higher-weight Series II, and the increased-tankage Series III. Later

bombers were the 1,977 Halifax B.Mk IIs with Merlin XXs or 22s and a two-gun dorsal turret, the 2,091 Halifax B.Mk IIIs with 1204-kW (1,615-hp) Bristol Hercules VI or XVI radials, the 904 Halifax B.Mk Vs based on the Mk II with revised landing gear, the 467 Halifax B.Mk VIs based on the Mk III but with 1249-kW (1,675-hp) Hercules 100s, and the 35 Halifax B.Mk VIIs that reverted to Hercules XVIs; there were also bomber subvariants with important modifications. The other variants retained the same mark number as the relevant bomber variant, and in the transport type these were the C.Mks II, VI and VII, in the maritime role GR.Mks II, V and VI, and in the airborne support role the A.Mks II, V and VII. Post-war development produced the C.Mk 8 and A.Mk 9 as well as the Halton civil transport, and total production was 6,178 aircraft.

HANDLEY PAGE HALIFAX B.Mk III

Role: Heavy night bomber
Crew/Accommodation: Seven
Power Plant: Four 1,615-hp Bristol Hercules XVI air-cooled radials
Dimensions: Span 30.12 m (98.83 ft); length 21.82 m (71.58 ft); wing area 116.3 m2 (1,250 sq ft)
Weights: Empty 17,346 kg (38,240 lb); MTOW 29,484 kg (65,000 lb)
Performance: Maximum speed 454 km/h (282 mph) at 4,115 m (13,500 ft); operational ceiling 7,315 m (24,000 ft); range 2,030 km (1,260 miles) with full warload
Load: Nine .303-inch machine guns, plus up to 5,897 kg (13,000 lb) of internally-stowed bombload

Handley Page Halifax Mk I

AVRO LANCASTER (United Kingdom)

Lancaster B.Mk III

B.Mk I), of which 3,435 were produced. Defensive armament was eight 7.7-mm (0.303-in) machine guns in three powered turrets: twin-gun nose and dorsal units, and a four-gun tail unit.

The first aircraft had 954-kW (1,280-hp) Merlin XXs or XXIIs, but later machines used the 1208-kW (1,620-hp) Merlin XXIVs. A feared shortage of Merlin inline engines led to the

Certainly the best night bomber of World War II, the Lancaster was conceived as a four-engined development of the twin-engined Type 679 Manchester, which failed because of the unreliability of its Rolls-Royce Vulture engines. The first Lancaster flew in January 1941 with 854-kW (1,145-hp) Rolls-Royce Merlin Xs and the same triple vertical tail surfaces as the Manchester, though these were later replaced by the larger endplate surfaces that became a Lancaster hallmark. The type was ordered into large-scale production as the Lancaster Mk I (later

AVRO LANCASTER Mk I

Role: Heavy night bomber
Crew/Accommodation: Seven
Power Plant: Four 1,640-hp Rolls-Royce Merlin 24 water-cooled inlines
Dimensions: Span 31.09 m (102 ft); length 21.18 m (69.5 ft); wing area 120.49 m² (1,297 sq ft)
Weights: Empty 16,780 kg (37,000 lb); MTOW 29,408 kg (65,000 lb)
Performance: Maximum speed 394 km/h (245 mph) at sea level; operational ceiling 6,706 m (22,000 ft); range 3,589 km (2,230 miles) with 3,182 kg (7,000 lb) bombload
Load: Eight .303-inch machine guns, plus up to 8,165 kg (18,000 lb) of bombs

The gun nose and cockpit of an Avro Lancaster

deliveries totalled 180 bringing overall Lancaster production to 7,377. After the war Lancasters were modified to perform a number of other roles.

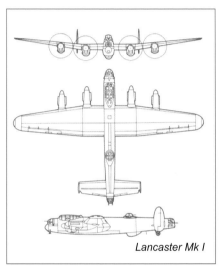

Lancaster Mk I

development of the Lancaster Mk II with 1294-kW (1,735-hp) Bristol Hercules VI or XVI radial engines, but only 301 of this model were built as performance was degraded and Merlins were in abundant supply. The Lancaster Mk I was soon supplemented by the Lancaster B.Mk III and Canadian-built Lancaster B.Mk X, both powered by Packard-built Merlins. Production of the Mk III and Mk X totalled 3,039 and 430 respectively. The final production version was the Lancaster B.Mk VIII with an American dorsal turret containing two 12.7-mm (0.5-in) heavy machine guns, and

BOEING B-29 and B-50 SUPERFORTRESS (U.S.A.)

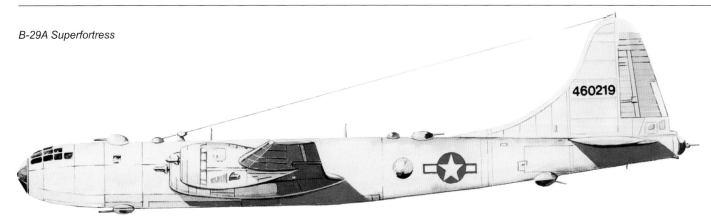

The B-29 was the world's first genuinely effective long-range strategic bomber, and was designed from January 1940 as the Model 345 to meet the U.S. Army Air Corps' extremely ambitious plan for a 'hemisphere defense' bomber. The type was an extremely advanced design with pressurized accommodation, remotely controlled defensive armament, a formidable offensive load, and very high performance including great ceiling and range. The first of three XB-29 prototypes flew in September 1942 with four Wright R-3550 twin-row radials, each fitted with two turbochargers. By this time, Boeing already had contracts for more than 1,500 production bombers. The XB-29s were followed by 14 YB-29 pre-production aircraft, of which the first flew in June 1943.

A prodigious effort was made to bring the Superfortress into full service, and a wide-ranging programme of subcontracting delivered components to four assembly plants. The type entered full service in time to make a major contribution to the war against Japan in World War II, which it ended with the A-

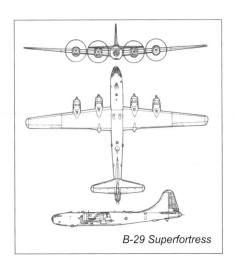

B-29 Superfortress

Boeing B-50D Superfortress

armament, and by 311 B-29Bs with no defensive armament but a radar-directed tail barbette. The type was also developed for reconnaissance and experimental roles, and was then revised with a sturdier structure and Pratt & Whitney R-4360 engines as the B-29D, which entered production as the B-50A. This was followed by its own series of bomber, reconnaissance and tanker aircraft.

bombings of Hiroshima and Nagasaki in August 1945.

Some 2,848 B-29s were complemented by 1,122 B-29 As with slightly greater span and revised defensive

---

BOEING B-29A SUPERFORTRESS
Role: Long-range, high-altitude day bomber
Crew/Accommodation: Ten
Power Plant: Four 2,200-hp Wright R-3350-23 Cyclone Eighteen air-cooled radials
Dimensions: Span 43.05 m (141.25 ft); length 30.18 m (99 ft); wing area 161.56 m² (1,739 sq ft)
Weights: Empty 32,369 kg (71,360 lb); MTOW 62,823 kg (138,500 lb)
Performance: Maximum speed 576 km/h (358 mph) at 7,620 m (25,000 ft); operational ceiling 9,708 m (31,850 ft); range 6,598 km (4,100 miles) with 7,258 kg (16,000 lb) bombload
Load: One 20-mm cannon and twelve .5-inch machine guns, plus up to 9,072 kg (20,000 lb) of bombs

ABOVE LEFT: A pair of B-29s

ABOVE: 1,000-lb Husky demolition bombs being dropped from a U.S. Far East Air Forces B-29

FAR LEFT: B-29 Superfortress

CONVAIR B-36 'PEACEMAKER' (U.S.A.)

B-36A 'Peacemaker'

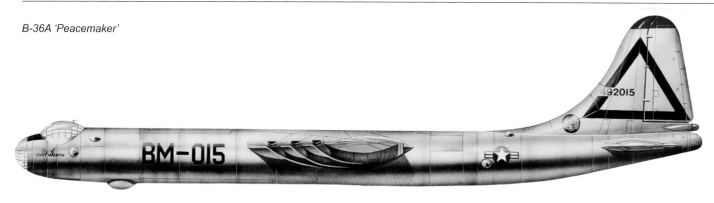

Designed as the Model 36 while the company was still Consolidated but built after it had become Convair, this extraordinary machine was the world's first genuinely intercontinental strategic bomber. The type resulted from an April 1941 requirement of the U.S. Army Air Corps for a machine able to carry a maximum bomb load of 32,659 kg (72,000 lb) but more realistically to deliver 4536 kg (10,000 lb) of bombs on European targets from bases in the United States. From four competing designs, the Model 36 was selected by the U.S. Army Air Forces for construction as the XB-36 prototype. This first flew in August 1946 and featured a pressurized fuselage and pusher propellers on the six 2237-kW (3,000-hp) R-4360-25 radial engines buried in the trailing edges of wings sufficiently deep to afford inflight access to the engines. The service trials model was the YB-36 with a raised cockpit roof, and this was subsequently modified as the YB-36A with four- rather than single-wheel main landing-gear units. These were features of the first production model, the B-36A unarmed crew trainer of which 22 were built without armament. The 104 B-36Bs introduced 2610-kW (3,500-hp) R-4360-41 engines and a defensive armament of

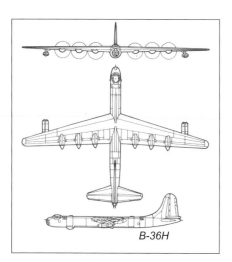

B-36H

Convair XB-36 prototype

Convair B-36 'Peacemaker'

16 20-mm cannon in nose, tail and six fuselage barbettes. Some 64 were later revised as B-36D strategic reconnaissance aircraft with greater weights and performance through the addition of four 2359-kg (5,200-lb) thrust General Electric J47-GE-19 turbojets in podded pairs under the outer wing, and in this role they complemented 22 aircraft which were built as such.

Later bombers with greater power and improved electronics were the 34 B-36Fs with 2833-kW (3,800-hp) R-04360-53s and J47-GE-19s, 83 B-36Hs with an improved flight deck, and 33 B-36Js with strengthened landing gear. There were also RB-36D, E, F and H reconnaissance versions, and even the GRB-36F with an embarked fighter for protection over the target area. Plans for jet- and even nuclear-powered versions resulted in no production variants.

CONSOLIDATED/CONVAIR B-36D

Role: Long-range heavy bomber

Crew/Accommodation: Fifteen, including four relief crew members

Power Plant: Six 3,500-hp Pratt & Whitney R-4360-41 air-cooled radials, plus four 2,359 kgp (5,200 lb s.t.) General Electric J47-GE-19 turbojets

Dimensions: Span 70.1 m (230 ft); length 49.4 m (162.08 ft); wing area 443 m² (4,772 sq ft)

Weights: Empty 72,051 kg (158,843 lb); MTOW 162,161 kg (357,500 lb)

Performance: Maximum speed 706 km/h (439 mph) at 9,790 m (32,120 ft); operational ceiling 13,777 m (45,200 ft); range 12,070 km (7,500 miles) with 4,535 kg (10,000 lb bombload)

Load: Twelve 20-mm cannon plus up to 39,009 kg (86,000 lb) of bombs

BOEING B-47 STRATOJET (U.S.A.)

B-47 Stratojet

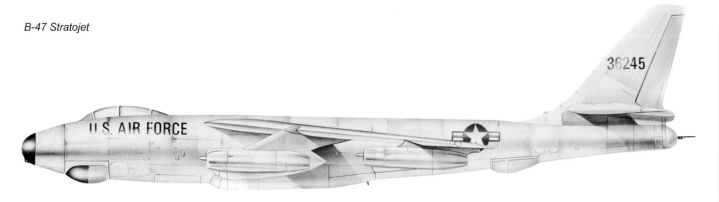

B-47E Stratojet

The B-47 was a great achievement, and as a swept-wing strategic bomber in the medium-range bracket it formed the main strength of the U.S. Strategic Air Command in the early 1950s. The U.S. Army Air Forces first considered a jet-powered bomber as early as 1944; at that time four companies were involved in producing preliminary designs for such a type. The Model 424 failed to attract real interest, but the later Model 432 was thought more acceptable and initial contracts were let. The company then recast the design as the Model 448 with the swept flying surfaces that captured German research data had shown to be desirable, but the USAAF was unimpressed. The design was finalized as the Model 450 with the six engines relocated from the fuselage to two twin-unit and two single-unit underwing nacelles.

In the spring of 1946, the USAAF ordered two Model 450 prototypes with the designation XB-47 and the first of these flew in December 1947. The type was notable for many of its features

Boeing B-47 Stratojet

including the 'bicycle' type landing gear, the twin main units of which retracted into the fuselage. The 10 B-47As were essentially development aircraft, and the first true service variant was the 399 B-47Bs, followed by 1,591 B-47Es with a host of operational improvements,

BOEING B-47E STRATOJET
Role: Heavy bomber
Crew/Accommodation: Three
Power Plant: Six 3,266-kgp (7,200-lb s.t.) General Electric J47-GE-25 turbojets, plus a 16,329-kgp (36,000-lb s.t.) rocket pack for Jet Assisted Take-Off (JATO)
Dimensions: Span 35.36 m (116 ft); length 32.92 m (108 ft); wing area 132.67 m² (1,428 sq ft)
Weights: Empty 36.631 kg (80,756 lb); MTOW 93,759 kg (206,700 lb) with JATO rocket assistance
Performance: Maximum speed 975 km/h (606 mph) at 4,968 m (16,300 ft); operational ceiling 12,344 m (40,500 ft); range 6,228 km (3,870 miles) with 4,536 kg (10,000 lb) bombload

including greater power, inflight refuelling capability and ejector seats. The B-47B and B-47E were both strengthened structurally later in their lives, leading to the designations B-47B-II and B-47E-II. There were also RB-47 reconnaissance together with several special-purpose and experimental variants.

ABOVE & LEFT: Boeing B-47 Stratojets

VICKERS VALIANT (UNITED KINGDOM)

Valiant B(K). Mk1

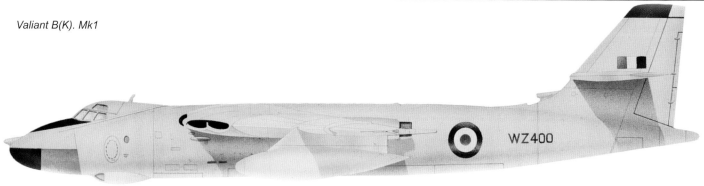

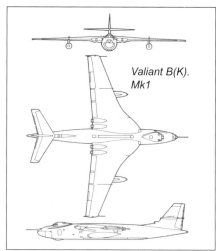

Valiant B(K). Mk1

The Valiant was the first of the U.K.'s trio of strategic V-bombers to enter service and, though not as advanced or capable as the later Avro Vulcan and Handley Page Victor, it was nonetheless a worthy warplane. The Type 667 was originated in response to a 1948 requirement for a high-altitude bomber to carry the British free-fall nuclear bomb that would be dropped with the aid of a radar bombing system. The type was based on modestly swept flying surfaces that included a shoulder-set cantilever wing with compound-sweep leading edges, a circular-section fuselage accommodating the five-man crew in its pressurized forward section, retractable tricycle landing gear and, in addition, four turbojets buried in the wing roots.

The prototype first flew in May 1951 with 2948-kg (6,500-lb) Rolls-Royce Avon RA.3 turbojets, improved to 3402-kg (7,500-lb) thrust Avon RA.7s in the second prototype that took over the flight test programme after the first had been destroyed by fire. The first five of 36

Valiant B.Mk 1 bombers served as pre-production aircraft, and this type began to enter squadron service in 1955. The type was used operationally as a conventional bomber in the Suez

A Vickers Valiant in camouflage

campaign of 1956, and was also used to drop the first British atomic and hydrogen bombs in October 1956 and May 1957 respectively. Production for the RAF totalled 104 aircraft in the form of

36 Valiant B.Mk 1 bombers, 11 Valiant B(PR).Mk. 1 strategic reconnaissace aircraft, 13 Valiant B(PR).Mk 1 multi-role aircraft usable in the bomber, reconnaissance and inflight refuelling tanker tasks, and 44 Valiant B(K).Mk 1 bomber and tanker aircraft. The Valiant B.Mk 2 did not pass the prototype stage, and all surviving aircraft were retired in 1965 as a result of fatigue problems.

VICKERS VALIANT B.Mk 1
Role: Strategic bomber
Crew/Accommodation: Five
Power Plant: Four 4,536-kgp (10,000-lb s.t.)
  Rolls-Royce Avon 28 turbojets
Dimensions: Span 34.85 m (114.33 ft); length
32.99 m (108.25 ft); wing area 219.4 m²
  (2,362 sq ft)
Weights: Empty 34,419 kg (75,881 lb); MTOW
63,503 kg (140,000 lb)
Performance: Maximum speed 912 km/h (492
  knots) at 9,144 m (30,000 ft); operational ceiling
  16,459 m (54,000 ft); range 7,242 km (3,908
  naut. miles) with maximum fuel
Load: No defensive armament, but internal
  stowage for up to 9,525 kg (21,000 lb) of bombs

BOEING B-52 STRATOFORTRESS (U.S.A.)

A B-52G Stratofortress in early form

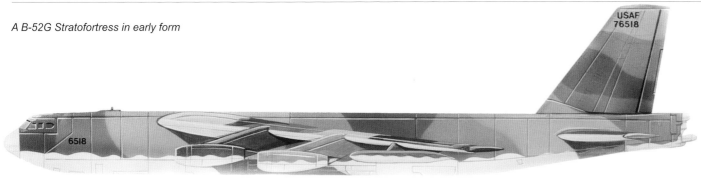

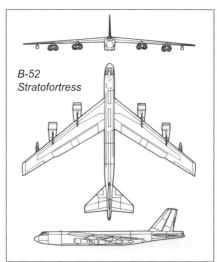

B-52 Stratofortress

In numerical terms, the B-52 is still the most important bomber in the U.S. Strategic Air Command inventory. It offers an excellent combination of great range and very large payload, though the type's radar signature is large and its operational capabilities are ensured only by constantly updated offensive and defensive electronic systems.

The Stratofortress was first planned as a turboprop-powered successor to the B-50, but was then recast as a turbojet-powered type using eight 3402-kg (7,500-lb) thrust Pratt & Whitney J57s podded in four pairs under the swept wings.

The B-52 employs the same type of 'bicycle' landing gear as the B-47, and after design as the Model 464 the XB-52 prototype first flew in April 1952 with a high-set cockpit that seated the two pilots in tandem. The current cockpit was adopted in the B-52A, of which three were built as development aircraft. The 50 B-52Bs introduced the standard nav/attack system, and the 35 B-52Cs had improved equipment and performance. These were in reality development models, and the first true service version

was the B-52D, of which 170 were built with revised tail armament. This model was followed by 100 B-52Es with improved navigation and weapon systems, 89 B-52Fs with greater power, 193 B-52Gs with a shorter fin, remotely controlled tail armament, integral fuel

tankage and underwing pylons for two AGM-28 Hound Dog stand-off nuclear missiles, and 102 B-52Hs, with Pratt & Whitney TF33 turbofans, a rotary-barrel cannon as tail armament, and structural strengthening for the low-altitude role.

The only version currently in service

is the B-52H, capable of carrying more than a 22,680-kg (50,000-lb) load. Apart from conventional weapons such as bombs, B-52H has an anti-shipping capability using Harpoon missiles, while for a nuclear mission it can carry up to twenty air-launched cruise missiles or a mix of these and gravity bombs. Other new missiles are also coming on stream for B-52H.

B-52 Stratofortress

BOEING B-52H STRATOFORTRESS
Role: Long-range bomber
Crew/Accommodation: Six
  Power Plant: Eight 7,718-kgp (17,000-lb s.t.)
  Pratt & Whitney TF33-P-3 turbofans.
Dimensions: Span 56.42 m (185 ft); length
  49.04 m (160 ft); wing area 371.6 m²
  (4,000 sq ft)
Weights: Empty 78,355 kg (172,740 lb); MTOW
  221,350 kg (488,000 lb)
Performance: Maximum speed 958 km/h
  (595 mph) at high altitude; operational ceiling
  16,750 m (55,000 ft); range 16,090 km (10,000
  miles)
Load: More than 22,680 kg (50,000 lb) of bombs
  or missiles

AVRO VULCAN (United Kingdom)

Vulcan B.Mk 2

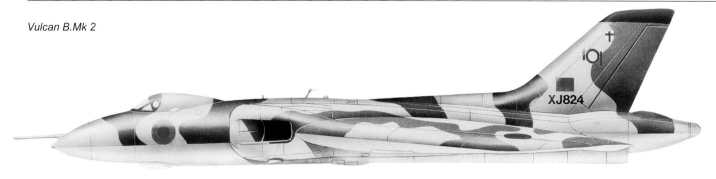

OPPOSITE: *XH558 is the only airworthy example remaining of the 134 Avro Vulcan V-bombers operated by the RAF from 1953–84*

The Type 698 was a massively impressive delta-winged bomber, and by any standards was an extraordinary aerodynamic feat that, with the Handley Page Victor and Vickers Valiant, was one of the U.K.'s trio of nuclear 'V-bombers' from the 1950s. The type was planned as a high-altitude bomber able to deliver the British free-fall nuclear bomb over long ranges. The first of two Type 698

prototypes flew in August 1952 with four 2,948-kg (6,500-lb) thrust Rolls-Royce Avon RA.3 turbojets, later replaced by 3,629-kg (8,000-lb) thrust Armstrong Siddeley Sapphire turbojets. The initial production model, the Vulcan B.Mk 1, had Olympus turbojets in variants

increased in thrust from 4,990 to 6,123-kg (11,000 to 13,500-lb).

In 1961 existing aircraft were modified to Vulcan B.Mk 1A standard with a bulged tail containing electronic counter-measures gear. The definitive model was the Vulcan B.Mk 2 with

provision for the Avro Blue Steel stand-off nuclear missile, a turbofan powerplant offering considerably greater fuel economy as well as more power, and a much-modified wing characterized by a cranked leading edge and offering greater area as well as elevons in place of the Mk 1's separated elevators and ailerons. The type was later modified as the Vulcan B.Mk 2A for the low-level role with conventional bombs and ECM equipment, and the Vulcan SR.Mk 2 was a strategic reconnaissance derivative.

Soon after the outbreak of the 1982 Falklands War, an RAF Vulcan attacked Port Stanley airfield; the flight from its Ascension Island base was then the largest ever operational sortie. Final retirement followed soon after.

Vulcan B.Mk 2A

A Royal Air Force Avro Vulcan

AVRO VULCAN B.Mk 2
Role: Long-range bomber
Crew/Accommodation: Five
Power Plant: Four 9,072 kgp (20,000 lb s.t.) Bristol Siddeley Olympus 301 turbojets
Dimensions: Span 33.83 m (111 ft); length 30.45 m (99.92 ft); wing area 368.29 m2 (3,964 sq ft)
Weights: Empty 48,081 kg (106,000 lb); MTOW 98,800 kg (200,180 lb)
Performance: Maximum speed 1,041 km/h (562 knots) Mach 0.98 at 12,192 m (40,000 ft); operational ceiling 19,912 m (65,000 ft); radius 3,701 km (2,300 miles) at altitude with missile
Load: Up to 9,525 kg (21,000 lb) of bombs, or one Blue Steel Mk 1 stand-off missile

TUPOLEV Tu-95 and Tu-142 'BEAR' (U.S.S.R.)

Tu-95 'Bear'

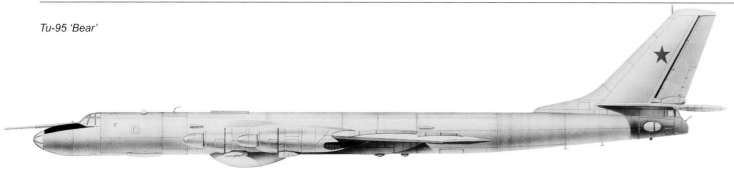

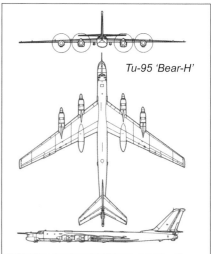

Tu-95 'Bear-H'

The Tu-95 prototype first flew in November 1952 and the type entered service in 1957. An extraordinary feature of this giant bomber was the adoption of massive turboprop engines, despite the official requirement for a speed of 900–950 km/h and a range of 14,000–15,000 km with a nuclear bomb.

'Bear-A' and 'Bear-B' were the original versions, the latter carrying the AS-3 'Kangaroo' missile semi-recessed under the fuselage, while retrofits later added inflight refuelling and, in some aircraft, strategic reconnaissance capabilities. Introduced in about 1963, the 'Bear-C' carried photographic and electronic

reconnaissance equipment. 'Bear-D' appeared in 1962 as a multi-sensor maritime reconnaissance and sea target acquisition version for the Soviet Navy. It was followed by 'Bear-E' for photographic reconnaissance and, from the mid-1970s,

by 'Bear-G' to carry AS-4 'Kitchen' missiles but was also used for electronic intelligence. All of these versions are now out of service. The 'Bear-H' first flew in 1979 and remains operational, armed with AS-15 'Kent' cruise missiles.

TUPOLEV Tu 142 'BEAR-F'
Role: Long-range anti-submarine warfare
Crew/Accommodation: Eleven to thirteen (mission-dependent)
Power Plant: Four 15,000-shp Kuznetsov NK-P 12M turboprops driving contra-rotating propellers
Dimensions: Span 50.04 m (164.17 ft); length 53.07 m (174.08 ft); wing area 289.9 m² (3,121 sq ft)
Weights: Empty 91,800 kg (202,384 lb); MTOW 185,000 kg (407,885 lb)
Performance: Maximum speed 855 km/h (531 mph); operational ceiling 11,000 m (36,000 ft); range 12,000 km (7,456 miles)
Load: Two 23-mm cannons and up to 9,000 kg (19,842 lb) of weaponry

A Tupolev Tu-95 and a McDonnell Douglas F-4B Phantom II

The TU-142 designation was applied to a long-range anti-submarine version of the Tu-95 for the Soviet Navy, first flown in 1968 and which remained in production until 1994. The ASW 'Bear-F' entered service in 1972 and remains operational with Russia and India. A communications relay variant became known to NATO as 'Bear-J' and continues in its role of providing an emergency link between the government and its nuclear submarines.

Tupolev Tu-95MS

HANDLEY PAGE VICTOR (United Kingdom)

Victor SR. Mk 2

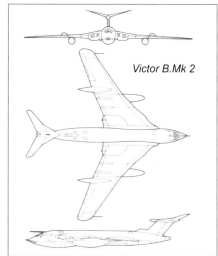

Victor B.Mk 2

The last of the United Kingdom's trio of nuclear 'V-bombers' to enter service, it is now the only one still in service, albeit as a tanker. The type was planned against the requirements of a 1946 specification for a bomber able to carry a free-fall nuclear bomb over long range at a speed and altitude too high for interception by the fighters of the day. The H.P.80 was based on what was in effect a pod-and-boom fuselage that supported crescent-shaped flying surfaces. For its time it was a very advanced type. The first of two prototypes flew in December 1952.

After considerable development, the type entered squadron service in November 1957 with 5012-kg (11,050-lb)

thrust Armstrong Siddeley Sapphire ASSa.7 Mk 202 turbojets. Production totalled just 50 aircraft that were formally designated Victor B.Mk 1H with better equipment and electronic counter-measures than the basic Victor B.Mk 1 that had originally been planned; soon

after delivery, 24 aircraft were modified to Victor B.Mk 1A standard with improved defensive electronics. Though planned with Sapphire ASSa.9 engines in a wing increased in span to 34.05 m (115 ft 0 in), the radically improved Victor B.Mk 2 was delivered with Rolls-Royce

HANDLEY PAGE VICTOR K.Mk 2

Role: Air-to-air refueller
Crew/Accommodation: Five
Power Plant: Four 9,344-kgp (20,600-lb s.t.)
 Rolls-Royce Conway Mk.201 turbo fans
Dimensions: Span 35.69 m (117 ft); length
 35.02 m (114.92 ft); wing area 204.38 m²
 (2,200 sq ft)
Weights: Empty 33,550 kg (110,000 lb); MTOW
 101,150 kg (223,000 lb)
Performance: Maximum speed 1,020 km/h (550
 knots) Mach 0.96 at 11,000 m (36,090 ft);
 operational ceiling 15,850 m (52,000 ft); range
 7,403 km (3,995 naut. miles) unrefuelled
Load: Up to 15,876 kg (35,000 lb)

Handley Page Victor

A British Royal Air Force Victor BK.Mk 2

Conway turbofans, initially 7824-kg (17,250-lb) thrust RCo. 11 Mk 200s but then in definitive-form 9344-kg (20,600-lb) thrust Conway Mk 201s. Production totalled 34 aircraft, and of these 21 were modified to Victor B.Mk 2R standard with provision for the Avro Blue Steel stand-off nuclear missile that allowed the Victor to avoid flight over heavily defended targets. Soon after this, the Victor was retasked to the low-level role as Soviet defensive capability was thought to have made high-altitude overflights little more than suicidal. Later conversions were the nine Victor B(SR).Mk 2 maritime reconnaissance and the tanker models that included 11 Victor K.Mk 1s, six Victor B.Mk 1A(K2P)s, 14 Victor K.Mk 1As and 24 Victor K.Mk 2s.

CONVAIR B-58 HUSTLER (U.S.A.)

B-58A Hustler

advances in aerodynamics, structures and materials, and was designed on Whitcomb area ruling principles with a long but slender fuselage that carried only a tall vertical tail and a small delta wing. This latter supported the nacelles for the four afterburning turbojets. The airframe was too small to accommodate sufficient fuel for both the outbound and return legs of the Hustler's mission, so the tricycle landing gear had very tall legs that raised the fuselage high enough off

The B-58 Hustler resulted from a 1949 U.S. Air Force requirement for a supersonic medium strategic bomber and was a stupendous technical achievement. In 1952 the Convair Model 4 was selected for development as an initial 18 aircraft. Convair's own experience in delta-winged aircraft, themselves based on German data captured at the end of World War II, was used in the far-sighted concept. The smallest possible airframe required

CONVAIR B-58A HUSTLER
Role: Supersonic bomber
Crew/Accommodation: Three
Power Plant: Four 7,076-kgp (15,600-lb s.t.) General Electric J79-GE-3B turbojets with reheat
Dimensions: Span 17.32 m (56.83 ft); length 29.49 m (96.75 ft); wing area 143.26 m² (1,542 sq ft)
Weights: Empty 25,202 kg (55,560 lb); MTOW 73,936 kg (163,000 lb)
Performance: Maximum speed 2,126 km/h (1,147 knots) Mach 2.1 at 12,192 m (40,000 ft); operational ceiling 19,202 m (63,000 ft); range 8,247 km (4,450 naut. miles) unrefuelled
Load: One 20-mm multi-barrel cannon, plus up to 8,820 kg (19,450 lb) of stores and fuel carrier in mission pod

Convair B-58A Hustler

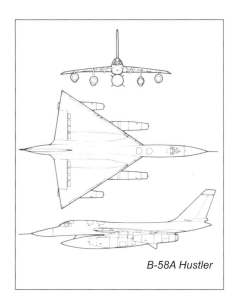

B-58A Hustler

the ground to accommodate a large underfuselage pod 18.90 m (62 ft 0 in) long. This pod contained the Hustler's nuclear bombload and also the fuel for the outward leg, and was dropped over the target. The crew of three was seated in tandem escape capsules.

In July 1954 the order was reduced to two XB-58 prototypes, 11 YB-58A pre-production aircraft and 31 pods. The first XB-58 flew in November 1956, and proved tricky to fly. Extensive development was undertaken with the aid of another 17 YB-58As ordered in February 1958 together with 35 pods; the last 17 YB-58As were later converted to RB-58A standard with ventral

reconnaissance pods. The type became operational in 1960, but as the high-altitude bomber was clearly obsolescent, full production amounted to only 86 B-58As plus 10 upgraded YB-58As. Training was carried out in eight TB 58A conversions of YB-58As.

LEFT & ABOVE: Convair B-58 Hustlers in desert storage

ROCKWELL B-1B LANCER (U.S.A.)

B-1A

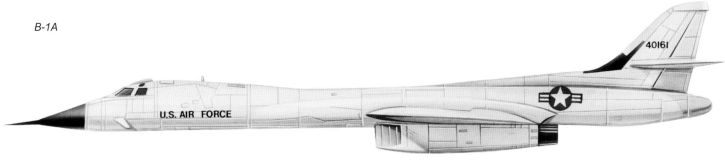

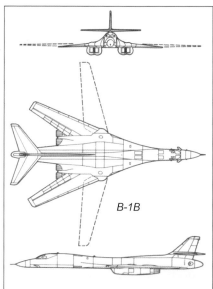

B-1B

Entering service from July 1985 to supersede the Boeing B-52 in the penetration bomber role, the B-1B resulted from a protracted development history that began in 1965 when the U.S. Air Force issued a requirement for an Advanced Manned Strategic Bomber. This was expected to have a dash capability of Mach 2.2+ for delivery of free-fall and stand-off weapons. The U.S. Department of Defense issued a request for proposals in 1969 and the Rockwell

submission was accepted as the B-l in 1970, and the full-scale development was soon under way as a complex variable-geometry type with General Electric F101 turbofans and variable inlets.

The prototype first flew in December 1974 and the flight test programme moved ahead without undue delay. In

June 1977, however, President Carter made the decision to scrap the programme in favour of cruise missiles, but the administration of President Reagan reactivated the programme in 1981 to procure just 100 B-1B bombers in the revised very low-level penetration role, using an automatic terrain-following

ROCKWELL B-1B

Role: Long-range low-level variable-geometry stand-off, strategic and conventional bomber
Crew/Accommodation: Four
Power Plant: Four 13,960-kpg (30,780-lb s.t.) General Electric F101-GE-102 turbofans with reheat
Dimensions: Span 41.66 m (136.68 ft); swept 23.84 m (78.23 ft); length 44.43 m (145.75 ft); wing area 181.2 m² (1,950 sq ft)
Weights: Empty 87,090 kg (192, 000 lb); MTOW 213,367 kg (477,000 lb)
Performance: Maximum speed 966 km/h (600 mph) at low level or Mach 1.2 at altitude; operational ceiling 15,240+ m (50,000+ ft); range 12,070 km (7,500 miles)
Load: Up to 56,699 kg (125,000 lb) of weapons as absolute maximum, including up to 24 nuclear bombs, 84 x 500 lb conventional bombs, sea mines, JDAM missiles or other weapons
Load: Two rear-firing 20-mm cannon, plus up to 9,979 kg (22,000 lb) of bombs

Rockwell B-1B Lancer

system. Other features included fixed inlets and modified nacelles (reducing speed to Mach 1.25) and a strengthened airframe and landing gear for operation at higher weights. Further changes were concerned with reduction of the type's already low radar signature, including some use of radar-absorbent materials.

The second and fourth B-1s were used from March 1983 to flight-test features of the B-1B, which itself first flew in October 1984 with the advanced offensive and defensive electronic systems. The second B-1B flew in May 1985 and became the first to join the Air Force in July 1985. From the ninth aircraft the type was built with revised weapons bays, the forward bay having a movable bulkhead allowing the carriage of 12 AGM-86B ALCMs internally, as well as additional fuel tanks and SRAMs. The final B-1B was delivered in April 1988, and currently some 77 are in the active inventory. Since 1993 emphasis has also been placed on giving the B-1B a conventional weapon capability, though remaining a nuclear bomber. Upgrading for new weapons continues.

A Rockwell B-1B Lancer landing at Robins Air Force Base, Georgia, U.S.A.

NORTHROP GRUMMAN B-2A SPIRIT (U.S.A.)

B-2A Spirit

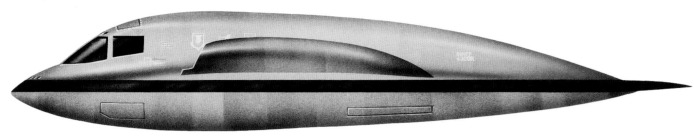

Developed at enormous cost during the late 1970s and 1980s, and first revealed in November 1988 for an initial flight in July 1989, the B-2 was designed as successor to the Rockwell B-1B in the penetration bomber role, although now intended to supplement it due partly to the tiny number built. Unlike the low-altitude B-1B, however, the B-2 is designed for penetration of enemy airspace at medium and high altitudes, relying on its stealth design, composite structure and defensive avionics suite to evade detection by an enemy until it has closed to within a few miles of its target,

B-2A is a costly but potentially decisive warplane

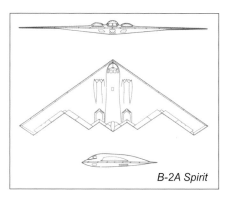

B-2A Spirit

NORTHROP B-2A SPIRIT
Role: Long-range subsonic stealth bomber
Crew/Accommodation: Two/three
Power Plant: Four 8,620-kgp (19,000-lb s.t.) General Electric F118-GE-100 turbofans
Dimensions: Span 52.43 m (172 ft); length 21.03 m (69 ft); wing area about 477.5 m^2 (5,140 sq ft)
Weights: Empty 56,700 kg (125,000 lb); MTOW 170,550 kg (376,000 lb)
Performance: Maximum speed Mach 0.8; operational ceiling 15,240 m (50,000 ft); range 11,100 km (6,900 miles) with a 14,515 kg (32,000 lb) load.
Load: Up to 18,145 kg (40,000 lb) in two bays

where attack accuracy is enhanced by use of the APQ-181 low-probability-of-intercept radar. Thereby, B-2A can strike at maximum defended and moving targets, allowing follow-up raids by non-stealth aircraft.

The B-2 is a design of the relaxed-stability type, and is a flying wing with highly swept leading edges and W-shaped trailing edges featuring all-horizontal flight-control surfaces (2-section elevons functioning as elevators and ailerons, and 2-section outer surfaces performing as drag rudders, spoilers and airbrakes) operated by a fly-by-wire control system. The design emphasis was placed on completely smooth surfaces with blended flightdeck and nacelle bulges. Radar reflectivity is very low because of the use of radiation-absorbent materials and a carefully optimized shape (including shielded upper-surface inlets), and the head-on radar cross-section is only about one-tenth of that of the B-1B.

Production of 132 B-2s was originally planned, but this total was progressively lowered until just 21 were completed for service, a figure including all six development aircraft raised to operational standard. The final B-2A was delivered in 1998 and full operational capability was achieved in 1999.

Northrop B-2 Spirit Stealth bomber

LIGHT/MEDIUM BOMBERS/STRIKE

LIGHT/ MEDIUM BOMBERS/STRIKE

The light bomber is arguably the oldest recorded form of combat aircraft. The first known illustration of an aerial attacker dates from 1326, as a bomb-carrying pennon kite, and thereby easily predates depictions in art of bomb-carrying balloons. Interestingly, more than a decade before the American Wright brothers achieved the world's first recognized manned and powered aeroplane flight, the first-ever contract to build a military heavier-than-air aeroplane had been issued to France's famed pioneer, Clément Ader, in 1892. Ader's aeroplane was to be a two-seater capable of carrying 75 kg (165 lb) of bombs; but the machine proved unable to fly during trials in 1897 and so the contract was not completed.

PAGE 166: Panavia Tornado GR4 02

PAGE 167: An F/A 18F Super Hornet flies alongside two Indian Navy Sea Harriers

RIGHT: Italy and Brazil collaborated on the development of the AMX International AMX close air support and interdiction jet, that entered service from 1989 and is capable of delivering 3,800 kg (8,378 lb) of free-fall and guided weapons

OPPOSITE: A Dassault Mirage 2000N (below) and an F-15 Eagle

In one of the first demonstrations of how aeroplanes could be used offensively in war, in January 1910 American Lt. Paul Beck dropped sandbags over Los Angeles from an aeroplane piloted by Louis Paulhan. More significantly, American pioneer Glenn Curtiss dropped dummy bombs over Lake Keuka in June that year, using buoys to indicate the outline of a battleship to be attacked from low level.

Then, in January 1911, Lt. Myron Crissy and Philip Parmalee released explosive bombs from their Wright biplane during live trials over San Francisco.

Italy was the first to take aeroplanes

to war, in 1911, and that November Second Lt. Giulio Gavotti piloted an aeroplane from which Cipelli grenades were thrown by hand onto Turkish forces at Taguira Oasis and Ain Zara (Libya), the first-ever recorded bombing raid by aeroplane. Fighting in Mexico provided the backdrop for the first aeroplane bombing of a warship when Didier Masson, supporting the forces of General Alvarado Obregon, attacked Mexican gunships in Guaymas Bay. During this conflict, Mexican generals often used the services of foreign pilots, and it is curious to note that in Mexico in November 1913 the very first aerial combat took place between aircraft, yet neither pilot who exchanged pistol fire was Mexican!

With the outbreak of World War I, tiny aircraft immediately undertook both nuisance and strategic bombing raids on the enemy, but in essence were the lightest of bombers. From a tactical standpoint, the first missions of real significance came on May 1915, when British aircraft attacked the railway system bringing up German reinforcements during the Neuve Chapelle offensive, thereby working in direct support of British ground forces. Areas around Courtrai and Menin were raided, plus the stations at Don, Douai and Lille, while for good measure three other aircraft bombed the German Divisional Headquarters at Fournes. The light bomber had established its importance as a tactical weapon and, despite the appearance of the much larger bombing aeroplanes possessing greater range and warload, the light bomber in developed forms

remained an essential part of air forces from this time forward.

Post World War I, the medium bomber bridged the gap between light and heavy types, although the definition became blurred as some air forces used payload carried as the defining factor, while others used range. Some difficulty in pinning down an exact definition continued until after World War II, when new light bomber jets, such as the RAF's Canberra that could carry a nuclear weapon to the U.S.S.R., caused further erosion of reasonable definitions.

Today, only a few air forces field heavy bombers, and it is probably true to say that the only truly modern medium bomber currently operational is the Russian Tu-22M Backfire, although even this is more often referred to as an intermediate-range bomber. Instead, many forces rely on smaller high-speed or subsonic jet attack aircraft armed with free-fall or precision-guided weapons. These, after all, can often carry a bomb load in excess of those managed by heavy bombers during World War II. 'Interdiction', 'strike', 'ground attack'

and 'close air support' are all modern-day terms for the varied traditional roles of the smaller bomber, and many (such as Tornado, Mirage 2000N and Sukhoi Su-24/Su-34) could, if called upon, carry out strategic as well as tactical attacks if the target was not too distant. Smaller jets have often been used at the outset of regional conflicts to deliver crippling blows against enemy forces, their size better suiting pinpoint attacks against high-value or critical targets. Indeed, air power in all forms has proven to be decisive in modern campaigns.

BREGUET 14 (France)

Bre.14B2

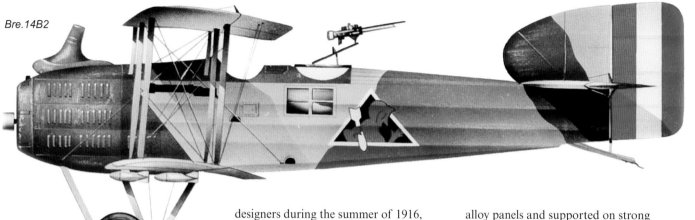

OPPOSITE: Replica of a Breguet Bre.14

The Breguet Bre. 14 was France's single most important and successful warplane of World War I, and perhaps the best known French combat plane until the advent of the Dassault Mirage III series. The type began to take shape on the drawing boards of the company's designers during the summer of 1916, and the first AV Type XIV flew in November 1916 with the AV (Avant, or forward) signifying that the plane was of the tractor type. Though not notable for its aesthetic qualities, the machine that soon became the Type 14 and later the Bre. 14 was immensely sturdy as a result of its steel, duralumin and wooden construction covered in fabric and light alloy panels and supported on strong landing gear of the spreader type. The pilot and gunner were located close together in the optimum tactical location, and the front-mounted Renault inline engine proved both powerful and reliable.

An initial 150 aircraft were ordered in the A.2 two-seat artillery observation category during April 1917, and by the end of that year orders had been placed for 2,650 aircraft to be produced by Breguet and five licensees in two-seat A.2 artillery and B.2 bomber variants, the latter with wings of increased span and flaps on the trailing edges of the lower wing. Other World War I variants were the Bre. 14B.1 single-seat bomber and Bre. 14S ambulance. Production up to the end of World War I totalled 5,300 aircraft with a variety of engine types, and more than 2,500 additional aircraft were built before production ended in 1928. Many of the postwar aircraft were of the Bre. 14 TOE type for use in France's colonial possessions. The Bre. 14 was finally phased out of French service only in 1932. Substantial exports were also made.

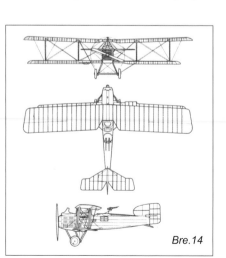

Bre.14

A Breguet Bre. 14 in Portuguese service

BREGUET Bre.14B2
Role: Fast day bomber/reconnaissance
Crew/Accommodation: Two
Power Plant: One 300-hp Renault 12 Fcy water-cooled inline
Dimensions: Span 14.91 m (48.92 ft); length 8.87 m (29.10 ft); wing area 51.1 m² (550 sq ft)
Weights: Empty 1,035 kg (2,282 lb); MTOW 1,580 kg (3,483 lb)
Performance: Maximum speed 195 km/h (121 mph) at sea level; operational ceiling 4,265 m (13,993 ft); range 485 km (301 miles) with full warload
Load: Two/three .303-inch machine guns, plus up to 260 kg (573 lb) of externally-carried bombs

Breguet Bre. 14

AIRCO (de HAVILLAND) D.H.9 and D.H.9A (United Kingdom)

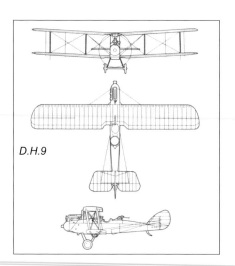

The D.H.9 was planned as a longer-range successor to the D.H.4. To speed production, the D.H.4's flying surfaces and landing gear were combined with a new fuselage that located the pilot and gunner close together and provided better streamlining for the engine, in this instance a 171.5-kW (230-hp) Galloway-built BHP engine. The type first flew in July 1917 and proved so successful that outstanding D.H.4 contracts were converted to the D.H.9, which therefore entered large-scale production with the 224-kW (300-hp) lightweight version of the BHP developed by Siddeley-Deasy and known as the Puma. The engine was unreliable and generally derated to 171.5 kW (230 hp), which gave the D.H.9

performance inferior to that of the D.H.4. As a result, the D.H.9 suffered quite heavy losses when it entered service during April 1918 over the Western Front, though it fared better in poorer defended areas, such as Macedonia and Palestine. Some 3,200 D.H.9s were built by Airco and 12 subcontractors.

Given the fact that the D.H.9's failing was its engine, it was hoped that use of the excellent 280-kW (375-hp) Rolls-Royce Eagle VIII would remedy the situation, but demands on this motor were so great that an American engine, the 298-kW (400-hp) Packard Liberty 12, was used instead to create the D.H.9A, which was perhaps the best strategic bomber of World War I. British production of 885 aircraft was complemented by 1,415 American-built Engineering Division USD-9 aircraft.

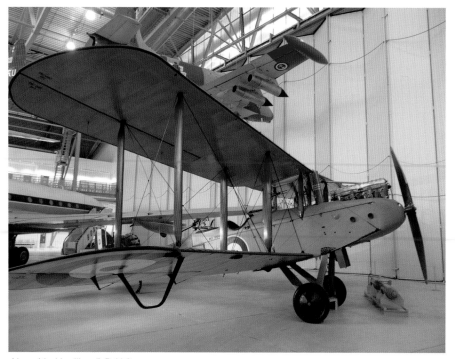

Airco (de Havilland) D.H.9

AIRCO D.H.9
Role: Light day bomber
Crew/Accommodation: Two
Power Plant: One 230-hp Siddeley-Deasy B.H.P. water-cooled inline
Dimensions: Span 12.92 m (42.4 ft); length 9.28 m (30.46 ft); wing area 40.32 m² (430 sq ft)
Weights: Empty 1,012 kg (2,230 lb); MTOW 1,508 kg (3,325 lb)
Performance: Maximum speed 177 km/h (110 mph) at 3,048 m (10,000 ft); operational ceiling 4.724 m (15,500 ft); endurance 4.5 hours
Load: Two .303-inch machine guns, plus up to 412 kg (908 lb) bombload

BREGUET 19 (France)

Bre. 19

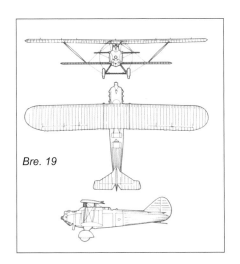

Bre. 19

F irst flown in March 1922 with a 336-kW (450-hp) Renault 12Kb inline engine, the Bre. 19 was planned as successor to the Bre. 14 but was produced in parallel with its predecessor for service with units based in metropolitan France. Though the Bre. 19 was similar in overall concept to the Bre. 14, it was a considerably more pleasing and aerodynamically refined design with unequal- rather than almost equal-span wings with single outward sloping I-type interplane struts, a circular-section rather than slab-sided fuselage, and a much cleaner landing gear arrangement with a spreader-type main unit. The structure was primarily of duralumin with fabric covering, though the forward fuselage as far aft as the gunner's cockpit was covered with duralumin sheet.

The prototype was followed by 11 development aircraft that were used to evaluate a number of engine types, and the Bre. 19 entered production in 1923. By 1927 some 2,000 aircraft had been delivered, half each in the B.2 bomber and A.2 spotter/ reconnaissance roles.

Most aircraft in French service were powered by the Renault 12K or Lorraine-Dietrich 12D/E engines, and with each type gave invaluable service mainly at home but also in France's colonial wars of the 1920s in Morocco and Syria. The Bre. 19 soldiered on into obsolescence, and late in its career equipped four night fighter squadrons before being relegated to the reserve and training roles during 1934. The type also secured considerable export success (direct sales and licensed production) mainly of the Bre. 19GR long-range variant. The Bre. 19 was also developed in Bidon (petrol can) and Super Bidon variants for a number of classic record-breaking distance flights.

Breguet Bre. 19TR

BREGUET Bre. 19 B2
Role: Light day bomber
Crew/Accommodation: Two
Power Plant: One 550-hp Renault 12Kc water-cooled inline
Dimensions: Span 14.8 m (48.5 ft); length 8.89 m (29.16 ft); wing area 50 m² (538.4 sqft)
Weights: Empty 1,485 kg (3,273 lb); MTOW 2,301 kg (5,093 lb)
Performance: Maximum speed 240 km/h (149 mph) at sea level; operational ceiling 7,800 m (25,590 ft); range 800 km (497 miles) with full warload
Load: Three/four .303-inch machine guns, plus up to 700 kg (1,543 lb) of bombs

JUNKERS Ju 87 (Germany)

Ju 87B-1

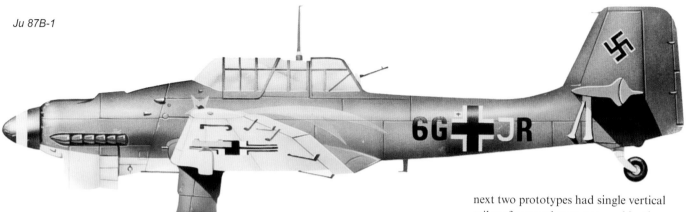

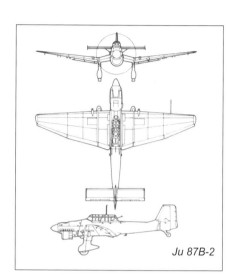

Ju 87B-2

The Ju 87 was planned as a dedicated dive bomber, a type known to the Germans as the Sturzkampfflugzeug or Stuka, and proved a decisive weapon in the opening campaigns of World War II. The type delivered its weapons with great accuracy, and came to be feared so highly that the appearance of its inverted gull wings and the sound of the 'Jericho trumpet' sirens on its landing gear legs often caused panic.

JUNKERS Ju 87B
Role: Dive bomber
Crew/Accommodation: Two
Power Plant: One 1,200-hp Junkers Jumo 211 Da water-cooled inline
Dimensions: Span 13.8 m (45.3 ft); length 11 m (36.83 ft); wing are a 31.9 m² (343.3 sq ft)
Weights: Empty 2,750 kg (6,063 lb); MTOW 4,250 kg (9,321 lb)
Performance: Maximum speed 380 km/h (237 mph) at 4,000 m (13,124 ft); operational ceiling 8,100 m (26,575 ft); range 600 km (372 miles) with full warload
Load: Three 7.9-mm machine guns, plus 1,000 kg (2,205 lb) bombload

The first of four prototypes flew late in 1935 as the Ju 87 V1 with the 477-kW (640-hp) Rolls-Royce Kestrel V inline engine and endplate vertical surfaces. The next two prototypes had single vertical tail surfaces and were powered by the 455-kW (610-hp) Junkers Jumo 210Aa inline, while the last prototype introduced a larger vertical tail. The type entered service in the spring of 1937 as the Ju 87A with the 477-kW (640-hp) Jumo 210C, and production of this variant totalled 210 aircraft.

Later variants included the Ju 87B

Junker Ju 87 replica

with the 895-kW (1,200-hp) Jumo 211D, a larger canopy and the wheel fairings replaced by spats; the Ju 87D dive-bomber and ground-attack type with the 1051-kW (1,410-hp) Jumo 211J in a revised cowling, a redesigned canopy, a still larger vertical tail, simplified landing gear, and upgraded offensive and defensive features; the Ju 87G anti-tank model with two 37-mm underwing cannon; the Ju 87H conversion of the Ju 87D as a dual-control trainer; and the Ju 87R version of the Ju 87B in the long-range anti-ship role. From 1941 the Ju 87's limitations in the face of effective anti-aircraft and fighter defences were fully evident, but Germany lacked a replacement and the type had to remain in service as increasingly specialized ground-attack and anti-tank aircraft. Production of the series totalled 5,709 aircraft.

HEINKEL He 111 (Germany)

He 111H-5

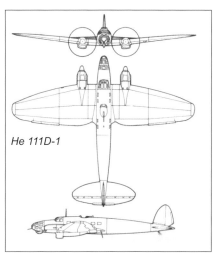

He 111D-1

The He 111 was Germany's most important bomber of World War II, and was built to the extent of 7,300 or more aircraft. The type was designed supposedly as an airliner, and in its first form it was basically an enlarged He 70 with two 492-kW (660-hp) BMW VI 6.0Z inline engines mounted on the wings. The first prototype flew in February 1935, and considerable development was necessary in another prototype, 10 pre-production aircraft, and finally another prototype before the He 111B began to enter military service with 746-kW (1,000-hp) Daimler-Benz DB 600 inlines, which were also used for the six He 111C

10-passenger airliners. The DB 600 was in short supply, so the He 111E used the 746-kW (1,000-hp) Junkers Jumo 211A and was developed in five subvariants to a total of about 190 aircraft.

The 70 He 111Fs combined the wing of the He 111G with Jumo 211A-3 engines, and at the same time the eight

He 111 Gs introduced a wing of straight rather than curved taper and was built in variants with BMW 132 radial or DB 600 inline engines. The He 111H was based on the He 111P and became the most extensively built model, some 6,150 aircraft being produced in many important subvariants, both built and

converted, up to the He 111H-23 with increasingly powerful engines (including the Jumo 211 and 213), heavier armament and sophisticated equipment. The He 111J was a torpedo bomber, and about 90 were delivered. Despite its late designation, the He 111P was introduced in 1939 and pioneered the asymmetric and extensively glazed forward fuselage in place of the original stepped design, and about 40 aircraft were built in subvariants up to the He 111P-6.

The oddest variant was the He 111Z heavy glider tug, which was two He 111H-6 bombers joined by a revised wing section incorporating a fifth Jumo 211F engine.

HEINKEL HE 111H-16
Role: Bomber
Crew/Accommodation: Five
Power Plant: Two 1,350-hp Junkers Jumo 211F-2 water-cooled inlines
Dimensions: Span 22.6 m (74.15 ft); length 16.4 m (53.81 ft); wing area 86.5 m² (931 sq ft)
Weights: Empty 8,680 kg (19,136 lb); MTOW 14,000 kg (30,865 lb)
Performance: Maximum speed 435 km/h (270 mph) at 6,000 m (19,685 ft); operational ceiling 6,700 m (21,982 ft); range 1,950 km (1,212 miles) with maximum bombload
Load: Two 20-mm cannon and five 13-mm machine guns, plus up to 3,600 kg (7,937 lb) of bombs

Heinkel He 111H-16

DORNIER Do 17 Family (Germany)

Do 217K

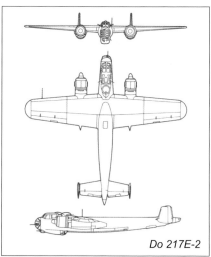

Do 217E-2

The origins of this important German bomber lie with a 1933 Deutsche Lufthansa requirement for a six-passenger mailplane, though this requirement was also responsible for the narrow 'pencil' fuselage that was one of the main hindrances to the type's later development as a warplane. The Do 17 first flew in the autumn of 1934, and its performance suggested a military development with the single vertical tail surface replaced by endplate surfaces to increase the dorsal gunner's field of fire. Six military prototypes were followed by two pre-production types, the Do 17E-1 bomber with a shortened but glazed nose

and 500-kg (1,102-lb) bomb load, and the Do 17F-1 photographic reconnaissance type, both powered by 559-kW (750-hp) BMW VI inlines.

There followed a number of experimental and limited-production variants before the advent of the Do 17Z definitive bomber, built in several subvariants with the 746-kW (1,000-hp)

BMW-Bramo 323 Fafnir radials in 1939 and 1940. Do 17 production was perhaps 1,200 aircraft, and from this basic type was developed the Do 215, of which 112 were produced with Daimler-Benz DB 601A inline engines. The two main models were the Do 215B-4 reconnaissance type and the Do 215B-5 night fighter. The Do 217, that first flew in September 1938, was

essentially a Do 17 with 802-kW (1,075-hp) DB 601A engines, a larger fuselage, and a revised empennage.

Production was 1,750 aircraft in three basic series: the Do 217E heavy bomber and anti-ship type with stepped forward fuselage and 1178-kW (1,580-hp) BMW 801 radial engines, the Do 217K and Do 217M heavy night bomber and missile-armed anti-ship types with unstepped forward fuselage plus 1268-kW (1,700-hp) BMW 801 radials and 1305-kW (1,750-hp) DB 603A inline engines, and the Do 217N night fighter and intruder types with radar, specialist weapon fit, and 1379-kW (1,850-hp) DB 603A inline engines.

DORNIER D0 17Z-2
Role: Medium bomber
Crew/Accommodation: Five
Power Plant: Two 1,000-hp BMW Bramo 323P Fafnir air-cooled radials
Dimensions: Span 18 m (59.06 ft); length 15.8 m (51.84 ft); wing area 55 m² (592 sq ft)
Weights: Empty 5,210 kg (11.488 lb); MTOW 8.590 kg (18.940 1b)
Performance: Maximum speed 410 km/h (255 mph) at 4,000 m (13,124 ft); operational ceiling 8,200 m (26,904 ft); radius 330 km (205 miles) with full bombload
Load: Eight 7.9-mm machine guns, plus up to 1,000 kg (2,205 lb) of bombs

The Do 217P, the final development of the Dornier Do 217 series

BRISTOL BLENHEIM (United Kingdom)

Blenheim Mk IF

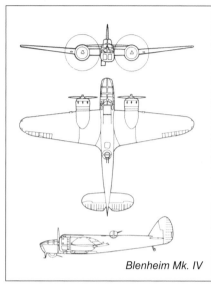

Blenheim Mk. IV

In 1934 Lord Rothermere commissioned Bristol to produce a fast and capacious light personal transport. This appeared as the Type 142 that first flew in April 1935 with two 485-kW (650-hp) Bristol Mercury VIS radials. The aircraft caused a great stir as it was 48 km/h (30 mph) faster than the U.K.'s latest fighter, and it was presented to the nation by the air-minded Rothermere after the Air Ministry asked for permission to evaluate the machine as a light bomber. As a result, Bristol developed the Type 142M bomber prototype that first flew in June 1936.

The type offered higher performance than current light bombers, and was ordered in large numbers for service from 1937 onwards.

The main variants were the original Blenheim Mk I of which 1,365 were built in the U.K. and 61 under licence (45 in Finland and 16 in Yugoslavia) with 626-kW (840-hp) Mercury VIII radials, the Blenheim Mk IF interim night fighter of which about 200 were produced as conversions with radar and a ventral pack of four machine guns, the generally improved Blenheim Mk IV of which 3,297 were built in the U.K. and another 10 under licence in Finland with 686-kW (920-hp) Mercury XV engines, more fuel and a lengthened nose, the Blenheim Mk IVF extemporized night fighter, the Blenheim Mk IVF fighter conversion, and the Blenheim Mk V of which 945 were built with 708-kW (950-hp) Mercury 25 or 30 engines and a solid nose housing four machine-guns in Mk VA bomber, Mk VB close support, Mk VC operational trainer and Mk VD tropicalized bomber subvariants. The Blenheim Mk IV was built in Canada as the Bolingbroke coastal reconnaissance and light bomber aircraft, of which 676 were built as Mk Is with Mercury VIIIs, Mk IVs with Mercury XVs and MK IV Ws with Pratt & Whitney R-1830 Wasp radials.

BRISTOL BLENHEIM Mk I
Role: Medium bomber
Crew/Accommodation: Three
Power Plant: Two 840-hp Bristol Mercury VIII air-cooled radials
Dimensions: Span 17.17 m (56.33 ft); length 12.11 m (39.75 ft); wing area 43.57m² (469 sq ft)
Weights: Empty 3,674 kg (8,100 lb); MTOW 5,670 kg (12,500 lb)
Performance: Maximum speed 459 km/h (285 mph) at 4,572 m (15,000 ft); operational ceiling 8,315 m (27,280 ft); range 1,810 km (1,125 miles) with full bombload
Load: Two .303-inch machine guns, plus up to 454 kg (1,000 lb) of bombs

Bristol Blenheim Mk.IV

SAVOIA-MARCHETTI SM. 79 SPARVIERO (Italy)

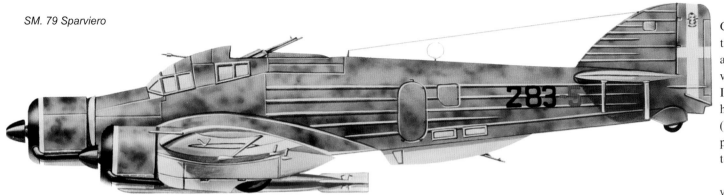

SM. 79 Sparviero

The SM. 79 Sparviero (Sparrowhawk) was Italy's most important bomber of World War II and, in its specialist anti-ship version, the best torpedo bomber of the war. The type was evolved from the company's earlier tri-motor types, and first flew in late 1934 as the SM. 79P prototype of a planned eight-passenger civil transport, and in this form was powered by three 455-kW (610-hp) Piaggio Stella radials. The type was a cantilever low-wing monoplane of mixed construction with retractable tailwheel landing gear, and its considerable capabilities soon prompted the adoption of a more warlike role with a revised cockpit, a ventral gondola, provision for offensive and defensive armament, and 582-kW (780-hp) Alfa Romeo 125 RC 35/126 RC 34 radial engines.

Production of the series totalled about 1,370 for Italy and for export, and the initial variant was the SM. 79-I bomber with 582-kW (780-hp) Alfa-Romeo 126 RC 34 radials and no windows in the fuselage sides. This type was successfully evaluated in the Spanish Civil War in both the level bomber and the torpedo bomber roles, and proved so admirable in the latter that a specialized variant was then ordered as the SM. 79-II torpedo bomber with 746-kW (1,000-hp) Piaggio P.XI RC 40 or 768-kW (1,030-hp) Fiat A.80 RC 41 radials and provision for two 450-mm (17.7-in) torpedoes.

The SM. 79-111 was an improved version of the SM. 79-11 without the ventral gondola and with heavier defensive armament. Production of the SM. 79-I, II and III totalled 1,230. Other variants were the SM. 79B twin-engined export version of the SM. 79-I with a variety of radials, the SM.79C (and SM. 79T long-range) prestige conversion of the SM. 79-I without dorsal and ventral protusions, the SM. 79JR model for Romania with two Junkers Jumo 211Da inline engines, the SM.79K version of the SM. 79-I for Yugoslavia, and the SM. 83 civil transport version.

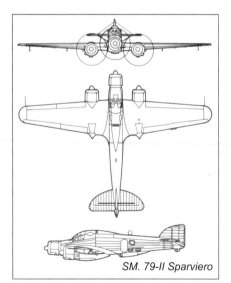

SM. 79-II Sparviero

A flight of four SM.79s showing their rear-cockpit-mounted machine guns

SAVOIA-MARCHETTI SM.79 SPARVIERO
Role: Bomber
Crew/Accommodation: Four
Power Plant: Three 780-hp Alfa Romeo 126 RC34 air-cooled radials
Dimensions: Span 21 m (69.55 ft); length 15.62 m (51.25 ft); wing area 61.7 m² (664.2 sq ft)
Weights: Empty 6,800 kg (14.991 lb); MTOW 10,500 kg (23,148 lb)
Performance: Maximum speed 430 km/h (267 mph) at 4,000 m (13,125 ft); operational ceiling 6,500 m (21,325 ft); range 1,900 km (1,180 miles) with full bombload
Load: Three 12.7-mm and two 7.7-mm machine guns, plus up to 1,250 kg (2,756 lb) of bombs or one torpedo

JUNKERS Ju 88 Family (Germany)

Ju 88A-4

The Ju 88 can be considered Germany's equivalent to the British Mosquito and with that type was certainly the most versatile warplane of World War II. Production of the Ju 88 family totalled about 15,000 aircraft. The type was schemed as a high-speed bomber and first flew in December 1936 with 746-kW (1,000-hp) Daimler-Benz

DB 600A inlines, subsequently changed to Junkers Jumo 211s of the same rating, a low/mid-set wing and, in the standard German fashion, the crew grouped closely together in an extensively glazed

nose section that proved comparatively vulnerable despite steadily heavier defensive armament. With the Jumo 211, the Ju 88A entered widespread service, being built in variants up to the Ju 88A-

17. Six manufacturers produced about 7,000 of this series alone.

The next operational bomber was the Ju 88S in three subvariants with the 1268-kW (1,700-hp) BMW 801G radial, smoother nose contours, and reduced bombload to improve performance; companion reconnaissance models were the two variants of the Ju 88T and the three variants of the longer-range Ju 88H. Production of the Ju 88H/S/T series totalled some 550 aircraft. From the Ju 88A was developed the Ju 88C heavy fighter; this had BMW 801A radials and a 'solid' nose for the heavy gun armament, together with radar in a few night fighter variants. The definitive night fighter series with steadily improving radar and effective armament was the Ju 88G, together with the improved Ju 88R version of the Ju 88C. Other series were the Ju 88D long-range reconnaissance and Ju 88P anti-tank aircraft. Development of the same concept yielded the high-performance Ju 188 and high-altitude Ju 388 series.

Ju 88A-4

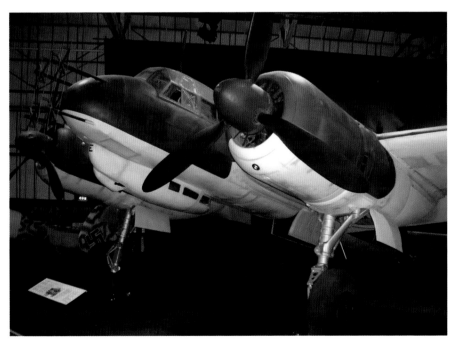

Junkers Ju 88 R-1 night fighter

JUNKERS Ju 88A-4
Role: Light fast bomber
Crew/Accommodation: Four
Power Plant: Two 1,340-hp Junkers Jumo 211J-1 water-cooled inlines
Dimensions: Span 20 m (65.63 ft); length 14.4 m (47.23 ft); wing area 54.5 m² (586.6 sq ft)
Weights: Empty 9,860 kg (21,737 lb); MTOW 14,000 kg (30,870 lb)
Performance: Maximum speed 470 km/h (292 mph) at 5,300 m (17,390 ft); operational ceiling 8,200 m (26,900 ft); range. 1.790 km (1,112 miles) with full bombload
Load: Two 13-mm and three 7.9-mm machine guns, plus up to 2,000 kg (4,409 lb) bombload

VICKERS WELLINGTON (United Kingdom)

Wellington B.Mk III

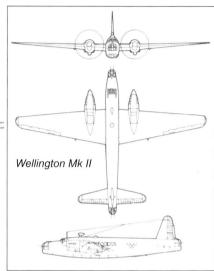

Wellington Mk II

The Wellington was the most important British medium bomber of World War II, and indeed during the early stages of the war was perhaps the only truly effective night bomber after the type was switched to this role in the aftermath of some disastrously heavy losses in early daylight raids. A Wellington of No. 149 Squadron was responsible for dropping the RAF's first 4,000-lb 'block buster' bomb during an attack on Emden in April 1941, and on the first RAF 'thousand bomber' raid on Germany (Cologne) in May 1942, no fewer than 599 of the 1,046 bombers used were Wellingtons.

Designed to meet a 1932 requirement, the prototype first flew in June 1936 with 682-kW (915-hp) Bristol Pegasus X radials. The type used the geodetic lattice-work form of airframe construction pioneered in the Vickers Wellesley by inventor Barnes Wallis, and was thus immensely strong. When production ceased in October 1945, no fewer than 11,461 Wellingtons had been produced in versions with the 746-kW (1,000-hp) Pegasus XVIII radial (the Wellington B.Mks I, IA and IC with steadily improved defensive capability, and the Wellington GR.Mk VIII with searchlight and provision for anti-submarine weapons), the 1,119-kW (1,500-hp) Bristol Hercules radial (the Wellington B.Mk III with the Hercules XI and B.Mk X with the Hercules VI or XVI, and the Wellington GR.Mks XI, XII, XIII and XIV with the Hercules VI or XVI and steadily improved anti-submarine equipment), the 783-kW (1,050-hp) Pratt & Whitney Twin Wasp radial (the Wellington B.Mk IV) and the 854-kW (1,145-hp) Rolls-Royce Merlin X inline (the Wellington B.Mks II and VI).

Wellingtons were extensively converted later in the type's career into alternative roles such as freighting and training. Several aircraft were also used as engine test-beds, and the basic concept was developed considerably further in the Type 294 Warwick that was designed as a heavy bomber but actually matured as a maritime reconnaissance aircraft.

Vickers Wellington Bomber

VICKERS WELLINGTON B.Mk IC
Role: Heavy bomber
Crew/Accommodation: Five/six
Power Plant: Two 1,050-hp Bristol Pegasus XVIII air-cooled radials
Dimensions: Span 26.27 m (86.18 ft); length 19.69 m (64.6 ft); wing area 78 m² (848 sq ft)
Weights: Empty 8,709 kg (19,200 lb); MTOW 12,927 kg (28,500 lb)
Performance: Maximum speed 378 km/h (235 mph) at 1,440 m (4,724 ft); operational ceiling 5,486 m (18,000 ft); range 2,575 km (1,600 miles) with 925 kg (2,040 lb) bombload
Load: Six .303-inch machine guns, plus up to 2,041 kg (4,500 lb) internally stowed bombload

AICHI D3A 'VAL' (Japan)

D3A2 'Val'

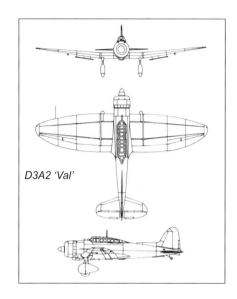

D3A2 'Val'

Designed as successor to the same company's D1A and first flown in 1938 with the 544-kW (730-hp) Kinsei 3 radial engine, the D3A was Japan's most important naval dive-bomber at the beginning of World War II, and played a major part in the Pearl Harbor attack. Known to the Allies as the 'Val', the D3A played a decisive part in Japan's expansionist campaign in South-East Asia and the South-West Pacific, but was eclipsed by American carrierborne fighters from mid-1942 onward.

The type's elliptical flying surfaces were aerodynamically elegant, and the combination of a lightweight structure and fixed but spatted landing gear provided good performance. Production aircraft were based on the second prototype, but with slightly reduced span and also a long dorsal fin to improve directional stability. Total construction

was 1,495 aircraft, and the main variants were the D3A1 and D3A2, which totalled 476 and 1,007 respectively.

The D3A1 entered service in 1940 with the 746-kW (1,000-hp) Kinsei 43

Aichi D3A2 'Val'

that was altered later in the production run to the 1,070-hp (798-kW) Kinsei 44 radial. The D3A2 was fitted with a propeller spinner and a modified rear cockpit canopy, and was powered by the 969-kW (1,300-hp) Kinsei 54 that could draw on greater fuel capacity for better

performance and range. The D3A2-K was a trainer conversion of the earlier models. From late 1942 the type was relegated to the land-based attack role, and then to second-line tasks such as training before final use as kamikaze attack aircraft.

AICHI D3A2 'VAL'
Role: Naval carrierborne dive bomber
Crew/Accommodation: Two
Power Plant: One 1,300-hp Mitsubishi Kinsei 54 air-cooled radial
Dimensions: Span 14.37 m (47.1 ft); length 10.23 m (33.6 ft); wing area 23.6 m² (254 sq ft)
Weights: Empty 2,618 kg (5,722 lb); MTOW 4,122 kg (9,087 lb)
Performance: Maximum speed 430 km/h (267 mph) at 9,225 m (20,340 ft); operational ceiling 10,888 m (35,720 ft); range 1,561 km (970 miles)
Load: Three 7.7-mm machine guns, plus up to 370 kg (816 lb) of bombs

DOUGLAS SBD DAUNTLESS (U.S.A.)

SBD-3 Dauntless

The SBD Dauntless was the most successful dive-bomber produced by the Americans during World War II, and assumed historical importance as one of the weapons that checked the tide of Japanese expansion in the Battles of the Coral Sea and Midway during 1942. The type began life as a development of the 1938 Northrop BT-1 after Northrop's acquisition by Douglas. The Douglas development was first flown in July 1938 as the XBT-2 low-wing monoplane with the 746-kW (1,000-hp) Wright R-1820-32 Cyclone radial engine, perforated split trailing-edge flaps that also served as airbrakes, and the main bomb carried under the fuselage on a crutch that swung it clear of the propeller before it was released in a steep dive.

The type began to enter U.S. Navy carrierborne and U.S. Marine Corps land-based service as the SBD-1, of which 57 were built with one trainable and two fixed 7.62-mm (0.3-in) machine guns. The 87 SBD-2s had greater fuel capacity and revised offensive armament. Next came the 584 SBD-3s which introduced the R-1820-52 engine, a bulletproof windshield, armour protection, self-sealing fuel tanks of greater capacity, and the definitive machine gun armament of two 12.7-mm (0.5-in) fixed guns and two 7.62-mm

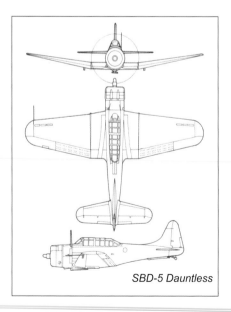

SBD-5 Dauntless

A U.S. Navy SBD Dauntless landing on aircraft carrier USS Ranger

DOUGLAS SBD-5 DAUNTLESS
Role: Naval carrierborne dive bomber
Crew/Accommodation: Two
Power Plant: One 1,200-hp Wright R-1820-60 Cyclone air-cooled radial
Dimensions: Span 12.66 m (41.54 ft); length 10.09 m (33.1 ft); wing area 30.19 m² (325 sq ft)
Weights: Empty 2,905 kg (6,404 lb); MTOW 4,853 kg (10,700 1b)
Performance: Maximum speed 410 km/h (255 mph) at 4,265 m (14,000 ft); operational ceiling 7,780 m (25,530 ft); range 1,795 km (1,115 miles) with 726 kg (1,600 lb) bombload
Load: Two .5-inch and two .303-inch machine guns, plus up to 1,021 kg (2,250 lb) of bombs

Two US Navy SBD-5 dive bombers.

(0.3-in) trainable guns. The 780 SBD-4s had a revised electrical system. The 3,025 SBD-5s had the 895-kW (1,200-hp) R-1820-60 engine and greater ammunition capacity. The 451 examples of the final SBD-6 had the yet more powerful R-1820-66 engine and increased fuel capacity.

Subvariants of this series were the SBD-1P, SBD-2P and SBD-3P photo-reconnaissance aircraft. The U.S. Army ordered an A-24 version of the SBD-3, further contracts specifying A-24A (SBD-4) and A-24B (SBD-5) aircraft, but these were not successful. The Fleet Air Arm received nine SBD-5s that were designated Dauntless DB.Mk I but not used operationally.

NORTH AMERICAN B-25 MITCHELL (U.S.A.)

B-25J Mitchell

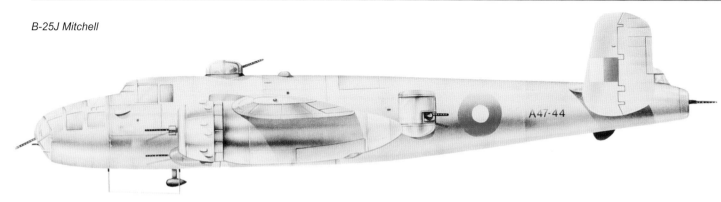

Immortalized as the mount of Doolittle's Tokyo Raiders when flown off the deck of USS *Hornet* in April 1942, the NA-40 was designed to meet a U.S. Army requirement for a twin-engined attack bomber, and emerged for its first flight in January 1939 as a shoulder-wing monoplane with tricycle landing gear and 820-kW (1,100-hp)

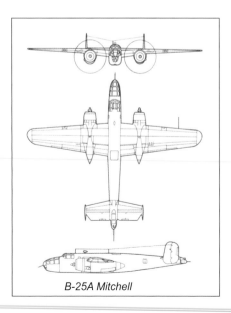

B-25A Mitchell

North American B-25J Mitchell in the Red Bull Air Race

Pratt & Whitney R-1830-S6C3-G radials that were soon replaced by 969-kW (1,300-hp) Wright GR-2600-A71 radials. The R-2600 was retained throughout the rest of the type's 9,816-aircraft production run. Further development produced the NA-62 design with the wing lowered to the mid-position, the fuselage widened for side-by-side pilot seating, the crew increased from three to five, greater offensive and defensive armament, and 1268-kW (1,700-hp) R-2600-9 engines. In this form the type entered production as the B-25, and the first of 24 such aircraft flew in August 1940.

Development models produced in small numbers were the B-25A (40 with armour and self-sealing fuel tanks) and B-25B (119 with power-operated dorsal and ventral turrets but with the tail gun position removed). The major production models began with the B-25C; 1,625 of this improved version were built with an autopilot, provision for an underfuselage torpedo, underwing racks for eight 113-kg (250-lb) bombs and, in some aircraft,

NORTH AMERICAN B-25C MITCHELL
Role: Medium bomber
Crew/Accommodation: Five/six
Power Plant: Two 1,700-hp Wright R-2600-19 Cyclone air-cooled radials
Dimensions: Span 20.6 m (67.58 ft); length 16.13 m (52.92 ft); wing area 56.67 m2 (610 sq ft)
Weights: Empty 9,208 kg (20,300 lb); MTOW 15,422 kg (34,000 lb)
Performance: Maximum speed 457 km/h (284 mph) at 4,572 m (15,000 ft); operational ceiling 6,041 m (21,200 ft); range 2,414 km (1,500 miles) with full bombload
Load: Four .5-inch machine guns, plus up to 1,361 kg (3,000 lb) of bombs

North American B-25 Mitchell

four 12.7-mm (0.5-in) machine guns on the fuselage sides to fire directly forward. The 2,290 B-25Ds were similar but from a different production line. A few experimental versions intervened, and the next series-built models were the B-25G

(405 with a 75-mm/2.95-in nose gun) and similar B-25H (1,000 with the 75-mm gun and between 14 and 18 12.7-mm machine guns).

The final production version was the B-25J (4,390 with R-2600-92 radials and

12 12.7-mm machine guns). Other variants included in the total were the F-10 reconnaissance, the AT-25 and TB-25 trainers, together with the PBJ versions, the last provided for the U.S. Navy.

DOUGLAS DB-7/A-20 HAVOC Series (U.S.A.)

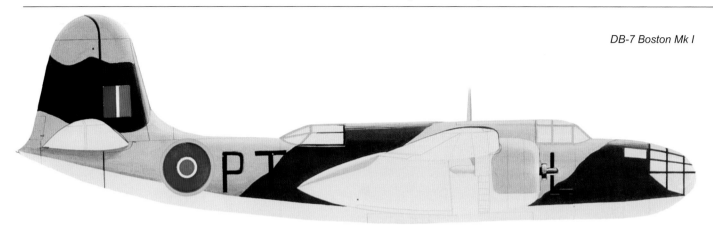

DB-7 Boston Mk I

OPPOSITE: Douglas DB-7 A-20 Havoc

The Model 7 was a basic twin-engined light bomber design that was evolved as a private venture and then went through a number of important forms during the course of an extensive production programme that saw the delivery of 7,478 aircraft in World War II up to September 1944. The type originated as a possible replacement for the U.S. Army's current generation of single-engined attack aircraft, and first flew as the Model 7B in October 1938 with 820-kW (1,100-hp) Pratt & Whitney R-1830 radials in place of the 336-kW (450-hp) engines of the originally proposed Model 7A. Initial orders came from France for a Douglas Bomber 7 (DB-7) variant with 895-kW (1,200-hp) R-1830-S3C4-G engines and a deeper fuselage, followed by the improved DB-7A with 1119-kW (1,500-hp) Wright R-2600-A5B engines.

Most of these aircraft were delivered to the U.K. after the fall of France, and were placed in service with the name Boston Mks I and II, though several were converted to Havoc radar-equipped night-fighters. A redesigned DB-7B bomber variant with larger vertical tail surfaces and British equipment became the Boston Mk III, and the same basic type was ordered by the U.S. Army as the A-20 Havoc. The latter were used mainly as reconnaissance aircraft, though a batch was converted to P-70 night fighter configuration. Thereafter the U.S. Army accepted large numbers of the A-20A and subsequent variants up to the A-20K with more power, heavier armament, and improved equipment. Many of these passed to the RAF and other British Commonwealth Air Forces in variants up to the Boston Mk V.

The steady increases in engine power maintained the performance of these types despite their greater weights and warloads. In addition to the Western Allies, the U.S.S.R. operated comparatively large numbers of the series received under Lend-Lease and often fitted with locally modified armament.

DOUGLAS A-20B HAVOC
Role: Light day bomber
Crew/Accommodation: Three
Power Plant: Two 1,600-hp Wright R-2600-11
  Double Cyclone air-cooled radials
Dimensions: Span 18.69 m (61.33 ft); length
  14.48 m (47.5 ft); wing area 43.1 m² (464 sq ft)
Weights: Empty 6,727 kg (14,830 lb); MTOW
  10,796 kg (23,800 lb)
Performance: Maximum speed 563 km/h
  (350 mph) at 3,658 (12,000 ft); operational
  ceiling 8,717 m (28,600 ft); range 1,328 km
  (825 miles) with 454 kg (1,000 lb) of bombs
Load: Three .5-inch and one or three .303-inch
  machine guns, plus 1,089 kg (2,400 lb)
  of bombs

A-20J Havoc

Douglas DB 7/A-20 Havoc

PETLYAKOV Pe-2 (U.S.S.R.)

Petlyakov Pe-2

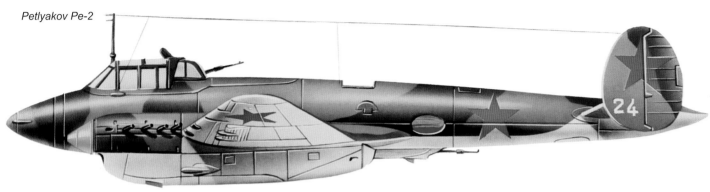

The Pe-2 was one of the U.S.S.R.'s most important tactical aircraft of World War II, and resulted from the VI-100 high-altitude fighter prototype with the 783-kW (1,050-hp) Klimov M-105 inlines. The planned role was then changed to dive-bombing, resulting in the PB-100 design for a dive-bomber with a crew of three rather than two, dive-brakes and other modifications, including provision of a bomb aimer's position and elimination of the pressure cabin. The type was of all-metal construction and a thoroughly modern

PETLYAKOV Pe-2
Role: Dive bomber
Crew/Accommodation: Three/four
Power Plant: Two 1,100-hp Klimov M-105R water-cooled inlines
Dimensions: Span 17.16 m (56.23 ft); length 12.66 m (41,54 ft); wing area 40.5 m² (435.9 sq ft)
Weights: Empty 5,876 kg (12,954 lb); MTOW 8,496 kg (18,730 lb)
Performance: Maximum speed 540 km/h (336 mph) at 5,000 m (16,404 ft); operational ceiling 8,800 m (28,871 ft); range 1,500 km (932 miles)
Load: One 12.7-mm and two 7.62-mm machine guns, plus up to 1,200 kg (2,646 lb) of bombs

concept with a cantilever low-set wing, endplate vertical tail surfaces, a circular-section fuselage, and retractable tailwheel landing gear. The aircraft entered service in November 1940 as the Pe-2 with two 902-kW (1,210-hp) VK-105RF engines,

and when production ended early in 1945 some 11,427 aircraft of the series had been built.

The versatility of the type is attested by the development and production of variants intended for the bombing,

reconnaissance, bomber destroyer, night fighter and conversion trainer roles. In addition to the baseline Pe-2, the main variants were the Pe-2R photo-reconnaissance type with cameras and greater fuel capacity, the Pe-2UT dual-control trainer with a revised cockpit enclosure over tandem seats, and the Pe-3 multi-role fighter, of which some 500 were built as 200 Pe-3 bomber destroyers and 300 Pe-3bis night fighters; the Pe-3 had the fixed nose armament of two 20-mm cannon, two 12.7-mm (0.5-in) and two 7.62-mm (0.3-in) machine guns plus one 12.7-mm gun in the dorsal turret, while the Pe-3bis entered production with a nose armament of one 20-mm cannon, one 12.7-mm machine gun and three 7.62-mm machine guns but ended with two 20-mm cannon, two 12.7-mm guns and two 7.62-mm guns.

Russian pilots and ground crew in front of a Petlyakov

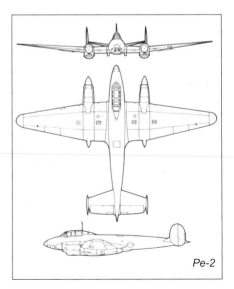

Pe-2

de HAVILLAND D.H.98 MOSQUITO (United Kingdom)

Mosquito B.Mk VI

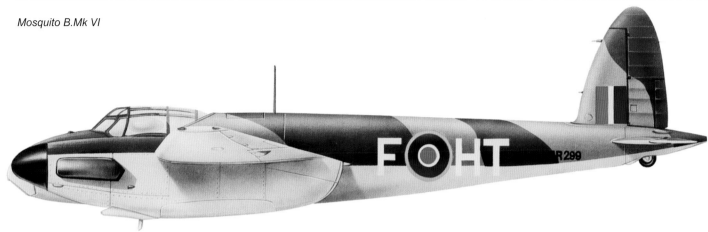

The trainer versions were the Mosquito T.Mk III, T.Mk 22 Canadian-built equivalent to the T.Mk III, T.Mk 27 version of the T.Mk 22 with Packard-built engines, T.Mk 29 conversion of the FB.Mk 26, and T.Mk 43 Australian-built equivalent to the T.Mk III.

The bomber versions were the basic Mosquito B.Mk IV, B.Mk VII Canadian-built type with underwing hardpoints, B.Mk IX high-altitude type with a single 1814-kg (4,000-lb) bomb, B.Mk XVI development of the B.Mk IX with pressurized cockpit, B.Mk 20 B.Mk 25 version of the B.Mk 20 and B.Mk 35 long-range high-altitude model.

Perhaps the most versatile warplane of World War II and certainly one of the classic warplanes of all time, the 7,785 Mosquitoes began from a private venture based on the company's composite plywood/balsa construction principal. It was planned as a high-performance but unarmed light bomber. The Mk I prototype flew in November 1940. Photographic reconnaissance, fighter, trainer and bomber variants followed.

The PR versions were the Mosquito PR.Mk IV with four cameras, PR.Mk VIII with two-stage Merlins, PR.Mk IX with greater fuel capacity, PR.Mk XVI with cockpit pressurization, PR.Mk 32 based on the NF.Mk XV, PR.Mk 34 with extra fuel in a bomb bay 'bulge', PR.Mk 40 Australian development of the FB.Mk 40, and PR.Mk 41 version of the PR.Mk 40 with two-stage engines.

The fighters were the Mosquito NF.Mk II night fighter, FB.Mk VI fighter-bomber with bombs and underwing rockets, NF.Mk XII and XIII with improved radar, NF. Mk XV conversion of the B. Mk IV for high-altitude interception, NF.Mk XVII conversion of the NF.Mk II with U.S. radar, FB.Mk XVIII anti-ship conversion or the FB.Mk VI with a 57-mm gun and rockets, NF.Mk XIX with British or U.S. radar, FB.Mk 21 Canadian-built FB.Mk VI, FB.Mk 26 version of the FB.Mk 21 with Packard-built Merlin engines, NF.Mk 30 high-altitude model with two-stage Merlins, TR.Mk 33 naval torpedo fighter, NF.Mk 36 higher-altitude equivalent to the NF.Mk 30, TR.Mk 37 version of the TR.Mk 33 with British radar, and FB.Mk 40 Australian-built equivalent of the FB.Mk VI.

de HAVILLAND D.H.98 MOSQUITO NF. Mk 36
Role: Night/all-weather fighter
Crew/Accommodation: Two
Power Plant: Two 1,690-hp Rolls-Royce Merlin 113 water-cooled inlines
Dimensions: Span 16.51 m (54.17 ft): length 12.34 m (40.5 ft); wing area 42.18 m² (454 sq ft)
Weights: Empty 7,257 kg (16,000 lb); MTOW 9,707 kg (21,400 lb)
Performance: Maximum speed 650 km/h (404 mph) at 8.717 m (28.600 ft); operational ceiling 10,972 m (36,000 ft); range 2.704 km (1,680 miles)
Load: Four 20-mm cannon (interception-guided by AI Mk 10 radar)

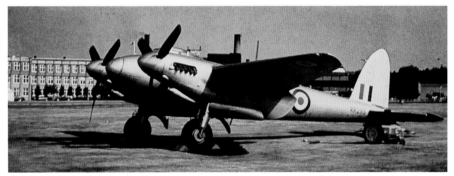
de Havilland D.H.98 Mosquito

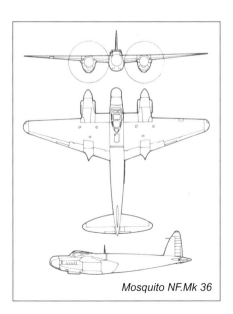
Mosquito NF.Mk 36

189

ILYUSHIN Il-2 (U.S.S.R.)

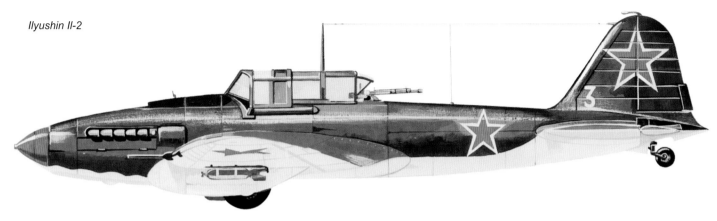

Ilyushin Il-2

The Il-2 was probably the finest ground-attack aircraft of World War II and was built to the extent of some 36,165 aircraft. The type began life as the TsKB-55 (alternatively BSh-2 or DBSh) two-seat prototype that first flew in December 1939 with the 1007-kW (1,350-hp) Mikulin AM-35 inline engine. Flight tests indicated that the type was too heavy because of its massive armour 'bath' structural core, so the basic design was developed into the single-seat TsKB-

57 that flew in October 1940 with a 1268-kW (1,700-hp) Mikulin AM-38 inline. This entered production as the single-seat BSh-2, a designation that was altered to Il-2 during April 1941, and by August production had risen to some 300 aircraft per month.

Early operations confirmed the design bureau's initial objections to the removal of the TsKB-55's rear gunner, for the Il-2 was found to be especially vulnerable to rear attack. The Il-2 was

therefore refined as the Il-2M with the cockpit extended aft for a rear gunner equipped with a 12.7-mm (0.5-in) machine gun but separated from the pilot by a fuel tank. The original two wing-mounted 20-mm cannon were replaced by 23-mm weapons offering greater armour-penetration capability, and provision was made for the eight 82-mm (3.2-in) rockets to be replaced by four 132-mm (5.2-in) weapons. Later the type was also produced in the aerodynamically

improved Il-2 Type 3 version with a 1320-kW (1,770-hp) engine, a refined canopy and faster-acting doors for the bomb cells in the wings that carried 200 2.5-kg (5.51-lb) anti-tank bomblets. There was also an Il-2 Type 3M variant with further aerodynamic refinement and a fixed forward-firing armament of two 37-mm cannon complemented by up to 32 82-mm (1 in) rockets on a two-stage zero-length installation. Other Il-2 versions were the Il-2T torpedo bomber with one 533-mm (21-in) torpedo under the fuselage and the Il-2U tandem-seat trainer. Production ended in late 1944 to allow for the much improved Il-10.

ILYUSHIN Il-2M
Role: Strike/close air support
Crew/Accommodation: Two
Power Plant: One 1,700-hp AM-38F
 water-cooled inline
Dimensions: Span 14.6 m (47.9 ft); length 11.6 m
 (38.06 ft); wing area 38.5 m² (414.41 sq ft)
Weights: Empty 4,525 kg (9,976 lb); MTOW
 6,360 kg (14,021 lb)
Performance: Maximum speed 404 km/h
 (251 mph) at 1,500 m (4,921 ft); operational
 ceiling 6,000 m (19,685 ft); range 765 km
 (475 miles) with full warload
Load: Two 23-mm cannon and two 7.62-mm
 machine guns, plus up to 600 kg (1,321 lb) of
 bombs or anti-armour rockets

Ilyushin Il-2 Type 3M

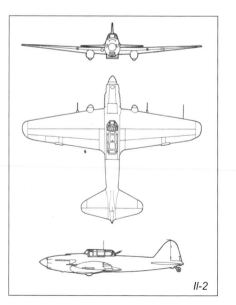

Il-2

MARTIN B-26 MARAUDER (U.S.A.)

B-26F Marauder

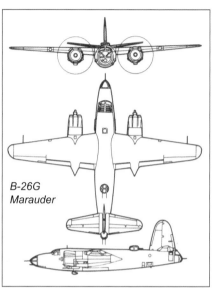

B-26G Marauder

The Marauder was designed to meet a particularly difficult specification issued in 1939 by the U.S. Army Air Corps for a high-performance medium bomber, and was ordered 'off the drawing board' straight into production without any prototype or even pre-production aircraft. The first B-26 flew in November 1940 with two 1380-kW (1,850-hp) Pratt & Whitney R-2800-5 radials as a highly streamlined mid-wing monoplane with tricycle landing gear. The type was able to deliver the required performance, but because of the high wing loading low-speed handling was poor, resulting in a spate of accidents.

Total production was 4,708 aircraft, and in addition to the 201 B-26s the main variants were the B-26A (139 aircraft) with 1380-kW (1,850-hp) R-2800-9 or -39 engines, greater fuel capacity and provision for an underfuselage torpedo, the B-26C (1,883) with 1491-kW (2,000-hp) R-2800-41 engines and, from the 642nd aircraft, a wing increased in span by 1.83 m (6 ft 0 in) as a means of reducing wing loading, though this was negated by inevitably increased weight, the B-26C (1,210) generally similar to the B-26B but from a different production line, the B-26F (300) which introduced a higher wing incidence angle to improve field performance, and the B-26G (893) generally similar to the B-26F. There were two target tug-gunnery trainer variants produced by converting bombers as 208 AT-23As (later TB-26Bs) and 375 AT-23Bs (later TB-26Cs); 225 of the latter were transferred to the U.S. Navy as JM-1s. There was also the new-build TB-26G crew trainer, and 47 of these 57 aircraft were transferred to the U.S. Navy as JM-2s. Comparatively large numbers of several models were used by the British and, to a lesser extent, the French and South Africans.

MARTIN B-26B MARAUDER

Role: Medium bomber
Crew/Accommodation: Seven
Power Plant: Two 2,000-hp Pratt & Whitney R-2800-41 Double Wasp air-cooled radials
Dimensions: Span 21.64 m (71 ft); length 17.75 m (58.25 ft); wing area 61.13 m² (658 sq ft)
Weights: Empty 10,660 kg (23,500 lb); MTOW 17,328 kg (38,200 lb)
Performance: Maximum speed 454 km/h (282 mph) at 4,572 m (15,000 ft); operational ceiling 4,572+ m (15,000+ ft); range 1,086 km (675 miles) with maximum bombload
Load: Twelve .5-inch machine guns, plus up to 1,815 kg (4,000 lb) of internally carried bombs, or one externally carried torpedo

Martin B-26G Marauder

191

CURTISS SB2C HELLDIVER (U.S.A.)

SB2C-1 Helldiver

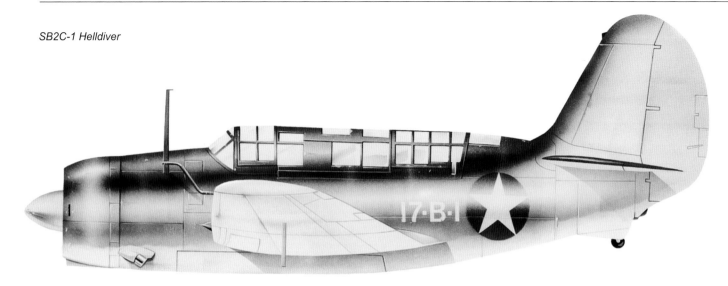

bomber/dive bomber role. The type was designed as a substantial all-metal monoplane of the low-wing variety with retractable tailwheel landing gear (complete with arrester hook), a substantial tail unit, and a deep oval-section fuselage characterized by extensive glazing over the rear compartment. The X2B2C-1 prototype flew in December 1940 but was lost in an accident only a short time later. The U.S. Navy had considerable faith in the type, however, and large-scale production had already been authorized to launch a programme that saw the eventual delivery of 7,200 aircraft. But because of the need to co-develop an A-25A version for the U.S. Army, the first SB2C-1 production aeroplane with the 1268-kW (1,700-hp) Wright R-2600-8 Cyclone 14 radial did

The SB2C was the third Curtiss design to bear the name Helldiver, the first two having been the F8C/02C biplanes of the early 1930s and SBC biplane of the late 1930s. The Model 84 (or SB2C) monoplane was designed in competition to the Brewster XSB2A Buccaneer as successor to the Model 77 (or SBC) biplane in the carrierborne scout

CURTISS SB2C-5 HELLDIVER
Role: Naval carrierborne bomber/reconnaissance
Crew/Accommodation: Two
Power Plant: One 1,900-hp Wright R-2600-20 Double Cyclone air-cooled radial
Dimensions: Span 15.15 m (49.75 ft); length 11.17 m (36.66 ft); wing area 39.2 m² (422 sq ft)
Weights: Empty 4,799 kg (10,580 lb); MTOW 7,388 kg (16,287 lb)
Performance: Maximum speed 418 km/h (260 mph) at 4,907 m (16,100 ft); operational ceiling 8,047 m (26,400 ft); range 1,875 km (1,165 miles) with 454 kg (1,000 lb) bombload
Load: Two 20-mm cannon and two .303-inch machine guns, plus up to 907 kg (2,000 lb) of bombs

Curtiss SB2C Helldiver

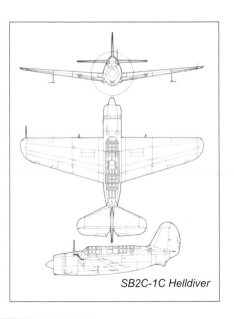

SB2C-1C Helldiver

not emerge until June 1942. The A-25A in fact entered only the most limited of army service, and the majority of the army's aircraft were reassigned to the U.S. Marine Corps in the land-based role with the designation SB2C-1A.

Other variants were the SB2C-1C with the four wing-mounted 12.7-mm (0.5-in) machine guns replaced by two 20-mm cannon, the SB2C-3 with the 1417-kW (1,900-hp) R-2600-20 engine, the SB2C-4 with underwing bomb/rocket

racks, the radar-fitted SB2C-4E, and the SB2C-5 with greater fuel capacity. Similar versions were built by Fairchild and Canadian Car & Foundry with the basic designation SBF and SBW respectively.

Curtiss SB2C Helldiver

193

GRUMMAN TBF AVENGER (U.S.A.)

TBF-1 Avenger

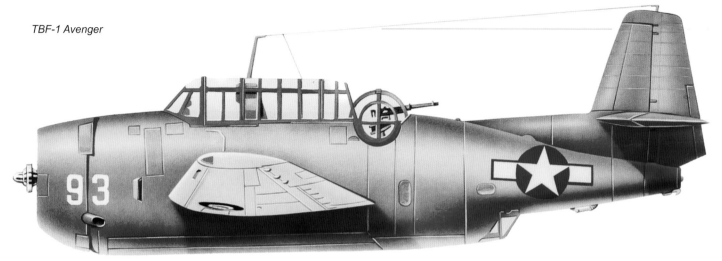

Despite a disastrous combat debut in which five out of six aircraft were lost, the TBF Avenger was a decisive warplane of World War II, and may rightly be regarded as the Allies' premier carrierborne torpedo bomber. The TBF resulted from a 1940 requirement for a successor to the Douglas TBD Devastator. Orders were placed for two Vought XTBU-1 prototypes in addition

to the two XTBF-1s, and the Grumman type first flew in August 1941 on the power of the 1268-kW (1,700-hp) Wright R-2600-8 Cyclone radial. The type was of typical Grumman design and construction, and despite the fact that it was the company's first essay in the field of carrierborne torpedo bombers, the Avenger proved itself a thoroughbred and immensely strong.

The type was ordered into production as the TBF-1 or, with two additional heavy machine-guns in the wings plus provision for drop tanks, TBF-1C; production totalled 2,291 aircraft. The Royal Navy also received the type as the Tarpon Mk I, later changed to Avenger Mk I. The Eastern Aircraft Division of General Motors was also brought into the programme to produce similar models as 550 TBM-1s

GRUMMAN TBF-1 AVENGER
Role: Naval carrierborne strike
Crew/Accommodation: Three
Power Plant: One 1,700-hp Wright R-2600-8 Double Cyclone air-cooled radial
Dimensions: Span 16.51 m (54.16 ft); length 12.23 m (40.125 ft); wing area 45.52 m² (490 sq ft)
Weights: Empty 4,572 kg (10,080 lb); MTOW 7,214 kg (15,905 lb)
Performance: Maximum speed 436 km/h (271 mph) at 3,658 m (12,000 ft); operational ceiling 6,828 m (22,400 ft); range 1,955 km (1,215 miles) with torpedo
Load: One .5-inch and two .303-inch machine guns, plus up to 726 kg (1,600 lb) of internally-stowed torpedo or bombs

Grumman TBF Avenger

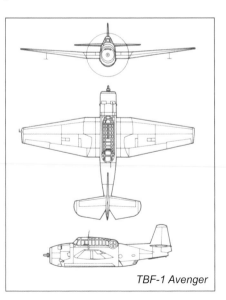

TBF-1 Avenger

and 2,336 TBM-1Cs (Avenger Mk IIs), and the only major development was the TBM-3. Eastern produced 4,657 of this model, which had been pioneered as the XTBF-3 with the 1417-kW (1,900-hp) R-2600-219 engine and strengthened wings for the carriage of drop tanks or rockets. Many of the aircraft were delivered without the initial model's heavy power-operated dorsal turret.

Late in World War II and after the war, the series was diversified into a host of other roles, each indicated by a special suffix, such as photo-reconnaissance, early warning, electronic warfare, anti-submarine search/attack, transport, and target towing. Total production was 9,839 aircraft.

Grumman TBM Avenger

MITSUBISHI Ki-67 HIRYU 'PEGGY' (Japan)

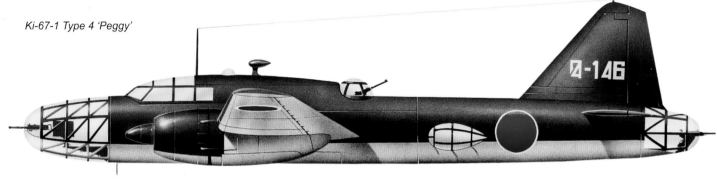

Ki-67-1 Type 4 'Peggy'

(6,393 lb) of explosives. Further production was to have been of the Ki-67-II version with two 1789-kW (2,400-hp) Mitsubishi Ha-214 radials; however, the only other production was in fact of the Ki-109 heavy fighter variant. This type was armed with a 75-mm (2.95-in) nose gun in the bomber destroyer role, and production totalled just 22 aircraft before the end of World War II. The Ki-67 was known to the Allies as the 'Peggy', however the Ki-109 received no reporting name.

In February 1941, Mitsubishi received instructions from the Imperial Japanese Army Air Force to design a tactical heavy bomber, and the company responded with a type that secured good performance and agility through the typically Japanese defects of minimal protection (armour and self-sealing fuel tanks) combined with a lightweight structure that was little suited to sustain battle damage.

The first of 19 Ki-67 prototypes and pre-production aircraft flew in December 1942 with two 1417-kW (1,900-hp) Mitsubishi Ha-104 radials. Production was delayed as the Japanese army considered a whole range of derivatives based on this high-performance basic aircraft, but in December 1943, the army belatedly decided to concentrate on just a single heavy bomber type capable of the level and torpedo bombing roles. The type entered production with the company designation Ki-67-I and

entered service as the Army Type 4 Heavy Bomber Model 1 Hiryu (Flying Dragon). Only 679 of these effective aircraft were built, all but the first 159 having provision for an underfuselage rack carrying one torpedo to give the type an anti-ship capability. Many were converted as three-seat Ki-67-I KAI kamikaze aircraft with the defensive gun turrets removed and provision made for two 800-kg (1,764-lb) bombs or 2900 kg

MITSUBISHI Ki-67-1 OTSU HIRYU 'PEGGY'
Role: Bomber
Crew/Accommodation: Eight
Power Plant: Two 1,900-hp Mitsubishi Ha-104 air-cooled radials
Dimensions: Span 22.5 m (73.82 ft); length 18.7 m (61.35 ft); wing area 65.85 m² (708.8 sq ft)
Weights: Empty 8,649 kg (19,068 lb); MTOW 13,765 kg (30,347 lb)
Performance: Maximum speed 537 km/h (334 mph) at 6,090 m (19,980 ft); operational ceiling 9,470 m (31,070 ft); range 2,800 km (1,740 miles) with 500 kg (1,102 lb) bombload
Load: One 20-mm cannon and four 12.7-mm machine guns, plus up to 1,080 kg (2,359 lb) of ordnance, including one heavyweight torpedo

Mitsubishi Ki-67-1B

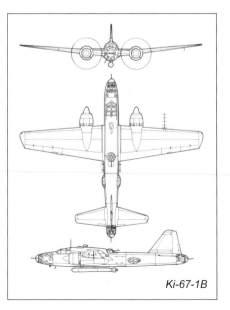

Ki-67-1B

DOUGLAS A-1 SKYRAIDER (U.S.A.)

A-1B Skyraider

hp) R-3350-24W radial and an armament of two 20-mm cannon plus 3629 kg (8,000 lb) of disposable stores, the 156 improved AD-2s with greater fuel capacity and other modifications, the 125 AD-3s with a redesigned canopy and longer-stroke landing gear as well as other improvements, the 372 AD-4s with the 2014-kW (2,700-hp) R-3350-26WA and an autopilot, the 165 nuclear-capable AD-4Bs with four 20-mm cannon, the 212 AD-5 anti-submarine search and attack aircraft with a widened fuselage for a side-by-side crew of two, the 713

The massive single-seat Skyraider was designed as a carrierborne dive- and torpedo-bomber, and the first of 25 XBT2D-1 Destroyer II prototype and service test aircraft flew in March 1945. The capabilities of the new aircraft were so impressive that large-scale production was ordered and it proved an invaluable U.S. tool in the Korean and Vietnam Wars.

The type went through a number of major marks, the most significant being the 242 AD-Is with the 1864-kW (2,500-

DOUGLAS AD-1 SKYRAIDER
Role: Naval carrierborne strike
Crew/Accommodation: One
Power Plant: One 2,500-hp Wright R-3350-24W air-cooled radial
Dimensions: Span 15.24 m (50.02 ft): length 12 m (39.35 ft); wing area 37.19 m² (400.3 sq ft)
Weights: Empty 4.749 kg (10.470 lb): MTOW 8.178 kg (18.030 1b)
Performance: Maximum speed 517 km/h (321 mph) at 5,580 m (18,300 ft): operational ceiling 7.925 m (26.000 ft): range 2,500 km (1,554 miles)
Load: Two 20-mm cannon, plus up to 2,722 kg (6,000 lb) of weapons

A U.S. Navy Douglas A-1H Skyraider

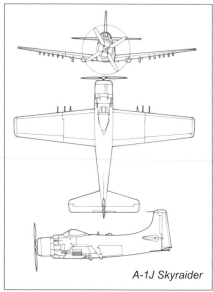

A-1J Skyraider

examples of the AD-6 improved version of the AD-4B with equipment for highly accurate low-level bombing, and the 72 examples of the AD-7 version of the AD-6 with the R-3350-26WB engine and strengthened structure. From 1962 all

FAR LEFT: Three Douglas A-1E Skyraiders

ABOVE: A U.S. Navy Douglas A-IJ Skyraider

OPPOSITE: This AD-4NA Skyraider was built for service in Korea as a ground-attack aircraft

surviving aircraft were redesignated in the A-l sequence. The Skyraider's large fuselage and greater load-carrying capability also commended the type for adaptation to other roles, and these roles were generally indicated by a letter suffix to the final number of the designation; E indicated anti-submarine search with radar under the port wing, N three-seat night attack, Q two-seat electronic counter-measures, S anti-submarine attack in concert with an E type, and W three/four-seat airborne early warning with radar in an underfuselage radome. Total production was 3,180 aircraft up to 1957, and from 1962 the series was redesignated in the A-l series.

ENGLISH ELECTRIC CANBERRA AND MARTIN B-57

Canberra B (I). Mk 6

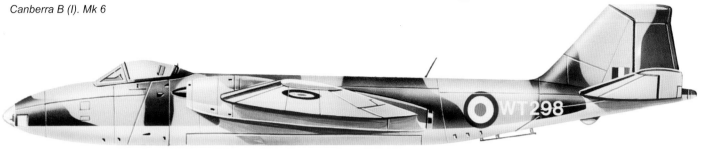

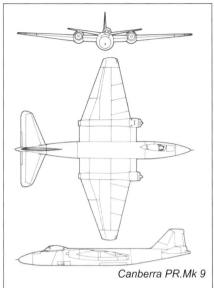

Canberra PR.Mk 9

The Canberra was planned as a nuclear-capable medium bomber with turbojet engines, and as a high-altitude type it was designed round a large wing and a crew of two using a radar bombing system. It matured as a medium/high-altitude type with optical bomb aiming by a third crew member and first flew in May 1949. Canberra was the first jet bomber produced in Britain, the RAF's first jet bomber, and the first aircraft in history to cross the Atlantic twice in a single day (1952). Its great development potential ensured that the type enjoyed a long first-line career as well as diversification into other roles. The main bomber stream began with the

Canberra B.Mk 2 powered by 2,948-kg (6,500-lb) Avon RA.3 Mk 101 turbojets, and then advanced to the B.Mk 6 with greater fuel capacity and 3,357-kg (7,400-lb) thrust Avon Mk 109s, the B.Mk 15 conversion of the B.Mk 6 with underwing hardpoints, the B.Mk 16 improved B.Mk 15, and the B.Mk 20

Australian-built B.Mk 6; there were also many export versions.

The intruder/interdictor series began with the Canberra B(I).Mk 6 version of the B.Mk 6 with underwing bombs and a ventral cannon pack, and continued with the B(I).Mk 8 multi-role version; there were also several export versions. The

ENGLISH ELECTRIC CANBERRA B.Mk 2
Role: Bomber reconnaissance
Crew/Accommodation: Two
Power Plant: Two 2,948-kgp (6,500-lb s.t.) Rolls-Royce Avon RA.3 Mk 101 turbojets
Dimensions: Span 19.49 m (63.96 ft); length 19.96 m (65.5 ft); wing area 89.2 m² (960 sq ft)
Weights: Empty 10,070 kg (22,200 lb); MTOW 20,865 kg (46,000 lb)
Performance: Maximum speed 917 km/h (570 mph) at 12,192 m (40,000 ft); operational ceiling 14,630 m (48,000 ft); range 4,281 km (2,660 miles)
Load: Up to 2,722 kg (6,000 lb) of ordnance all carried internally

English Electric Canberra PR.9

reconnaissance models began with the Canberra PR.Mk 3 based on the B.Mk 2, and then moved through variants including the PR.Mk 7 equivalent of the B.Mk 6, and the PR.Mk 9 high-altitude model with increased span, extended centre-section chord, and 4,990-kg (11,000-lb) thrust Avon Mk 206s; there were also a few export models. Other streams included trainer, target tug and remotely controlled target drone models. The last surviving Canberras were mostly

of reconnaissance and electronic warfare types, but not exclusively. The importance of the Canberra is also attested by the fact that it became the first non-U. S. type to be manufactured under licence in the U.S. after World War II. This variant was the Martin B-57, the first version of which was the B-57A with Wright J65-W-1 (licence-built Armstrong Siddeley Sapphire) turbojets.

The main production model was the B-57B, an extensively adapted night

intruder with two seats in tandem and a fixed armament of four 20-mm cannon plus eight 12.7-mm (0.5-in) machine guns as well as the standard bomb bay and underwing loads. Other variants were the B-57C dual-control version of the B-57B, and the B-57E target-tug version of the B-57B. The aircraft were also extensively converted as RB-57 photo-reconnaissance and EB-57 electronic-warfare platforms, the most radical such version being the General

Dynamics-produced RB-57F with span increased to 37.19 m (122 ft 0 in) for ultra-high flight with two 8,165-kg (18,000-lb) thrust Pratt & Whitney TF33-P-11 turbofans and, in underwing nacelles, two 1,497-kg (3,300-lb) thrust Pratt & Whitney J60-P-9 turbojets.

English Electric Canberra bomber

TUPOLEV Tu-16 'BADGER' (U.S.S.R.)

Tu-16 'Badger'

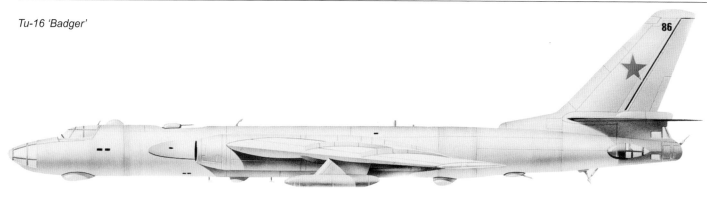

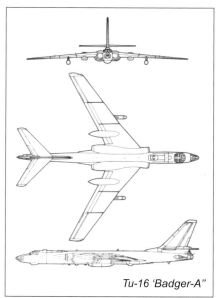

Tu-16 'Badger-A"

A great technical achievement in the fields of aerodynamics and structures by the Tupolev design bureau, the Tu-16 twin-jet intermediate-range strategic bomber first flew as the type 88 prototype in April 1952, with production at Kazan beginning in 1953 and later at Kuibyshev. In May 1954 nine bombers flew over Red Square and later that year the Tu-16KS missile carrier flew for the first time.

By 1963, all 1,500 or thereabouts production aircraft had been delivered, although other versions followed by conversion of existing models.

The baseline 'Badger-A' bomber was originally equipped with free-fall weapons while the 'Badger-B' was developed as a launcher for anti-ship missiles, but later became a free-fall bomber. The 'Badger-C' was an anti-ship type carrying either one AS-2 'Kipper' under the fuselage or two AS-6 'Kingfish' missiles under the wings. The 'Badger-D' was an electronic and/or maritime reconnaissance platform while 'Badger-E' first appeared in 1955 as a photo-reconnaissance and electronic

TUPOLEV Tu-16 'BADGER-G'
Role: Missile-carrying bomber, reconnaissance, electronic warfare
Crew/Accommodation: Six to nine dependent on mission
Power Plant: Two 8,750-kgp (19,290-lb s.t.) Mikulin AM-3M turbojets
Dimensions: Span 32.93 m (108 ft); length 34.8 m (114.2 ft); wing area 164.65 m² (1,772 sq ft)
Weights: Empty 40,000 kg (88,185 lb); MTOW 77,000 kg (169,756 lb)
Performance: Maximum speed 941 km/h (585 mph) at 11,000 m (36,090 ft); operational ceiling 12,200 m (40,026 ft); radius 2,895 km (1,800 miles) unrefuelled with full warload
Load: Three 23-mm cannon, plus up to 9,000 kg (19,842 lb) of bombs

Ariel view of an Egyptian Tu-16 'Badger'

intelligence version. The 'Badger-F' was a conversion of 'Badger-A' for sea reconnaissance. The 'Badger-G' became a very important anti-ship and anti-radar missile carrier with two AS-5 'Kelt' or, in its 'Badger-G (Modified)' form with AS-6 'Kingfish' missiles under its wings. The 'Badger-H', 'J', 'K', and 'L' were all developed as air force or naval electronic warfare aircraft optimized for the escort and/or stand-off, locator jamming, revised locator jamming and electronic intelligence/jamming roles respectively. Many of the older aircraft were finally converted into either of two types of in-flight refuelling tanker. By 1998, the Tu-16 was out of service in Russia. However, the same basic type is produced in China as the Xi'an H-6 bomber and anti-ship missile carrier, after receipt of a licence in 1957.

Tupolev Tu-16 'Badger'

McDONNELL DOUGLAS A-4 SKYHAWK (U.S.A.)

A-4S Super Skyhawk

Nicknamed 'Heinemann's Hot Rod' after its designer, the Skyhawk was conceived as a private-venture successor to the AD Skyraider. At this time the U.S. Navy envisaged a turboprop-powered machine in the role, but Douglas produced its design to offer all the specified payload/range capability in an airframe that promised higher-than-specified performance and about half the planned maximum take-off weight. The concept was sufficiently attractive for the service to order two XA4D-1 prototypes, and the first of these flew in June 1954 as a low-wing delta monoplane with integral fuel tankage and the 3,266-kg (7,200-lb)

Wright J65-W-2 version of a British turbojet, the Armstrong Siddeley Sapphire. Production deliveries began in October 1956 and continued to February 1979 for a total of 2,960 aircraft.

The first version was the A4D-1 (A-4A from 1962), of which just 19 were delivered with the 3,493-kg (7,700-lb) thrust Wright J65-W-4 and an armament of two 20-mm cannon and 2,268 kg (5,000 lb) of disposable stores. The main successor variants were the 542 A4D-2s (A-4Bs) with more power and inflight-refuelling capability, the 638 A4D-2Ns (A-4Cs) with terrain-following radar and more power, the 494 A4D-5s (A-4Es) with the 3,856-kg (8,500-lb) thrust Pratt & Whitney J52-P-6 turbojet and two additional hardpoints for a 3,719-kg (8,200-lb) disposable load, the 146 A-4Fs

McDONNELL DOUGLAS A-4E SKYHAWK
Role: Naval carrierborne strike
Crew/Accommodation: One
Power Plant: One 3,856-kgp (8,500-lb s.t.) Pratt
& Whitney J52-P-6A turbojet
Dimensions: Span 8.38 m (27.5 ft); length
12.23 m (40.125 ft); wing area 24.16 m²
(260 sq ft)
Weights: Empty 4,469 kg (9,853 lb); MTOW
11,113 kg (24,500 lb)
Performance: Maximum speed 1,083 km/h
(673 mph) at sea level; operational ceiling
11,460 m (37,600 ft); range 1,865 km
(1,160 miles) with 1,451-kg (3,200- lb)
bombload
Load: Two 20-mm cannon, plus up to 3,719 kg
(8,200 lb) of weapons

One TA-4SU leading two A-4SU Super Skyhawks of the Republic of Singapore Air Force

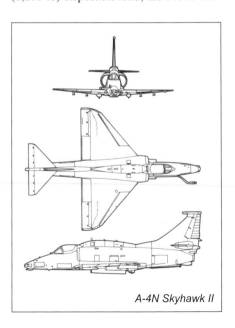

A-4N Skyhawk II

with a dorsal hump for more advanced electronics, the 90 examples of the A-4H based on the A-4E for Israel with 30-mm cannon and upgraded electronics, the 162 A-4Ms with an enlarged dorsal hump and more power, and the 117 examples of the A-4N development of the A-4M for Israel. There were a number of TA-4 trainer models, and other suffixes were used to indicate aircraft built or rebuilt for export. There is currently a considerable boom in upgraded aircraft, some (such as Argentina's refurbished A-4AR Fightinghawks) only now going back into service.

A McDonnell Douglas A-4M Skyhawk of the U.S. Marine Corps

SUKHOI Su-7 'FITTER' Family (U.S.S.R.)

Su-7B 'Fitter'

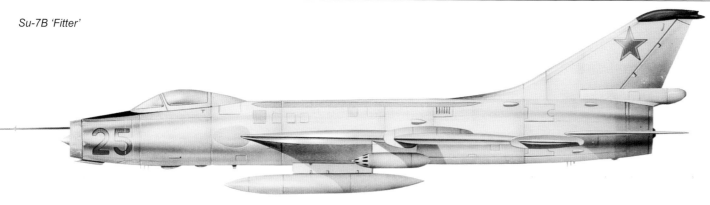

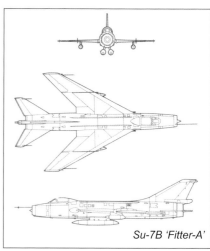

Su-7B 'Fitter-A'

Though now virtually obsolete and no longer in Russian service, in its time the Su-7 had a superb reputation as a ground-attack fighter able to absorb practically any amount of combat damage yet still deliver its ordnance with accuracy. On the other side of the coin, however, the type was given an engine so prodigiously thirsty that at least two hardpoints were used for drop tanks rather than ordnance.

Various S-1 and S-2 prototypes flew in the mid-1950s, the latter introducing a slab tailplane, and during 1958 the Su-7 was ordered with the 9,000-kg (19,841-lb) thrust Lyulka AL-7F turbojet as the service version of the S-2 2 pre-production derivative of the S-2 with an area-ruled fuselage. The type was developed in steadily improved Su-7 variants, known to NATO by the reporting name 'Fitter-A', with greater power, soft-field capability and six rather than four hardpoints. This effective yet short-range type was then transformed into the far more potent Su-17 with variable-geometry outer wing panels. The Su-71G prototype of 1966 confirmed that field performance and range were markedly improved. With the 10,000-kg (22,046-lb) AL7F-1 turbojet in early aircraft and the 11,200-kg (24,691-lb) thrust AL-21F-3/F-3A in later aircraft, the variable-geometry type was extensively built up to 1990 for Soviet, Warsaw Pact and Allied use.

The main Soviet and Warsaw Pact models were delivered as Su-17 variants known to NATO as the 'Fitter-C, 'Fitter-D' with a lengthened nose, 'Fitter-H' with a new weapon system, and 'Fitter-K' as the most advanced version and having ten weapon pylons. The main export variant was the Su-20 with inferior electronics to the Soviet 'Fitter-C', while the Su-22 became a Third-World export model with the 11,500-kg (25,353-lb) Tumansky R-29BS-300 or later AL-21F3 turbojet and inferior electronics. The final models in Russian service were for reconnaissance, but many remain flying with other air forces.

SUKHOI SU-7BMK FITTER A'

Role: Strike-fighter
Crew/Accommodation: One
Power Plant: One 9,600-kgp (21,164-lb s.t.) Lyuika AL-7F-1 turbojet with reheat
Dimensions: Span 8.77 m (28.77 ft); length 16.8 m (55.12 ft); wing area 34.5 m² (371.4 sq ft)
Weights: Empty 8,616 kg (18,995 lb); MTOW 13,500 kg (29,762 lb)
Performance: Maximum speed 1,160 km/h (720 mph) Mach 0.95 at 305 m (1,000 ft); operational ceiling 13,000+ m (42,650 ft); radius 460 km (285 miles) with 1,500 kg (3,307 lb) warload

Sukhoi Su-7BKL attack fighter

NORTH AMERICAN A-5 VIGILANTE (U.S.A.)

RA-5G Vigilante

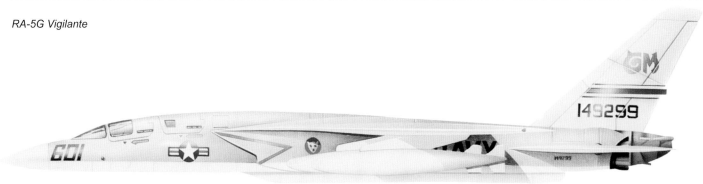

RA-5C Vigilante

The Vigilante was designed as a Mach 2 all-weather strike aircraft to provide the U.S. Navy with a carrierborne type able to deliver strategic nuclear weapons, and the design known as the North American General Purpose Attack Weapon was ordered in the form of two YA3J-1 prototypes. The first of these flew in August 1958 with two 7326-kg (16,150-lb) thrust General Electric J79-GE-2 afterburning turbojets aspirated via the first variable-geometry inlets fitted on any operational warplane. The overall design was of great sophistication, and included wing spoilers for roll control in conjunction with differentially operating slab tailplane halves that worked in concert for pitch control. Considerable problems were caused by the design's weapon bay, which was a longitudinal tunnel that contained fuel cells as well as the nuclear weapon in a package that was ejected to the rear as

NORTH AMERICAN A-5A VIGILANTE
Role: Naval carrierborne nuclear bomber
Crew/Accommodation: Two
Power Plant: Two 7,324-kgp (16,150-lb s.t.) General Electric J79-GE-2/4/8 turbojets with reheat
Dimensions: Span 16.15 m (53 ft); length 23.11 m (75.83 ft); wing area 71.45 m² (769 sq ft)
Weights: Empty 17,009 kg (37,498 lb); MTOW 36.287 kg (80,000 lb)
Performance: Maximum speed 2,229 km/h (1,203 knots) Mach 2.1 at 12.192 m (40,000 ft); operational ceiling 14,326 m (47,000 ft); range 3,862 km (2,084 naut. miles) with nuclear weapons

North American A-5A Vigilante

the Vigilante flew over the target.

The A3J-1 began to enter service in June 1961 with the 7711-kg (17,000-lb) thrust J79-GE-8, and just over a year later the type was redesignated A-5A. These 57 aircraft were followed by the A-5B long-range version with additional fuel in a large dorsal hump, wider-span flaps, blown leading-edge flaps, and four underwing hardpoints. Only six of this variant were built as a change in the U.S. Navy's strategic nuclear role led to the Vigilante's adaptation for the reconnaissance role with additional tankage and cameras in the weapon bay and side-looking airborne radar in a ventral canoe fairing. Production of this RA-5C model totalled 55 with 8101-kg (17,860-lb) thrust J79-GE-10 engines and revised inlets, in addition, extra capability was provided by 59 conversions (53 A-5As and the six A-5Bs).

OPPOSITE: RA-5C Vigilante

ABOVE: A North American RA-5C Vigilante with two LTV A-7C Corsairs and a Grumman KA-6D Intruder

BLACKBURN BUCCANEER (United Kingdom)

Buccaneer S.Mk 2B

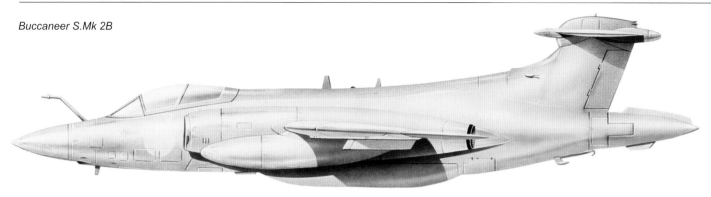

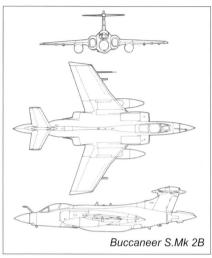

Buccaneer S.Mk 2B

This superb aircraft was planned as a B-103 to meet the NA.39 requirement for a carrierborne low-level transonic strike warplane, and was designed with a boundary layer control system for the wings and tailplane, an area-ruled fuselage, a sizeable weapon bay with a rotary door carrying the main weapons, and a vertically split tail cone that could be opened into larger-area air brakes. The prototype was the first of 20 pre-production aircraft, and first flew in April 1958 with two 3,175-kg (7,000-lb) thrust de Havilland

Gyron Junior DGJ. 1 turbojets.

Forty Buccaneer S.Mk 1s were ordered with the 3,221-kg (7,100-lb) thrust Gyron Junior 101, and these began to enter service in July 1962. To overcome the S.Mk 1's lack of power,

the 84 Buccaneer S.Mk 2s were powered by the 5,105-kg (11,200-lb) thrust Rolls-Royce Spey Mk 101 turbofan, and with this engine displayed an all-round improvement in performance. The Royal Navy received its first aircraft in

October 1965. The type had greater range than the S.Mk 1, but was also equipped for inflight refuelling. The similar Buccaneer S.Mk 50 was procured by South Africa, this model also having a 3,629-kg (8,000-lb) thrust Bristol Siddeley Stentor rocket motor for improved 'hot and high' take-off.

With the demise of the Navy's large carriers, some 70 S.Mk 2s were reallocated to the RAF from 1969 Buccaneer S.Mk 2As. Updated aircraft with provision for the Martel ASM became Buccaneer S.Mk 2Bs, and another 43 new aircraft were ordered to this standard. Further upgrades were made to RAF aircraft to extend their service career.

OPPOSITE: Blackburn Buccaneer S.Mk 1

BLACKBURN BUCCANEER S.Mk 2
Role: Low-level strike
Crew/Accommodation: Two
Power Plant: Two 5,035-kgp (11,100-lb s.t.) Rolls-Royce Spey Mk 101 turbofans
Dimensions: Span 13.41 m (44 ft); length 19.33 m (63.42 ft); wing area 47.82 m² (514.7 sq ft)
Weights: Empty 13,517 kg (29,800 lb); MTOW 28,123 kg (62,000 lb)
Performance: Maximum speed 1,040 km/h (561 knots) Mach 0.85 at 76 m (250 ft); operational ceiling 12,192 m (40,000+ ft); radius 1,738 km (938 naut. miles) with full warload
Load: Up to 3,175 kg (7,000 lb) of ordnance, including up to 1,815 kg (4,000 lb) internally, the remainder, typically Martel or Sea Eagle anti-ship missiles, being carried externally under the wings

A Blackburn Buccaneer S.MK 2 with wings folded

DASSAULT ÉTENDARD Family (France)

Super Étendard

Super Étendard

By the middle of the 1950s the growing complexity of modern warplanes was beginning to dictate types of such size, weight, cost and lengthy gestation that considerable thought was given to lightweight attack fighters that could be developed comparatively quickly and cheaply for use on small airfields or even semi-prepared airstrips that would remove the need to build the large and costly air bases that were becoming increasingly vulnerable. NATO formulated the requirement, and

one of several contenders was the Étendard (Standard). Three prototypes were built, one of them with company funding, and the first of these flew in July 1956 as the Étendard II with two 1,100-kg (2,425-lb) thrust Turbomeca Gabizo turbojets; the second prototypes had the 2,200-kg (4,850-lb) thrust Bristol Siddeley Orpheus BOr. 3 turbojet. The competition was won by the Fiat G91, but the company's own

Etendard IV prototype, the Etendard IVM, larger than its half-brothers and designed to accommodate more powerful engines, first flew in July 1956 and soon attracted naval interest as a carrierborne attack fighter.

One prototype and six pre-production aircraft validated revisions such as folding wingtips, naval equipment, a large rudder, beefed-up landing gear, and the 4,400-kg (9,700-lb)

thrust SNECMA Atar 8B turbojet. Production totalled 90 aircraft, including 21 of the Étendard IVP reconnaissance/tanker variant. From 1970 Dassault revised the basic type as the Super Étendard, and the first of two prototype conversions flew in October 1974. This model was given aerodynamic and structural revisions for transonic performance, and a modern nav/attack system including Agave multi-role radar for targeting of the AM.39 Exocet anti-ship missile. Seventy Super Étendards were delivered to the French Navy from 1978, plus 12 to Argentina, with many French aircraft being modified to have the ability to carry ASMP nuclear stand-off missiles.

DASSAULT SUPER ÉTENDARD
Role: Carrierborne strike fighter
Crew/Accommodation: One
Power Plant: One 5,000-kgp (11,023-lb s.t.) SNECMA Atar 8K50 turbojet with reheat
Dimensions: Span 9.60 m (31.50 ft); length 14.31 m (46.90 ft); wing area 28.40 m² (307.00 sq ft)
Weights: Empty 6,300 kg (14,330 lb); MTOW 12,000 kg (26,455 lb)
Performance: Maximum speed 1,200 km/h (746 mph) at sea level; operational ceiling 13,700 m (45,000 ft); radius of action 880 km (547 miles) with one Exocet
Load: Two 30-mm cannon, plus up to 2,087 kg (4,600 lb) of externally carried weapons/missiles/fuel

A Dassault Super Étendard strike fighter

OPPOSITE: A Dassault Étendard IVM of the French Navy

GRUMMAN A-6 INTRUDER (U.S.A.)

A-6E Intruder

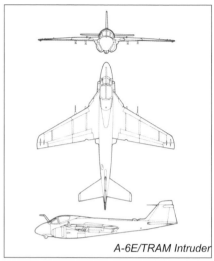

A-6E/TRAM Intruder

A fter the Korean War, the U.S. Navy wanted a jet-powered attacker able to undertake the pinpoint delivery of large warloads over long ranges and under all weather conditions. The resulting specification attracted 11 design submissions from eight companies, and at the very end of 1957 the G-128 design was selected for development as the A2F. Eight YA2F-1 development aircraft were ordered, and the first of these flew in April 1960 with two 3,856-kg (8,500-lb) thrust Pratt & Whitney J52-P-6 turbojets. In 1962 the type was designated A-6, and in February 1963 the first of 482 A-6A

production aircraft were delivered with 4,218-kg (9,300-lb) thrust J52-P-8A/B engines, a larger rudder, and the world's first digital nav/attack system. The Intruder had high maintenance requirements, but proved itself a superb attack platform during the Vietnam War.

The next three models were conversions and comprised 19 A-6B day interdictors with simplified avionics and capability for the AGM-78 Standard anti-radar missile, 12 A-6C night attack aircraft with forward-looking infra-red and low-light-level TV sensors in an

underfuselage turret, and 58 KA-6D 'buddy' refuelling tankers with a hose and drogue unit in the rear fuselage. This paved the way for the definitive A-6E attack model with J52-P-8B or -408 engines and an improved nav/attack system based on solid-state electronics for greater reliability and reduced servicing requirements. Large numbers of A-6As were converted to this standard, with 205 A-6Es and A-6E/TRAM also newly built before all production ended in February 1992; TRAM aircraft featured the Target Recognition and Attack Multisensor package in a small undernose turret. The Intruder has now been withdrawn from service.

GRUMMAN A-6E/TRAM INTRUDER
Role: Naval carrierborne all-weather heavy strike (bomber)
Crew/Accommodation: Two
Power Plant: Two 4,218-kgp (9,300-lb s.t.) Pratt & Whitney J52-P-8B turbojets
Dimensions: Span 16.15 m (53 ft); length 16.69 m (54.75 ft); wing area 49.15 m² (529 sq ft)
Weights: Empty 12,525 kg (27,613 lb); MTOW 26,580 kg (58,600 lb) for carrier use
Performance: Maximum speed 1,036 km/h (644 mph) Mach 0.85 at sea level; operational ceiling 13,600 m (44,600 ft); range 1,738 km (1,080 miles) with full load
Load: Up to 8,165 kg (18,000 lb) of weapons – all externally carried

Grumman A-6E Intruder

OPPOSITE: A U.S. Navy Grumman A-6E Intruder

BRITISH AIRCRAFT CORPORATION TSR-2 (United Kingdom)

TSR-2

This is one of history's great 'aircraft that might have been'. The TSR-2 resulted from attempts, started as early as the 1950s, to produce a successor to the English Electric Canberra for long-range interdiction and reconnaissance. There were considerable difficulties in defining the type of aircraft required, and in envisaging the appropriate technology. Eventually it was announced in 1959 that the concept offered by the partnership of

English Electric and Vickers-Armstrong was to be developed as the TSR-2 weapons system providing the capability for supersonic penetratior of enemy airspace at very low level for the accurate delivery of conventional and/or nuclear weapons. In configuration the TSR was a

high-wing monoplane with tandem seating for the crew of two, highly swept wings with downturned tips and wide-span blown trailing-edge flaps to provide STOL performance, and a swept tail unit, the surfaces of which provided control in all three planes. The onboard electronic

suite included an air-data system, inertial navigation system, forward-looking radar, and side-looking radar the data of which were integrated via an advanced computer to provide terrain-following capability and, on the pilot's head-up display and navigator's head-down displays, navigation cues and information relevant to weapon arming and release.

The result was an advanced but potentially formidable warplane that first flew in September 1964. As was only to be expected in so complex a machine, there were a number of problems. These were in the process of being solved when rising costs and political antipathy persuaded the Labour government to cancel the project in April 1965. Only the first of four completed aircraft had flown, and this had accumulated only 13 hours 14 minutes of flying time during 24 flights.

TSR-2

BAC TSR-2 at the RAF Museum, Cosford, England

BRITISH AIRCRAFT CORPORATION TSR-2
Role: Long range, low-level strike and
  reconnaissance
Crew/Accommodation: Two
Power Plant: Two 13,800-kgp (30,600- lb s.t)
  Bristol-Siddeley Olympus B.01.22R turbojets
  with reheat
Dimensions: Span 11.32 m (37.14 ft) length
  27.14 m (89.04 ft); wing area 65.30 m²
  (702.90 sq ft)
Weights: Empty 24,834 kg (54,750 lb) MTOW
  46,357 kg (102,200 lb)
Performance: Maximum speed 1,344+ km/h
  (725+knots) Mach 1.1+ at sea level; operational
  ceiling 17,374+ m (57,000+ ft); radius 1,853 km
  (1,000 naut. miles)
Load: Up to 4,536 kg (10,000 lb) of weaponry/fuel

DASSAULT MIRAGE IV (FRANCE)

Mirage IVA

Atar 9K engines, inflight refuelling probe and definitive nav/attack system. Mirage IVA production totalled 62 aircraft. Twelve aircraft were later converted as Mirage IVR strategic reconnaissance platforms with the CT52 mission package in the erstwhile bomb station, and from 1983 another 18 aircraft were converted as Mirage IVP missile carriers (plus one more later because of attrition loss). These were given a new nav/attack system and upgraded electronic defences, and were designed for low-level penetration of enemy airspace as the launchers for the ASMP nuclear-tipped stand-off missile. The strategic/tactical bomber role was finally ended in 1996, leaving only a single squadron of reconnaissance aircraft.

Requiring a supersonic delivery platform for the atomic bomb that was then the French nuclear deterrent weapon, the French Air Force in 1954 issued a requirement for a bomber offering long-range as well as high speed. Dassault headed a consortium that looked first at the development of the Sud-Ouest S.O. 4050 Vautour but from 1956 turned its attentions to the potential of an earlier aborted Dassault twin-engined night fighter design. This resulted in the design of the Mirage IV of what was in essence a scaled-up Mirage

III with two engines and provision for a 60-kiloton AN22 free-fall bomb semi-recessed under the fuselage.

The prototype first flew in June 1959 on the power of two 6,000-kg (13,228-lb) thrust SNECMA Atar 9 turbojets, and soon demonstrated its ability to maintain Mach 2 speed at high altitude. There followed three pre-production aircraft

with slightly larger overall dimensions and two 6,400-kg (14,110-lb) thrust Atar 9C turbojets. The first of these flew in October 1961, and was more representative of the Mirage IVA production model with a circular radome under the fuselage for the antenna of the bombing radar. The last of these three aircraft was fully representative in its

Mirage IVA

Dassault Mirage IVPs refuelling from a C-135FR tanker (SIRPA 'Air)

DASSAULT MIRAGE IVA
Role: Supersonic strategic bomber
Crew/Accommodation: Two
Power Plant: Two 7,000-kgp (15,432-lb s.t.) SNECMA Atar 09K turbojets with reheat
Dimensions: Span 11.85 m (38.88 ft); length 23.50 m (77.08 ft); wing area 78.00 m² (839.58 sq ft)
Weights: Empty 14,500 kg (31,965 lb); MTOW 31,600 kg (69,665 lb)
Performance: Maximum speed 2,124 km/h (1,146 knots) Mach 2.2 at 11,000 m (36,088 ft); operational ceiling 20,000 m (65,616 ft); radius 1,600+ km (994+ miles) unrefuelled
Load: One megaton range nuclear bomb carried semi-recessed beneath fuselage

GENERAL DYNAMICS F-111 'Aardvark' (U.S.A.)

EF-111A Raven

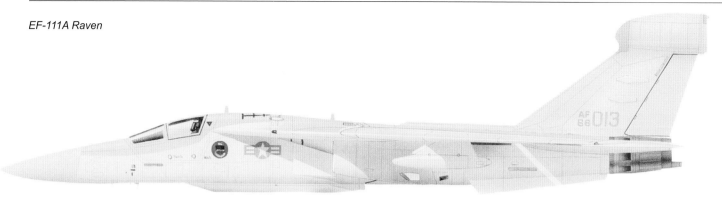

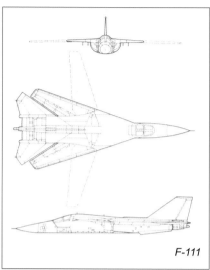

F-111

The F-111 was the world's first operational 'swing-wing' aircraft and remained in service as the U.S. Air Force's most potent all-weather long-range interdiction platform until July 1997, when it was belatedly named Aardvark. However, it remained operational with the Australian Air Force. The type originated from a 1960 requirement for a strike platform with the variable-geometry wings, the positions of which at minimum sweep would provide semi-STOL field performance at very high weights, at intermediate sweep long cruising range at high subsonic speed, and at maximum sweep very high dash performance. So versatile a tactical warplane suggested to the Department of Defense's civilian leadership the economic advantages of cheaper development and production costs if this land-based type could also be used as a basis for a new fleet defence fighter. Despite technical objections, the Tactical Fighter Experimental requirement was drawn up and orders placed for 23 pre-production aircraft (18 F-111As and five F-111Bs). The first of these flew in December 1964, but weight and

General Dynamics F-111 'Aardvark'

GENERAL DYNAMICS F-111F
Role: Long-range, low-level variable-geometry strike
Crew/Accommodation: Two
Power Plant: Two 11,385-kgp (25,100-lb s.t.) Pratt & Whitney TF30-P-111 turbofans with reheat
Dimensions: Span 19.2 m (63.00 ft), swept 9.73 m (31.95 ft); length 22.4 m (73.5 ft); wing area 48.77 m² (525 sq ft)
Weights: Empty 21,700 kg (47,840 lb); MTOW 45,360 kg (100,000 lb)
Performance: Maximum speed Mach 2.5 at altitude or 1,471 km/h (91,4 mph) Mach 1.2 at sea level; operational ceiling 17,650 m (57,900 ft); range over 4,667 km (2,900 miles)
Load: One 22-mm multi-barrel cannon, plus up to 11,340 kg (25,000 lb) of ordnance/fuel

performance problems led to the July 1968 cancellation of the F111B. The F111A also had problems before and after its March 1968 operational service debut in Vietnam, but despite an indifferent powerplant it matured into an exceptional combat aircraft. The most important tactical models were 158 F-111As with 8,391-kg (18,500-1b) thrust TF30-P-3 engines, 24 F-111Cs for Australia with the FB-111A's longer-span wings, 96 F-111Ds with 8,890-kg (19,600-1b) thrust TF30-P-9s, 94 F-111Es with 8,890-kg (19,600-lb) thrust TF30-P-103s, and 106 F-111Fs with 11,385-kg (25,100-lb) thrust TF30-P-111s and improved electronics; 42 of the F-111As were modified into EF-111A Raven electronic platforms for service from 1981; Ravens were retired in 1998. There is also a strategic model in the form of 76 FB-111As with wings of 2.13 m (7 ft 0 in) greater span, two extra wing hardpoints, 9,185-kg (20,150-lb) thrust TF30-P-7 engines, and revised electronics; many of these were later converted into F-111G tactical aircraft for use in the European theatre by the U.S.A.F. as conventionally armed aircraft (now retired), with some also going to the RAAF.

F-111 'Aardvark'

219

VOUGHT A-7 CORSAIR II (U.S.A.)

A-7P Corsair

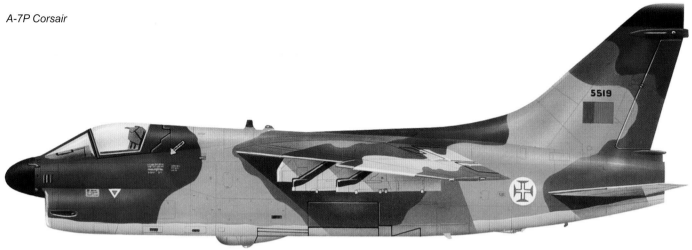

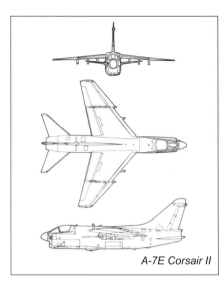

A-7E Corsair II

The A-7 was developed with great speed on the aerodynamic basis of the F-8 Crusader to provide the U.S. Navy with a medium-weight replacement for the lightweight Douglas A-4 Skyhawk in the carrierborne attack role, and in March 1964 the navy ordered three YA-7A prototypes. The first of these flew in September 1965 with the 5148-kg (11,350-1b) thrust Pratt & Whitney TF30-P-6 non-afterburning turbofan, and the flight test programme moved ahead with great speed. This allowed the Corsair II to enter service during February 1967 in the form of the A-7A with the same engine as the YA-7A. Production totalled 199 aircraft of this initial model, and was followed by 196 examples of the A-7B with the 5534-kg (12,200-lb) thrust TF30-P-8 that was later upgraded to -408 standard, and by 67 examples of the A-7C with the 6078-kg (13,400-lb) thrust TF309-P-408 and the armament/avionics suite of the later A-7E variant.

In December 1965 the U.S. Air Force decided to adopt a version with a different engine, the Rolls-Royce Spey turbofan in its licence-built form as the Allison TF41. The USAF series was now named Corsair II, and the first model was the A-7D, of which 459 were built with the 6577-kg (14,500-lb) thrust TF41-A-1, a 20-mm six-barrel rotary cannon in place of the Corsair II's two 20-mm single-barrel cannon, a much improved nav/attack package and, as a retrofit, manoeuvring flaps and the 'Pave Penny' laser tracker. This model was mirrored by the Navy's A-7E, of which 551 were built with the 6804-kg (15,000-lb) thrust TF41-A-2 and, as a retrofit, a forward-looking infra-red sensor. There have been some two-seat versions and limited exports, but nothing came of the A-7 Plus radical development that was evaluated as the YA-7F with advanced electronics and the combination of more power and a revised airframe for supersonic performance.

Three Vought A-7D Corsairs flying in formation

VOUGHT A-7E CORSAIR II
Role: Naval carrierborne strike
Crew/Accommodation: One
Power Plant: One 6,804-kgp (15,000-lb s.t.) Allison/Rolls-Royce TF41-A-1 turbofan
Dimensions: Span 11.8 m (38.75 ft); length 14.06 m (46.13 ft); wing area 34.83 m² (375 sq ft)
Weights: Empty 8.592 kg (18,942 lb); MTOW 19,051 kg (42,000 lb)
Performance: Maximum speed 1,060 km/h (572 knots) at sea level; operational ceiling 13,106 m (43,000 ft); range 908 km (489 naut. miles) with 2,722 kg (6,000 lb) bombload
Load: One 6-barrel 20-mm cannon, plus up to 6,804 kg (15,000 lb) of weapons

OPPOSITE: Vought A-7 Corsair II

BRITISH AEROSPACE HARRIER Family (United Kingdom)

Harrier GR.Mk 3

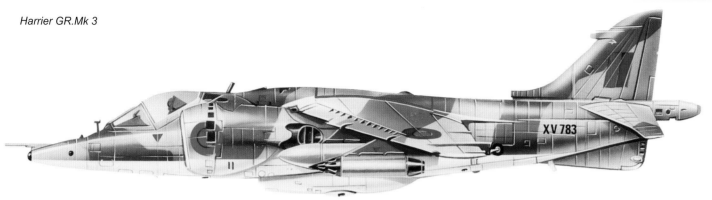

Harrier GR.Mk 3

The Harrier was the world's first operational VTOL combat aircraft, and at its core is the remarkable Rolls-Royce (Bristol Siddeley) Pegasus vectored-thrust turbofan. The type was pioneered in the form of six P. 1127 prototypes. The first of these made its initial hovering flights, in tethered mode, during October 1960, and the first transition flights between direct-thrust hovering and wingborne forward flight followed during September 1961. Such was the potential of this experimental type that nine Kestrel F(GA).Mk 1 evaluation aircraft were built for a

combined British, U.S. and West German trials squadron.

The Harrier became the operational version, and the main types were the

Harrier GR.Mk 1 with the 8,618-kg (19,000-lb) thrust Pegasus Mk 101, the GR.Mk 1A with the 9,072-kg (20,000-lb) thrust Pegasus Mk 102, and the

BRITISH AEROSPACE HARRIER GR. Mk 7
Role: Close air support and interdiction
Crew/Accommodation: One
Power Plant: One 9,775-kgp (21,550-lb s.t.) Rolls-Royce Pegasus 11 Mk 105 vectored-thrust turbofan
Dimensions: Span 9.25 m (30.33 ft); length 14.53 m (47.66 ft); wing area 21.37 m² (230 sq ft)
Weights: Empty 6,831-7,123 kg (15,060-15,705 lb); MTOW 14,515 kg (32,000 lb)
Performance: Maximum speed Mach 0.98; radius of action 1,111 km (691 miles) with two 1,000-lb bombs, three BL 755s and two drop tanks
Load: Two 25-mm externally mounted cannon plus up to 4,900 kg (10,800 lb) of ordnance/fuel

AV-8B Harriers aboard the USS Bataan

GR.Mk 3 with the 9,752-kg (21,000-lb) thrust Pegasus Mk 103 and revised nose accommodating a laser ranger and marked-target seeker. Combat-capable two-seat trainers were also built.

The U.S. Marine Corps used the Harrier as the AV-8A single-seater (of which many were upgraded to AV-8C standard) and TAV-8A two-seater examples were exported to Spain with the local name Matador.

A much improved variant of Harrier was developed by McDonnell Douglas and BAe as the Harrier II, first flown in 1981 and featuring a larger wing of composite construction with leading-edge root extensions, other aerodynamic improvements, better avionics and more engine power, allowing twice the payload or range. Various models of the Pegasus 11 engine have been fitted, the most powerful being the 10,795-kg (23,800-lb)

thrust Pegasus 11-61 in late U.S. Marine Corps aircraft (designated F402-RR-408A), as also used in Spanish Matador IIs and Italian trainers.

U.S. Marine Corps Harrier IIs are designated AV-8B, while the current RAF version is the GR.Mk 7, upgraded from GR. Mk 5/5As to permit night attack. The companies have also developed the Harrier II Plus with APG-65 radar for expanded roles. Naval versions of Harrier

became Sea Harrier, now in its latest F/A Mk 2 form for the Royal Navy.

A victim of defence cuts in Britain, the Harriers will be decommissioned in 2011 to be replaced by the Joint Strike Fighter by the end of the decade.

British Aerospace Harrier GR9

223

SEPECAT JAGUAR (France/United Kingdom)

Jaguar GR.Mk 1A

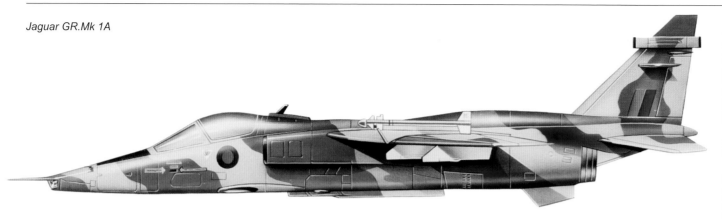

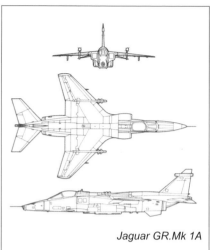

Jaguar GR.Mk 1A

In the early 1960s, the British and French Air Forces each showed interest in a dual-role supersonic warplane able to function as a tandem-seat operational trainer and single-seat attack aircraft. The similarity of the two requirements suggested a collaborative design, development and production programme, and in May 1965 the British and French governments signed an agreement for such a programme. Several British and French designs were studied before the

Breguet Br. 121 concept was selected as the basis for the new warplane, the development of which was undertaken by

the Société Européenne de Production de l'Avion École de Combat at d'Appui Tactique (SEPECAT) formed by the

SEPECAT JAGUAR INTERNATIONAL
Role: Low-level strike fighter and maritime strike
Crew/Accommodation: One
Power Plant: Two 3,811-kgp (8,400-lb s.t.) Rolls-Royce/Turboméca Adour Mk 811 turbofans with reheat
Dimensions: Span 8.69 m (28.5 ft); length 15.52 m (50.92 ft) as single-seater, without probe; wing area 24 m² (258.33 sq ft)
Weights: Empty 7,000 kg (15,432 lb); MTOW 15,700 kg (34,613 lb)
Performance: Maximum speed 1,350 km/h (839 mph) Mach 1.1 at sea level; radius of action 852 km (529 miles) with 3,629 kg (8,000 lb) warload
Load: Two 30-mm cannon, plus up to 4,536 kg (10,000 lb) of weapons, including bombs, rockets or air-to-surface missiles, plus two short-range air-to-air missiles

SEPECAT Jaguar GR.Mk 1A fighters of the Royal Air Force's No 54 Squadron

LEFT & BELOW: SEPECAT Jaguars

with greater power and a more advanced nav/attack system, and in GR. Mk 3 form) plus Jaguar E and Jaguar B trainers (40 and 38 aircraft respectively for the French and British air forces).

There has also been the Jaguar International for the export market, with overwing hardpoints for air-to-air missiles as standard, uprated engines and, in Indian aircraft, an improved nav/attack system including radar in some aircraft. Customers were Ecuador, Nigeria, Oman and India, plus others built in India by HAL as Shamshers (Indian total of 131 aircraft).

British Aircraft Corporation and Breguet. An equivalent engine grouping combined Rolls-Royce and Turboméca for the selected Adour afterburning turbofan.

The Jaguar first flew in September 1968 as a conventional monoplane with swept flying surfaces and retractable tricycle landing gear, a shoulder-set wing being selected as this provided good ground clearance for the wide assortment of disposable stores carried on four underwing hardpoints in addition to a centreline hardpoint under the fuselage.

Such were the capabilities of the aircraft that major production was initiated, with variants as the Jaguar A and S single-seat attack aircraft (160 and 165 aircraft respectively for the French and British air forces, of which the latter has considerably upgraded its aircraft

TUPOLEV Tu-22M 'BACKFIRE' (U.S.S.R.)

Tu-22M 'Backfire'

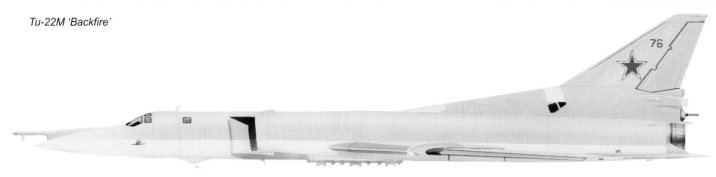

Tu-22M 'Backfire-G'

Known to NATO as the 'Backfire', the Tu-22M is the world's only modern medium bomber, and was conceived to make nuclear or conventional strikes against targets in Western Europe and China, plus attack aircraft carriers and other large ships in a maritime role. It was specified to require a 2,000 km/h dash speed and Mach 0.9 low-level penetration speed while armed with AS-4 'Kitchen' missiles. It was to be a supersonic 'swing-wing' successor to the Tu-16 'Badger' via the interim supersonic Tu-22 'Blinder'.

The new bomber first flew in August 1969 and 'Backfire-A' pre-series aircraft appeared from 1971. Tu-22M2 'Backfire-B' initial large-scale production aircraft joined the Soviet air force from 1975, fitted with new avionics and two cannon in the tail, but most importantly offering a range of 2,753 nautical miles and speed of 972 knots.

The Tu-22M3 'Backfire-C' entered

TUPOLEV Tu-22M 'BACKFIRE-C'
Role: Bomber/reconnaissance with variable-geometry wing
Crew/Accommodation: Four
Power Plant: Two 25,000-kgp (55,115 lb-s.t.) Samara NK-25 turbofans with reheat
Dimensions: Span 34.28 m (112.5 ft), swept 23.3 m (76.4 ft); length 42.46 m (139.33 ft); wing area 183.58 m² (1,976 sq ft)
Weights: MTOW 124,000 kg (273,373 lb) without JATO rockets
Performance: Maximum speed 2,000 km/h (1,243 mph) Mach 1.8 at high altitude; operational ceiling 14,000 m (45,925 ft); radius of action 2,200 km (1,367 miles) with one 'Kitchen' missile and unrefuelled
Load: Two 23-mm cannon, plus 24,000 kg (52,910 lb) of weapons, including three AS-4 'Kitchen' missiles or a mix with AS-16 'Kickback' short-range missiles on a rotary launcher, nuclear or conventional bombs, mines, etc.

A Tupolev Tu-22M and an F-16A Fighting Falcon

service in 1983 and introduced uprated NK-25 engines, modified forward fuselage with larger wedge air inlets and other improvements, making it over twice as combat-capable as the Tu-22M2. Since 1992, M3s have been further upgraded to M5s, with changes including those to the radar and missiles carried. Tu-22MP and Tu-22MR are electronic warfare and reconnaissance versions respectively. Tu-22 operators are the Russian air force and navy plus Ukraine.

Tupolev Tu-22M 'Backfire'

227

YAKOVLEV Yak-38 'FORGER' (U.S.S.R.)

Yak-38 'Forger'

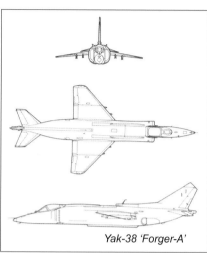

Yak-38 'Forger-A'

The Yak-38 (or Yak-36M for prototype) was the first-ever and so far only Soviet operational vertical take-off (VSTOL) combat aeroplane, of which 231 were built for the navy, but was withdrawn from service in the early 1990s. Supersonic replacements to be used as carrierborne interceptors, the Yakovlev Yak-41 and Yak-43 (the former known to NATO as 'Freestyle' and first flown in 1987) were

subsequently abandoned before reaching service status.

The 'Forger' prototype first flew in January 1971, with the thrust-vectoring turbojet in the rear fuselage complemented by two small liftjets in the forward fuselage and mounted almost

vertically to exhaust downward. A fully automatic control system was employed during take-off/landing, to ensure correct use of engines and jet reaction nozzles/aerodynamic controls used in association with devices on board ship. Subsequently, short take-offs became

more common than vertical, using similar methods of control.

The 'Forger-A' was a single-seat type designed principally to provide Soviet naval forces with experience in the operation of such aircraft. The type is therefore limited in terms of performance, warload and electronics, but still provided Soviet aircraft carriers/cruiser carriers with useful interception and attack capabilities in areas too distant for the involvement of land-based air defences. The original production 'Forger-A' had less powerful liftjets than the improved Yak-38M 'Forger-A' of 1984 onwards service. The Yak-38UV was known to NATO as 'Forger-B' and was the tandem two-seat conversion trainer variant with the fuselage lengthened to accommodate the second cockpit.

YAKOVLEV Yak-38M 'FORGER-A'
Role: Vertical take-off and landing naval strike fighter
Crew/Accommodation: One
Power Plant: One 6,700-kgp (14,770-lb s.t.) Soyuz R-28V-300 vectored-thrust turbojet plus two 3,250 kgp (7,165 lb s.t.) Rybinsk RD-36 lift turbojets
Dimensions: Span 7.3 m (24 ft); length 15.5 m (51 ft); wing area 18.5 m² (199 sq ft)
Weights: MTOW 11,700 kg (25,794 lb)
Performance: Maximum speed 1,164 km/h (723 mph) Mach 0.95 at sea level; operational ceiling 12,000 m (39,370 ft); radius of action 371 km (230 miles)
Load: Up to 2,000 kg (4,409 lb) of externally carried weapons, including two AA-8 'Aphid' air-to-air missiles

Yakovlev Yak-38

FAIRCHILD REPUBLIC A-10 THUNDERBOLT II (U.S.A.)

A-10A Thunderbolt II

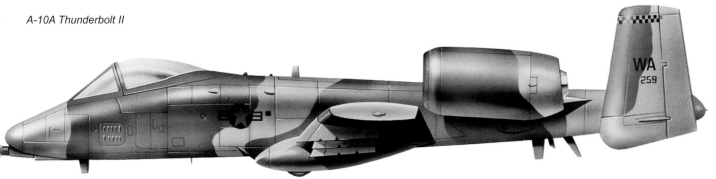

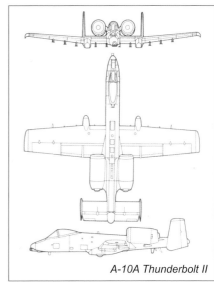

A-10A Thunderbolt II

First flown in May 1972 as the YA-10A after Republic Aviation had become a division of Fairchild, the Thunderbolt II was developed to meet the U.S. Air Force's Attack Experimental requirement of 1967. The two YA-10A prototypes were competitively evaluated against the two YA-9s produced by Northrop, and the Fairchild Republic design was declared winner of the competition in January 1973. The requirement called for a specialist close-support and anti-tank aircraft offering high rates of survival from ground fire, a high-subsonic speed combined with good low-speed manoeuvrability, and a heavy weapon load.

The particular nature of its role dictated the Thunderbolt IIs peculiar

Fairchild Republic A-10 Thunderbolt II

FAIRCHILD REPUBLIC A-10A THUNDERBOLT II
Role: Close air support
Crew/Accommodation: One
Power Plant: Two 4,112-kgp (9,065-lb s.t.) General Electric TF34-GE-100 turbofans
Dimensions: Span 17.53 m (57.5 ft); length 16.25 m (53.33 ft); wing area 47.01m² (506 sq ft)
Weights: Empty 12,700 kg (28,000 lb); MTOW 23,586 kg (52,000 lb)
Performance: Maximum speed 707 km/h (439 mph) without external weapons; operational ceiling 10,575 m (34,700 ft); radius of action 763 km (474 miles)
Load: One 30-mm multi-barrel cannon, plus up to 7,250 kg (16,000 lb) of externally carried weapons

configuration with two turbofan engines located high on the fuselage sides between the wings and tailplane, and straight flying surfaces that restrict outright performance but enhance take-off performance and agility at very low level. To reduce the effect of anti-aircraft fire, all major systems are duplicated, extensive armour is carried, and vulnerable systems such as the engines are both duplicated and shielded as much as possible from ground detection and thus from ground fire.

The first of 713 production aircraft were delivered in 1975, and though the type remains in valuable service in both A-10A attack and OA-10A lightly-armed forward air control variants, many have been passed to U.S. Air National Guard and Air Force Reserve units.

The core of the A-10A is the massive GAU-8/A Avenger seven-barrel cannon that occupies most of the forward fuselage and carries 1,174 rounds of 30-mm anti-tank ammunition delivering a pyrophoric penetrator of depleted uranium. A large load of other weapons, both 'smart' and 'dumb', can be carried on no fewer than 11 hardpoints.

LEFT: An A-10 Thunderbolt II deploys flairs over Afghanistan

OPPOSITE: An A-10 Thunderbolt II takes off on combat mission

PANAVIA TORNADO (Italy/United Kingdom/Germany)

Tornado F.Mk 3

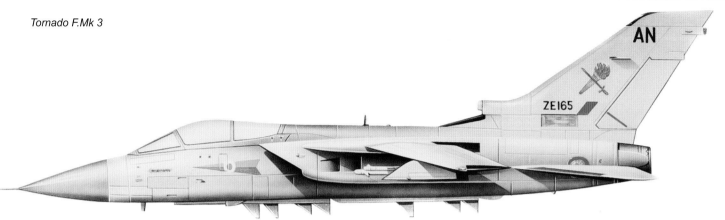

Tornado F.Mk 3

Currently one of the NATO alliance's premier front-line aircraft types, the Tornado was planned from the late 1960s as a multi-role combat aircraft able to operate from and into short or damaged runways for long-range interdiction missions at high speed and very low level. The keys to the mission are variable-geometry wings able to sweep from 25°

spread to 67° fully swept and carrying an extensive array of high-lift devices on their leading edges and trailing edges, advanced high by-pass turbofan engines that offer low fuel burn at cruise speed and high afterburning thrust, and an advanced sensor and electronic suite. This suite is based on a capable nav/attack system that includes attack and terrain-following radars, an inertial navigation system, and a triplex fly-by-wire control system.

The first of the Tornado prototypes flew in August 1974, and after a protracted development the first production Tornados for the RAF and Luftwaffe were handed over in June 1979, followed eventually by the first for Italy (in 1981). The three main variants are the Tornado IDS baseline interdiction and strike warplane, the Tornado ADV air-defence fighter with different radar and weapons (including four semi-recessed Sky Flash air-to-air missiles) in a longer

fuselage, and the Tornado ECR electronic combat and reconnaissance type. The British RAF version of the IDS was delivered as the Tornado GR.Mk 1, while Tornado GR.Mk 1A became the reconnaissance derivative and GR.Mk 1B a maritime attack model carrying two Sea Eagle missiles; GR.Mk 4/4As are current upgrades of Mk 1/1As. The air defence variant interceptor for the RAF is currently flown in F.Mk 3 version, while Italy is leasing 24 pending Eurofighter deliveries. Including exports of IDS/ADVs to Saudi Arabia, total Tornado production amounted to 781 IDS/ECRs and 194 ADVs.

PANAVIA TORNADO IDS

Role: All-weather, low-level strike and reconnaissance
Crew/Accommodation: Two
Power Plant: Two 7,257-kgp (16,000-lb s.t.) Turbo-Union RB199 Mk 103 turbofans with reheat
Dimensions: Span 13.9m (45.6 ft), swept 8.6 m (28.2 ft); length 16.7 m (54.8 ft); wing area 26.6 m² (286.3 sq ft)
Weights: Empty 14,000 kg (30,864 lb); MTOW 28,000 kg (61,729 lb)
Performance: Maximum speed Mach 2.2 clean or 1,483 km/h (921 mph), Mach 1.2 at 152 m (500 ft); operational ceiling 15,240+ m (50,000+ ft); radius of action typically 1,482 km (921 miles) with four 1,000-lb bombs, two Sidewinders and two drop tanks
Load: Two 27-mm cannon, plus up to 9,000 kg (19,842 lb) of externally carried weaponry and fuel

Royal Air Force Panavia Tornado GR.4

OPPOSITE: A Panavia Tornado IDS of the German Air Force

LOCKHEED MARTIN F-117 NIGHTHAWK (U.S.A.)

F-117A Nighthawk

F-117A Nighthawk

The world's first fully 'stealth' aircraft to reach operational status, the F-117 was developed to penetrate dense threat environments during the hours of darkness and destroy critical or high-value enemy targets with amazing accuracy. Its strange shape and secret nature comes from its ability to counter radar, infra-red, visual, contrails, engine smoke, acoustic and electromagnetic signatures.

Development began with two small XST Have Blue technology demonstrators, the first flown in December 1977, and five FSD flight test aircraft (first flown in January 1981). Delivery of 59 F-117As to the USAF

started in August 1982 and initial operational capability was achieved in October 1983.

The public did not hear of the aircraft until 1988. Its first combat use came in December 1989 when two aircraft dropped laser-guided bombs on barracks in Panama during Operation Just Cause, while during the 1991 Gulf War 42 flew 1,271 missions.

The F-117A's airframe is of the 'lifting body' type, with the outer faceted skin formed from flat surfaces arranged at angles to overcome enemy radars. All aspects of the design were carefully considered, including the air intakes which have heated grids to block radar energy, while the engine nozzles are horizontal slots that produce a thin exhaust plume that is mixed with cold air and quickly dispersed. No radar is carried, the pilot instead relying on sophisticated navigation and attack systems, automated mission planning, and forward/downward-looking infra-red devices.

LOCKHEED MARTIN F-117A

Role: Low-observability strike
Crew/Accommodation: One
Power Plant: Two 4,899-kgp (10.800-lb s.t.)
General Electric F404-GE-F1D2 non-reheated turbofans
Dimensions: Span 13.20 m (43.44 ft); length 20.09 m (65.92 ft); wing area 84,82 m² (913 sq ft)
Weights: MTOW 23,814 kg (52,500 lb)
Performance: Maximum speed 1,040 km/h (646 mph); radius of action 1,111 km (691 miles) with full weapon load, unrefuelled
Load: Two laser-guided 2,000-lb bombs in the bay or other weapons up to 2,268 kg (5,000 lb)

Lockheed Martin F-117 Nighthawk

OPPOSITE: Lockheed Martin F-117 Nighthawk

EUROFIGHTER TYPHOON

The Eurofighter Typhoon is a twin-engine canard delta-wing multi-role aircraft designed and built by a consortium of three companies: Alenia Aeronautica, BAE Systems, and EADS working through a holding company Eurofighter GmbH, which was formed in 1986. The project is managed by the NATO Eurofighter and Tornado Management Agency, which acts as the prime customer.

EUROFIGHTER TYPHOON
Role: Multi-role fighter
Crew/Accommodation: One
Power Plant: Two Eurojet EJ200 reheated tubofans, max thrust each of 90kn (20,000 lbs)
Dimensions: Span 10.9 m (35.11 ft); length 15.09 m (52.4 ft); wing area 50.0m m² (538 sq ft)
Performance: Maximum speed Mach 2.0
Load: Various bombs

The series production of the Eurofighter Typhoon is progressing, and the aircraft is being procured under three separate contracts (or 'tranches'), each covering aircraft with generally improved capabilities. The aircraft has entered service with the British Royal Air Force, the German Luftwaffe, the Italian Air Force, the Spanish Air Force and the Austrian Air Force. Saudi Arabia has signed a contract worth £4.43 billion (approx. €6.4 billion or $9.5 billion) for 72 aircraft.

The first production contract was signed on 30 January 1998 between Eurofighter GmbH, Eurojet and NETMA. The procurement totals were as follows: UK 232, Germany 180, Italy 121, and Spain 87. Production was again allotted according to procurement:

British Aerospace (37%), DASA (29%), Aeritalia (19.5%), and CASA (14%).

On 2 September 1998, a naming ceremony was held at Farnborough, England when the Typhoon name was formally adopted, initially for export aircraft only. This was reportedly resisted by Germany, perhaps because the Hawker Typhoon was a fighter-bomber aircraft which served with the RAF during the World War II against German targets. The name 'Spitfire II' (after the famous British World War II fighter, the Supermarine Spitfire) had also been considered and rejected for the same reason early in the development programme. In September 1998 contracts were signed for production of 148 Tranche 1 aircraft and procurement of long lead-time items for Tranche 2

aircraft. In March 2008 the final aircraft out of Tranche 1 was delivered to the German Luftwaffe, with all successive deliveries being at the Tranche 2 standard. On 21 October 2008, the first two of 91 Tranche 2 aircraft, ordered four years before, were delivered to RAF Coningsby.

In October 2008, the Eurofighter nations were considering splitting the 236-fighter Tranche 3 into two parts. In June 2009, RAF Air Chief Marshal Sir Glenn Torpy suggested that the RAF fleet might only be 123 jets instead of the 232 previously planned. In spite of this reduction in the number of required aircraft, on 14 May 2009, British Prime Minister Gordon Brown confirmed that the UK would move ahead with the third batch purchase. A contract for the first part, Tranche 3A, was signed at the end of July 2009 for 112 aircraft split across the four partner nations, including 40 aircraft for the UK, 31 for Germany, 21 for Italy and 20 for Spain. These 40 UK aircraft were said to have fully covered that nation's obligations in the project by Air Commodore Chris Bushell, due to cost overruns in the project.

The Typhoon is of lightweight construction (82% composites consisting of 70% carbon fibre composites and 12% glass reinforced composites) with an estimated lifespan of 6,000 flying hours.

The fighter achieves high agility at both supersonic and lower speeds by having a relaxed stability design. It has a quadruplex digital fly-by-wire control system providing artificial stability, as

OPPOSITE: RAF Eurofighter EF-200 Typhoon

BELOW: Two Eurofighters and an AWACS aircraft

RIGHT: Eurofighter Typhoon

manual operation alone could not compensate for the inherent instability. The fly-by-wire system is described as 'carefree' by preventing the pilot from exceeding the permitted manoeuvre envelope.

Roll control is primarily achieved by use of the wing flaperons. Pitch control is by operation of the foreplanes and flaperons, the yaw control is by rudder. Control surfaces are moved through two independent hydraulic systems that are incorporated in the aircraft, which also supply various other items, such as the canopy, brakes and undercarriage. Each hydraulic system is powered by a 4000 psi engine-driven gearbox.

Navigation is via both GPS and an inertial navigation system. The Typhoon can use Instrument Landing System (ILS) for landing in poor weather.

The aircraft employs a sophisticated and highly integrated Defensive Aids Sub-System named Praetorian (formerly called EuroDASS). Threat detection is provided by a Radar Warning Receiver (RWR) and

a Laser Warning Receiver (LWR), though only for UK Typhoons. Protection is provided by Chaff, Jaff and Flares, Electronic Counter Measures (ECM) and a Towed Radar Decoy (TRD).

Praetorian monitors and responds automatically to the outside world. It provides the pilot with an all-round prioritized assessment of Air-to-Air and Air-to-Surface threats. It can respond to single or multiple threats.

The aircraft also features an advanced ground proximity warning system based on the TERPROM Terrain Referenced Navigation (TRN) system used by the Panavia Tornado but further enhanced and fully integrated into the cockpit displays and controls.

LOCKHEED MARTIN F-35 LIGHTNING II

Martin expects to reduce government cost estimates by 20%.

While the United States is the primary customer and financial backer, the United Kingdom, Italy, the Netherlands, Canada, Turkey, Australia, Norway and Denmark have agreed to contribute U.S.$4.375 billion toward the development costs of the programme. Total development costs are estimated at more than U.S.$40 billion (underwritten largely by the United States), while the purchase of an estimated 2,400 planes is expected to cost an additional U.S.$200 billion. The nine major partner nations plan to acquire over 3,100 F-35s through 2035, making the F-35 one of the most numerous jet fighters.

The Lockheed Martin F-35 Lightning II is a family of fifth-generation, single-seat, single-engine stealth multi-role fighters. When it enters service it will be one of the most advanced fighter aircraft in the world, performing ground attack, reconnaissance and air defence missions. The F-35 has three main models; one is a conventional take-off and landing variant, the second is a short take-off and vertical-landing variant, and the third is a carrier-based variant.

The F-35 is descended from the X-35, the product of the Joint Strike Fighter (JSF) programm. JSF development is being principally funded by the United

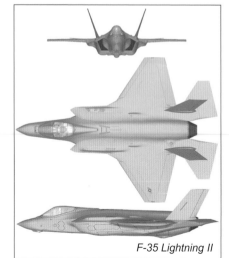

F-35 Lightning II

States, with the United Kingdom and other partner governments providing additional funding. It is being designed and built by an aerospace industry team led by Lockheed Martin. The F-35's first flight took place on 15 December 2006.

The United States intends to buy a total of 2,443 aircraft for an estimated U.S.$323 billion, making it the most expensive defence programme ever. The U.S.A.F.'s budget data in 2010, along with other sources, projects the F-35 to have a flyaway cost that ranges between U.S.$89 million and U.S.$200 million over the planned production of F-35's, depending on the variant. Lockheed

---

LOCKHEED MARTIN F-35 LIGHTNING II
Role: Strike aircraft
Crew/Accommodation: One
Power Plant: 1× Pratt & Whitney F135 afterburning turbofan
Dimensions: Span 13.1m (4ft); length 15.7 m (51.5 ft)
Weights: MTOW 31,800 kg (70,000 lb)
Performance: Maximum speed mach 1.6.
Load: Guns: General Dynamics GAU-22/A Equalizer 25 mm (0.984 in) 4-barrelled Gatling cannon, internally mounted with 180 rounds. Hardpoints: 6 external pylons on wings with a capacity of 15,000 lb (6,800 kg) and 2 internal bays with 2 pylons each for a total weapons payload of 18,000 lb (8,100 kg) and provisions to carry combinations of Missiles: Air-to-air, AIM-120, AMRAAM, AIM-132 ASRAAM, AIM-9X Sidewinder, IRIS-T, Joint Dual Role Air Dominance Missile (JDRADM), Air-to-ground: AGM-154 JSOW, AGM-158 JASSM Bombs: Mark 84, Mark 83 and Mark 82 GP bombs, Mk.20 Rockeye II cluster bomb, Wind Corrected Munitions Dispenser capable: Paveway-series laser-guided bombs, Small-diameter bomb, JDAM-series, B61 nuclear bomb.

There are three levels of international participation. The levels generally reflect the financial stake in the programme, the amount of technology transfer and subcontracts open for bid by national companies, and the order in which countries can obtain production aircraft. The United Kingdom is the sole 'Level 1' partner, contributing U.S.$2.5 billion, which was about 10% of the planned development costs under the 1995 Memorandum of Understanding that brought the U.K. into the project. Level 2 partners are Italy, which is contributing U.S.$1 billion; and the Netherlands, U.S.$800 million. Level 3 partners are Canada, U.S.$475 million; Turkey, U.S.$195 million; Australia, U.S.$144 million; Norway, U.S.$122 million and Denmark, U.S.$110 million. Israel and Singapore have joined as Security Co-operative Participants (SCP).

OPPOSITE ABOVE: A Lockheed Martin Lightning II lands at Edwards Air Force Base, California

RIGHT: An F-35 Lightning Joint Strike Fighter test aircraft

MITSUBISHI F-2

The Mitsubishi F-2 multi-role fighter is manufactured by Mitsubishi Heavy Industries (MHI) and Lockheed Martin for the Japan Air Self-Defense Force, with a 60/40 split in manufacturing between Japan and the U.S.A. Production started in 1996 and the first aircraft entered service in 2000.

Work started in the 1980s under the FS-X programme, and began in earnest with a Memorandum of Understanding between Japan and the U.S. It would lead to a new fighter based on the General Dynamics (post-1993 Lockheed Martin) F-16 Fighting Falcon, and in particular the F-16 Agile Falcon proposal. Lockheed Martin was chosen as the major subcontractor to Mitsubishi Heavy Industries, and the two companies co-developed and co-produced the aircraft. Some of the early developmental works

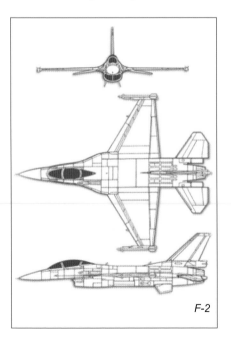

F-2

were actually done under General Dynamics, who sold its aircraft division to Lockheed Martin in 1993.

It is essentially an execution of the F-16 Agile Falcon proposal: a late-1980s plan for an enlarged F-16 which was passed over by the U.S. in favour of an all-new fighter programme (Joint Strike Fighter). The F-2 used the wing design of the F-16 Agile Falcon, but much of the electronics were further updated to 1990s standards. The overall concept of the enlarged F-16 by General Dynamics was intended as a cheap counter to the then

emerging threat of Su-27/MiG-29.

In October 1987, Japan selected the F-16 as the basis of its new secondary fighter to replace the ageing Mitsubishi F-1 and supplement its main air superiority fighter, the F-15J as well as the F-4EJ. The programme involved technology transfer from the U.S.A. to Japan, and responsibility for cost sharing was split 60% by Japan and 40% by the U.S.A. Also during the 1980s, General Dynamics (who developed the F-16) had proposed its F-16 Agile Falcon to the U.S.A.F. While the U.S.

would pass over the design concept in favour of all-new types (F-22/JSF) and upgrades to its existing fleet, the enlarged F-16 would find a home in Japan.

The F-2 programme was controversial, because the unit cost, which includes development costs, is roughly four times that of a Block 50/52 F-16, which does not include development costs. Inclusion of development costs distorts the incremental unit cost (this happens with most modern military aircraft), though even at the planned

MITSUBISHI F-2
Role: Strike aircraft
Crew/Accommodation: One (or 2 for the F-B)
Power Plant: 1 General Electric F110-GE-129
  turbofan. Dry thrust: 76 kN (17,000 lbf). Thrust
  with afterburner: 120-125 kN (29,500 lbf)
Dimensions: Wing span 11.13 m (36 ft 6 in);
  wing area 34.84 m² (375 ft²)
Weights: MTOW 23,814 kg (52,500 lb)
Performance: Maximum speed mach 2.0
Load: 20-mm JM61A1 cannon, plus maximum
  weapon load of 8,085 kg, AAMs: AIM-9
  Sidewinder, AIM-7 Sparrow, Mitsubishi AAM-3,
  Mitsubishi AAM-4 (from FY2010). Air-to-ground
  weapons include: ASM-1 and ASM-2 anti-ship
  missiles, various free-fall bombs with GCS-1 IIR
  seeker heads, JDAM, others: J/AAQ-2 FLIR

procurement levels the price per aircraft was somewhat high. The initial plan of 141 F-2s would have reduced the unit cost by up to U.S.$ 10 million per unit, not including reduced cost from mass-production. As of 2008, 94 aircraft were planned. Also controversial are the amounts claimed to be paid to the American side as various licensing fees, although making use of the pre-existing technology was much cheaper than trying to develop it from scratch.

The Japanese may eventually make up to 94, at a cost of roughly U.S.$ 110 million each in 2004 dollars. Much of the

F-16 technology used in the F-2 was the subject of some political debate in the U.S. and Japan in the early 1990s. The technology transfers were authorized, however, and the project proceeded.

The F-2's maiden flight was on 7 October 1995. Later that year, the Japanese government approved an order for 141 (but that was soon cut to 130), to enter service by 1999; structural problems resulted in service entry being delayed until 2000. Because of issues with cost-efficiency, orders for the aircraft were curtailed to 98 in 2004.

On 31 October 2007, an F-2B

crashed during take-off and subsequently caught fire at Nagoya Airfield in central Japan. The jet was being taken up on a test flight by Mitsubishi employees after major maintenance and before being delivered to the JSDF. Both test pilots survived the incident with only minor injuries. It was eventually determined that improper wiring caused the crash.

OPPOSITE & ABOVE: An F-2 fighter arriving at Andersen Air Force Base, Guam

SUKHOI T-50 PAK FA

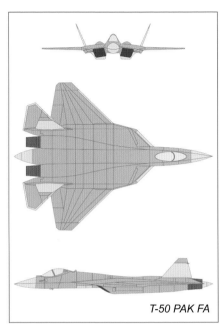

T-50 PAK FA

Russian aircraft carriers. There will be a competition between the Sukhoi, Mikoyan and Yakovlev design bureaus to choose the new naval aircraft.

Although most of the information about the PAK FA is classified, it is believed from interviews with people in

The current prototype is Sukhoi's T-50. The PAK FA, when fully developed, is intended to replace the MiG-29 Fulcrum and Su-27 Flanker in the Russian inventory and serve as the basis of the Sukhoi/HAL FGFA project being developed with India. A fifth-generation jet fighter, it is designed to directly compete with Lockheed Martin's F-22 Raptor and F-35 Lightning II. The

T-50 performed its first flight on 29 January 2010. Its second flight was on 6 February and its third on 12 February. As of 31 August 2010, it made 17 flights in total.

The aircraft's maiden flight took place on 29 January 2010 at KNAAPO's Komsomolsk-on-Amur Dzemgi Airport; the aircraft was piloted by Sergey Bogdan and the flight lasted for 47 minutes.

A second airframe is planned to join the flight testing later in the fourth quarter of 2010. These first two aircraft will lack radar and weapon control systems, while the third and fourth aircraft, to be added in 2011, will be fully functional test aircraft.

Navalized Sukhoi T-50 PAK FAs will be deployed on the Russian aircraft carrier *Admiral Kuznetsov* and future

SUKHOI T-50 PAK FA
Role: Fighter aircraft
Crew/Accommodation: One
Power Plant: 2 new unnamed engines by NPO Saturn and FNPTS MMPP Salyut of 175 kN each. Prototype with AL-41F1 of 147 kN each, definitive version with new engine >157 kNDimensions: Length: 9.8 m (65.9 ft) Wing span 14 m (46.6 ft); Wing area 78.8 m² (848.1 ft²
Weights: MTOW 37,000 kg (81,570 lb)
Performance: 2,100 km/h (Mach 2)
Load: Guns: None on prototype. Apparent provision for a cannon (most likely GSh-301). Possible two 30-mm cannons

the Russian Air Force and Defence Ministry that it will be stealthy, have the ability to supercruise, be outfitted with the next generation of air-to-air, air-to-surface, and air-to-ship missiles, incorporate a fix-mounted AESA radar with a 1,500-element array and have an 'artificial intellect'.

According to Sukhoi, the new radar will reduce pilot load and the aircraft will have a new data link to share information between aircraft.

Composites are used extensively on the T-50 and comprise 25% of its weight and almost 70% of the outer surface. It is estimated that the titanium alloy content of the fuselage is 75%. Further reductions in structural weight, drag and radar signature are achieved by the use of three-dimensional thrust vectoring engines. Sukhoi's concern for minimizing RCS (and drag) is also shown by the provision of two tandem main weapons bays in the centre fuselage, between the

engine nacelles. Each is estimated to be between 4.9–5.1m long. The main bays are augmented by bulged, triangular-section bays at the wing root.

The Moskovsky Komsomolets reported that the T-50 has been designed to be more manoeuvrable than the F-22 Raptor at the cost of making it less stealthy than the F-22.

The PAK-FA SH121 radar complex includes three X-Band AESA radars located on the front and sides of the

aircraft. These will be accompanied by L-Band radars on the wing leading edges. L-Band radars are proven to have increased effectiveness against VLO targets which are optimized only against X-Band frequencies, but their longer wavelengths reduce their resolution.

The PAK-FA will feature an IRST optical/IR search and tracking system.

The PAK FA was expected to use a pair of Saturn 117S engines on its first flights. The 117S (AL-41F1A) is a major upgrade of the AL-31F based on the AL-41F intended to power the Su-35BM, producing 142 kN (32,000 lb) of thrust in afterburner and 86.3 kN (19,400 lb) dry. In fact, PAK FA already used a completely new engine in its first flight, as stated by NPO Saturn. The engine is not based on the Saturn 117S. The engine generates a larger thrust and has a complex automation system to facilitate flight modes such as manoeuvrability. Exact specifications of the new engine are still secret. It is expected that each engine will be able to independently vector its thrust upward, downward or from side to side. Vectoring one engine up with the other one down can produce a twisting force. Therefore the PAK FA would be the first fifth-generation fighter with full 3-D thrust vectoring along all three aircraft axes: pitch, yaw and roll. This engine layout, however, would compromise IR and radar stealth.

OPPOSITE & LEFT: Sukhoi T-50 PAK FA

MARITIME PATROL

Few people fully appreciate the importance of maritime aircraft in the annals of aviation. Two years before the Wright brothers flew for the first time in their powered *Flyer*, Austrian Wilhelm Kress 'hopped' his tandem-wing powered seaplane from the Tullnerbach reservoir (in 1901), experiments which preceded even the famous Potomac river trials by American Samuel Pierpoint Langley. Maritime aircraft were widely used during World War I, both in floatplane form and as flying-boats. The German Navy made particular use of floatplanes as naval station defence fighters and for reconnaissance patrol and fighter escort, while Claude Dornier became responsible for several giant flying-boats from 1915 that were produced as Zeppelin-Lindau R-type prototypes under the patronage of Count von Zeppelin of airship fame. Although these Dornier-designed aircraft were not significant to the German war effort, it gave the young designer the means to go on and conceive some of the finest flying-boats of the inter-war period.

Other fighting nations also produced maritime aircraft, not least the truly beautifully-styled small Italian Macchi flying-boat fighters and maritime patrol aircraft that were operational from 1917. Overall, though, it was Britain that led the world in the development and use of large flying-boats, aircraft which performed brilliantly in combating both German U-boat submarines and Zeppelin airships. Interestingly, the best of these was without question the R.N.A.S.'s Felixstowe F.2A/F.3, developed by Sqdn. Cdr. John C. Porte from the earlier and less successful American Curtiss H.12 Large America which could trace its ancestry to an original pre-war flying-boat intended to attempt a transatlantic flight. Despite its bulk and weight, the Felixstowe had the added virtue of being highly manoeuvrable, and on 4 June 1918 this was put to the test when three F2As defended a fourth aircraft (which had alighted due to a fuel blockage) from 14 attacking enemy seaplanes, shooting down six in the process. Indeed, as testimony to the Felixstowe design, Curtiss went on to produce a version as the F-5L for the U.S. Navy, as an American-built example of a British-improved flying-boat of Curtiss original design!

Flying-boats were ideally suited to long over-water flights, and post-war were highly developed for both military and commercial use. They remained much prized during World War II for an expanded number of roles, including spotter-reconnaissance and air-sea rescue, the latter often by small craft launched from ships at sea as well as from land and coastal waters. But it was the large flying-boats that made such an impact on anti-submarine warfare and convoy escort. The RAF Short Sunderland, for example, proved so successful that the final aircraft were not retired by the RAF until 1959, having first become operational in 1938, while the American Consolidated PBY Catalina was used from 1941 in a whole gamut of roles and became the most-produced flying-boat of all time.

Germany, as others, built fine flying-boats, among the best remembered being the unorthodox Blohm und Voss Bv 138 for reconnaissance and some giant types

LEFT: The Dassault Atlantique 2 has been developed from the original Atlantic of 1961 first appearance, which was originally conceived to offer NATO forces a standardized long-range maritime patrol and anti-submarine landplane. Atlantic was the first European landplane specifically designed for anti-submarine and anti-surface vessel use

OPPOSITE: A British Aerospace Nimrod

from the same company. The sleek
Dornier Do 24, despite its capability to
carry bombs, is thought never to have
been employed on any offensive mission.
Instead, Germany placed its faith partly
in the Focke-Wulf Fw 200 Condor

landplane for long-range maritime
reconnaissance and maritime bomber
duties as one of the few German four-
engined bombers of that war. This
proved extremely successful in its
combined operations with German U-

boats against Allied convoys until
confronted by fighters from new escort
carriers or catapult-launched from
merchant ships. It may be said, therefore,
that Condor led the way to post-war
preferences towards landplanes and, since

the 1950s, most of the world's purpose-
built maritime patrol aircraft have been
of landplane design.

CONSOLIDATED PBY CATALINA (U.S.A.)

PBY-1 Catalina

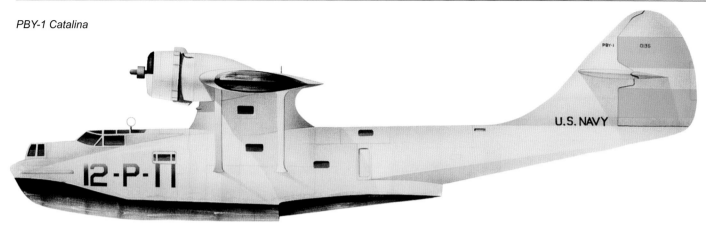

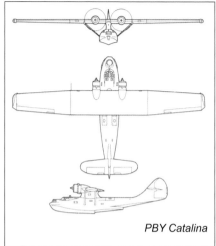

PBY Catalina

In the early 1930s, the U.S. Navy issued a requirement for a patrol flying boat that offered greater range and payload than the Consolidated P2Y and Martin P3M then in service. Design proposals were received from Consolidated and Douglas, and single prototypes of each were ordered. The Douglas type was restricted to a single XP3D-1 prototype, but the Consolidated Model 28 became one of the most important flying-boats ever developed. The XP3Y-1 prototype first flew in March 1935 and was a large machine with a wide two-step hull, a strut-braced parasol wing mounted on top of a massive pylon that accommodated the flight engineer, and stabilizing floats that retracted in flight to become the wingtips and so reduce drag.

The type clearly possessed considerable potential and after being reworked as a patrol bomber was ordered into production as the PBY-1, of which 60 were built with 671-kW (900-hp) R-1830-64 radial engines. The following PBY-2 had equipment improvements, and production totalled 50. Next came 66 PBY-3s with 746-kW (1,000-hp) R-1830-66 engines and 33 PBY-4s with 783-kW (1,050-hp) R-1830-72 engines. The generally improved PBY-5 with 895-kW (1,200-lb) R-1830-82 or -92 engines was the definitive flying-boat model and many hundreds were built, complemented by many PYB-5A and 5B amphibians, including those for Lend-Lease to Britain. The Naval Aircraft Factory produced 156 of a PBN-1 Nomad version of the PBY-5 with aerodynamic and hydrodynamic improvements, and 235 of a comparable amphibian model were built by Consolidated as the PBY-6A for the U.S. Navy, U.S.A.A.F. and Russia, making 2,398 Catalinas built by Consolidated. The basic type was also produced in Canada by Canadian Vickers and Boeing, plus in the U.S.S.R. as the GST, while the U.K. adopted the aircraft in several variants with the name Catalina that has since been generally adopted for all PBY models.

CONSOLIDATED PBY-5 (RAF CATALINA Mk IV)
Role: Long-range maritime patrol bomber flying-boat
Crew/Accommodation: Nine
Power Plant: Two 1,200-hp Pratt & Whitney R-1830-92 Twin Wasp air-cooled radials
Dimensions: Span 37.10 m (104 ft); length 19.47 m (63.88 ft); wing area 130.1 m² (1,400 sq ft)
Weights: Empty 7,809 kg (17,200 lb); MTOW 15,436 kg (34,000 lb)
Performance: Cruise speed 182 km/h (113 mph) at sea level; operational ceiling 5,517 m (18,100 ft); range 4,812 km (2,990 miles) with full warload
Load: Two .5-inch and two .303-inch machine guns, plus up to 1,816 kg (4,000 lb) of torpedoes, depth charges or bombs carried externally

Consolidated PBY Catalina with floats

OPPOSITE: Consolidated PBY Catalina

SHORT SUNDERLAND Family (United Kingdom)

Sunderland Mk I

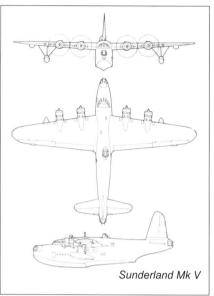

Sunderland Mk V

The Sunderland was the U.K.'s premier maritime reconnaissance flying-boat of World War II, and derived ultimately from the S.23 class of civil 'Empire' flying-boats. The prototype flew in October 1937 with 753-kW (1,010-hp) Bristol Pegasus XXII radials, and was the first British flying-boat to have power-operated defensive gun turrets. The prototype

SHORT SUNDERLAND Mk V
Role: Anti-submarine/maritime patrol
Crew/Accommodation: Seven
Power Plant: Four 1,200-hp Pratt & Whitney R-1830-90B Twin Wasp air-cooled radials
Dimensions: Span 34.39 m (112.77 ft); length 26 m (85.33 ft); wing area 156.6 m² (1,687 sq ft)
Weights: Empty 16,783 kg (37,000 lb); MTOW 27,250 kg (60,000 lb)
Performance: Maximum speed 343 km/h (213 mph) at 1,525 m (5,000 ft); operational ceiling 5,455 m (17,900 ft); range 4,300 km (2,690 miles) with maximum fuel
Load: Six .5-inch machine guns and eight .303-inch machine guns, plus up to 908 kg (2,000 lb) of bombs/depth charges

A Short Sunderland passing under Tower Bridge, London

proved most satisfactory, and production of this variant totalled 90 before it was overtaken on the lines by the Sunderland Mk II with 794-kW (1,065-hp) Pegasus XVIII radials and a power-operated dorsal turret in place of the Mk I's two 7.7-mm (0.303-in) beam guns in manually operated waist positions.

These 43 boats were in turn succeeded by the Sunderland Mk III, which was the most extensively built variant with 456 being built. This variant had a hull revised with a faired step, and some boats were to the Sunderland Mk IIIA standard with ASV. Mk III surface-search radar. The Sunderland Mk IV was developed for Pacific operations and became the S.45 Seaford, of which a mere 10 examples (three prototypes and seven production boats) were built with 1253- and 1283-kW

Short Sunderland

(1,680- and 1,720-hp) Bristol Hercules XVII and XIX radials respectively. The last Sunderland variant was the Mk V, of which 150 were built with 895-kW (1,200-hp) Pratt & Whitney R-1830-90B radials and ASV. Mk VIC radar under the wingtips; the more powerful engines allowed the type to operate at cruising rather than maximum engine revolutions, which improved engine life and aided economical running.

Sunderlands were also used for civil transport, the first of 24 Sunderland Mk IIIs being handed over to British Airways in March 1943. The boats were later brought up to more comfortable standard as Hythes, and were then revised as Sandringhams with R-1830-92 radials and, in addition, neat aerodynamic fairings over the erstwhile nose and tail turret positions.

ARADO AR 196 (Germany)

Ar 196A-3

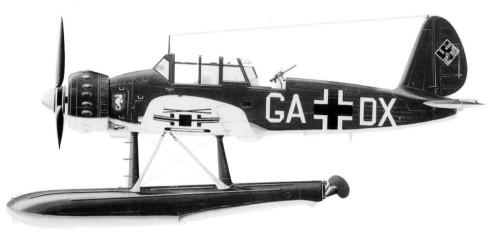

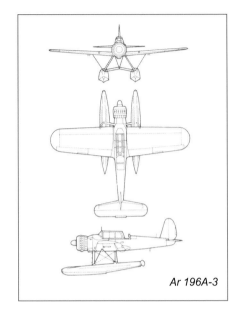

Ar 196A-3

The Ar 196 was designed to meet a 1936 requirement for a floatplane reconnaissance aircraft to succeed the same company's Ar 95 biplane, and was intended for catapult-launched use from German major surface warships, though a secondary coastal patrol capability was also envisaged. The type clearly had more than a passing kinship with the Ar 95, but was an all-metal monoplane and was designed for use on either twin floats or a combination of one main and two outrigger floats. Several proposals had been received in response to the requirement, and orders were placed for Arado monoplane and Focke-Wulf biplane prototypes.

Initial evaluation in the summer of 1937 removed the Focke-Wulf contender from the running and, after testing of the two alighting gear arrangements, the Arado type was ordered into production as the Ar 196A with twin floats. Total construction was 546 aircraft, including machines built in Dutch and French factories under German control.

The type was built in two main streams for shipboard and coastal use. The shipboard stream comprised 20 Ar 196A-1s with two wing-mounted 7.92-mm (0.312-in) machine guns and 24 strengthened Ar 196A-4s based on the Ar 196A-3. The coastal stream comprised 391 examples of the Ar 196A-2 with two 20-mm wing-mounted cannon and the strengthened Ar 196A-3 with a variable-pitch propeller, and 69 examples of the Ar 196A-5 with better radio and a twin rather than single machine-gun installation for the radio-operator/gunner. The Ar 196 was used in most of the German theatres during World War II.

ARADO Ar 196A-3
Role: Shipborne reconnaissance floatplane
Crew/Accommodation: Two
Power Plant: One 960-hp BMW 132K air-cooled radial
Dimensions: Span 12.4 m (40.68 ft); length 11 m (36.09 ft); wing area 28.4 m² (305.6 sq ft)
Weights: Empty 2,990 kg (6,593 lb); MTOW 3,730 kg (8,225 lb)
Performance: Maximum speed 310 km/h (193 mph) at 4,000 m (13,120 ft); operational ceiling 7,000 m (22,960 ft); range 1,070 km (665 miles)
Load: Two 20-mm cannon and two 7.9-mm machine guns, plus 100 kg (210 lb) of bombs

Arado Ar 196A floatplane

VOUGHT OS2U KINGFISHER (U.S.A.)

OS2U-2 Kingfisher

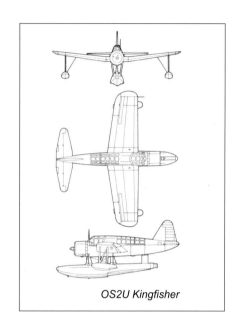

OS2U Kingfisher

To replace its O3U Corsair biplane operated by the U.S. Navy in the scouting role, Vought produced its VS.310 design with a cantilever monoplane wing in the low/mid-position, a portly fuselage with extensive glazing, and provision for fixed landing gear that could be of the tailwheel or float type, the latter based on a single central float and two stabilizing floats under the wings.

The U.S. Navy ordered a single XOS2U-1 prototype, and this first flew in March 1938 in landplane configuration with the 336-kW (450-hp) Pratt & Whitney R-985-4 Wasp Junior radial; in May of the same year the type was first flown in floatplane form. The trial programme was completed successfully, and the type was ordered into production as the OS2U-1 with the R-985-48 engine. Production totalled 54 aircraft, and in August 1940 these became the first catapult-launched observation/scout aircraft to serve on American capital ships. Further production embraced 158 examples of the OS2U-2 with the R-985-50 engine and modified equipment, and 1,006 examples of the OS2U-3 with the R-985-AN-2 engine, self-sealing fuel tanks, armour protection, and armament comprising two 7.7-mm (0.303-in) machine guns (one fixed and the other trainable) and two 147-kg (325-lb) depth charges. The type was also operated by inshore patrol squadrons in the anti-submarine air air-sea rescue roles, proving an invaluable asset. Some aircraft were supplied to Central and South American nations, and 100 were transferred to the Royal Navy as Kingfisher Mk I trainers and catapult-launched spotters. Nothing came of the planned OS2U-4 version with a more powerful engine and revised flying surfaces that included a straight-tapered tailplane and narrow-chord wings with full-span flaps and square-cut tips.

VOUGHT-SIKORSKY 0S2U-3 KINGFISHER
Role: Shipborne (catapult-launched) reconnaissance
Crew/Accommodation: Two
Power Plant: One 450-hp Pratt & Whitney R-985-AN-2 or -8 air-cooled radial
Dimensions: Span 10.95 m (35.91 ft); length 10.31 m (33.83 ft); wing area 24.34 m² (262.00 sq ft)
Weights: Empty 1,870 kg (4,123 lb); MTOW 2,722 kg (6,000 lb)
Performance: Maximum speed 264 km/h (164 mph) at 1,676 m (5,500 ft); operational ceiling 3,962 m (13,000 ft); radius 1,296 km (805 miles)

A Royal Australian Air Force Vought OS2U Kingfisher

AVRO SHACKLETON (United Kingdom)

Shackleton AEW.Mk 2

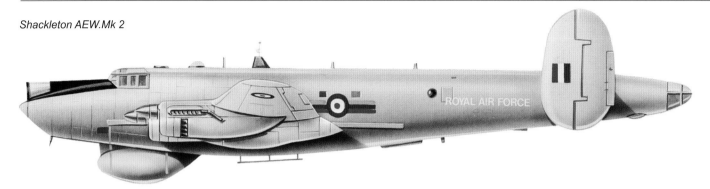

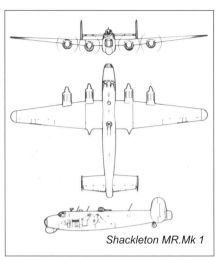

Shackleton MR.Mk 1

To give the Lancaster a long-range capability at high altitude, Avro planned the Lancaster Mk IV, but this Type 694 emerged as so different an aeroplane that it was given the name Lincoln. The prototype flew in June 1944 and, although plans were laid for 2,254 aircraft, British post-war production amounted to only 72 Lincoln B.Mk1s and 465 Lincoln B.Mk 2s. Canada completed one Lincoln B.Mk XV, but Australia built 43 Lincoln B.Mk 30s and 30 Lincoln B.Mk 30As, and 20 of these were later modified to Lincoln B.Mk 31 standard together with a longer nose accommodating search radar and two operators.

Meanwhile, experience with the Lancaster in the maritime role after World War II made the British decide to develop a specialized aeroplane as the Lincoln GR.Mk III with the wing and landing gear of the bomber married to a new fuselage, revised empennage, and Rolls-Royce Griffon engines, each driving a contra-rotating propeller unit. Later renamed Shackleton, the first example of the new type flew in March 1949, leading to production of the Shackleton GR.Mk 1 (later MR.Mk 1) with two Griffon 57As and two Griffon 57s and the Shackleton MR.Mk 1A with four Griffon 57As. The Shackleton MR.Mk 2 had revised armament and search radar with its antenna in a retractable 'dustbin' rather than a chin radome, while the definitive Shackleton MR.Mk 3 was considerably updated, lost the dorsal turret but gained underwing hardpoints and changed to tricycle landing gear. Eight MR.Mk3s also went to the South African Air Force. Twelve MR.Mk 2s were converted in the 1970s into Shackleton AEW.Mk 2 airborne early-warning aircraft for the RAF, especially equipped with specialist radar, remaining in service until the arrival of Boeing E-3s.

AVRO SHACKLETON AEW.Mk 2
Role: Airborne early warning
Crew/Accommodation: Ten
Power Plant: Four 2,456-hp Rolls-Royce Griffon 57A water-cooled inlines
Dimensions: Span 36.52 m (119.83 ft); length 28.19 m (92.5 ft); wing area 135.45 m² (1,458 sq ft)
Weights: Empty 25,583 kg (56,400 lb); MTOW 44,452 kg (98,000 lb)
Performance: Cruise speed 322 km/h (200 mph) at 3,050 m (10,000 ft); operational ceiling 5,852 m (19,200 ft); endurance 16 hours
Load: None, other than APS 20 long-range search radar

A British Royal Air Force Arvro Shackleton

OPPOSITE: Avro Shackleton

SP-3G Orion

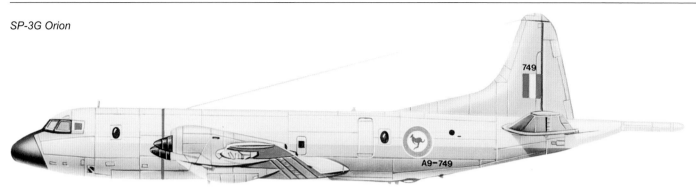

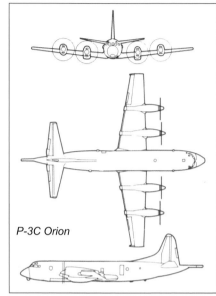

P-3C Orion

In 1957 the U.S. Navy required a maritime patrol type to supplant the piston-engined Lockheed P2V Neptune, and stressed the urgency of the programme by agreeing to the development of the type on the basis of an existing civil airframe. Lockheed's Model 85 proposal was therefore based on the airframe/powerplant combination of the relatively unsuccessful Model 188 Electra turboprop-powered airliner, though with the fuselage shortened by 2.24 m (7 ft 4 in) as well as modified to include a weapons bay in the lower fuselage.

The YP3V-l prototype first flew in November 1959, and while the initial production variant was delivered from August 1962 with the designation P3V-1, it was redesignated P-3A in 1962. By the end of U.S. Orion production in 1996, 649 had been delivered to the U.S. Navy and forces abroad while others continued to be built by Kawasaki in Japan. The

original 157 P-3As were powered by 3,356-kW (4,500-shp) Allison T56-A-10W turboprops and, though the initial aircraft had the same tactical system as the P2V-7, the 109th and later aircraft had the more advanced Deltic system that was then retrofitted to the earlier machines. The 145 P-3Bs were given the same Deltic system, but were powered by

LOCKHEED ORION P-3C Update III ORION
Role: Long-range maritime patrol and
  anti-submarine
Crew/Accommodation: Ten
Power Plant: Four 4,910-shp Allison T56-A-14
  turboprops
Dimensions: Span 30.38 m (99.66 ft);
  length 35.6 m (116.8 ft); wing area 120.8 m²
  (1,300 sq ft)
Weights: Empty 27,892 kg (61,491 lb); MTOW
  64,410 kg (142,000 lb)
Performance: Maximum speed 761 km/h
  (466 mph) at 4,572 m (1 5,000 ft); operational
  ceiling 10,485 m (34,400 ft); radius of action
  3,836 km (2,384 miles)
Load: Up to 9,072 kg (20,000 lb) of weapons and
  sonobuoys

U.S. Navy Lockheed Martin P-3 Orion

3,661-kW (4,910-shp) T56-A-14 engines and were delivered with provision for the launch of AGM-12 Bullpup air-to-surface missiles. The final version was the P-3C, which retains the airframe/powerplant combination of the P-3B but was given the A-NEW ASW avionics system with new sensors and controls. In 1975 the first of a series of Update models was introduced, aimed to increase operational effectiveness, the last being Update III, in 1984. There were also several export models including the CP-140 Aurora for Canada that combined the P-3C's airframe and powerplant with the electronics of the Lockheed S-3 Viking carrierborne anti-submarine platform; the related Canadian CP-140A Arcturus has no ASW equipment and is used for surveillance. The U.S. Navy also took in electronic surveillance models as EP-3 Aries IIs, plus various transport, trainer and the research models RP-3, while an airborne early warning version P-3AEW went to U.S. Customs.

A P-3A Orion on patrol over the Atlantic on 22 January 1964

255

BRITISH AEROSPACE NIMROD (United Kingdom)

Nimrod MR.Mk 2

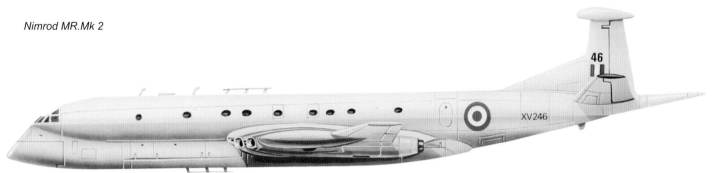

The Nimrod was developed on the aerodynamic and structural basis of the Comet 4 airliner as a jet-powered maritime patroller to replace the piston-engined Avro Shackleton. The Nimrod looks remarkably similar to the Comet 4, but features a fuselage shortened by 1.98 m (6 ft 6 in) and deepened to allow the incorporation of a weapons bay 14.78 m (48 ft 6 in) long below the wide tactical compartment, a turbofan powerplant for much improved reliability and range (especially in the patrol regime with two engines shut down), and highly advanced

mission electronics including radar, MAD and an acoustic data-processing system using dropped sonobuoys. Wings, tailplane and landing were similar to those of Comet 4C, though the landing gear was strengthened, and the first prototype flew in May 1967 as a conversion of a Comet 4C. Successful

trials led to production of 46 Nimrod MR.Mk 1s with EMI ASV-21D search radar and Emerson ASQ-10A magnetic anomaly detector in a tail 'sting'.

A variant of this baseline version became the Nimrod R.Mk 1, a special electronic intelligence variant of which three were produced. Further

Nimrod MR.MK 1

development in the electronic field led to the improved Nimrod MR.Mk 2, of which 35 were produced by conversion of MR.Mk 1 airframes with EMI Searchwater radar, Loral ESM in wingtip pods (to complement the original Thomson-CSF ESM system in a fintop fairing), and a thoroughly upgraded tactical suite with a Marconi ASQ-901 acoustic data-processing and display system allowing use of many active and passive sonobuoy types. Redelivery of Mk 2s began in 1979, the addition of inflight refuelling later adding a 'P' to the designation.

Under current development is the Nimrod 2000 or MRA.Mk 4, initially for the RAF from 2003 and 21 are being produced by major rework of existing aircraft, having new mission

BRITISH AEROSPACE NIMROD MR.Mk 2P

Role: Long-range maritime reconnaissance/
  anti-submarine
Crew/Accommodation: Twelve
Power Plant: Four 5,440-kgp (11,995-lb s.t.)
  Rolls-Royce Spey Mk 250 turbofans
Dimensions: Span 35 m (114.83 ft); length
  39.32 m (129 ft); wing area 197 m² (2,121 sq ft)
Weights: Empty 39,000 kg (86.000 lb); MTOW
  87,090 kg (192,000 lb)
Performance: Maximum speed 926 km/h
  (576 mph) at 610 m (2,000 ft);
  operational ceiling 12,802 m (42,000 ft);
  endurance 12 hours
Load: Up to 6,120 kg (13,500 lb) including up to
  nine Stingray lightweight anti-submarine
  torpedoes, Harpoon missiles, depth charges,
  mines and/or cluster bombs

British Aerospace Nimrod tanker

systems, a 2-man cockpit with modern LCD screen displays, new wings and other components, BMW Rolls-Royce BR710 turbofans, Searchwater 2000 radar, other advanced avionics and more.

On 5 November 2007, XV235 was involved in a midair incident over Afghanistan when the crew noticed a fuel leak during air-to-air refuelling. After transmitting a mayday call, the crew landed the aircraft successfully. The incident came only a month before the issue of the report of a Board of Enquiry into the 2 September 2006 fatal accident to XV230 in (likely) similar circumstances. The RAF subsequently suspended air-to-air refuelling operations for this type.

British Aerospace Nimrod MR.2 (XV254)

CIVIL AIRCRAFT

CIVIL PISTON-ENGINED TRANSPORTS

The 'stick and string' aeroplanes that pioneered flying in the early years of the 20th century had enough difficulty keeping the pilot aloft without the added complication of a commercially viable payload. And yet, hardly had the Wright brothers recovered from the exhilaration of their first-ever powered flights than a letter arrived from a businessman, enquiring whether they could transport minerals by air over a 26-km (16-mile) hop in West Virginia, for which they would be paid $10 per ton. Politely, the offer was turned down for practical reasons.

However, a much developed Wright Model B biplane was used in November 1910 to carry the first-ever air freight, this time 542 yards of silk transported between Dayton and Columbus. The cost of the flight to the Morehouse-Martens Company was a staggering $5,000, yet the flight generated such interest in the company's Home Dry Goods Store that, by cutting some silk into small pieces for sale as souvenirs attached to postcards, Morehouse-Martens showed an overall

PAGE 258: Airbus A380

PAGE 259: Boeing 787 Dreamliner

BELOW: Lockheed Super Constellation

OPPOSITE: Cessna Grand Caravan

profit from the venture of over $1,000.

This and similar high-publicity flights were little more than advertising stunts, but already in 1910 the first-ever commercial passenger airline had begun operating in Germany, carrying over 34,000 passengers without injury until November 1913. Known as Delag, the airline had been founded by Count von Zeppelin and consequently operated giant airships. At the start of the following year, in 1914, the first-ever scheduled airline services using an aeroplane (Benoist flying-boat) began in Florida, but these lasted only a few months.

Even while World War I raged at its bloodiest, British and German civil airline companies were registered for post-war activities, allowing operations to start in 1919. Progress in aeroplane development had, by then, made commercial operations viable. Very little time passed before other airlines began to appear, able to call upon cheap ex-military aircraft that could be crudely converted for their new peacetime roles, while the first purpose-designed commercial transports were but a step away.

JUNKERS F 13 (Germany)

F 13

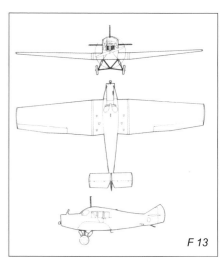

F 13

From its DI single-seat fighter and CLI two-seat escort fighter and close-support warplane of 1918, both all-metal monoplanes that saw limited service in World War I, Junkers developed Europe's single most important transport of the 1920s, the classic F 13 low-wing monoplane with a single nose-mounted engine and fixed tail wheel landing gear. This used the metal construction patented by Dr Hugo Junkers in 1910 for thick-section cantilever monoplane wings and was the world's first all-metal purpose-designed commercial transport.

The F 13 first flew in June 1919, and was based on nine spars braced with welded duralumin tubes and covered in streamwise corrugated duralumin skinning to create an immensely strong and durable structure. The accommodation comprised an open cockpit for two pilots and an enclosed cabin for four passengers. The cockpit was later enclosed, and the engine of the first machine was a 119-kW (160-hp) Mercedes D.IIIa inline, which was superseded in early production aircraft by the 138-kW (185-hp) BMW IIIa inline that offered much superior performance.

Production continued to 1932, and amounted to at least 320 and probably 350 aircraft in more than 60 variants with a host of modifications and different engines, the most frequent being the 156-kW (210-hp) Junkers L-5 inline.

The main operator of the type was Junkers Luftverkehr, which operated more than 60 aircraft in a period between 1921 and 1926, in the process flying some 15,000,000 km (9,300,000 miles) and carrying nearly 282,000 passengers. The airline then became part of Deutsche Luft-Hansa (later Deutsche Lufthansa) which still had 43 such aircraft in service in 1931. The other F 13s were used by civil and military operators in most parts of the world. The fact that the type was immensely strong, needed little maintenance, and could operate from wheel, ski or float landing gear, made the F 13 especially popular with operators in remoter areas.

JUNKERS F 13

Role: Light passenger transport
Crew/Accommodation: One, plus up to four passengers
Power Plant: One 185 hp BMW III A water-cooled inline
Dimensions: Span 14.47 m (47.74 ft) length 9.6 m (31.5 ft); wing area 39 m² (419.8 sq ft)
Weights: Empty 1.150 kg (2.535 lb); MTOW 1,650 kg (3,638 lb)
Performance: Cruise speed 140 km/h (75.5 mph) at sea level; operational ceiling 3,000 m (9.843 ft); range 725 km (450 miles)
Load: Up to 320 kg (705 lb) payload

The Junkers F 13 was a light but enduring commercial transport

FOKKER F.VII-3m (Netherlands)

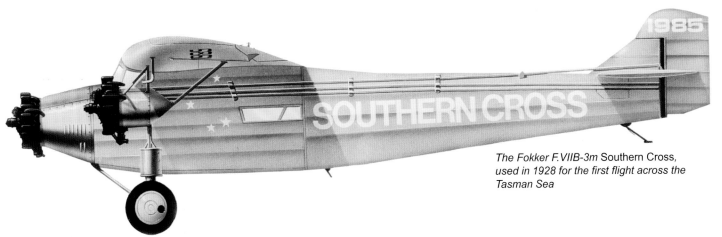

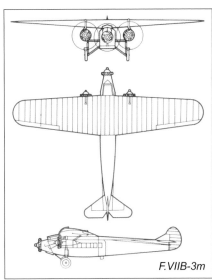

The Fokker F.VIIB-3m Southern Cross, used in 1928 for the first flight across the Tasman Sea

F.VIIB-3m

In 1924–25, Fokker built five examples of its F.VII powered by the 268-kW (360-hp) Rolls-Royce Eagle inline engine, and then evolved the eight-passenger F.VIIA that first flew in March 1925 with a 298-kW (400-hp) Packard Liberty 12 engine and a number of aerodynamic refinements and simple three-strut rather than multi-strut main landing gear units. The type undertook a successful demonstration tour of the United States, and orders were received there and in Europe for 42 aircraft with inline or radial engines in the class between 261 and 391 kW (350 and 525 hp); licensed production was also undertaken in several countries.

The type was a typical Fokker construction, with a welded steel-tube fuselage and tail unit covered in fabric, and a high-set cantilever wing of thick section and wooden construction. For the Ford Reliability Tour of the United States, Fokker produced the first F.VIIA-3m with a powerplant of three 179-kW

(240-hp) Wright Whirlwind radials mounted one on the nose and the others on the main landing gear struts below the wing.

All subsequent production was of the three-engined type, and many F.VIIAs were converted. The F.VIIA-3m spanned 19.30 m (63 ft 3.75 in), but to meet the requirement of Sir Hubert Wilkins for a long-range polar

exploration type, a version was produced as the F.VIIB-3m with wings spanning 21.70 m (71 ft 2.5 in). This also became a production type. Dutch construction of the two F. VII-3m models was 116 aircraft, and large numbers were built under licence in seven countries. The British and American models were the Avro Ten and Atlantic F.7. The type was also adopted by the U.S. Army Air

Corps and U.S. Navy as the C-2 and RA respectively. The F.VII-3m was of great importance in the development of European and third-world transport for passengers and freight, and was also used extensively for route-proving and record-breaking flights.

Richard Byrd claimed to have flown over the North Pole in the Josephine Ford *on 9 May 1926*

FOKKER F.VIIB-3m
Role: Passenger Transport
Crew/Accommodation: Two, plus up to 8 passengers
Power Plant: Three 240-hp Gnôme-Rhône Titan air-cooled radials (the aircraft was equipped with various makes/powers of European and U.S. radials)
Dimensions: Span 21.70 m (71.19 ft); length 14.20 m (46.56 ft); wing area 71.20 m² (722 sq ft)
Weights: Empty 3,050 kg (6,724 lb); MTOW 5,250 kg (11,574 lb)
Performance: Maximum speed 185 km/h (115 mph) at sea level; operational ceiling 4,875 m (15,994 ft); range 837 km (520 miles) with full payload
Load: Up to 1,280 kg (2,822 lb)

FORD TRI-MOTOR (U.S.A.)

Tri-Motor

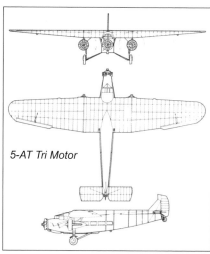

5-AT Tri Motor

The much-loved Ford Tri-Motor was the result of Henry Ford purchasing the Stout Metal Airplane Company in 1925, which had developed the Pullman 6-passenger monoplane, and progressing on to the larger design. Remembered for its corrugated all-metal construction, it gained the nickname 'Tin Goose'.

FORD 4-AT-E TRI-MOTOR
Role: Passenger transport
Crew/Accommodation: Two, plus up to 11 passengers
Power Plant: Three 300-hp Wright J-6 air-cooled radials
Dimensions: Span 22.56 m (74 ft); length 15.19 m (49.83 ft); wing area 72.93 m² (785 sq ft)
Weights: Empty 2,948 kg (6,500 lb); MTOW 4,595 kg (10,130 lb)
Performance: Cruise speed 172 km/h (107 mph) at sea level; operational ceiling 5,029 m (16,500 ft); range 917 km (570 miles)
Load: Up to 782 kg (1,725 lb)

The legendary Ford Tri-Motor 'Tin Goose'

From his 2-AT Pullman, powered by a single 298-kW (400-hp) Packard Liberty inline engine, William B. Stout had evolved the 3-AT with three uncowled radial engines mounted two on the wings and one low on the nose. This was unsuccessful, but paved the way for th 4-AT that first flew in June 1926 with three 149-kW (200-hp) Wright Whirlwind J-4 radials located two under the wings in strut-braced nacelles and one in a neat nose installation. The 4-AT accommodated two pilots in an open cockpit and eight passengers in an enclosed cabin.

The type was produced in variants that ranged from the initial 4-AT-A to the 4-AT-E with 224-kW (300-hp) Whirlwind J-6-9 radials and provision for 12 passengers. Production totalled 81 aircraft and was complemented from 1928 by the 5-AT with 13 passengers, span increased by 1.17 m (3 ft 10 in), and

three 313-kW (420-hp) Pratt and Whitney Wasp radials. Production continued up to 1932, and these 117 aircraft included variants up to the 5-AT-D with 17 passengers in a cabin given greater headroom by raising the wing 0.203 m (8 in). Other variants were four

6-ATs based on the 5-AT but with Whirlwind J-6-9 engines, one 7-AT conversion of a 6-AT with a 313-kW Wasp, one 8-AT conversion of a 5-AT with only the nose engine, one 9-AT conversion of a 4-AT with 224-kW Pratt and Whitney Wasp Junior radials,

one 11-AT conversion of a 4-AT with three 168-kW (225-hp) Packard diesel engines. Army and Navy versions were the C-3, C-4 and C-9, and the JR and RR respectively.

Ford Tri-Motor

JUNKERS Ju 52/3 (Germany)

Ju 52/3m g7e

OPPOSITE: Ju 52/1m replica at the Western Canada Aviation Museum, Winnipeg, Manitoba, Canada

First flown in October 1930 with a single 541-kW (725-hp) BMW VII engine, the Ju 52 was produced to the extent of just six aircraft as civil transports with various engines. The type was of typical Junkers concept for the period, with corrugated alloy skinning on an angular airframe, fixed but faired tailwheel landing gear, and a low-set wing trailed by typical Junkers full-span slotted ailerons/flaps. The Ju 52 would clearly benefit from greater power, and the

company therefore developed the Ju 52/3m ce tri-motor version that first flew in April 1931 with 410-kW (550-hp) Pratt & Whitney Hornet radials. The type was produced in Ju 52/3m ce, de, fe and ge

civil variants, the last with accommodation for 17 passengers on the power of three 492-kW (660-hp) BMW 132A-1 radials. Development then veered to German military needs, resulting in the Ju 52/3m g3e interim bomber-transport pending the arrival of purpose-designed aircraft. Then the type was built as Germany's main transport and airborne forces aircraft of World War II.

The main variants in an overall production total of about 4,850 aircraft were the Ju 52/3m g4e bomber-transport with a heavier payload and a tailwheel in place of the original skid, the Ju 52/3m g5e with 619-kW (830-hp) BMW 132T-2 radials, the Ju 52/3m g6e improved transport, the Ju 52/3m g7e with an autopilot and a larger loading hatch, Ju 52/3m g8e multi-role transport with conversion kits for specialized roles, Ju 52/3m g9e airborne forces version with a glider-tow attachment and BMW 132Z radials, Ju 52/3m g12e civil and military transport with 596-kW (800-hp) BMW 132L radials, and Ju 52/3m g14e final transport version with improved armament and armour protection. There were also small numbers of the later Ju 252 and Ju 352 developments with more power and retractable landing gear.

Ju 52/3m

Junkers Ju 52

JUNKERS Ju 52/3m g4e
Role: Military transport (land- or water-based)
Crew/Accommodation: Three, plus up to 18 troops
Power Plant: Three 830 hp BMW 132T-2 air-cooled radials
Dimensions: Span 29.25 m (95.97 ft); length 18.9 m (62 ft); wing area 110.5 m² (1,189.4 sq ft)
Weights: Empty 6,510 kg (14,354 lb); MTOW 10,500 kg (23,1571b)
Performance: Cruise speed 200 km/h (124 mph) at sea level; operational ceiling 5,000 m (18,046 ft); range 915 km (568 miles) with full payload
Load: Three 7.9-mm machine guns and up to 2,000 kg (4,409 lb) payload

BOEING MODEL 247 (U.S.A.)

Model 247D

The Model 247 was the logical development of the other pioneering Boeing aircraft, most notably the Model 200 Monomail and Model 215. The Model 200 was a mailplane with limited passenger capacity, and introduced the cantilever monoplane wing, semi-monocoque fuselage and retractable landing gear. The Model 215 was an extrapolation of the Model 200's concept into the bomber category, and introduced larger size and a twin-engined powerplant. The Model 247 was slightly smaller and lighter than the Model 215, and has many claims to the title of world's first 'modern' air transport as it had features such as all-metal construction, cantilever wings, pneumatic de-icing of the flying surfaces, a semi-monocoque fuselage, retractable landing gear, and fully enclosed accommodation for two pilots, a stewardess, and a planned 14 passengers. Passenger capacity was in fact limited to 10, but with this load the Model 247 could in fact both climb and maintain cruising altitude on just one engine.

The type first flew in February 1933 but, despite its undoubted technical merits, was not a great commercial success. The reasons for this were two-fold: firstly it was not available soon enough for all the airlines wishing to purchase such a modern design; and secondly the aircraft was sized to the requirement of Boeing Air Transport and therefore lacked the larger capacity needed by some potential purchasers. Thus the 60 United Air Lines examples (formed from BAT in 1931) were completed by only 15 more aircraft for companies or individuals. A Model 247 ordered by Roscoe Turner and Clyde Pangbourne for the 1934 England to Australia 'MacRobertson' air race introduced drag-reducing NACA engine cowlings and controllable-pitch propellers, and these features proved so successful that they were retrofitted to most aircraft, which became the Model 247Ds.

BOEING 247D
Role: Passenger transport
Crew/Accommodation: Two crew, one cabin crew plus up to ten passengers
Power Plant: Two 550-hp Pratt & Whitney Wasp S1H1G air-cooled radials
Dimensions: Span 22.56 m (74 ft); length 15.72 m (51.58 ft): wing area 77.67 m² (836 sq ft)
Weights: Empty 4,148 kg (9,144 lb); MTOW 6,192 kg (13,650 1b)
Performance: Cruise speed 304 km/h (189 mph); operational ceiling 7,742 m (25,400 ft); range 1,199 km (745 miles)
Load: Up to 998 kg (2,200 lb)

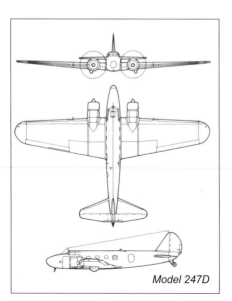

Model 247D

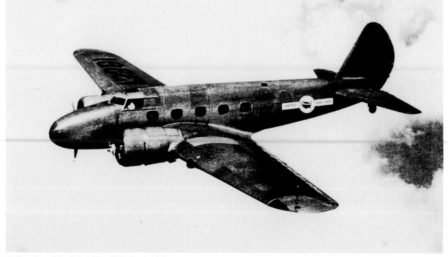

A Boeing Model 247 of United Airlines

LOCKHEED L10 ELECTRA (U.S.A.)

XR20-1

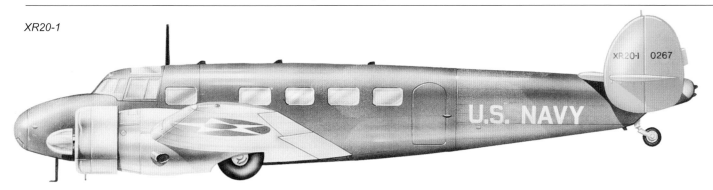

After cutting its teeth on a series of single-engined light transports that also achieved many record long-distance flights, Lockheed decided to move a step up into the potentially more lucrative twin-engined transport market with the Model 10 Electra that offered lower capacity but higher performance than contemporary Boeing and Douglas aircraft. The Electra was an advanced type of all-metal construction with endplate vertical tail surfaces, retractable tailwheel landing gear and other advanced features. The first machine flew in February 1934 with a pair of Pratt & Whitney Wasp Junior SB radials and, though the type's 10-passenger capacity was thought by many to be too small for airline operators, production totalled 148 aircraft in major variants such as 101 Electra 10-As with 336-kW (450-hp) Wasp Juniors and accommodation for 10 passengers, 18 Electra 10-Bs with 328-kW (440-hp) Wright R-975-E3 Whirlwinds, eight Electra 10-Cs with Wasp SC1s, and 15 Electra 10-Es with 447-kW (600-hp) Wasp S3H1s.

Nothing came of the projected Electra 10-D military transport, but 26 civil Electras were later impressed with the designation C-36A to C to supplement the single XC-36 high-altitude research type, three C-36s with 10-seat accommodation and the single C-37 used by the Militia Bureau. The XR20 and XR30 were single U.S. Navy and U.S. Coast Guard aircraft.

The L-12 Electra Junior was a scaled-down version intended mainly for feederlines and business operators, and first flew in June 1936. Some 114 were built in Model 12 and improved Model 12-A forms with accommodation for five passengers, and many of the 73 civil aircraft were later impressed for military service. Here they shared the C-40 designation with the machines built for the U.S. Army Air Corps.

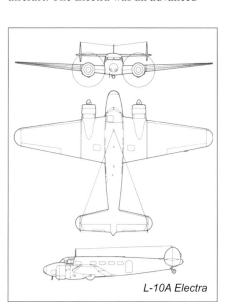

L-10A Electra

Lockheed L-10A Electra

LOCKHEED L10-A ELECTRA
Role: Passenger transport
Crew/Accommodation: Two plus up to ten passengers
Power Plant: Two 450-hp Pratt & Whitney R-1340 Wasp Junior SB air-cooled radials
Dimensions: Span 16.76 m (55 ft); length 11.76 m (38.58 ft); wing area 42.59 m² (458.5 sq ft)
Weights: Empty 2,927 kg (6.454 lb); MTOW 4,672 kg (10,300 lb)
Performance: Maximum speed 306 km/h (190 mph) at 1,525 m (5,000 ft); operational ceiling 5,915 m (19,400 ft); range 1,305 km (810 miles)
Load: Up to 816 kg (1,800 lb)

SIKORSKY S-42 (U.S.A.)

S-42A

In August 1931, Pan American Airways issued a requirement for a new type of flying-boat. This was needed for the transatlantic service that the airline intended to inaugurate, and called for a type carrying a crew of four and at least 12 passengers over a range of 4023 km

(2,500 miles) at a cruising speed of 233 km/h (145 mph). At the end of 1932, the airline contracted with Martin for its M-130 and with Sikorsky for its S-42. The latter was related to the S-40 amphibian to be used on Pan American's routes across the Caribbean and South America.

The S-40 had been based on the S-38 and retained the earlier design's combination of a central pod for 40 passengers and a crew of six, with a twin-boom tail and a parasol wing braced to a 'lower wing' that also supported the stabilizing floats. The larger and more

powerful S-42 was a parasol-winged flying-boat with a wholly conventional boat hull, a high-set braced tailplane with twin vertical surfaces, the wing braced directly to the hull and supporting the two stabilizing floats as well as four radial engines on the leading edges. The first S-42 was delivered in August 1934, and the type flew its first service during that month between Miami and Rio de Janeiro. The type was used mainly on the airline's South American and transpacific routes (including pioneering flights across the South Pacific to New Zealand). Total production was 10 boats including three S-42s with the 522-kW (700-hp) Pratt & Whitney Hornet S5D1G, three-S-42A boats with 559-kW (750-hp) Hornet S1EG radials and longer-span wings, and four S-42B boats with further refinements and Hamilton Standard constant-speed propellers, permitting 907-kg (2,000-lb) increase in maximum take-off weight.

S-42

The Sikorsky S-42 was based on a substantial hull

SIKORSKY S-42B

Role: Intermediate/short-range passenger transport flying-boat

Crew/Accommodation: Four and two cabin crew, plus up to 32 passengers

Power Plant: Four 800-hp Pratt & Whitney R-1690 Hornet air-cooled radials

Dimensions: Span 35.97 m (118.33 ft); length 20.93 m (68.66 ft); wing area 124.5 m² (1,340 sq ft)

Weights: Empty 9,491 kg (20,924 lb); MTOW 19,504 kg (43,000 lb)

Performance: Cruise speed 225 km/h (140 mph) at 610 m (2,000 ft); operational ceiling 4,878 m (16,000 ft); range 1,207 km (750 miles) with full payload

Load: Up to 3,626 kg (7,995 lb)

DOUGLAS DC-3 and Military Derivatives (U.S.A.)

DC-3

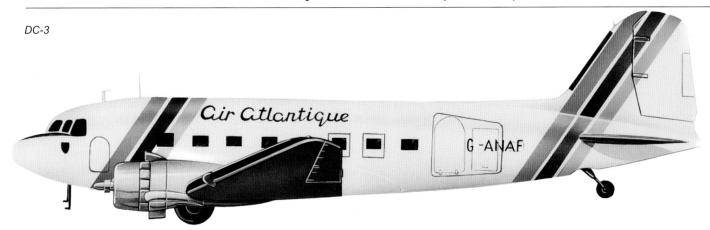

The DC-3 can truly be said to have changed history, for this type opened the era of 'modern' air travel in the mid-1950s and became the mainstay of the Allies' air transport effort in World War II. Production of 10,349 aircraft was completed in the United States; at least another 2,000 were produced under licence in the U.S.S.R. as the Lisunov Li-2, and 485 were built in Japan as the Showa (Nakajima) L2D.

The series began with the DC-1 that first flew in July 1933 as a cantilever low-wing monoplane of all-metal construction (except fabric-covered control surfaces) with enclosed accommodation and features such as retractable landing gear and trailing-edge flaps. From this prototype was developed the 14-passenger DC-2 production model, which was built in modest numbers but paved the way for the Douglas Sleeper Transport that first flew in December 1935 as an airliner for transcontinental night flights with 16 passengers in sleeper berths. From this was evolved the 24-passenger DC-3. This latter was produced in five series with either the Wright SGR-1820 Cyclone or Pratt & Whitney R-1830 Twin Wasp radial as the standard engine. The type was ordered for the U.S. military as the C-47 Skytrain (U.S. Army) and R4D (U.S. Navy), while the British adopted the name Dakota for aircraft supplied under the terms of the Lend-Lease Act.

The type was produced in a vast number of variants within the new-build C-47, C-53, C-117 and R4D series for transport, paratrooping, and glider-towing duties, while impressed aircraft swelled numbers and also designations to a bewildering degree. After the war, large quantities of these monumentally reliable aircraft were released cheaply to civil operators, and the series can be credited with the development of air transport in most of the world's remoter regions.

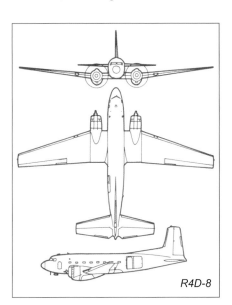

R4D-8

A Scandinavian Airlines DC-3

DOUGLAS DC-3A
Role: Passenger transport
Crew/Accommodation: Three plus two cabin crew and up to 28 passengers
Power Plant: Two 1,200-hp Pratt & Whitney Twin Wasp S1C3-G air cooled radials
Dimensions: Span 28.96 m (95 ft); length 1965m (64.47 ft); wing area 91.7 m² (987 sq ft)
Weights: Empty 7,650 g (16,865 lb); MTOW 11,431 kg (25,200 lb)
Performance: Maximum speed 370 km /h (230 mph) at 2,590 m (8,500 sq ft); operational ceiling 7,070 m (23,200 ft); range 3,420 km (2,125 miles)
Load: Up to 2,350 kg (5,180 lb)

FOCKE-WULF Fw 200 CONDOR (Germany)

Fw 200G

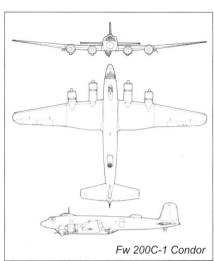

Fw 200C-1 Condor

The Fw 200 was developed as a transatlantic passenger and mail aircraft that might appeal to Deutsche Lufthansa. The first of three prototypes flew during July 1937 with 652-kW (750-hp) Pratt and Whitney Hornet radials and room for a maximum of 26 passengers in two cabins; the next two aircraft had 537-kW (720-hp) BMW 132G-1 radials. Eight Fw 200A preproduction transports were delivered to Lufthansa and single examples to Brazilian and Danish airliners. Four Fw 200B airliners with 619-kW (830-hp) BMW 132H engines followed. Some of

these later became the personal transports of Nazi VIPs.

The Condor's real claim to fame rests with its Fw 200C series, Germany's most important maritime reconnaissance bomber of World War II. This was

pioneered by a maritime reconnaissance prototype ordered by Japan but never delivered. Ten Fw 200C-0 pre-production aircraft were delivered as six maritime reconnaissance and four transport aircraft, and there followed a steadily

more diverse sequence of specialized aircraft that were hampered by a structural weakness in the fuselage aft of the wing but nevertheless played a major part in the Atlantic and Arctic convoy campaigns. The Fw 200C-1 was a reconnaissance bomber with a 1750-kg (3,757-1b) bomb load, and the Fw 200C-2 was an aerodynamically refined variant. The Fw 200C-3 had 895-kW (1,200-hp) BMW-Bramo 323R-2 Fafnir radials, structural strengthening, and improved defensive and offensive armament in four subvariants. The main model was the Fw 200C-4 with radar, and there were two 11- and 14-passenger transport derivatives of this. The Fw 200C-6 was the C-3 modified as launcher for two Henschel Hs 293 anti-ship missiles, while the Fw 200C-8 was another missile carrier with improved radar. Total production was 276 aircraft.

FOCKE-WULF Fw 200C-3 CONDOR
Role: Long-range maritime reconnaissance bomber
Crew: Accommodation: Seven
Power Plant: Four 1,200-hp BMW Bramo 323 R-2 Fafnir air-cooled radials
Dimensions: Span 32.84 m (107.74 ft); length 23.85 m (78.25 ft); wing area 118m² (1,290 sq ft)
Weights: Empty 17,000 kg (37,485 lb); MTOW 22,700 kg (50,045 lb)
Performance: Cruise speed 335 km/h (208 mph) at 4,000 m (13,124 ft); operational ceiling 6,000 m (19,685 ft); range 3,560 km (2,211 miles)
Load: One 20-mm cannon, three 13-mm and two 7.9-mm machine guns, plus up to 2,100 kg (4,630 lb) of bombs

Focke-Wulf Fw 200 V5

DORNIER Do 26 (Germany)

Do 26

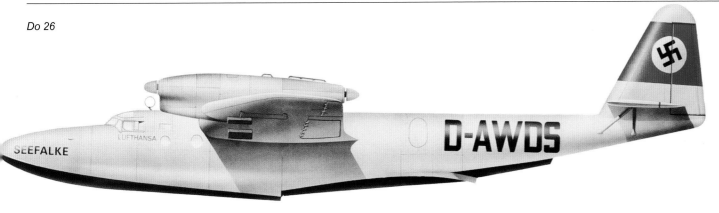

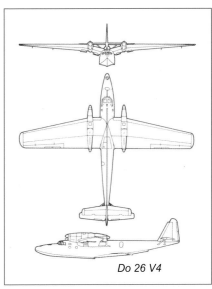

Do 26 V4

Dornier built many types of flying boat, but the type that offered the cleanest aerodynamics and the most pleasing lines was, without doubt, the Do 26. The type had its origins in the transatlantic mail services developed in the 1930s, and was designed to carry a flight crew of four and 500 kg (1,102 lb) of mail between Lisbon and New York. The all-metal design was based on a slender two-step hull carrying a shoulder-mounted gull wing and a simple tail unit with braced tailplane halves. The four engines were located in the angles of the gull wings as push/pull tandem pairs in single nacelles that offered minimum resistance. Junkers Jumo 205C/D diesel engines each delivering 447-kW (600-hp) were chosen for their reliability and low specific fuel consumption, and the two pusher engines were installed on mountings that allowed them to be tilted up at 10° at take-off so that the three-blade propeller units were clear of the spray from the hull.

The flying boats were stressed for catapult launches from support ships, and Deutsche Lufthansa ordered three aircraft during 1937. The first of these flew in May 1938, and the two machines completed before the outbreak of World War II were delivered to the airline with the designation Do 26A. These were never used for their intended North Atlantic route, and completed just 18 crossings of the South Atlantic. The third machine was to have been the Do 26B with provision for four passengers, but was completed as the first of an eventual four Do 26D military flying boats in the long-range reconnaissance and transport roles. These were powered by 522-kW (700-hp) Jumo 205Ea engines and carried a bow turret armed with a single 20-mm cannon in addition to three 7.92-mm (0.312-in) machine guns in one dorsal and two waist positions.

DORNIER Do 26A
Role: Long-range mail transport
Crew/Accommodation: Four
Power Plant: Four 700-hp Junkers Jumo 205C liquid-cooled diesels
Dimensions: Span 30.00 m (98.42 ft); length 24.60 m (80.71 ft); wing area 120 m² (1,291.67 sq ft)
Weights: Empty 10,700 kg (23,594 lb); MTOW 20,000 kg (44,100 lb)
Performance: Maximum speed 335 km/h (208 mph) at sea level; operational ceiling 4,800 m (15,748 ft); range 9,000 km (5,592 miles) with full payload
Load: Up to 500 kg (1,103 lb)

The Dornier 26 had very clean lines in the air

BOEING 314 (U.S.A.)

Boeing Model 314A

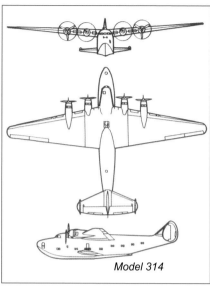

Model 314

The Model 314 was the greatest flying-boat ever built for the civil air transport role. It was designed to the requirement of Pan American Airways for the transatlantic service which the airline had requested from the U.S. Bureau of Air Commerce as early as January 1935. The airline already operated the Martin M-130 and Sikorsky S-42 flying-boat airliners, but wanted a 'state-of-the-art' type for this new prestige route. Boeing designed its Model 314 on the basis of the wings and modified tailplane of the Model 294

(XB-15) experimental bomber married to a fuselage accommodating a maximum of 74 passengers in four cabins. The engines were a quartet of 1119-kW (1,500-hp) Wright GR-2600 Double Cyclone radials with fuel for a range of 5633 km (3,500 miles). Some of the fuel

was stored in the two lateral sponsons that stabilized the machine on the water and also served as loading platforms.

The first aeroplane flew in June 1938, and the original single vertical tail was soon replaced by twin endplate surfaces that were then supplemented by a central

fin based on the original vertical surface but without a movable rudder. The Model 314 entered service in May 1939 as a mailplane, and the first passengers were carried in June of the same year.

The six Model 314s were later joined by six Model 314As (including three for the British Overseas Airways Corporation) with more fuel and 1193-kW (1,600-hp) engines driving larger-diameter propellers. Six of the aircraft were used in World War II by the American military in the form of C-98s and B-314s.

BOEING 314A

Role: Long-range passenger flying-boat
Crew/Accommodation: Three, plus seven cabin crew and up to 74 passengers
Power Plant: Four 1,600-hp Wright GR-2600 Double Cyclone air-cooled radials
Dimensions: Span 46.33 m (152 ft); length 32.31 m (106 ft); wing area 266.35 m² (2,867 sq ft)
Weights: Empty 22,801 kg (50,268 lb); MTOW 37,422 kg (82,500 lb)
Performance: Cruise speed 295 km/h (183 mph) at sea level; operational ceiling 4,084 m (13,400 ft); range 5,632 km (3,500 miles)
Load: Up to 6,713 kg (14,800 lb)

The Boeing Model 314 was undoubtedly the finest flying-boat airliner ever built.

OPPOSITE: Boeing 314 'Yankee Clipper'

LOCKHEED CONSTELLATION Family (U.S.A.)

EC-121K

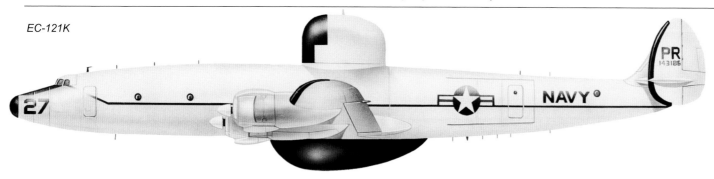

OPPOSITE: Lockheed C-121A Constellation

This was surely one of the classic aircraft of all time, developed as an elegant yet efficient airliner but also of great military importance as the basis of the world's first long-range airborne early warning and electronic warfare aircraft. The design was originated in 1939 to provide Pan American Airways and Transcontinental and Western Air with an advanced airliner for use on long-range domestic routes. The Lockheed design was centred on refined aerodynamics, pressurized accommodation and high power for sustained high-altitude cruising at high speed, and tricycle landing gear was incorporated for optimum field performance and passenger comfort on the ground.

The type first flew in January 1943, and civil production was overtaken by the needs of the military during World War II; the L-49 thus became the U.S. Army's C-69, of which 22 were completed before Japan's capitulation and the cancellation of military orders. Some aircraft then on the production line were completed as 60-seat L-049 airliners, but the first true civil version was the 81-seat L-649 with 1864-kW (2,500-hp) Wright 749C-18BD-1 radials. Further airliners were the L-749 with additional fuel, the L-1049 Super Constellation with the fuselage lengthened by 5.59 m (18 in 4 in) for the accommodation of 109 passengers, and the L-1649 Starliner with a new, longer-span wing and 2535-kW (3,500-hp) Wright 988TC-18EA-2 radials fed from increased fuel tankage for true intercontinental range. Production of the series totalled 856 including military variants that included the C-121 transport version of the L-749, the R70 naval transport version of the L-1049, and the PO-1 and VW-2 Warning Star airborne early warning aircraft. These R7O, PO-1 and VW-2 aircraft were later redesignated in the C-121 series that expanded to include a large number of EC-121 electronic warfare aircraft.

LOCKHEED L749 CONSTELLATION
Role: Long-range passenger transport
Crew/Accommodation: Four and two cabin crew, plus up to 81 passengers
Power Plant: Four 2,500-hp Wright 749C-18BD-1 Double Cyclone air-cooled radials
Dimensions: Span 37.49 m (123 ft); length 29.03 m (95.25 ft); wing area 153.3 m² (1,650 sq ft)
Weights: Empty 27,648 kg (60,954 lb); MTOW 47,627 (105,000 lb)
Performance: Cruise speed 557 km/h (346 mph) at 9,072 m (20,000 ft); operational ceiling 10,886 m (24,000 ft); range 3,219 km/h (2,000 miles) with 5,124 (13,500 lb) payload plus reserves
Load: Up to 6,690 kg (14,750 lb) with 6,124 kg (13,500 lb)

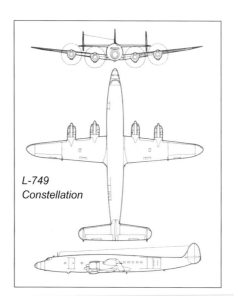

L-749 Constellation

An L-049E

CONVAIR CONVAIRLINER Series (U.S.A.)

440 Convairliner

OPPOSITE: Convair freighter

The CV-240 series was developed in the hope of producing a successor to the legendary Douglas DC-3, and though the type was in every respect good, with features such as pressurized accommodation and tricycle landing gear that kept the fuselage level on the ground, it failed to make a decisive impression on a market saturated by the vast number of C-47s released on to the civil market when they became surplus to military requirements. The spur for the type's original design was a specification issued in 1945 by American Airlines for a modern airliner to supersede the DC-3 and offer superior operating economics.

The CV-110 prototype first flew in July 1946 with 1566-kW (2,100-hp) Pratt & Whitney R-2800-S1C3-G radial engines and pressurized accommodation for 30 passengers. Even before this prototype flew, however, American Airlines had revised its specification and now demanded greater capacity. It proved a comparatively straightforward task to increase capacity to 40 passengers by lengthening the fuselage by 1.12m (3 ft 8 in), and in this form the airliner became the CV-240. No prototype was built, the company flying its first production example in March 1947. The CV-240 entered service in June 1948, and 176 were built as airliners. There followed the 44-passenger CV-340 with 1864-kW (2,500-hp) R-2800-CB-16 or 17 engines and a fuselage stretch of 1.37 m (4 ft 6 in), and finally the similar CV-440 with aerodynamic refinements and high-density seating for 52 passengers. Turboprop conversions were later made to produce the CV-540, 580, 600 and 640 series. Variants for the military were the T-29 U.S.A.F. crew trainer, the C-131 air ambulance and transport for the U.S.A.F., and the R4Y transport for the U.S. Navy.

CONVAIR 440 CONVAIRLINER
Role: Short-range passenger transport
Crew/Accommodation: Two plus up to 52 passengers
Power Plant: Two 2,500 hp Pratt & Whitney R-2800-CB16/17 Double Wasp air-cooled radials
Dimensions: Span 31.10 m (105. 33 ft); length 24.84 m (81.5 ft); wing area 85.47 m^2 (920 sq ft)
Weights: Empty 15,111 kg (33,314 lb); MTOW 22,544 kg (49.700 lb)
Performance: Cruise speed 465 km/h (289 mph) at 6,096 m (20,000 ft); operational ceiling 7,590 m (24,900 ft); range 459 km (285 miles) with maximum payload
Load: Up to 5,820 kg (12,836 lb)

CV-580

CV-440 Metropolitan

AIRSPEED AMBASSADOR (United Kingdom)

AS. 57 Ambassador

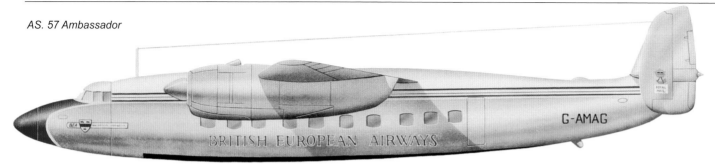

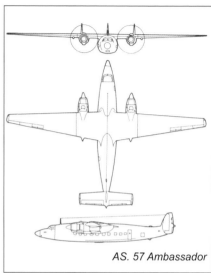

AS. 57 Ambassador

The Ambassador was one of the most elegant aircraft ever built, and resulted from the Brabazon Committee's 1943 recommendation for a 30-seat short/medium-range airliner to be built after World War II within the context of reviving the U.K.'s airline network and civil aircraft production capability.

The AS.57 was designed in the closing stages of the war with a high aspect ratio wing set high on the circular-section pressurized fuselage, which ended in an upswept tail unit with triple vertical surfaces; the main units of the tricycle landing gear retracted into the rear part of the two engine

nacelles slung under the inner portions of the wing.

The first Ambassador flew in July 1947 and, with two Bristol Centaurus radials, had very promising performance. Just over one year later, an order for 20 aircraft was received from BEA, but the programme was then beset by a number

of technical problems during its development. This delayed the Ambassador's service entry until March 1952, and meant that the initial 20-aircraft order was the only one fulfilled as this piston-engined type had been overtaken in performance and operating economics by the turboprop-powered

Vickers Viscount. Even so, the 'Elizabethan' class served BEA with great popularity for six years, and the aircraft were then acquired by five other operators. The second and third prototypes went on to important subsidiary careers as test beds for turboprops, such as the Bristol Proteus, the Napier Eland, and the Rolls-Royce Dart and Tyne.

AIRSPEED AMBASSADOR
Role: Short-range passenger transport
Crew/Accommodation: Three, plus three cabin crew and 47/49 passengers
Power Plant: Two 2,700-hp Bristol Centaurus 661 air-cooled radials
Dimensions: Span 35.05 m (115 ft); length 24.69 m (81 ft); wing area 111.48 m² (1,200 sq ft)
Weights: Empty 16,277 kg (35,884 lb); MTOW 23,590 kg (52,000 lb)
Performance: Cruise speed 483 km/h (300 mph) at 6,096 m (20,000 ft); range 1,159 km (720 miles) with maximum payload
Load: Up to 5,285 kg (11,650 lb)

The Airspeed Ambassador was the epitome of aerodynamic elegance

BOEING STRATOCRUISER and C-97 Series (U.S.A.)

Stratocruiser

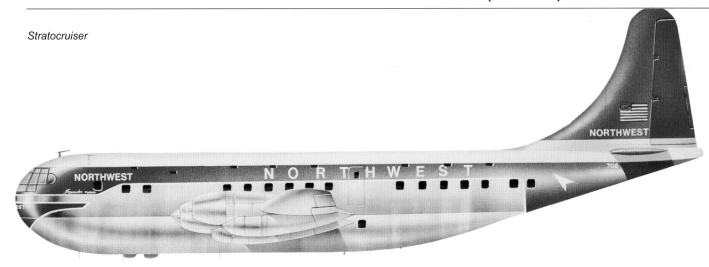

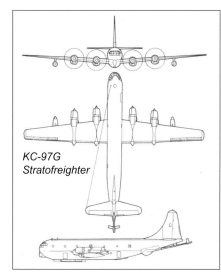

*KC-97G
Stratofreighter*

The Model 377 was a commercial transport developed from the C-97 military transport, which itself evolved as the Model 367 to combine the wings, engines, tail unit, landing gear and lower fuselage of the B-29 bomber with a new upper fuselage lobe of considerably larger radius and so create a pressurized 'double-bubble' fuselage. This provided considerable volume, and also provided the Model 377 with its distinctive two-deck layout. The Model 377-10-9

prototype was based on the YC-97A with Pratt & Whitney R-4360 radial engines, and first flew in July 1947.

The aircraft was later delivered to Pan American Airways, which soon became the world's largest operator of the Stratocruiser, with 27 of the 55 aircraft built. Ten of them were fitted

with additional fuel tankage as Super Stratocruisers, and these were suitable for the transatlantic route. At a later date, all Pan Am's aircraft were modified with a General Electric CH-10 turbocharger on each engine for an additional 37.3 kW (50 hp) of power for high-altitude cruise. The other major operator of the type was

BOAC, which bought six new aircraft and then found this particular type so useful that is secured another 11 from other operators.

The Stratocruiser was available in Model 377-10-26, -28, -29, -30 and -32 variants with interior arrangements that catered for anything between 58 and 112 day passengers, or alternatively 33 night passengers accommodated in five seats as well as 28 upper- and lower-deck berths. The standard accommodation was on the upper deck, with access to the 14-person cocktail lounge on the lower deck via a spiral staircase.

Strange derivatives of the C-97/Stratocruiser became the Guppy series of 'outsized' transports developed by Aero Spacelines, starting with the Pregnant Guppy in 1962. Each featured a huge fuselage extension to allow carriage of very bulky freight.

BOEING 377 STRATOCRUISER
Role: Long-range passenger transport
Crew/Accommodation: Five and five cabin crew, plus up to 95 passengers
Power Plant: Four 3,500-hp Pratt & Whitney R-4360B3 Double Wasp air-cooled radials
Dimensions: 43.03 m (141.19 ft); length 33.63 m (110.33 ft); wing area 159.79 m² (1,720 sq ft)
Weights: Empty 35,797 kg (78,920 lb); MTOW 67,131 kg (148,000 lb)
Performance: Maximum speed 603 km/h (375 mph) at 7,625 m (25,000 ft); operational ceiling 9,754 m (32,000 ft); range 7,360 km (4,600 miles) with full fuel
Load: Up to 13,608 kg (30,000 lb)

Aero Spacelines Guppy-201

de HAVILLAND CANADA DHC-2 BEAVER (Canada)

DHC-2 Beaver

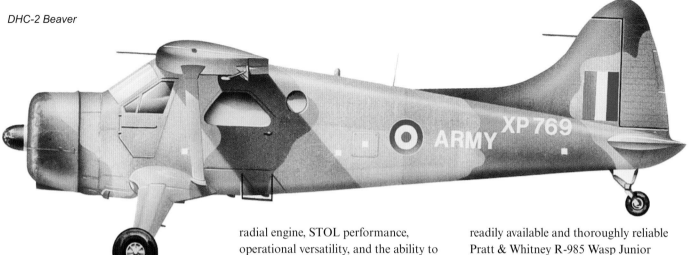

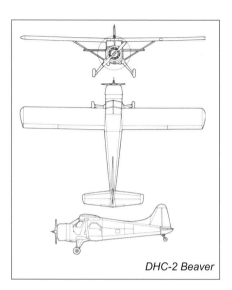

DHC-2 Beaver

The DHC-2 Beaver was designed from 1946 especially to meet a specification issued by the Ontario Department of Lands and Forests, and resulted in a superb aircraft that fully met the overall Canadian need for a bushplane to replace pre-World War II types such as the Noorduyn Norseman and various Fairchild aircraft. Key features of the design were the rugged reliability of the airframe and single radial engine, STOL performance, operational versatility, and the ability to carry wheels, skis or floats on the main units of its tailwheel landing gear, whose wide track gave the type exceptional stability on the ground, snow or water. The DHC-2 was designed round the readily available and thoroughly reliable Pratt & Whitney R-985 Wasp Junior engine, and emerged for its first flight in August 1947 as a braced high-wing monoplane together with sturdy fixed landing gear.

The only model to achieve mass production was the Beaver I, of which 1,657 were produced with the ability to carry the pilot and a basic payload of seven passengers or 680 kg (1,500 lb) of freight. No fewer than 980 of these Beaver Is were bought by the U.S. Army and U.S. Air Force with the basic designation L-20 (from 1962 U-6); six were YL-20 service test aircraft, 968 were L-20A production aircraft, and six were L-20B production aircraft with different equipment. One Beaver II was produced with the 410-kW (550-hp) Alvis Leonides radial, and there were also a few Turbo-Beaver IIIs with the 431-kW (578-ehp) Pratt & Whitney Canada PT6A-6/20 turboprop and provision for 10 passengers. Production of this classic type ended in the mid-1960s as de Havilland Canada concentrated on more ambitious aircraft.

de HAVILLAND CANADA DHC-2 BEAVER I
Role: Light utility transport
Crew/Accommodation: One plus up to six passengers
Power Plant: One 450 hp Pratt & Whitney R-985AN-6B Wasp Junior air-cooled radial
Dimensions: 14.62 m (48.00 ft); length 9.23 m (30.25 ft); wing area 23.20 m² (250.00 sq ft)
Weights: Empty 1,294 kg (2,850 lb); MTOW 2,313 kg (5,100 lb)
Performance: Maximum speed 257 km/h (160 mph) at 1,524 m (5,000 ft); operational ceiling 5,486 m (18,000 ft); range 756 km (470 miles) with full payload
Load: Up to 613 kg (1,350 lb)

The de Havilland Canada DHC-2 Beaver

DOUGLAS DC-7 (U.S.A.)

DC-7C

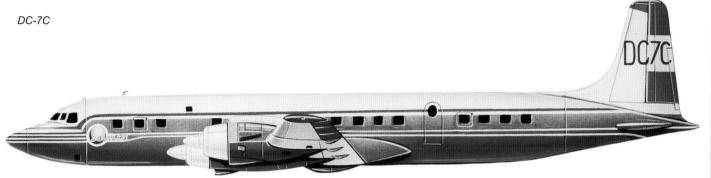

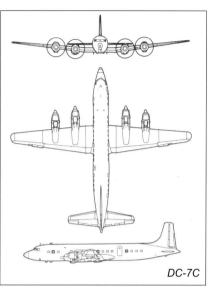

DC-7C

In its C-54 military guise, the DC-4 proved an invaluable long-range transport in World War II. The type's reliability is attested by the fact that only three aircraft were lost in the course of 80,000 or more oceanic crossings. Capacity was limited, however, and Douglas developed to army order the similar but pressurized XC-112A with a longer fuselage. This first flew in February 1946 and was thus too late for the war. With no military orders forthcoming, Douglas marketed the type as the civil DC-6 that later spawned a military C-118 Liftmaster derivative. And from the DC-6B passenger transport, the company developed the DC-7 to meet an American Airlines' requirement for an airliner to compete with TWA's Lockheed Super Constellation. The DC-7 had a lengthened fuselage, beefed-up landing gear and the same 2424-kW (3,250-hp) Wright R-3350 Turbo-Compound engines as the Super Constellation.

The type first flew in May 1953 and entered production as the DC-6 transcontinental transport, of which 105 were built. To provide transatlantic range, Douglas developed the DC-7B with additional fuel capacity in longer engine nacelles. Production of this variant totalled 112 aircraft, but the model proved to possess only marginally adequate capability in its intended role, and was therefore superseded by the DC-7C, often called the Seven Seas. This became one of the definitive piston-engined airliners, and production totalled 120. The type had 2535-kW (3,400-hp) R-3350-18EA-1 engines, a fuselage lengthened by 1.02 m (3 ft 4 in) to allow the carriage of 105 passengers and, most importantly, increased fuel capacity in parallel-chord inboard wing extensions that also possessed the additional benefit of moving the engines farther from the fuselage and so reducing cabin noise.

DOUGLAS DC-7C

Role: Long-range passenger transport
Crew/Accommodation: Four and four/five cabin crew, plus up to 105 passengers
Power Plant: Four 3,400-hp Wright R-3350-18EA-1 Turbo-Compound air-cooled radials
Dimensions: Span 38.86 m (127.5 ft); length 34.21 m (112.25 ft); wing area 152.08 m² (1,637 sq ft)
Weights: Empty 33,005 kg (72,763 lb); MTOW 64,864 kg (143,000 lb)
Performance: Cruise speed 571 km/h (355 mph) at 5,791 m (19,000 ft); operational ceiling 6,615 m (21,700 ft); range 7,410 km (4,605 miles) with maximum payload

Douglas DC-7

BRITTEN-NORMAN BN2 ISLANDER Family (United Kingdom)

BN2A Islander

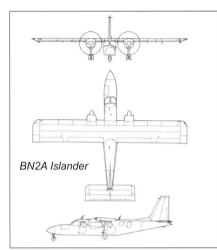

BN2A Islander

The Islander was designed as a simple feeder liner for operators in remoter areas, and was schemed as a low-maintenance type of all-metal construction with fixed tricycle landing gear, a high-set wing mounting the two reliable piston engines, and a slab-sided fuselage with 'wall-to-wall' seating accessed by one door on the starboard side and two on the port side. The first Islander flew in June 1965 with two 157-

kW (210-hp) Continental IO-360-B engines. The type was underpowered and had too high a wing loading. This meant

the adoption of a wing spanning 1.22 m (4 ft 0 in) more, and a power plant of two 194-kW (260-hp) Lycoming O-540-E

engines. The result was the BN2 model that entered service in August 1967.

Later variants became the refined

BRITTEN-NORMAN BN2B-20
Role: Light short-field utility/passenger transport
Crew/Accommodation: One, plus up to nine passengers
Power Plant: Two 260-hp Lycoming O-540-E4C5 air-cooled flat-opposed
Dimensions: Span 14.94 m (49 ft); length 10.97 m (36 ft); wing area 30.2 m² (325 sq ft)
Weights: Empty 1,866 kg (4,114 lb); MTOW 2,993 kg (6,600 lb)
Performance: Cruise speed 263 km/h (164 mph) at 2,440 m (8,000 ft); operational ceiling 3,444 m (11,300 ft); range 1,763 km (1,096 miles) with optional wingtip tanks for IFR flying
Load: Up to1,082 kg (2.386 lb) disposable load

Britten-Norman BN2A Islander

BN2A and the heavier BN2B with an interior of proved design and smaller-diameter propellers for lower cabin noise levels. Options have included an extended nose providing additional baggage volume. The current piston-engined models are the BN2B-26 and the BN2B-20, the latter with more powerful engines. The type has also been produced in Defender and other militarized models with underwing hardpoints and options for weapons and/or sensors that can optimize the aircraft for a number of important roles in the electronic warfare arena. Turbine power became an increasingly attractive alternative during the Islander's early production career, and the result was the BN2T with two 239-kW (320-shp) Allison 250-B17C turboprops, which remains available. The largest derivative became the Trislander with a third engine added at the junction of the enlarged vertical tail and the mid-set tailplane. The Trislander was given a lengthened fuselage for 17 passengers.

Britten-Norman BN-2T Islander

CIVIL TURBOPROP-ENGINED TRANSPORTS

It was as long ago as 1926 that British Dr A.A. Griffith first suggested that a turbine engine could be used to produce not only jet exhaust but also the power needed to turn a propeller via a reduction gear. During World War II Rolls-Royce developed its Derwent turbojet engine and, from this, conceived a turboprop derivative as the Trent, which drove a five-blade propeller. Incredibly, an early Gloster Meteor fighter prototype was used to flight-test the Trent, in September 1945, and thereby became the first aeroplane in history to fly on turboprop power alone.

BELOW; EMBRAER EMB-120 Brasilia

OPPOSITE; SAAB 340 of American Airlines

The wartime Brabazon Committee recommended that a turboprop-powered short/medium-range airliner should be developed among other types, and what was originally named the Brabazon IIB eventually appeared in 1948 as the Vickers Viscount, the world's first turbine-powered airliner of either turboprop or turbojet varieties. The Dart engines chosen provided the required mix of high performance and fuel economy and, although virtually all large commercial jetliners were eventually to adopt turbojets for greatest performance gains from turbine power, turboprops remained the favoured engine type for many of the smaller airliners to this day.

Of course, it should not be overlooked that some of the world's largest aircraft have also used turboprop power, including giant Soviet and Ukrainian types, while another historic first for turboprop power came in December 1957 when a BOAC Bristol Britannia 312 flew from London to New York and was thereby the first-ever turbine airliner to undertake a transatlantic passenger service.

VICKERS VISCOUNT (United Kingdom)

Viscount 800

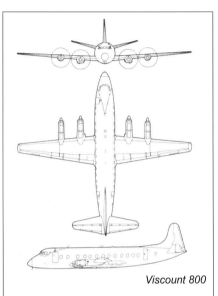

Viscount 800

The Type 630 Viscount was the world's first turbine-powered airliner to enter service. The aircraft was developed as the Vickers VC2 (originally the Brabazon IIB) to meet a requirement for a 24-seat short/medium-range airliner with a turboprop powerplant. The specification was issued during World War II by the Brabazon Committee that was charged with assessing the U.K.'s post-war civil air transport needs, and the prototype Type 630 was designed as a 32-passenger airliner of attractive design and orthodox construction based on a cantilever low-wing monoplane layout with retractable tricycle landing gear. The first example flew in July 1948 with four 738-kW (990-shp) Rolls-Royce Dart RDa.l Mk 502 turboprops in slim wing-mounted nacelles. The type had too low a capacity to attract any real commercial interest, but was then revised in accordance with the requirement of British European Airways for an airliner with pressurized accommodation for between 40 and 59 passengers. This Type 700 became the first production version with a powerplant of four 1044-kW (1,400-shp) Dart Mk 506s or, in the Type 700D, four 1193-kW (1,600-shp) Dart Mk 510s. These latter engines also powered the Type 800 with a lengthened fuselage for between 65 and 71 passengers. The Type 810 was structurally strengthened for operation at higher weights, and was powered by 1566-kW (2,100-shp) Dart RDa.7/1 Mk 525s. Total production was eventually 444 aircraft and the type made the world's first turbine-powered commercial airline flight on 29 July 1950 at the beginning of a two-week experimental service between London and Paris. The Viscount was sold in many parts of the world, and made good though not decisive inroads into the lucrative American market.

VICKERS VISCOUNT 810

Role: Short-range passenger transport
Crew/Accommodation: Three and two cabin crew plus up to 71 passengers
Power Plant: Four 2,100-shp Rolls-Royce Dart R.Da 7/1 Mk. 525 turboprops
Dimensions: Span 28.5 m (93.76 ft); length 26.11 m (85.66 ft); wing area 89.46 m² (963 sq ft)
Weights: Empty 18,753 kg (41,565 lb); MTOW 32,886 kg (72,500 lb)
Performance: Maximum speed 563 km/h (350 mph) at 6,100 m (20,000 ft); operational ceiling 7,620 m (25,000 ft); range 2,775 km (1,725 miles) with maximum payload
Load: Up to 6,577 kg (14,500 lb)

BEA Vickers Viscount

BRISTOL BRITANNIA (United Kingdom)

Britannia

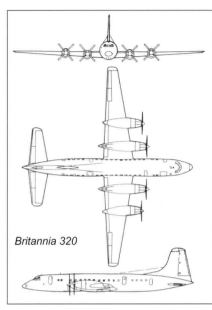

Britannia 320

Probably the finest turboprop airliner ever built, the Britannia was so delayed by engine problems that it was overtaken by jet-powered airliners and thus failed to fulfil its great commercial promise. The type was one of eight types proposed by five companies to meet a BOAC requirement shortly after the end of World War II for a Medium-Range Empire airliner with pressurized accommodation for 36 passengers. The Type 175's proposed powerplant of four Bristol Centaurus radials was more than adequate for the specified load, so the design was enlarged to 48-passenger capacity. The Ministry of Supply ordered three prototypes, but the design was further amended and, when the first machine flew in August 1952, it had provision for 90 passengers on the power of four 2088-kW (2,800-ehp) Bristol Proteus turboprops. This paved the way for the first production model, the Britannia Series 100 which entered service in 1957 with 2819-kW (3,780-ehp) Proteus 705s; 15 of these were built for BOAC.

There followed eight Britannia Series 300s with the fuselage lengthened by 3.12 m (10 ft 3 in) for a maximum of 133 passengers carried over transatlantic routes, and 32 Britannia Series 310s with 3072-kW (4,120-ehp) Proteus 755s and greater fuel capacity. Only two were built of the final Britannia Series 320 with 3318-kW (4,450-ehp) Proteus 765s, while production of the Britannia for the civil market in total numbered just 60 aircraft. The last variant was the Britannia Series 250 modelled on the Series 310 but intended for RAF use as 20 Britannia C.Mk Is and three C.Mk 2s. Exactly the same basic airframe was used by Canadair as the core of two aircraft, the CL-28 Argus maritime patroller with 2535-kW (3,400-hp) Wright R-3350-EA1 Turbo-Compound piston engines, together with the CL-44 long-range transport with 4273-kW (5,730-ehp) Rolls-Royce Tyne 515 Mk 10 turboprops.

BRISTOL BRITANNIA 310 Series
Role: Long-range passenger transport
Crew/Accommodation: Four, four cabin crew and up to 139 passengers
Power Plant: Four 4,120-ehp Bristol Siddeley Proteus 755 turboprops
Dimensions: Span 43.37 m (142.29 ft); length 37.87 m (124.25 ft); wing area 192.78 m² (2,075 sq ft)
Weights: Empty 37,438 kg (82,537 lb); MTOW 83,915 kg (185,000 lb)
Performance: Cruise speed 660 km/h (410 mph) at 6,401 m (21,000 ft); operational ceiling 9,200+ m (30,184 ft); range 6,869 km (4,268 miles) with maximum payload
Load: Up to 15,830 kg (34,900 lb)

Royal Air Force Bristol Britannia

FOKKER F.27 FRIENDSHIP and 50 (Netherlands)

F. 27 Mk 200 Friendship

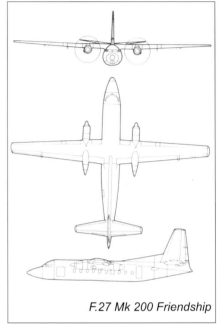

F.27 Mk 200 Friendship

After World War II Fokker sought to recapture a slice of the airliner market with a type matching the best of its classic interwar airliners. After long deliberation, the company fixed on a short/medium-range type powered by two Rolls-Royce Dart turboprops on the high-set wing. The first of two prototypes flew in November 1955. The Friendship entered service in December 1958 as the F.27 Mk 100 with two 1279-kW (1,715-shp) Dart RDa. 6 Mk 514-7 engines for the carriage of between 40 and 52 passengers, and was followed by successively upgraded models such as the F.27 Mk 200 with 1529-kW (2,050-shp) Dart RDa. 7 Mk 532-7 engines, the F.27 Mks 300 and 400 Combiplane derivatives of the Mks 100 and 200 with reinforced cabin floors and a large cargo door on the port side of the forward fuselage. The F.27 Mk 500 introduced a fuselage lengthened by 1.50 m (4ft 11 in) for between 52 and 60 passengers. The last variant was the F.27 Mk 600 convertible

FOKKER 50
Role: Short-range passenger transport
Crew/Accommodation: Two and two cabin crew, plus up to 58 passengers
Power Plant: Two 2,250-shp Pratt & Whitney PW 125B turboprops
Dimensions: Span 29 m (95.15 ft); length 25.25 m (82.83 ft); wing area 70 m² (754 sq ft)
Weights: Empty 12,741 kg (28,090 lb); MTOW 18,990 kg (41,865 1b)
Performance: Cruise speed 500 km/h (270 knots) at 6,096 m (20,000 ft): operational ceiling 7,620 m (25,000 ft); range 1,125 km (607 naut. miles) with 50 passengers
Load: Up to 5,262 kg (11,600 lb)

A Fokker 50 at Antwerp Airport

variant of the Mk 400 without the reinforced floor.

Military variants became the F.27 Mks 400M and 500M Troopship, and specialized maritime reconnaissance models were the unarmed F.27 Maritime and armed F.27 Maritime Enforcer. F.27 production ended with the 579th aircraft, which was delivered in 1987. The basic Mks 100, 200 and 300 were licence-built in the United States as the Fairchild F-27A, B and C to the extent of 128 aircraft, and the same company also produced a variant with its fuselage stretched by 1.83m (6 ft 0 in) as the FH-227, of which 79 were produced. The durability of the Friendship's basic design was attested by the follow-up development of the Fokker 50, a thoroughly updated 58-passenger version with Pratt & Whitney Canada PW125B or PW127B turboprops driving six-blade propellers. The first Fokker 50 was delivered in August 1987.

Fokker 27 cargo plane

ANTONOV An-22 ANTHEUS 'COCK' (U.S.S.R.)

Antonov An-22 'Cock'

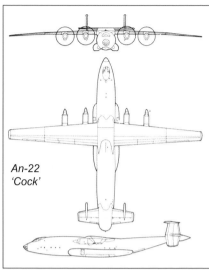

An-22 'Cock'

In its time the An-22 Antei (Antheus) was the world's largest aircraft although now beaten by the turbofan and 73.3-m (240.5-ft) span An-124 and 88.4-m (290-ft) An-225. An-22 was designed for the twin tasks of military heavy transport and support for the resources exploitation industry in Siberia (flying typically in civil Aeroflot markings). The specification for the type was issued in 1962, and the first example flew in February 1965. The type was first revealed in the West, where it had the NATO reporting name 'Cock' during the Paris air show of June 1965. At that time

it was reported that the design could also be developed as a 724-passenger airliner, but this proposal came to nothing.

Given the type's highly specialized role and size, it is not surprising that production was limited to only about 60 aircraft, all completed by 1974 and many

still flying. Keynotes of the design are four potent turboprops driving immense contra-rotating propeller units, and an upswept tail unit with twin vertical surfaces at about three-fifths span. The 14-wheel landing gear allows operations into and out of semi-prepared airstrips,

and comprises a twin-wheel nose unit and two six-wheel units as main units; the latter are three twin-wheel units in each of the two lateral sponson fairings that provide an unobstructed hold. The upswept tail allows in the rear-fuselage a hydraulically operated ramp/door arrangement for the straight-in loading of items as large as tanks or complete missiles. The hold is 32.7 m (107 ft 3 in) long and 4.4 m (14 ft 5 in) wide and high, and has four overhead travelling gantries as well as two 2500-kg (5,511-lb) capacity winches for the loading of freight.

ANTONOV An-22 ANTHEUS 'COCK'
Role: Long-range freight transport
Crew/Accommodation: Five plus up to 29
  passengers/troops in upper cabin
Power Plant: Four 14,805-shp Kuznetsov
  NK 12MA turboprops
Dimensions: Span 64.4 .m (211.29 ft);
  length 57.31 m (188 ft); wing area 345 m²
  (3,713.6 sq ft)
Weights: Empty 118,727 kg (261,748 lb);
  MTOW 225,000 kg (496,040 lb)
Performance: Cruise speed 580 km/h (360 mph);
  operational ceiling 10,000 m (32,808 ft); range
  5,000 km (2,698 naut. miles) with maximum
  payload
Load: Up to 60,000 kg (132,340 lb)

Antonov An-22

OPPOSITE: Antonov An-22 Antheus 'Cock'

EMBRAER EMB-110 BANDEIRANTE Family (Brazil)

EMB-110 Bandeirante

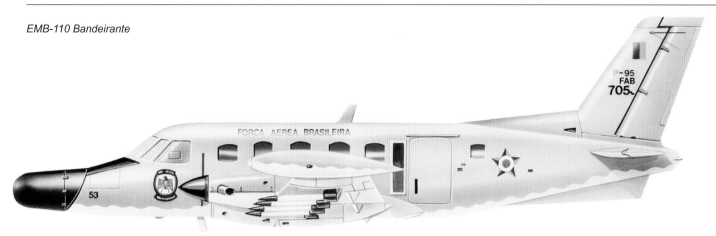

OPPOSITE: EMBRAER EMB-110 Bandeirante

The Empresa Brasileira de Aeronautica SA was created in 1969 to promote the development of an indigenous Brazilian aircraft industry, and began operation in January 1970. The company has had astonishing international success, particularly with a number of interesting light transports that most recently include the ERJ 135 and 145 regional turbofan jets. Early success came with the EMB-110 Bandeirante (Pioneer), whose design origins lie in the period before EMBRAER's creation. The EMB-110 was evolved under the leadership of Max Holste as a utility light transport to meet the multi-role requirements of the Brazilian ministry of aeronautics, and first flew in October 1968 in the form of a YC-95 prototype.

The Bandeirante is of all-metal construction and of typical light transport configuration with low-set cantilever wings, a conventional fuselage and tail unit, retractable tricycle landing gear, and two wing-mounted Pratt & Whitney Canada PT6A turboprop engines. The accommodation varies with model and role, but the EMB-110P2 is typical of the series with seating for 18–19 passengers. The type has been produced in a number of civil variants such as the 15-passenger EMB-110C feederliner, 7-passenger executive EMB-110E, all-cargo EMB-110K1, 18-passenger EMB-110P export model, a higher-capacity model with a fuselage stretch of 0.85 m (2 ft 9.5 in) in EMB-110P1 mixed or all-cargo and EMB-110P2 passenger subvariants, and the EMB-110P/41 higher-weight model in EMB-110P1/41 quick-change and EMB-110P2/41 passenger subvariants. The EMB-110P2A accommodates 21 passengers. Large-scale production for the Brazilian Air Force resulted in a number of C-95 utility transport, R-95 survey and SC-95 transport and search-and-rescue models. Also produced was the EMB-111 Patrulha coastal patrol version operated as the P-95 with search radar, a tactical navigation system, wingtip tanks and provision for underwing weapons. Bandeirante production ended in 1994.

EMB-110 Bandeirante

EMBRAER EMB-110 Bandeirante

EMBRAER EMB-110P1A BANDEIRANTE
Role: Short-range passenger/cargo transport
Crew/Accommodation: Two plus up to 19 passengers
Power Plant: Two 750-shp Pratt & Whitney PT6A-34 turboprops
Dimensions: Span 15.32 m (50.26 ft); length 15.08 m (49.47 ft); wing area 29.1 m² (313 sq ft)
Weights: Empty 3,630 kg (8,010 lb); MTOW 5,900 kg (13,010 lb)
Performance: Cruise speed 417 km/h (259 mph); operational ceiling up to 6,860 m (22,500 ft); range 1,898 km (1,179 miles)
Load: Up to 1,565-kg (3,450-lb) passenger version or 1,724-kg (3,800-lb) cargo-carrier

CASA C-212 AVIOCAR (Spain)

C-212 Aviocar

This simple yet effective light transport aircraft was developed to replace the Spanish Air Force's miscellany of obsolete transports. CASA conceived the type with the civil as well as military markets in mind, and thus schemed the type with STOL capability, highly cost-effective operation, great reliability, and simple maintenance. The resulting Aviocar is of all-metal construction and of typical airlifter configuration with an upswept tail unit above a rear ramp/door that provides straight-in access to the rectangular-section cabin; in the latest C-212 Series 300/400 forms, the cabin is 7.275 m (23.88 ft) long in passenger layout and 6.55 m (21.5 ft) in cargo layout, with a width at the floor of 2.1 m (6.92 ft) and 1.87 m (6.17 ft) respectively, and 1.8m (5.92 ft high. The tricycle landing gear is fixed, and the attachment of the main units to external fairings leaves the hold entirely unobstructed.

The first C-212 first flew in March 1971, and it soon became clear that CASA had designed the right type as orders arrived from third-world civil operators as well as air forces. Spanish production has been complemented by Indonesian construction by IPTN.

More than 460 have been ordered of all versions, going to over 50 civil operators plus military/government agencies in 24 countries. Until recently the Series 300 Aviocar was the current production version, the last with all electro-mechanical instrumentation. For the latest Series 400, first flown in 1997, display screens provided a 'glass cockpit' environment. The military version is designated C-212M, while specialized variants for maritime patrol, anti-submarine, counter-insurgency, search and rescue, electronic warfare and other missions carry the designations 'MP', 'ASW and 'DE Patrullero'.

CASA C-212 AVIOCAR Series 400, unless stated
Role: Short, rough field-going utility transport
Crew/Accommodation: Two plus up to 2–6 passengers
Power Plant: Two 900-shp AlliedSignal TPE331-10R-513C turboprops for Series 300 and two 925 shp TPE331-12JR-701Cs for Series 400
Dimensions: Span 20.275 m (66.5 ft); length 16.154m (53 ft); wing area 41 m² (441.3 sq ft)
Weights: Empty 3,780 kg (8.333 lb) for Series 300; MTOW 8,100 kg (17,857 lb)
Performance: Cruise speed 361 km/h (225 mph) at 3,050 m (10,000 ft); operational ceiling 7,925 m (26,000 ft); range 1,594 km (990miles)
Load: Up to 2,320 kg (5,115 lb) of passengers or 2,800 kg (6,172 lb) of cargo for Series 300, 2,950 kg (6,504 lb) for Series 400

U.S. Air Force CASA C-212 Aviocar

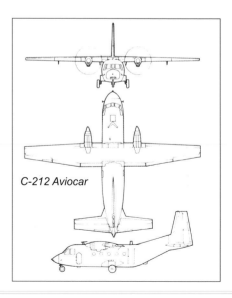

C-212 Aviocar

SHORTS 360 (United Kingdom)

Shorts 360

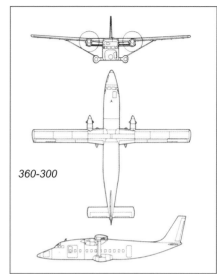

360-300

After the success of its SC.7 Skyvan series, Shorts decided to produce a larger and more refined derivative as the SD3-30 that then became the Shorts 330 with retractable tricycle landing gear and accommodation for 30 passengers. The type entered service in August 1976, and has proved most successful. Even so, the company appreciated that a larger-capacity type would broaden the series' market appeal, and the result was the Shorts 360. Market research indicated that capacity 20 per cent greater than that of the Shorts 330 was really desirable, and it was in 36-passenger configuration that the first Shorts 360 flew in June 1981 on the power of two 990-kW (1,327-shp) Pratt & Whitney Canada PT6A-65R turboprops.

The Shorts 360 is similar to its predecessor in being a high-wing monoplane with aerofoil-section lifting struts that brace the high aspect ratio wing to the sponsons that accommodate the main units of the retractable tricycle landing gear, but differs in having a single vertical tail in place of twin endplate surfaces, the lengthening of the forward fuselage by 0.91 m (3 ft 0 in) to allow the incorporation of an extra three-seat passenger row, and revision of the rear fuselage to improve aerodynamic form and permit the addition of another extra three-seat passenger row.

The Shorts 360 entered service in December 1982, and the type's only major improvement to date has been the introduction from 1986 of 1063-kW (1,424-shp) PT6A-65AR engines to produce the Shorts 360 Advanced. The maximum passenger payload is 3184 kg (7,020 lb), but in the type's alternative freight configuration the payload is somewhat increased to 3765 kg (8,300 lb).

Shorts 360

SHORTS 360-300
Role: Short-range passenger transport/freighter
Crew/Accommodation: Two and two cabin crew, plus up to 37 passengers
Power Plant: Two 1,424-shp Pratt & Whitney Canada PT6A-67R turboprops
Dimensions: Span 22.80 m (74.79 ft); length 21.58 m (70.94 ft): wing area 42.18 m² (454.00 sq ft)
Weights: Empty 7,870 kg (17.350 lb): MTOW 12,292 kg (27.100 lb)
Performance: Maximum speed 401 km/h (216 knots) at 3,048 m (10,000 ft); operational ceiling 3,930 m (12,900 ft); range 1,178 km (732 miles) with 36 passengers
Load: Up to 4,536 kg (10,000 lb) for freighter version.

CESSNA CARAVAN Series (U.S.A.)

Caravan I

OPPOSITE: Cesna 208 Grand Caravan

The Model 208 Caravan can be considered as Cessna's replacement for the elderly Model 185 Skywagon in the light utility transport role. The Model 208 offers its operators considerably greater capacity and performance, combined with more advanced features such as tricycle landing gear and the turboprop powerplant that runs off fuel that can be obtained anywhere in the world and also offers great reliability and better operating economics.

The first Model 208 flew in December 1982, and the first deliveries of production aircraft followed in 1985. The type can operate on sturdy wheeled or float landing gear, and is otherwise a conventional high-wing monoplane with a fuselage of slightly odd appearance because it has been optimized for the freight role in its long parallel upper and lower lines and large loading door in the side at easy loading/unloading height.

Current versions are the basic Caravan with a PT6A-114 engine, a cabin volume of 7.19 m³ (254 cu ft) plus optional 2.37 m³ (82.7 cu ft) external cargo pod, and with maximum seating for 14 persons; Caravan Floatplane, without external cargo pod but with baggage capacity in floats; the large Grand Caravan with a 675-shp PT6A-114A engine and cabin volume of 9.63 m³ (340 cu ft) plus a 3.16 m³ (111.5 cu ft) cargo pod; and Super Cargomaster, a cargo version of Grand Caravan. There is also a U-27A military version for U.S. foreign military sales programme.

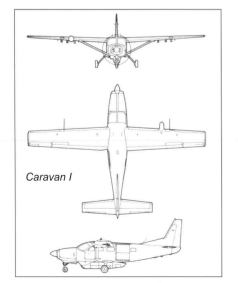

Caravan I

Cesna Caravan on floats

CESNA GRAND CARAVAN
Role: Commercial and military short field-capable utility transport
Crew/Accommodation: One plus up to 14 passengers
Power Plant: One 675-shp Pratt & Whitney Canada PT6A-114A turboprop
Dimensions: Span 15.88 m (52.08 ft); length 12.67 m (41.58 ft); wing area 25.96 m² (279.4 sq ft)
Weights: Empty 2,064 kg (4,550 lb); MTOW 3,856 kg (8,500 lb)
Performance: Cruise speed 324 km/h (202 mph) at 3,050 m (10,000 ft); operational ceiling 8,780 m (28,800 ft); range 1,783 km (1,109 miles)
Load: 1,921 kg (4,235 lb) useful load
Note: operational ceiling artificially restricted for passenger comfort

SAAB 340 and 2000 (Sweden)

Saab 340

addition to the two prototypes.
Certification was achieved in May 1984,
and the type entered service in the
following month. In November 1985,

In January 1980, Saab and Fairchild agreed to undertake the collaborative design and development of a turboprop-powered small transport for the civil market. This was initially known as the Saab-Fairchild SF-340 and planned in the form of a low-wing monoplane featuring a wing of high aspect ratio with long-span slotted flaps and retractable tricycle landing gear with twin wheels on each unit. Construction is of the all-metal type, with selective use of composite materials in some areas, and while Saab was

responsible for the fuselage, assembly and flight testing, Fairchild built the wings, tail unit and nacelles. The type was planned as a passenger transport with provision for 34 passengers in addition to a flight crew of two or three plus one flight attendant, but the cabin was schemed from the beginning for easy

completion in the passenger/freight or alternative 16-passenger executive/corporate transport roles.

The first machine flew in January 1983 with 1215-kW (1,630-hp) General Electric CT7-5A turboprops, and the certification programme was undertaken by the first production machine in

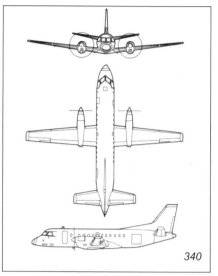

340

SAAB 340B Plus
Role: Regional passenger transport
Crew/Accommodation: Two and one cabin crew, plus up to 37 passengers
Power Plant: Two 1,870-shp General Electric CT7-9B turboprops
Dimensions: Span 21.44 m (70.33 ft); length 19.73 m (64.75 ft); wing area 41.81 m^2 (450.00 sq ft)
Weights: Empty 8,255 kg (18,135 lb); MTOW 13,155 kg (29,000 lb)
Performance: Typical cruise speed 528 km/h (328 mph); operational ceiling 7,620 m (25,000 ft); range 1,551 km (964 miles) with 35 passengers
Load: Up to 3,795 kg (8,366) lb

Saab 340

Fairchild indicated its unwillingness to continue with the programme, which thereupon became a Saab responsibility. Fairchild continued as a subcontractor until 1987, giving Saab time to complete additional construction facilities in Sweden. Early aircraft were limited to a maximum take-off weight of 11,794 kg (26,000 lb). Later machines were given CT7-5A2 turboprops driving larger-diameter propellers, and were cleared for higher weights. Since 1994 the standard version has been the 340B Plus (replacing the 340B of 1989–94 deliveries, which in turn had replaced the 340A). Production was expected to end in 1999, along with production of the 50–58-seat Saab 2000 (first flown in 1992).

A Saab 340A of Estonian Air

BOMBARDIER de HAVILLAND DASH 8Q (Canada)

Dash 8Q Series 100

The DHC-8 was developed to the same basic operating philosophy as the 50-passenger DHC-7, but was sized for 40 passengers in the commuterliner role. As with other de Havilland Canada transports, STOL capability was a primary consideration and the type was made attractive to potential operators by its fuel-economical turboprop engines driving propellers of large diameter, which turn slowly and so generate considerably less noise than fast-turning propellers of

smaller diameter. Other features include a large cargo-loading door in the port side of the fuselage aft of the wing, retractable tricycle landing gear with twin-wheel main units, and a T-tail keeping the tailplane well clear of the disturbed airflow behind the wings and propellers.

The first of four pre-production aircraft flew in June 1983. The type entered revenue-earning service in December 1984. The baseline variant is now the Dash 8Q Series 100A with 2,000-shp Pratt & Whitney Canada PW120A turboprops. In its basic commuterliner

layout, this carries a crew of three (two flight crew and one cabin attendant) and between 37–39 passengers. The same

Dash 8Q

de HAVILLAND CANADA DASH 8Q Series 100A
Role: Short field-capable passenger transport
Crew/Accommodation: Two, plus up to 39 passengers
Power Plant: Two 2,000-shp Pratt & Whitney Canada PW120A turboprops
Dimensions: Span 25.91 m (85 ft); length 22.25 m (73 ft); wing area 54.4 m² (585 sq ft)
Weights: Empty 10,310 kg (22,730 lb); MTOW 15,649 kg (34,500 lb)
Performance: Cruise speed 491 km/h (303 mph); operational ceiling 7,620 m (25,000 ft); range 1,365 km (848 miles)
Load: Up to 3,887 kg (8,570 lb)

QuantasLink Bombardier de Havilland Dash 8Q

Bombardier de Havilland Dash 8Q

seating capacities apply to the Series 100B (PW121 engines) and Series 200A and B (PW123 series engines), all engines being of 2,150-shp rating. Seating jumps to 50–56 for the Series 300A, B and E, whose PW123 series engines are rated at 2,380 shp, 2,500 shp and 2,380 shp respectively. With these versions, the fuselage length increases to 25.68 m (84,25 ft). The largest versions are the Series 400A and B with 5,071-shp PW150A engines, 32.84 m (107.75 ft) length fuselages and seating for 70 and 72–78 passengers respectively.

EMBRAER EMB-120 BRASILIA (Brazil)

EMB-120 Brasilia

The type was designated EMB-120 and later named Brasilia, and metal was cut for the first aircraft in May 1981. Six aircraft were produced for the test and certification programmes, and the first machine flew in July 1983 as a low-wing monoplane with a circular-section fuselage, a T-tail, retractable tricycle landing gear, and a powerplant of two wing-mounted 1118-kW (1,500-shp) Pratt & Whitney Canada PW115 turboprop engines. Though designed as a

The Brazilian government and EMBRAER were both highly encouraged by the EMB-110's penetration of the world market for commuterliners and feederliners. From this success, there emerged plans for an EMB-12X series of three pressurized types sharing a fuselage of common diameter but different lengths. Of these only the EMB-121 Xingu business transport actually entered production. In September 1979 EMBRAER decided to

move a step further up the size ladder with a pressurized 30-seat regional airliner, and this retained the overall configuration of the earlier 20-passenger EMB-120 Araguaia.

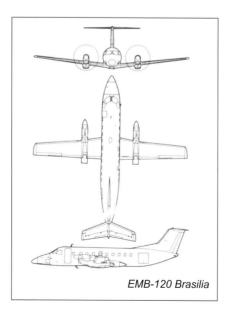

EMB-120 Brasilia

EMBRAER EMB-120 Brasilia.

EMBRAER EMB-120 BRASILIA
Role: Short-range passenger transport
Crew/Accommodation: Two and one cabin crew, plus up to 30 passengers
Power Plant: Two 1,600-shp Pratt & Whitney PW115 turboprops
Dimensions: Span 19.78 m (64.90 ft); length 20.00 m (65.62 ft); wing area 39.43 m² (424.42 sq ft)
Weights: Empty 6,878 kg (15,163 lb); MTOW 11,500 kg (25,353 lb)
Performance: Maximum speed 556 km/h (300 knots) at 7,620 m (25,000 ft); operational ceiling 9,083 m (29,800 ft); range 1,751 km (945 naut. miles) with 30 passengers

regional airliner with 30 seats, the Brasilia has a large cargo door in the port side of the rear fuselage, and is also available in freight and mixed-traffic versions, the former offering a payload of 3470-kg (7,650-lb) and the latter the capacity for 26 passengers and 900 kg (1,984 lb) of cargo. The Brasilia has an airstair door on the port side of the forward fuselage to reduce demand on external support at small airports, and for the same reason is also offered with a Garrett auxiliary power unit in the tail cone as an option. Later aircraft are powered by a pair of 1343-kW (1,800-shp) PW118 turboprops for improved performance at higher weights.

An EMBRAER EMB-120 Brasilia of United Express

305

CIVIL JET-ENGINED TRANSPORTS

The turboprop, turbojet and turbofan are related in that all are turbine engines and therefore 'jets'. Because of this, it is slightly misleading to title only this section as 'Jet'-engined transports, having separated out the propeller-driven aircraft. Yet, in the common usage of the term 'jet', most people think only of an engine without a propeller.

By the early years of World War II, several British companies were engaged in jet propulsion research, as were others abroad. In 1941 de Havilland began the design of what ultimately became the Goblin engine, used successfully on its Vampire fighter. The company also required a larger turbojet engine to power a proposed jet airliner, the engine and airliner eventually becoming the Ghost and Comet respectively. The Ghost adopted the same simple form of the smaller Goblin and Ghost 50 form was the first turbojet engine to obtain civil Type Approval. With Ghost 50s buried neatly into its wing roots, the de Havilland Comet first flew in 1949, gained it certificate of airworthiness in 1952 and entered commercial service later that year.

What was a British triumph soon turned to tragedy, however, when in March 1953 a Comet 1 on its delivery flight in stages to Australia crashed on take-off in Pakistan. Then, in May, a BOAC Comet 1 was lost near Calcutta, the first fatal accident for a turbojet airliner while on a scheduled service. British and foreign jetliner manufacturers learned from the tragedies.

While de Havilland developed and produced superior models of the Comet that later performed well in commercial use, Boeing had meantime flown the prototype of a jet which it had developed as a private venture against the perceived needs of the U.S.A.F. for a tanker/transport able to service present and future high-speed combat aircraft while suiting commercial applications. This was known as the Model 367-80 and, in 1954, was ordered for the U.S.A.F. as the KC-135. Importantly, in July 1955 Boeing gained the necessary official clearance to permit production of the commercial variant as the Model 707, to be built simultaneously with the military KC-135. Backed by vast military orders and with many potential worldwide customers for its jetliner, Boeing never looked back. Indeed, the last 707-based airframe did not leave the production line until 1992, although for the final decade production was at a low rate to satisfy only the need to provide airframes for specialized military aircraft. By then, of course, a wide range of Boeing jetliners had been created.

Despite early setbacks, Britain still managed to claim the first transatlantic passenger services using a turbojet airliner when BOAC inaugurated Comet 4 flights

OPPOSITE: The Boeing 747, one of the most successful of its type

ABOVE: The hugely impressive Airbus A380 is now in full production

between London and New York in October 1958. However, the Boeing 707 was in a class of its own and in 1959 was used for the first trans-Pacific jetliner service and, in the hands of Pan-American World Airways, the first round-the-world passenger jetliner service. Turbojet airliners from France, the Soviet Union and elsewhere soon got in on the act, and it was the combined talent of

France and Britain that a decade later went on to win the battle to produce a viable supersonic airliner against strong competition from the Soviet Union and to a lesser extent the U.S.A.

Today, the vast majority of the world's larger airliners are built by just two companies, Boeing of the U.S.A. and the rival European Airbus Industrie. Boeing, having taken over McDonnell

Douglas, has a very extensive range that spans from the smallest Model 717 to the huge Model 747 and includes the extremely important C-17 Globemaster III military transport and also the new 787 Dreamliner. Whereas Airbus has the new A380 added to its list of highly successful products, this being the world's first ultra-large, full double-deck, long-range airliner.

307

de HAVILLAND D.H.106 COMET (United Kingdom)

D.H. 106 Comet 4

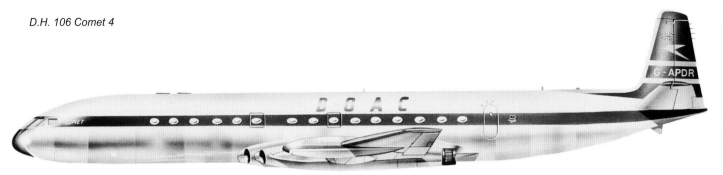

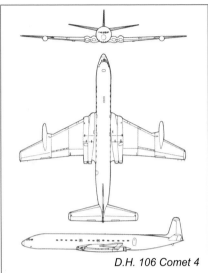

D.H. 106 Comet 4

The Comet was the world's first turbojet-powered airliner but failed to secure the financial advantages of this potentially world-beating lead because of technical problems. The type was planned from 1944 in response to the far-sighted Type IV specification resulting from the Brabazon Committee's wartime deliberations into the shape of British air transport needs after the end of World War II. It first flew in July 1949 with four de Havilland Ghost 50 centrifugal-flow turbojets. The type entered service in January 1952 as the Comet 1 with multi-wheel bogies rather than the two prototypes' single wheels on the main landing gear units. The Comet 1 was used initially as a freighter and only later as a passenger-carrying airliner, and deliveries to the British Overseas Airways Corporation totalled nine between January 1951 and September 1952; there followed 10 Comet 1As with greater fuel capacity.

One crash in 1953 and two in 1954 resulted in the type's grounding, and it was then established that fatigue failures at the corners of the rectangular window frames were to blame. Rounded windows were introduced on the 44-passenger Comet 2, of which 12 were built with a 0.91-m (3-ft) fuselage stretch and axial-flow Rolls-Royce Avon 503 engines, but these BOAC aircraft were diverted to the RAF as 70-passenger Comet C.Mk 2s. The Comet 3 was precursor to a transatlantic version that entered service as the 78-seat Cornet 4 with Avon 524 engines in May 1958, when the conceptually more advanced Boeing Model 707 and Douglas DC-8 were already coming to the fore of the market. Some 27 were built. Derivatives were the 18 shorter-range Comet 4Bs with a shorter wing but longer fuselage for 99 passengers, and the 29 Comet 4Cs combining the wing of the Comet 4 with the Comet 4B's fuselage.

de HAVILLAND D.H. 106 COMET 4
Role: Intermediate-range passenger transport
Crew/Accommodation: Three, plus four cabin
 crew and up to 78 passengers
Power Plant: Four 4,649-kgp (10,250-lb s.t.)
 Rolls-Royce Avon RA29 turbojets
Dimensions: Span 35 m (114.83 tt); length
 33.99 m (111.5 ft); wing area 197 m²
 (2,121 sq ft)
Weights: Empty 34,200 kg (75,400 lb); MTOW
 72,575 kg (160,000 lb)
Performance: Cruise speed 809 km/h (503 mph)
 at 12,802 m (42,000 ft); operational ceiling
 13,411+ m (44,000+ft); range 5,190 km (3,225
 miles) with full load
Load: Up to 9,206 kg (20,286 lb)

A Comet 4B of British European Airways

BOEING 707 and 720 (U.S.A.)

Boeing 707-300C

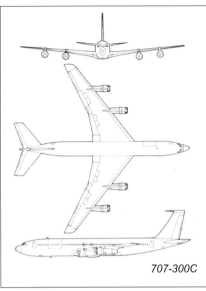

707-300C

Though preceded into service by the de Havilland Comet, the Model 707 must rightly be regarded as the world's first effective long-range jet transport. In an exceptionally bold technical and commercial move, Boeing decided during August 1952 to develop, as a private venture, the prototype of an advanced transport with military as well as civil applications. This Model 367-80 prototype first flew in July 1954 with 4309-kg (9,500-lb) thrust Pratt & Whitney JT3P turbojets, and in October of the same year the company's

faith in its capabilities was rewarded by the first of many orders for the KC-135A inflight refuelling tanker derived from the 'Dash 80'. Once the U.S. Air Force had given clearance, the company then started marketing the type as the 707 civil transport with a slightly wider fuselage, and in October 1955 Pan American took the bold step of ordering the 707 for its long-haul domestic network in the United States.

A total of 1,010 707s and closely related 720s was built in the last decade (1982-92), but only as airframes for military special versions, while U.S.A.F. KC-135s and C-135/137s were delivered during 1957–66 (808 aircraft) plus 12 to France. The major commercial variants were the Model 707-120 transcontinental airliner with 6123-kg (13,500-lb) thrust Pratt & Whitney JT3C turbojets, the Model 707-120B with JT3D turbofans, the Model 707-220 with 7938-kg (17,500-lb) thrust JT4A turbojets, the Model 707-320 intercontinental airliner with longer wing and fuselage plus 7938-kg (17,500-lb thrust JT4A turbojets, the

Model 707-320B with aerodynamic refinements and turbofans, the Model 707-320C convertible or freighter variants with turbofans, and the Model 707-420 with 7983-kg (17,600-lb) thrust Rolls-Royce Conway turbofans. The model 720 was aerodynamically similar to the Model 707-120 but had a shorter fuselage plus a new and lighter structure optimized for the intermediate-range

role. There was also a Model 720B turbofan-powered variant.

BOEING 707-320C

Role: Long-range passenger/cargo transport
Crew/Accommodation: Three, plus five/six cabin crew, plus up to 189 passengers
Power Plant: Four 8,618 kgp (19,000 lb s.t.) Pratt & Whitney JT3D-7 turbofans
Dimensions: Span 44.42 m (145.71 ft); length 45.6 m (152.92 ft); wing area 283.4 m2 (3050 sq ft)
Weights: Empty 66,224 kg (146,000 lb); MTOW 151,315 kg (333,600 lb)
Performance: Cruise speed 886 km/h (550 mph) at 8,534 m (28,000 ft); operational ceiling 11,885 m (39,000 ft); range 6,920 km (4,300 miles) with maximum payload
Load: Up to 41,453 kg (91,390 lb)

Egypt Air Boeing 707

SUD-EST CARAVELLE (France)

Caravelle VI-N

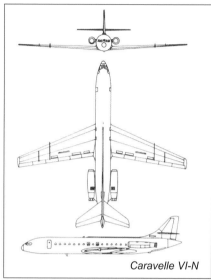

Caravelle VI-N

The Caravelle was France's first jet-powered airliner, the world's first short/medium-range jet airliner, and also the world's first airliner with its engines pod-mounted on the sides of the rear fuselage. The type resulted from a 1951 French civil aviation ministry requirement, and out of submissions from six manufacturers the S.E.210 was selected for hardware development in the form of two prototypes. The first of these flew in May 1955 with two 4536-kg (10,000-lb) thrust Rolls-Royce Avon RA.26 turbojets and had

accommodation for 52 passengers.

Successful evaluation paved the way for the Caravelle I with its fuselage lengthened by 1.41 m (4 ft 7.5 in) for 64 passengers. The 19 Caravelle Is had 4763-kg (10,500-lb) Avon RA. 29 Mk 522s, while the 13 Caravelle IAs had Avon RA.29/1 Mk 526s. Next came 78 Caravelle IIIs with 5307-kg (11,700-lb) thrust Avon RA.29/3 Mk 527s, and all but one of the Mk I aircraft were upgraded to this standard. The Caravelle VI followed in two forms: the 53 VI-Ns had 5534-kg (12,200-lb) Avon RA.29/ 6 Mk 531s and the 56 VI-Rs had thrust-reversing 5715-kg (12,600-lb) thrust Avon Mk 532R or 533R engines.

Considerable refinement went into the Super Caravelle 10B, of which 22 were built. This first flew in March 1964 with extended wing roots, double-slotted flaps, a larger tailplane, a lengthened fuselage for 104 passengers, and 6350-kg (14,000-lb) thrust Pratt & Whitney JT8D-7 turbofans. The 20 Super Caravelle 10Rs used the Mk VI airframe with JT8D-7 engines, and 20 were built. The final models were the six Caravelle

IIRs for mixed freight and passenger operations, and the 12 Caravelle 12s lengthened for 140-passenger accommodation and powered by 6577-kg (14,500-lb) thrust JT8D-9s.

AÉROSPATIALE (SUD AVIATION) CARAVELLE 12

Role: Short-range passenger transport
Crew/Accommodation: Two, four cabin crew, plus up to 140 passengers
Power Plant: Two 6,577-kgp (14,500-lb s.t.) Pratt & Whitney JT8D-9 turbofans
Dimensions: Span 34.30 m (112.5 ft); length 36.24 m (118.75 ft); wing area 146.7 m² (1,579 sq ft)
Weights: Empty 31,800 kg (70,107 lb); MTOW 56,699 kg (125,000 lb)
Performance: Maximum speed 785 km/h (424 knots) at 7,620 m (25,000 ft); operational ceiling 12,192 m (40,000+ ft); range 1,870 km (1,162 miles) with full payload
Load: Up to 13,200 kg (29,101 lb)

Caravelle 12

DOUGLAS DC-8 (U.S.A.)

DC-8-50

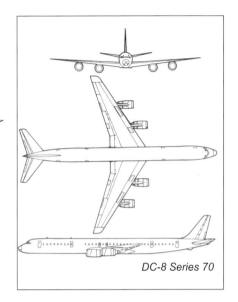

DC-8 Series 70

A fter planning the DC-7D with four 4273-kW (5,730-shp) Rolls-Royce Tyne turboprop engines, Douglas decided instead to challenge the Boeing Model 707 in the market for turbojet-powered airliners. The result was the DC-8, a worthy type that nevertheless trailed the Model 707 because of its later start and the availability of only a single fuselage length. In an effort to catch up with the Model 707, Douglas produced nine test aircraft with three different types of engine, and the first of these

flew in May 1958. Total production of the initial five series was 294 built over a period of nine years. These series were the DC-8-10 domestic model with 6123-kg (13,500-lb) thrust Pratt & Whitney

JT3C-6 turbojets, the similar DC-8-20 with uprated engines for 'hot-and-high' routes, the DC-8-30 intercontinental model, typically with 7620-kg (16,800-lb) thrust JT4A-9 turbojets, the similar DC-

DOUGLAS DC-8-63
Role: Long-range passenger transport
Crew/Accommodation: Four and four cabin
  crew, plus up to 251 passengers
Power Plant: Four 8,618-kgp (19,000-lb s.t.)
  Pratt & Whitney JT3D-7 turbofans
Dimensions: Span 45.24 m (148.42 ft);
  length 57.1 m (187 ft); wing area 271.93
  m² (2,927 sq ft)
Weights: Empty 71,401 kg (157,409 lb);
  MTOW 158,760 kg (350,000 lb)
Performance: Cruise speed 959 km/h (517
  knots) at 10,973 m (36,000 ft); operational
  ceiling 12,802 m (42,000 ft); range
  6,301 km (3,400 naut. miles) with full
  payload
Load: Up to 30,126 kg (55,415 lb)

Douglas DC-8

311

8-40 with 7938-kg (17,500-lb) thrust Rolls-Royce Conway Mk 509 turbofans, and the DC-8-50 with Pratt & Whitney JT3D turbofans and a rearranged cabin for 189 passengers. The DC-8F Jet Trader was based on the DC-8-50 but available in all-freight or convertible-freight/passenger layouts.

From 1967 production was of the JT3D-powered Super Sixty series, of which 262 were produced. This series comprised the DC-8 Super 61 with the fuselage stretched by 11.18 m (36 ft 8 in) for 259 passengers, the DC-8 Super 62 with span increased by 1.83 m (6 ft 0 in) and length by 2.03 m (6 ft 8 in) for 189

passengers carried over very long range, and the DC-8 Super 63 combining the Super 61's fuselage and Super 62's wing. These models could be delivered in all-passenger, all-freight, or convertible-freight/passenger configurations. Finally came the Super Seventy series, which comprised Super 61, 62, and 63 aircraft

converted with General Electric/SNECMA CFM56 turbofans with the designations DC-8 Super 71, 72, and 73 respectively.

ABOVE & OPPOSITE: NASA DC-8
Airborne Science Program research aircraft

VICKERS VC10 (United Kingdom)

VC10

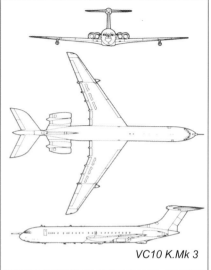

VC10 K.Mk 3

In 1957 the British Overseas Airways Corporation issued a requirement for an airliner able to carry a 15422-kg (34,000-lb) payload over a range of 6437 km (4,000 miles) on the operator's Commonwealth routes. Vickers responded with its Type 1100 design. This was optimized for BOAC's route network, which included many 'hot-and-high' airports with short runways, with a large wing left uncluttered for its primary lifting task by the location of the four engines in paired pods on the sides of the rear fuselage below the tall T-tail. Other features were the retractable tricycle landing gear and six-abreast seating in the pressurized circular-section fuselage.

The first VC10 flew in July 1962, and the type entered service with BOAC in April 1964 with 9525-kg (21,000-lb) thrust Rolls-Royce Conway RCo. 42 turbofans, a crew of 10 and a payload of between 115 and 135 passengers. BOAC took 12 such aircraft, and other customers were Ghana Airways (two), British United Airways (three), and the Royal Air Force (14VC10 C.Mk Is with a revised wing, greater fuel capacity and Conway RCo.43 engines).The prototype was also revised to production standard and was then sold to Laker Airways.

Development evolved the Type 1150 that entered production as the Super VC 10 with Conway RCo.43 engines, greater fuel capacity and a fuselage lengthened by 3.96 m (13 ft 0 in). BOAC took 17 such aircraft and East African Airways another five. Because of its large wing, the VC 10 had inferior operating economics to the Boeing Model 707, and most airports upgraded their facilities to cater for the Model 707 and Douglas DC-8.

The RAF bought from airlines VC10s and Super VC 10s for conversion as VC10 K.Mks 2, 3 and 4 inflight refuelling tankers (14 aircraft). Many VC 10 C.Mk Is were also adapted as two-point tanker transports with the designation VC10 C.Mk1(K).

VICKERS/BRITISH AIRCRAFT CORPORATION SUPER VC-10

Role: Long-range passenger transport
Crew/Accommodation: Five and seven cabin crew, plus up to 180 passengers
Power Plant: Four 9,888-kgp (21,800-lb) Rolls-Royce Conway RC0.43D Mk 550 turbofans
Dimensions: Span 44.55 m (146.17 ft); length 52.32 m (171.66 ft); wing area 272.40 m² (2,932 sq ft)
Weights: Empty 71,940 kg (158,594 lb); MTOW 151,950 kg (335,000 lb)
Performance: Maximum speed 935 km/h (505 knots) at 9,449 m (31,000 ft); operational ceiling 11,582 m (38,000 ft); range 7,596 km (4,720 miles) with full payload
Load: Up to 27,360 kg (60,321 lb)

Vickers VC10

BOEING 727 (U.S.A.)

Model 727-100

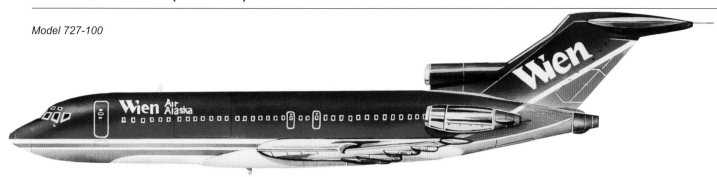

The Model 727 was conceived as a short/medium-range partner to the Model 707, with the primary task of bringing passengers to the larger airports used by the long-range type. The type was designed for as much construction commonality as possible with the Model 707, and among other features was designed to use the same fuselage cross-section. The design team considered 70 concepts before finalizing its concept for the Model 727 as a fairly radical type able to meet the apparently conflicting requirements for high cruising speed at the lowest possible altitude and minimum seat/mile costs. Other factors that had to

be taken into account were frequent take-off/landing cycles, the need for fast 'turn-round' time, and the need for low take-off noise so that the type could use airports close to urban areas. The Model 727 emerged with three rear-mounted engines, a T-tail, and an uncluttered wing with triple-slotted flaps along its trailing edges. Independence of airport services was ensured by an auxiliary

power unit and a ventral airstair/door.

The Model 727 first flew in February 1963, and production has reached 1,831 in two main variants. The basic variant is the Model 727-100, which was also

produced in convertible and quick-change convertible derivatives. Then came the Model 727-200 lengthened by 6.1 m (20 ft) and featuring the structural modifications required for operation at higher weights; the latest version is the Advanced 727-200 with a performance data computer system to improve operating economy and safety. Also operational in smaller numbers is the Model 727F, which was produced to the special order of small-package operator Federal Express; this variant has no fuselage windows and can carry 26,649-kg (58,750-lb) of freight.

BOEING 727-200
Role: Intermediate-range passenger transport
Crew/Accommodation: Three and four cabin crew, plus up to 189 passengers
Power Plant: Three 7,257-kgp (16,000-lb s.t.) Pratt & Whitney JT8D-17 turbofans
Dimensions: Span 32.9 m (108 ft); length 46.7 m (153.17 ft); wing area 153.3 m² (1,650 sq ft)
Weights: Empty 46,164 kg (101,773 lb); MTOW 95,028 kg (209,500 lb)
Performance: Cruise speed 982 km/h (530 knots) at 7,620 m (25,000 ft); operational ceiling 11,582+ m (38,000+ ft); range 5,371 km (2,900 naut. miles)
Load: Up to 18,597 kg (41,000 lb)

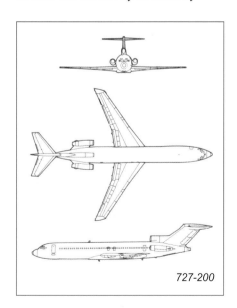

727-200

Boeing 727F

BRITISH AIRCRAFT CORPORATION ONE-ELEVEN (United Kingdom)

BAC One-Eleven 500

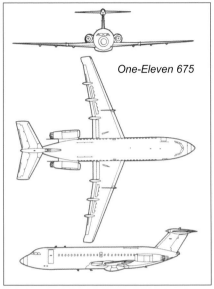

One-Eleven 675

This pioneering airliner was conceived as the Hunting H.107 short-range airliner with accommodation for 59 passengers, and to provide the type with excellent field performance and low cabin noise levels it was decided to use aft-mounted engines; this left the wing uncluttered and therefore better able to perform its primary function, and dictated the use of a T-tail to lift the tailplane well clear of the jet exhausts. Hunting was bought by BAC and the H.107 became the BAC 107. There was little airline enthusiasm for an airliner with so small a passenger payload, and the basic concept was therefore enlarged to provide 79-

passenger capacity. This was redesignated the BAC 111, and later the One-Eleven. The design was finalized with a circular-section pressurized fuselage with a ventral airstair let into the underside of the fuselage under the tail unit, a low-set wing of modest sweep with Fowler trailing-edge flaps, and a variable-incidence tailplane at the very top of the vertical tail surfaces.

The prototype flew in August 1963 with two 4722-kg (10,410-lb) thrust Rolls-Royce Spey Mk 506 turbofans, and was lost in a fatal crash some two months later

as a result of a 'deep stall' occasioned by the aft engine/T-tail configuration. After this problem had been cured, useful sales were secured for the basic One-Eleven Series 200 with Spey Mk 506s, the One-Eleven Mk 300 with 5171-kg (11,400-lb) thrust Spey Mk 51 Is, the generally similar but higher-weight One-Eleven Mk 400 for U.S. airlines, the stretched One-Eleven Series 500 for 119 passengers, and the 'hot and high' One-Eleven Series 475 with the fuselage of the Series 400 plus the wings and powerplant of the Series 500. The

One-Eleven production line was bought by Romaero in Romania where nine One-Elevens were built for a short time, the first Romaero 1-11 flying in 1982.

BRITISH AIRCRAFT CORPORATION ONE-ELEVEN 500
Role: Short-range passenger transport
Crew/Accommodation: Two and three/four cabin crew, plus up to 119 passengers
Power Plant: Two 5,692-kgp (12,500-lb s.t.) Rolls-Royce Spey 512-DW turbofans
Dimensions: Span 28.5 m (92.5 ft); length 32.61 m (107 ft); wing area 95.78 m² (1,031 sq ft) Weights: Empty 24,758 kg (54,582 lb); MTOW 47,000 kg (104,500 lb)
Performance: Maximum speed 871 km/h (470 knots) at 6,400 m (21,000 ft); range 2,380 km (1,480 miles) with full passenger load
Load: Up to 11,983 kg (26,418 lb) including belly cargo

British Aircraft Corporation One-Eleven

ILYUSHIN Il-62 (U.S.S.R.)

Il-62M

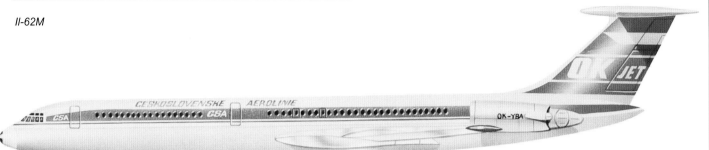

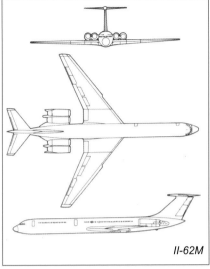

Il-62M

The Il-62 (known to NATO as 'Classic') was developed as a long-range airliner to complement and then to supplant the Tupolev Tu-114 on domestic and international routes. The Soviets specified high levels of comfort and performance in the hope that this would result in a type that would gain a measure of the export success that had eluded earlier Soviet airliners. The first U-62 flew in january 1963 with four 7,500-kg (16,535-lb) thrust Lyulka Al-7 turbojets as the planned 10,500-kg (23,150-lb) thrust Kuznetsov nK-8-4 turbofans were not yet ready for flight. Clearly the design had been influenced by that of the Vickers vC10 in its configuration, with a large wing, a T-tail, rear-mounted engines, and retractable tricycle landing gear. This similarity was also carried over into the flight test programme for, like the vC10, the 11-62 required lengthy development for the problem of its deep-stall tendency to be overcome. The nK-4 turbofans were introduced later in the test programme, which involved two prototypes and three pre-production aircraft.

The initial Il-62 production version entered service in September 1967 with accommodation for between 168 and 186 passengers, and cascade-type thrust reversers were fitted only on the outer engines. In 1971 there appeared the Il-62M with 11,000-kg (24,250-lb) thrust Soloviev d-30KU turbofans with clamshell-type thrust reversers, and the improved specific fuel consumption of this more advanced engine type combined with additional fuel capacity (a fuel tank in the fin) to improve the payload/range performance to a marked degree over that of the Il-62. Other improvements were a revised flight deck, new avionics, and wing spoilers that could be operated differentially for roll control. The Il-62MK of 1978 introduced structure, landing gear and control system modifications to permit operations at higher weights. All production ended in the mid-1990s.

ILYUSHIN Il-62M CLASSIC

Role: Long-range passenger transport
Crew/Accommodation: Five, four cabin crew, plus up to 186 passengers
Power Plant: Four 11,500-kgp (25,350-lb s.t.) Soloviev D-30KU turbofans
Dimensions: Span 43.2 m (141.75 ft); length 53.12 m (174.28 ft); wing area 279.6 m² (3,010 sq ft) Weights: Empty 69,400 kg (153,000 lb); TOW 165,000 kg (363,760 lb)
Performance: Cruise speed 900 km/h (485 knots) at 12,000 m (39,370 ft); operational ceiling 13,000+ m (42,650+ ft); range 8,000 km (4,317 naut. miles) with full payload
Load: Up to 23,000 kg (50,700 lb)

Ilyushin Il-62M

MD-80

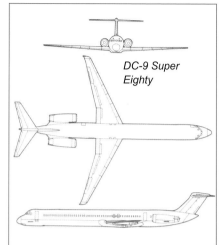

DC-9 Super Eighty

Planned as a medium-range partner to the DC-8, the DC-9 was then recast as a short-range type to compete with the BAC One-Eleven. Having learned the sales disadvantages of a single-length fuselage with the DC-8, Douglas planned the DC-9 with length options, and decided to optimize the efficiency of the wing by pod-mounting engines on the fuselage sides under a T-tail. The type first flew in February 1965 and built up an excellent sales record based on low operating costs and fuselage length tailored to customer requirements. The success of the type also demanded so high a level of production investment, however, that Douglas was forced to merge with McDonnell.

The variants of the initial production series were the DC-9-10 with Pratt & Whitney JT8D turbofans and 90 passengers, the DC-9-15 with uprated engines, the DC-9-20 for 'hot-and-high' operations with more power and span increased by 1.22 m (4 ft 0 in), the DC9-30 with the fuselage stretched by 4.54 m (14 ft 10.75 in) for 119 passengers, the DC-9-40 with a further stretch of 1.92 m (6 ft 3.5 in) for 132 passengers, and the DC-9-50 with more power and a further stretch of 2.44 m (8 ft 0 in) for 139 passengers. Developments for the military were the C-9A nightingale aeromedical transport based on the DC-9-30, and the C-9B Skytrain II fleet

DOUGLAS DC-9-10

Role: Short-range passenger transport
Crew/Accommodation: Two and three cabin crew, plus up to 90 passengers
Power Plant: Two 6,580-kgp (14,500-lb s.t.) Pratt & Whitney JT8D-9 turbofans
Dimensions: Span 27.2 m (89.42 ft); length 31.8 m (104.42 ft); wing area 86.8 m² (934.3 sq ft)
Weights: Empty 23,060 kg (50,848 lb); MTOW 41,142 kg (90,700 lb)
Performance: Cruise speed 874 km/h (471 knots) at 9,144 m (30,000 ft); operational ceiling 12,497 m (41,000 ft); range 2,038 km (1,100 naut. miles) with maximum payload
Load: Up to 8,707 kg (19,200 lb)

MD-83

logistic transport combining features of the DC-9-30 and -40. Production totalled 976, and from 1975 McDonnell Douglas offered the DC-9 Super Eighty series with a longer fuselage and the refanned JT8D (-200 series) turbofan. This first flew in October 1979, and variants became the DC-9 Super 81 (now MD-81) with JT8D-209s and a fuselage stretched by 4.34 m (14ft 3 in) for 172 passengers, the DC-9 Super 82 (now MD-82) with JT8D-217s, the DC-9 Super 83 (now MD-83) with JT8D-219s and extra fuel, the DC-9 Super 87 (now MD-87) with JT8D-217Bs and a fuselage shortened by 5.0 m (16 ft 5 in), and the DC-9 Super 88 (now MD-88) development of the MD82 with JT8D-217Cs and an electronic flight instruments system combined with a flight-management computer and inertial navigation system. Mcdonnell also produced the MD-90 series, based on the MD-8C but with electronic engine controls, modernized flight deck, a fuselage lengthened to 46.51 m (152.6 ft), Internation Aero Engines turbofans and many other improvements. First flown in 1993, it is now also a Boeing type since the merger of Boeing and Mcdonnell Douglas.

Alitalia MD-80 taxiiing on runway

BOEING 737 (U.S.A.)

Model 737-200

737-400

The short/medium range Model 737 became the small brother to the 707 and 727, and completed the Boeing family of airliners covering the full spectrum of commercial operations at the time of the company's November 1964 decision to design such a type. The Model 737 is currently the world's best-selling airliner, with more than 4,000 ordered. Originally intended for short sectors, the Model 737 first flew in April 1967. Despite the somewhat different appearance of the two aircraft, Boeing managed about 60 per cent commonality of structure and systems between the Models 727 and 737.

The initial variant was the Model 737-100 for 100 passengers, but only a few were built before production switched to the larger 737-200 for 130 passengers, offering also convertible, quick-change convertible, and advanced derivatives. In 1984 came the 737-300 with an advanced technology flight deck, 9072-kg (20,000-lb) thrust CFM56-3 turbofans (instead of the previous Pratt & Whitney JT8Ds) and further lengthening for 128–149 passengers, while in February 1988 the 737-400 flew offering up to 168 passengers in a 3.05-m (10-ft) longer fuselage, with the basic engine option of

BOEING 737-300
Role: Short/medium-range passenger transport
Crew/Accommodation: Two and four cabin crew, plus 149 passengers
Power Plant: Two 9,072-kgp (20,000-lb s.t.) CFM International CFM56-3B or 3C1 turbofans
Dimensions: Span 28.9 m (94.75 ft); length 33.4 m (109.58 ft); wing area 105.44 m² (1,135 sq ft)
Weights: Empty 32,704 kg (72,100 lb); MTOW 56,472 kg (124,500 lb)
Performance: Cruise speed 908 km/h (564 mph) at 7,925 m (26,000 ft); operational ceiling 11,278 m (37,000 ft); range 4,184 km (2,600 miles) with 124 passengers
Load: 16,030 kg (35,270 lb)

Boeing 737

9,980-kg (22,000-lb) CFM 56-35s. The 737-500 for 108–132 passengers flew in June 1989, the basic engines derated to 8,391-kg (18,500-lb) thrust. Next

generation versions are the 108–140-passenger 737-600, 128–149-passenger 737-700, 162–189-passenger 737-800 and largest 737-900, offering CFM56-7B

engines on larger wings. The 737-700 and -800 first flew in 1997.

Air-Berlin Boeing 737

321

FOKKER F.28 FELLOWSHIP and 100 (Netherlands)

F.28 Fellowship Mk 1000

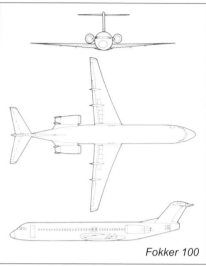

Fokker 100

The F.28 Fellowship was designed as a complement to the turboprop-powered F.27 with slightly higher passenger capacity and considerably improved performance through the use of a twin-turbofan powerplant. Initial design work began in 1960, and Fokker opted for a T-tail configuration and rear-mounted Rolls-Royce Spey engines to provide an uncluttered wing. The first of three F.28 prototypes flew in May 1967, and the certification and delivery of the initial production machines were achieved at the same time in February 1969.

The first production version was the F.28 Mk 1000 for 65 passengers on two 4468-kg (9,850-lb) thrust Spey Mk 555-15s, and a subvariant was the F.28 Mk 1000C with a large cargo door on the port side of the forward fuselage for all-freight or mixed-freight/passenger services. Subsequent models have been the F.28 Mk 2000 with its fuselage stretched by 2.21 m (7 ft 3 in) for 79 passengers, and the F.28 Mks 3000 and 4000 with the fuselages of the Mks 1000 and 2000 respectively, span increased by 1.57 m (6 ft 11.5 in), and two 4491-kg (9,900-lb) thrust Spey Mk 555-15Ps.

In order to keep the type matched to current airline demands, in November 1983 Fokker announced an updated and stretched Fokker 100 version. This was given a revised wing of greater efficiency and spanning 3.00 m (9 ft 9.5 in) more than that of the F.28, a larger tailplane, a fuselage stretched by 5.74 m (18 ft 10in) by plugs forward and aft of the wing to increase capacity to 107 passengers, and Rolls-Royce Tay 620-15 or Tay 650 turbofans. At the same time, the interior was completely remodelled, composite materials were introduced, and an electronic flight instrument system was introduced. The first Fokker 100 flew in November 1986, and 278 were delivered before production was brought to an end in 1997 following the company's bankruptcy.

OPPOSITE: A KLM Cityhopper Fokker 100

Fokker F.28

FOKKER 100
Role: Short-range jet passenger transport
Crew/Accommodation: Two and four cabin crew, plus up to 109 passengers
Power Plant: Two 6,282-kgp (13,850-lb s.t.) Rolls-Royce Tay 620-15 or 6,850-kgp (15,100-lb s.t.) Tay 650 turbofans
Dimensions: Span 28.08 m (92.13 ft); length 35.53 m (116.57 ft); wing area 93.5 m² (1,006.5 sq ft) Weights: Empty 24,593 kg (54,218 lb) with Tay 620s; MTOW 43,090 kg (95,000 lb) standard
Performance: Cruise speed 765 km/h (475 mph) at 8,534 m (28,000 ft); operational ceiling 10,668 m (35,000 ft); range 2,389 km (1,485 miles) at standard MTOW with 107 passengers and Tay 620 engines
Load: 11,242–12,147 kg (24,784–26,780 lb) with Tay 620s

BOEING 747 (U.S.A.)

Model 747-100

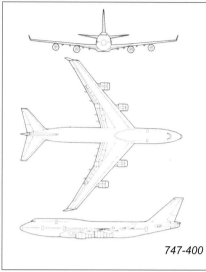

747-400

K nown universally as the 'Jumbo Jet', the Model 747 introduced the 'wide-body' airliner concept. It is the world's largest airliner, and is the mainstay of the Western world's long-range high-capacity routes. After failing to win the U.S. Air Force's CX-HLS competition for a long-range logistic freighter, Boeing decided to capitalize on its work by developing the basic concept into a civil transport. Initial thoughts centred on a 430-seat type with a 'double bubble' fuselage configuration in which each lobe would be about 4.57m (15 ft) wide. This failed to secure major airline interest, so Boeing finally opted for a 'big brother' to the Model 707 using basically the same layout but with a fuselage large enough to accommodate a cabin 6.13 m (20 ft 1.5 in) wide and 56.39 m (185 ft 0 in) long. The type first flew in February 1969 and, with more than 1,300 aircraft ordered, the Model 747 is still in development and production with a choice of General Electric, Pratt & Whitney and Rolls-Royce turbofan engines.

The main variants have been the initial Model 747-100 with a maximum weight of 322,051 kg (710,000 lb) and strengthened Model 747-100B, the Model 747-200 (also offered in convertible and freighter versions) with further structural strengthening, greater fuel capacity and uprated engines for a maximum weight of 377,842 kg (833,000 lb), the Model 747SP long-range version with the fuselage reduced in length by 14.35 m (47 ft 1 in) for a maximum of 440 passengers, the Model 747SR short-range version of the Model 747-100B with features to cater for the higher frequency of take-off/landing cycles, the Model 747-300 with a stretched upper deck increasing this area's accommodation from 16 first-class to 69 economy-class passengers, and the current Model 747-400 with structural improvements to reduce weight, a two-crew flight deck with the latest cockpit displays and instrumentation, extended wings with drag-reducing winglets on the international versions, lean-burn turbofans, and extra fuel for longer range.

OPPOSITE: Virgin Atlantic Boeing 747-400

BOEING 747-400

Role: Long-range passenger/cargo transport
Crew/Accommodation: Two, plus 420 passengers in a 3-class configuration or other layouts up to 568 passengers.
Power Plant: Four 26,263-kgp (57,900-lb s.t.) General Electric CF6-80C2B or 25,741-kgp (56,750-lb s.t.) Pratt & Whitney PW 4000 series or 26,308-kgp (58,000-lb s.t.) Rolls-Royce RB211-524G or higher rated H turbofans.
Dimensions: Span 64.44 m (211.4 ft); length 70.66 m (231.83 ft); wing area 520.25 m² (5,600 sq ft)
Weights: Empty 182,256 kg (402,400 lb) typically; MTOW up to 394,625 kg (870,000 lb)
Performance: Cruise speed 939 km/h (507 knots) at 10.670 m (35,000 ft); cruise altitude 12,500 m (41,000 ft); design range up to13,418 km (8,342 miles)
Load: Un to 65.230 kg (143,800 lb) with cargo

Boeing 747-400

AÉROSPATIALE/BAC CONCORDE (France/United Kingdom)

Concorde

OPPOSITE: An Air France Concorde

City from Paris on 30 May 2003. British Airways retired its Concorde fleet on 24 October 2003.

The world's first supersonic air transport, the Concorde originated from separate French and British projects which were considered too expensive for single-nation development. The two efforts were therefore amalgamated in 1962 by an inter-governmental agreement. The French and British airframe contractors were Sud-Aviation and the British Aircraft Corporation, which eventually became parts of Aérospatiale and British Aerospace respectively. The project matured as a medium-sized type with a delta wing and a slender fuselage; the wing has an ogival leading edge, and the aerodynamically clean forward section of the fuselage has a 'droop snoot' arrangement to provide the crew with an adequate field of vision for take-off and landing.

The French were responsible for the wings, the rear cabin section, the flying controls, and the air-conditioning, hydraulic, navigation and radio systems; the British were tasked with the three forward fuselage sections, the rear fuselage and vertical tail, the engine nacelles and ducts, the engine installation, the electrical, fuel and oxygen systems, and the noise and thermal insulation. A similar collaborative arrangement was organized between Rolls-Royce and SNECMA for the design and construction of the engines.

The first of two prototypes, one from each country, flew in March 1969, and these two machines had slightly shorter nose and tail sections than later aircraft. The type has proved an outstanding technical success, but political and environmental opposition meant that only two pre-production and 14 production aircraft were built.

The 2000 Paris air crash largely saw the end of Concorde's service. Air France made its final commercial Concorde, landing in the United States in New York

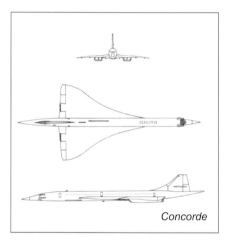

Concorde

AÉROSPATIALE/BAC CONCORDE
Role: Supersonic passenger transport
Crew/Accommodation: Three and four cabin crew, plus up to 144 passengers
Power Plant: Four 17,260-kgp (38,050-lb s.t.) Rolls-Royce/SNECMA Olympus 593 Mk610 turbojets with reheat
Dimensions: Span 25.6 m (84 ft): Length 67.17 m (203.96 ft); wing area 358.25 m² (3,856 sq ft)
Weights: Empty 77,110 kg (170,000 lb); MTOW 181,400 kg (400,000 lb)
Performance: Maximum speed 2,333 km/h (1,450 knots) Mach 2.05 at 16,600 m (54,500 ft); operational ceiling 18,288 m (60,000 ft); range 7,215 km (4,483 miles)
Load: Typically 11,340 kg (25,000 lb)

A British Airways Concorde

DC-10-10

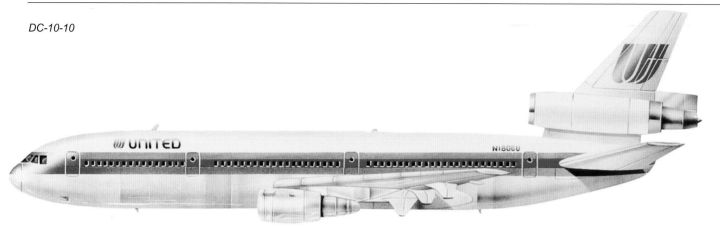

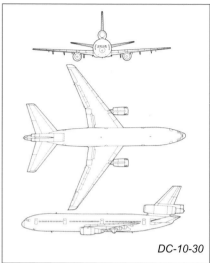

DC-10-30

Douglas began work on the design of the DC-10 in 1966 in response to a requirement of American Airlines for a wide-body airliner offering the same sort of range as the Boeing Model 747 with a smaller payload. With orders for 55 aircraft and options for another 55 received, Douglas launched production in April 1968. The design matured as a basically conventional low-wing monoplane with swept flying surfaces,

tricycle landing gear and three turbofan engines (one under each wing and the third on a vertical pylon above the rear fuselage with the vertical tail above it).

The first example flew in August 1970, by which time Douglas had amalgamated with McDonnell. A total of 386 commercial and 60 military DC-10s were ordered, the last (a KC-10A) delivered in April 1990. These included the DC-10-10 with 18,144-kg (40,000-lb

thrust General Electric CF-6 turbofans for 380 passengers and which first entered service in August 1971, the DC-10-10CF convertible freight passenger transport, the DC-10-15 with 21,092-kg (46,500-lb) thrust CF6-50 engines and higher weights, the DC-10-30 intercontinental transport with the span increased by 3.05 m (10 ft 0 in), 22,226-kg

MCDONNELL DOUGLAS MD-11 airliner
Role: Long/intermediate-range passenger/cargo transport
Crew/Accommodation: Two, eight cabin crew and 250–410 passengers
Power Plant: Three 27,896-kgp (61,500-lb s.t.) General Electric CF6-80C2D1F or 27,215–28,123-kgp (60,000–62,000-lb s.t.) Pratt & Whitney PW 4460/4462 turbofans
Dimensions: Span 51.7 m (169.5 ft); length 61.62 m (202.17 ft) with G.E. engines; wing area 338.91 m² (3,648 sq ft)
Weights: Empty (operating) 130,165 kg (286,965 lb); MTOW 273,314 kg-285,990 kg (602,555–630,500 lb)
Performance: Maximum speed 946 km/h (588 mph) at 9,450 m (31,000 ft); operational ceiling 12,800 m (42,000 ft); range 12,668 km (7,871 miles) with 298 passengers, no auxiliary tanks
Load: Typically 51,272 kg (113,035 lb) or up to 90,787 kg (200,151 lb) for freighter (including tare weight)

(49,000-lb thrust CF6-50A/C engines, extra fuel and a two-wheel additional main landing gear unit between the standard units, the DC-10-30F freighter and DC-10-30CF convertible freighter, the DC-10-40 intercontinental version of the 30 with 22,407-kg (49,400-lb) thrust and later 24,040-kg (53,000-lb) thrust Pratt & Whitney JT9D turbofans, and 60 KC-10A Extender transport/tankers for the U.S. Air Force. The MD-11 is an updated version that first flew in January 1990. A total 192 had been ordered in airliner, freighter and combi forms, but production ended in the year 2000. MD-11 features include drag-reducing winglets on extended wings, a lengthened fuselage for up to 410 passengers, advanced avionics and a choice of modern high-thrust General Electric or Pratt & Whitney engines.

A McDonnell Douglas DC-10-30

LOCKHEED L-1011 TRISTAR (U.S.A.)

L-1011-1 TriStar

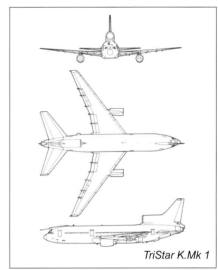

TriStar K.Mk 1

The TriStar was planned to meet an Eastern Airlines' requirement for a wide-body airliner optimized for short- and medium-range operations with a large number of passengers, and was planned in parallel with its engine, the Rolls-Royce RB.211 turbofan, initially offered at a 19,051-kg (42,000-lb) thrust rating. Development problems with the engine broke Rolls-Royce and nearly broke Lockheed, both companies having to be rescued by their respective governments. Construction began in 1968, and the first TriStar flew in November 1970.

Certification was delayed until April 1972 by the two companies' financial problems, and the L-1101-1 variant entered service in the same month with RB.211-22B engines and provision for up to 400 passengers at a maximum take-off weight of 195,045-kg (430,000-lb). The L-1011-100, which was the same basic airliner with RB.211-22B engines but with the fuel capacity and weights of the L-1011-200, which first flew in 1976 with 21,772-kg (48,000-lb) thrust RB.211-524 engines and a maximum take-off weight of up to 216,363 kg (477,000 lb) depending on the fuel load. The final production model was the L-1011-500 for very long-range operations, with 22,680-kg (50,000-lb) thrust RB.211-524B engines, increased fuel capacity, the fuselage shortened by 4.11 m (13 ft 6 in) for the accommodation of between 246 and 330 passengers, and the wings increased in span by 2.74 m (9 ft 0 in) as part of the new active control system that also saw a reduction in tailplane size. Sales failed to match Lockheed's marketing forecasts, and production ended in 1984 with the 250th aircraft. TriStars modified with the L-1011-500's engines and given a strengthened airframe and landing gear for higher gross weights (including more fuel for extended range) became L-101l-250s. Other conversions included several ex-airline aircraft converted as TriStar K.Mk 1 tankers and KC.Mk 1 tanker/freighters for the RAF.

A Royal Air Force L-1011 TriStar tanker

LOCKHEED L-1011 TRISTAR
Role: Intermediate-range passenger transport
Crew/Accommodation: Three, six cabin crew, plus up to 400 passengers (charter)
Power Plant: Three 19,051-kgp (42,000-lb s.t.) Rolls-Royce RB211-22 turbofans
Dimensions: Span 47.35 m (155,33 ft); length 54.46 m (178.66 ft); wing area 321.1m² (3,456 sq ft)
Weights: Empty 106,265 kg (234,275 lb); MTOW 195,045 kg (430,000 lb)
Performance: Cruise speed 796 km/h (495 mph) at 9,140 m (30,000 ft); operational ceiling 12,800 m (42,000 ft); range 4,635 km (2,880 miles) with maximum payload
Load: Up to 41,152 kg (90,725 lb)

AIRBUS INDUSTRIE A300 (France/Germany/Spain/U.K.)

A300B4

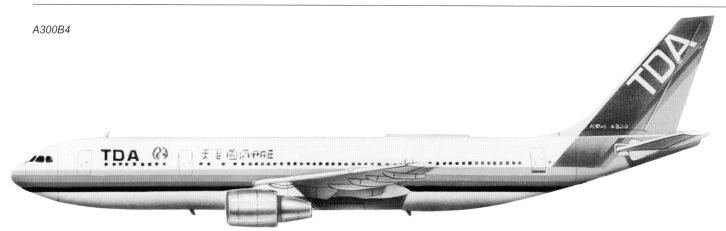

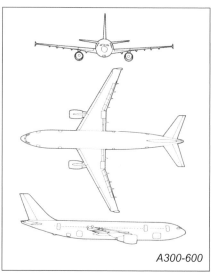

A300-600

The Airbus Consortium was founded in 1970 to manage this European challenge to the American 'big three' of airliner production: Boeing, Lockheed and McDonnell Douglas. A number of national designs had already been studied before the consortium was created to design, develop and build a 250-seat airliner powered by two British or American turbofans. The political and economic difficulties as the programme got underway were considerable, and the two sponsoring and largest shareholding countries became France and West Germany joined by the United Kingdom and Spain that have smaller shareholdings. All became industrial participants, joined as associate members by Belgium and the Netherlands.

The first A300B1 flew in October 1972, and this was lengthened by 2.65 m (8ft 8 in) to create the basic production model, the A300B2-100 with General Electric CF6-50 engines; variants became the A300B2-200 with leading-edge flaps, the A300B2-220 with Pratt & Whitney JT9D-59A turbofans, and the A300B2-

AIRBUS A300-600
Role: Long/intermediate-range passenger transport
Crew/Accommodation: Two and six cabin crew plus up to 361 passengers
Power Plant: Two 25,400-kgp (56,000-lb s.t.) Pratt & Whitney PW4156 or 26,310-kgp (58,000-lb s.t.) PW4158 turbofans, or General Electric CF6-80C2As of 26,762–27,895 kgp (59,000-61,500 lb s.t.)
Dimensions: Span 44.84 m (147.1 ft); length 54.08 m (177.4 ft); wing area 260 m² (2,799 sq ft)
Weights: Empty 90,100 kg (198,636 lb); MTOW 165,000 kg (363,760 lb) typically
Performance: Maximum speed 891 km/h (554 mph) at 9,450 m (31,000 ft); operational ceiling 12,200 m (40,000 ft); range 6,852 km (4,260 miles) with G E engines and 266 passengers

A Korean Air Airbus A300-622

300 with higher take-off and landing weights. Then came the A300B4-100 long-range version offered with CF6 or JT91 engines, the strengthened A300B4-200 with still higher weights and the A300B4-200FF with a two-crew cockpit.

The A300C4 first flew in 1979 as a convertible freighter based on the A300B4, while an all-freight model became F4. In July 1983 the first flight took place of the A300-600, the only version currently available as new, itself

available in passenger, extended range (R), convertible (C) and freighter (F) variants. Total A300 sales are well over 500 aircraft

A Lufthansa A300

BOEING 767 and 777 (U.S.A.)

Model 767-200

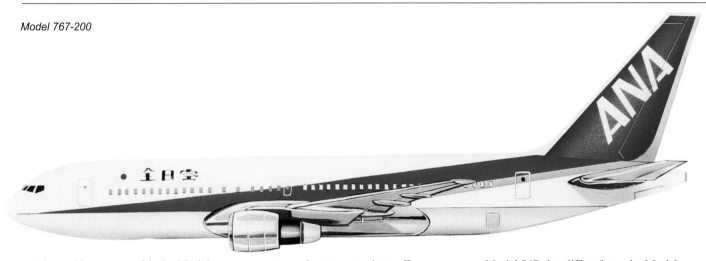

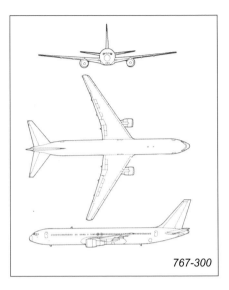

767-300

Planned in concert with the Model 757, the Model 767 is a wide-body transport with a cabin width of 4.72 m (15.5 ft) compared with 3.53 m (11.58 ft) for the Model 757. Even so, the Models 757 and 767 have so much in common that pilots can secure a single rating for both types. Drafting was undertaken with the aid of computer-aided design techniques. The type was schemed as a high-capacity airliner for medium-range routes, and present versions offer accommodation for 181 and 350 passengers plus a choice of General Electric CF6-80C2B, Pratt & Whitney PW4052/4056/4060/4062, or Rolls-Royce RB211-524G4 or H turbofans. The Model 767 also differs from the Model 757 in having larger wings of increased sweep, but similar features are the tail unit, landing gear and engine pods.

The first Model 767 flew in September 1981 and, with the cancellation of the planned Model 767-100 with a shorter fuselage for the carriage of a maximum of 180

BOEING 767-300
Role: Intermediate-range passenger transport
Crew/Accommodation: Two/three, six cabin crew plus up to 290 passengers
Power Plant: Two General Electric CF6-80C2B or Pratt & Whitney PW4050/4060 series turbofans, ranging from 23,814–28,123 kgp (52,500–62,000 lb s.t.)
Dimensions: Span 47.57 m (156.08 ft); length 54.94 m (180.25 ft); wing area 283.35 m² (3,050 sq ft)
Weights: Empty 86,954 kg (191,700 lb); MTOW 159,211 kg (351,000 lb)
Performance: Maximum speed 906 km/h (563 mph) at 11,887 m (39,000 ft); operational ceiling 13,000+ m (42,650+ ft); range 6,920 km (4,300 miles)
Load: Up to 39,145 kg (86,300 lb)

Boeing 777

passengers, the Model 767-200 became the basic variant, with a typical maximum take-off weight of 136,077 kg (300,000 lb) and range of 8,465 km (5,260 miles).The extended- range Model 767-200ER has additional fuel in a second centre section tank for greater range, while the Model 767-300 provides greater capacity, and has its length stretched from 48.51 m (159.17 ft) to 54.94 m (180.25 ft). Variants include the extended-range 767-300ER and 767-300F freighter. Latest version is the 767-400, launched in 1997 and offering accommodation for 303 passengers in 2-class layout and a range of 10460 km (6,500 miles). Well over 800 767s have been ordered. The model 777 first flew in June 1994 as a long-range wide-body airliner of increased size for up to 550 passengers.

A Delta Airlines 767

BOEING 757 (U.S.A.)

Model 757-200

In the later part of 1978, Boeing announced its intention of developing a new generation of advanced-technology airliners. The two definitive members of this family were the Models 757 and 767, while the Model 777 was less certain. The Model 757 retained the same narrow fuselage cross-section as the Model 727, and could be regarded as the Model 727's successor in the carriage of between 150 and 239 passengers over short- and medium-range routes, while the latest

757-300 (launched 1996) can carry up to 289 persons. Where Boeing offered considerable improvement, however, was in a new standard of fuel efficiency

expected to offer 45 per cent fuel savings per passenger/mile by comparison with contemporary types. The Model 757 was therefore first offered with Rolls-Royce

757-200

BOEING 757-200

Role: Intermediate-range passenger transport
Crew/Accommodation: Two, four cabin crew plus
  up to 239 passengers
Power Plant: Two 18,189-kgp (40,100-lb s.t.)
  Rolls-Royce RB211-535E4 or 17,350-kgp
  (38,250-lb s.t.) Pratt & Whitney PW2037 or
  other turbofans
Dimensions: Span 38.05 m (124.83 ft); length
  47.32 m (155.25 ft); wing area 185.25 m²
  (1,994 sq ft)
Weights: Empty from 57,970 kg (127,800 lb);
  MTOW 115,666 kg (255,000 lb)
Performance: Cruise speed 950 km/h (590 mph)
  at 8,230 m (27,000 ft); operational ceiling
  13,000+ m (42,650+ ft); range 7,278 km (4,525
  miles) with PW2037 engines and maximum
  payload

Boeing 757-200

RB211-535 or General Electric CF6-32C1 turbofans in underwing pods; General Electric then dropped the CF6-32 engine, and Pratt & Whitney entered the lists with the PW2037.

The type was originally planned in Model 757-100 short-fuselage and Model 757-200 long-fuselage variants; launch customers all opted for the latter with RB211 engines, and the shorter variant was then dropped. The Model 757-200 first flew in February 1982.

Freighter, PF Package Freighter and M combi models are also available, the PF and M each having a large main-deck cargo door. For delivery to customers from 1999, the latest 757-300 is a stretched version for 240–289 passengers, with strengthened wings and landing gear and maximum take-off weight increased to 122,470 kg (270,000 lb).

A British Airways Boeing 757-200

AIRBUS INDUSTRIE A310 (France/Germany/Spain/U.K.)

A310

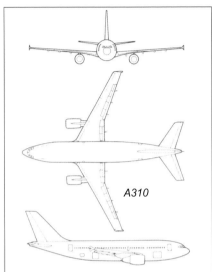

A310

A major problem facing the design team of the Airbus family of airliners was the lack of clear signals from potential purchasers both in Europe and elsewhere in the world. The A310 resulted from an Airbus programme designed to produce a large-capacity airliner for the short-haul market. At one time, the programme encompassed no fewer than 11 proposals designed to attract the widest possible spectrum of potential buyers. The final A310 was designed to satisfy the emerging market for a 200-seater offering the same type of fuel economy as the A300, and was indeed designed for the highest possible

AIRBUS A310-300

Role: Intermediate-range passenger transport
Crew/Accommodation: Two flight and six cabin crew, plus up to 280 passengers
Power Plant: Two 23,586-kgp (52,000-lb s.t.) Pratt & Whitney PW4152 or 4156A or 24,267-kgp (53,500-lb s.t.) General Electric CF6-80C2A2 or more powerful CF6-80C2A8 turbofans
Dimensions: Span 43.9 m (144.0 ft); length 44.66 m (153.08 ft); wing area 219 m² (2,357 sq ft)
Weights: Empty 80,800 kg (178,113 lb); MTOW 164,000 kg (361,558 lb)
Performance: Maximum speed 903 km/h (561 mph) at 10,670 m (35,000 ft); operational ceiling 13,000+ m (42,650 ft); range up to 9,630 km (5,988 miles) with P & W engines and 220 passengers

Airbus Industrie A310

commonality with the A300. Thus the A310 may be regarded as a short-fuselage derivative of the A300, with other features including aerodynamically clean outer wing areas without vortex generators, offering a lift coefficient usefully higher than that of the A300.

The type was first flown in April 1982, entering service in 1983. It was proposed in A310-100 short-range and A310-200 medium-range versions, but the former was dropped in favour of different-weight versions of the A310-200 optimized for the two roles. The

A310-300 is a longer range version with drag-reducing wingtip fences (retrospectively applied to the A310-200) and a tailplane trim tank, available in the weight options for the A310-200. Convertible and freight versions are designated A310C and A310F.

An Air Portugal Airbus A310

337

AIRBUS INDUSTRIE A340 (France/Germany/Spain/U.K.)

A340-300

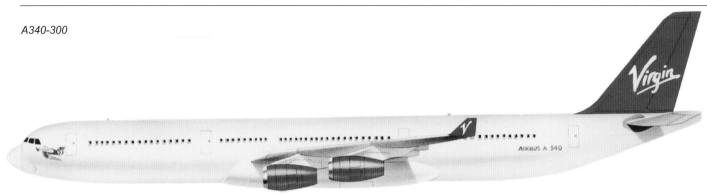

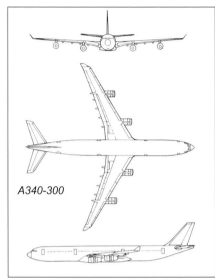

A340-300

The A340 was launched on 5 June 1987, at which time it was the largest aircraft to achieve production status in Europe. A340-200 is the reduced capacity version with a length of 59.39 m (194.83 ft), while the A340-300 is the standard-length model for up to 440 passengers. Singapore Airlines was the first operator (in 1996) to receive an ultra-long-range and higher weight A340-300E. Further versions are the A340-400E as a variant of A340-300 but with a 6.4m (21.0 ft) fuselage stretch and CFM56-5C4 engines, the A340-500 short-fuselage and longer-range variant of the A340-600 with

engine options including Rolls-Royce Trents, the stretched A340-600 with more engine power for 378 passengers in 3-class layout (enlarged and improved wings), and the proposed A340-800 for up to 400 passengers (MTOW 275,000 kg/606,270 lb). First flight of the -200 was October 1991.

Lufthansa was the first customer for the A340 as a replacement for DC-10s

and these entered service in March 1993.

In June 1993 the A340-200 prototype set several international distance records in its class by flying non-stop from Paris to New Zealand.

Another first for the A340 series was their being fitted with toilet facilities, especially for handicapped passengers, plus a collapsible wheelchair for inflight use.

The Airbus A330 is a twin-engined variant, first flown in November 1992, and corresponds in size to the A340-300.

AIRBUS A340-300

Role: Long-range passenger transport
Crew/Accommodation: Two pilots and cabin crew plus up to 440 passengers.
Power Plant: Four 14,152-kgp (31,200-lb s.t.) CFM International CFM56-5C2 turbofans initially, with 14,742 kgp (32,500 lb s.t.), -5C3 and 15,442 kgp (34,0001b s.t.), -5C4s optional
Dimensions: Span 60.3 m (197.83 ft); length 63.69 m (208.92 ft); wing area 363.1 m² (3,908.37 sq ft)
Weights: Empty 126,870 kg (279,700 lb); MTOW 257,000 kg (566,587 lb)
Performance: Cruise speed 890 km/h (553 mph); range 12,225 km (7,600 miles); operational ceiling 12,200m (40,000 ft);
Load: About 47,690 kg (105,139 lb)

ABOVE & OPPOSITE: Airbus Industrie A340s in Swiss and German liveries

SATIC A300-600ST SUPER TRANSPORTER 'BELUGA'

A300-600ST 'Beluga'

A300-600ST 'Beluga'

From 1971, the Airbus Industrie Consortium transported major assemblies of aircraft sections between their various manufacturing and assembly plants using a fleet of four converted Boeing Stratocruisers. These, known as 'Super Guppies', had proved successful but were in need of replacement. They were finally retired in October 1997.

There being no suitable replacement available with a huge open fuselage cross-section for outsized cargo, the consortium developed its own outsize transporter. The result is the SATIC

A300-600ST 'Beluga' Airbus Super Transporter which flew for the first time on 13 September 1994. SATIC (Special

Aircraft Transport International Company) was formed jointly by Deutsche Aerospace Airbus and

SATIC A300-600ST 'BELUGA'
Role: Heavy-lift freighter
Crew/Accommodation: Pilot and co-pilot plus 2
 handlers with folding seats in the cockpit
Power Plant: Two 26,762-kgp (59,000-lb s.t.)
 General Electric CF-6-80C2A8 turbofans
Dimensions: Span 44.84 m (147.083 ft); length
 56.16 m (184.25 ft); wing area 260 m²
 (2,798.6 sq ft)
Weights: MTOW 150,000 kg (330,693 lb)
Performance: Cruise speed 778 km/h (484 mph);
 range 1,666 km (1,035 miles)
Load: Up to 45,500 kg (100,310 lb)

SATIC A300-600ST Super Transporter 'Beluga'

Aérospatiale in 1991 to build the aircraft. The 600ST has 80 per cent of spares in common with the basic aircraft, the A300-600R Airbus, with corresponding low maintenance costs.

The design employs five major conversions or modifications over the original A300 airframe. These are an increase from 5.3 m (17.4 ft) to 7.4 m (24.3 ft) in the fuselage diameter, the lowering of the cockpit to below and

forward of the freight floor level, reinforcement of the cargo floor, installation of an upper deck cargo door, and the redesigning and reinforcement of the tail plane surfaces.

The cockpit layout is identical to the A300-600R. Payloads are inserted through the main forward freight door, the largest ever fitted to an aircraft, which opens upwards above the cockpit. The aircraft can be loaded or unloaded

by two men within 45 minutes turn-round schedule, compared with two hours, by 8 to 10 men for the Super Guppy. Maximum payload has increased to 45.5 tonnes, held in a cargo compartment of 1,400 cubic metres volume.

Four Belugas had been delivered by 1998, with the fifth and last delivered in 2001.

Airbus became aware that other industries could require 'super transport'

availability, including the European Space Agency, and in 1996 Airbus Transport International was formed to offer charter services using any spare Beluga capacity from the main Airbus activities.

Super Transporter 'Beluga'

341

AIRBUS INDUSTRIE A380

The Airbus A380 is a double-deck, wide-body, four-engine airliner manufactured by the European corporation Airbus, a subsidiary of EADS. The largest passenger airliner in the world, the A380 made its maiden flight on 27 April 2005 from Toulouse, France, and made its first commercial flight on 25 October 2007 from Singapore to Sydney with Singapore Airlines. The aircraft was known as the Airbus A3XX during much of its development phase, but the nickname Superjumbo has since become associated with it.

The A380's upper deck extends along the entire length of the fuselage, and its width is equivalent to that of a widebody aircraft. This allows for an A380-800's cabin with 5,146 square feet (478.1 m²) of floor space; 49% more floor space than the next-largest airliner, the Boeing 747-400 with 3,453 square feet (320.8 m²), and provides seating for 525 people in a typical 3-class configuration or up to 853 people in all-economy class

configurations. The postponed freighter version, the A380-800F, is offered as one of the largest freight aircraft, with a payload capacity exceeded only by the Antonov An-225. The A380-800 has a design range of 15,200 km (8,200 nmi; 9,400 mi), sufficient to fly from New York to Hong Kong for example, and a cruising speed of Mach 0.85 (about 900 km/h or 560 mph at cruising altitude).

The first aircraft delivered (MSN003, registered 9V-SKA) was handed over to Singapore Airlines on 15 October 2007 and entered into service on 25 October 2007 with an inaugural flight between Singapore and Sydney (flight number SQ380). Passengers bought seats in a charity online auction paying between $560 and $100,380. Two months later, Singapore Airlines CEO Chew Choong Seng said that the A380 was performing better than both the airline and Airbus had anticipated, burning 20% less fuel per passenger than the airline's existing 747-400 fleet.

Emirates was the second airline to take delivery of the A380 on 28 July 2008 and began flights between Dubai and New York on 1 August 2008. Qantas followed on 19 September 2008, starting

AIRBUS INDUSTRIE A380-800F
Role: Long-range passenger transport.
Cockpit crew: Two
Seating capacity: Up to 853 plus crew
Power Plant: Four GP7270 (A380-861) Trent 970/B (A380-841), Trent 972/B (A380-842) GP7277 (A380-863F), Trent 977/B (A380-843F)
Thrust: Four 311 kN (70,000 lbf) - 355 kN (80,000 lbf)
Dimensions: Span 79.75 m (261.6 ft); length 72.73 m (238.6 ft); height 24.45 m (80.2 ft); wing area 845 m² (9,100 sq ft)
Weights: Empty weight 276,800 kg (610,000 lb) 252,200 kg (556,000 lb). MTOW 569,000 kg (1,250,000 lb)
Performance: Maximum speed at cruise altitude (945 km/h, 587 mph, 510 knots)

flights between Melbourne and Los Angeles on 20 October 2008. By the end of 2008, 890,000 passengers had flown on 2,200 A380 flights totalling 21,000 hours.

In February 2009 the millionth A380 passenger flying with Singapore Airlines was recorded. In May 2009 it was reported that the A380 had carried 1.5 million passengers during 41,000 flight hours and 4,200 flights. Air France received its first A380 on 30 October 2009, arriving at Charles de Gaulle Airport. Lufthansa received its first A380 on 19 May 2010. By July 2010 the 31 A380s then in service had flown 156,000 hours with passengers in 17,000 flights, transporting 6,000,000 passengers between 20 international destinations.

OPPOSITE: A380 during test flights

ABOVE: Quantas A380

343

BOEING 787 DREAMLINER

The Boeing 787 Dreamliner is a long-range, mid-sized, wide-body, twin-engine jet airliner developed by Boeing Commercial Airplanes. It seats 210 to 330 passengers, depending on variant. Boeing states that it is the company's most fuel-efficient airliner and the world's first major airliner to use composite materials for most of its construction. The 787 consumes 20% less fuel than the similarly-sized Boeing 767. Its development and production has involved a large-scale collaboration with numerous suppliers.

Originally scheduled to enter service in May 2008, the aircraft's maiden flight took place on 15 December 2009 in the Seattle area and it is currently undergoing flight testing with the goal of receiving its type certificate in late 2010, and to enter service in 2011.

Boeing announced on 15 July 2010 that the first delivery could slip into 2011, and on 27 August 2010 confirmed that the first delivery, to launch customer All Nippon Airways, would be delayed until early 2011 due to a blowout in the Trent

1000 on 2 August at Rolls-Royce's test facility, although Rolls-Royce claims that a lack of engines is unrelated to the test incident. In August 2010 it was also announced that Boeing was facing a U.S.$1 billion compensation claim from Air India due to the delays for the 27 787s it has on order. In October 2010, Boeing announced that its deliveries of parts from suppliers would be frozen for two weeks while dealing with delays from Alenia.

The longest-range 787 variant can fly 14800 to 15700 km (8,000 to 8,500 nautical miles), enough to cover the Los Angeles to Bangkok or New York City to Taipei routes. It will have a cruising airspeed of Mach 0.85 (903 km/h/561 mph, at typical cruise altitudes). External features include raked wingtips and

BELOW & OPPOSITE: The 787 is Boeing's most fuel-efficient airliner

engine nacelles with noise-reducing serrated edges. The two different engine models compatible with the 787 use a standard electrical interface to allow an aircraft to be fitted with either Rolls-Royce or General Electric engines.

BOEING 787 DREAMLINER
Role: Long-range passenger transport.
Cockpit crew: Two
Seating capacity: Up to 330 plus crew
Power Plant: Two General Electric GEnx or
  Rolls-Royce Trent 1000
Thrust: Two 53,000 lbf (240 kN), 64,000 lbf (280
  kN) or 71,000 lbf (320 kN)
Dimensions: Span 60.1 m (197 ft 3 in); length
  62.8 m (206 ft); height 80.2 ft (24.45 m);
  wing area 16.9 m (55 ft 6 in)
Weights: Empty 115,000 kg (254,000 lb)
  MTOW 247,000 kg (545,000 lb)
Performance: Maximum speed at cruise altitude
  490 knots, 913 km/h at 35,000 ft/10,700 m)

SPECIALIZED AIRCRAFT

SPECIAL MISSION AIRCRAFT

'Special mission' can signify a complete range of tasks, not all of them military, the common factor often being the application of electronic sensors or emitters in one form or another. Intelligence-gathering, communications relay or jamming, airborne early warning and surveillance are typical military roles, undertaken by uniquely equipped variants of existing large transport aircraft or by purpose-designed types, while survey, remote sensing and pollution control are among non-military roles for aircraft often based on small commercial transports or civil lightplanes.

It was during World War II that special mission aircraft began to ply their trade, with early examples including RAF Vickers Wellington bombers fitted with huge 14.6 m (48 ft) diameter degaussing rings to fly over and explode German magnetic mines. But it was during the Vietnam War that special mission aircraft really got underway, typified by the U.S.'s need to jam enemy radars during raids on the North, to prevent surface-to-air missiles and radar-guided guns from claiming so many of its aircraft. Such electronic warfare aircraft, used to escort the fighter-bombers, greatly reduced losses.

The three aircraft chosen to represent 'special mission' types are all U.S., although such aircraft have been produced in many countries. Interestingly, one of the most incredible special mission aircraft to appear recently has been the Scaled Composites Proteus, a uniquely-configured sensor platform suited to both military and civil uses, including communications relay, earth and ocean resources monitoring and much else besides, with an early application expected to be for telecommunications and data relay. Missions are greatly assisted by an on-station endurance of up to 18 hours.

PAGE 346: BAe Hawk

PAGE 347: Cessna Citation Excel

LEFT: Interior of a Boeing E-3 Sentry

NORTHROP GRUMMAN E-2 HAWKEYE (U.S.A.)

E-2C Hawkeye

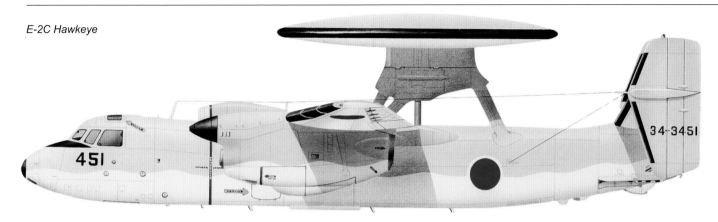

Tracer for aircraft carrier operations in this role, but Tracer was based on the Tracker ASW aircraft and so, despite its over-fuselage radome, was not a purpose design. The first W2F-1 aerodynamic prototype flew in October 1960, while the second machine, which flew in April 1961, introduced the original APS-96 surveillance radar (with its antenna in a large-diameter rotodome) and the advanced data-processing system that

Grumman developed its G-89 concept as the world's first purpose-designed airborne early warning platform to meet a U.S. Navy requirement for the aerial component of the Naval Tactical Data System. The Grumman design was selected in March 1957. Interestingly, it had been preceded by the Grumman E-1B

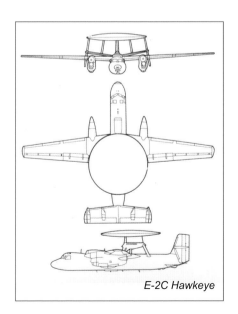

E-2C Hawkeye

Two Northrop Grumman E-2Cs

allowed the three-man tactical crew to watch and control all air activity within a large radius. The first aircraft were delivered with the designation W2F-1, but these 62 aircraft entered service from January 1964 as E-2As. This model was limited to overwater operations, but from 1969 most aircraft were modified to the E-2B standard adding overland capability. This resulted from the combination of APS-120 radar and a new central computer; other improvements were inflight refuelling capability and larger vertical tail surfaces.

In January 1971 Grumman flew the prototype of the E-2C that entered service in November 1973 with the more capable and digital APS-125 radar able to detect air targets out to a range of 370 km (230 miles), even in ground clutter, and also able to track more than 250 air and surface targets simultaneously, allowing the tactical crew to control 30 or more interceptions at the same time. Later aircraft were given the APS-138 radar for the tracking of 600 targets to a range of 483 km (300 miles) and enhanced electronic support measures capability.

NORTHROP GRUMMAN E-2C HAWKEYE
Role: Naval carrierborne airborne early warning and control
Crew/Accommodation: Five
Power Plant: Two 5,100-hp Allison T56-A427 turboprops
Dimensions: Span 24.6 m (80.6 ft); length 17.6 m (57.7 ft); wing area 65.03 m² (700 sq ft)
Weights: Empty 18,363 kg (40,484 lb); MTOW 24,687 kg (54,426 lb)
Performance: Maximum speed 626 km/h (389 mph); operational ceiling 11,278 m (37,000 ft); endurance 5.3 hours at 200 naut. miles from base
Load: None, other than special-to-task onboard equipment

From 1988 the APS-139 radar added the capability to track even stationary targets. A total of 166 E-2Cs was built up to 1995, with 139 going to the U.S. Navy and most of the remainder exported. Production has since been restarted to provide the U.S.N with 36 new Hawkeye 2000s featuring AN/APS-145 radar able to track over 2,000 targets and guide interceptors to 40 enemy targets simultaneously.

Two Advanced Hawkeye E-2D aircraft conducting a test flight near St. Augustine, Florida

NORTHROP GRUMMAN EA-6 PROWLER (U.S.A.)

EA-6B Prowler

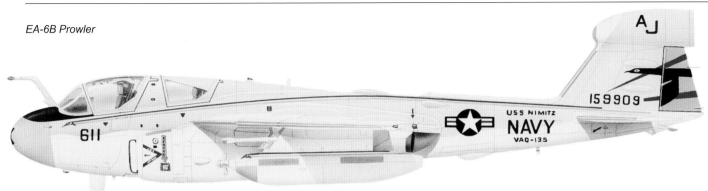

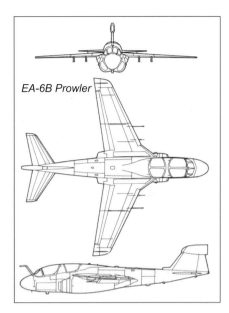

EA-6B Prowler

From early in the programme to develop the A2F Intruder strike aircraft, the U.S. Navy realized the importance of producing a support version fitted with the specialized electronic systems that could aid passage through enemy airspace. The result was the development of the EA-6A (initially the A2F-1Q) as an electronic support variant that also retained partial attack capability. The first example of this variant flew in 1963 as a conversion from YA-6A (initially YA2F-1) standard,

and was followed by another two YA-6A and four A-6A conversion and by 21 new-build aircraft. The variant became distinguishable by its revised vertical tail surfaces, which were surmounted by the large fairing that accommodated the receiver antennae for the electronic warfare system, which had internal and external jammers.

In 1966, the U.S. Navy called for a dedicated electronic warfare variant, and

this appeared as the EA-6B Prowler with its fuselage lengthened by 1.37 m (4 ft 6 in) to allow the insertion of a stretched cockpit accommodating, in addition to the standard two crew, two specialist operators for the ALQ-99 system to detect, localize and analyze enemy radar emissions before finding the right jamming set-on frequency for any of the five jammer pods carried under the fuselage and wings. Since entering

service in 1971 the EA-6B has undergone enormous electronic development in the form of steadily more comprehensive and wide-ranging standards known as the Expanded Capability, Improved Capability, Improved Capability 2, Defensive Electronic Counter-Measures, and Advanced Capability, together with aerodynamic and powerplant enhancements. Some 127 Prowlers remained in service in 1998/99 with the U.S. Navy and Marines and, with the 1998 retirement of U.S.A.F. EF-111A Ravens, Prowlers now provide the stand-off jamming requirements of the three services.

PAGE 352: Northrop Grumman EA-6B Prowler

NORTHROP GRUMMAN EA-6B PROWLER
Role: Naval carrierborne, all-weather electronic warfare
Crew/Accommodation: Four
Power Plant: Two 5,080-kgp (11,200-lb s.t.) Pratt & Whitney J52-P-408 or 5,443-kgp (12,000-lb s.t.) J52-P-409s
Dimensions: Span 16.16 m (53 ft); length 18.24 m (59.83 ft); wing area 49.15 m² (529 sq ft)
Weights: Empty 14,320 kg (31,572 lb); MTOW 29,480 kg (65,000 lb)
Performance: Maximum speed 1,047 km/h (651 mph); operational ceiling 12,560 m (41,200 ft); range 1,770 km (1,100 miles)
Load: Up to in excess of 11,340 kg (25,000 lb) of electronic broad-band jammers and other specialized electronic warfare systems within the AN/ALQ-99F tactical jamming system, and HARM missiles

An EA-6B Prowler launching from U.S.S. Harry S. Truman

BOEING E-3 SENTRY (U.S.A.)

E-3A Sentry

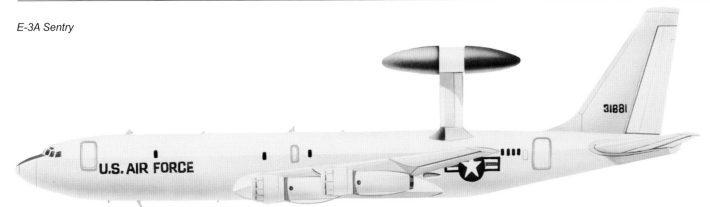

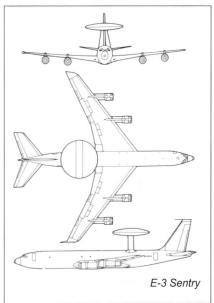

E-3 Sentry

O ne of the most expensive but important current military aircraft, the Sentry is a highly capable Airborne Warning and Control System type, designed for three-dimensional surveillance of a massive volume of air and the direction of aerial operations within that volume as a force multiplier. The type is based on the Model 707-300B airliner, and two EC-137D prototypes were used to evaluate the Westinghouse APY-1 and Hughes APY-2 radars. The former was chosen for the 34 E-3A production aircraft, which were delivered

between 1977 and 1984. The first 24 aircraft for the U.S.A.F. were Core E-3As with only an overland capability, CC-1 computer, nine situation display consoles and two auxiliary display units, while the last 10 were Standard E-3As with additional overwater sensor capability, a

faster CC-2 computer, secure voice communications, and Joint Tactical Information Distribution System.

The Standard E-3A type (though with improved APY-2 radar and provision for self-defence AAMs) was ordered for the multi-national NATO

BOEING E-3D SENTRY
Role: Airborne early warning and command
Crew/Accommodation: Four, plus 17 AWACS specialists
Power Plant: Four 10,886-kgp (24,000-lb s.t.) CFM International CFM56-2A-2 or-3 turbofans
Dimensions: Span 44.43 m (145.75 ft); length 46.62 m (152 ft); wing area 284.40 m² (3,050 sq ft)
Weights: Empty 77,238 kg (170,277 lb); MTOW 151,995 kg (335,000 lb)
Performance: Maximum speed 805 km/h (500 mph) at 8,839 m (29,000 ft); operational ceiling 11,430 m (37,500 ft); range 9,250 km (5,760 miles)
Load: Nil

Boeing E-3D Sentry

early warning force, and these 18 aircraft were delivered between January 1982 and April 1985. Another five were delivered to Saudi Arabia as E-3A/Saudi aircraft with slightly less capable electronics and four 9979-kg (22,000-lb) thrust CFM56-A2-2 turbofans. The Core E-3As (and two EC-137Ds) were later raised to E-3B standard with the CC-2 computer, 14 display consoles, JTIDS, improved ECM capability, and limited overwater sensor capability, while the Standard E-3As were raised to E-3C standard with five extra situation display consoles and the 'Have Quick-A' communications system. The type also has the capability to carry small underwing pylons, which could carry AIM-9 Sidewinder AAMs for modest self-defence facility. Comparable aircraft for the RAF and French Air Force are seven E-3Ds (that is, Sentry AEW.Mk 1s) and four E-3Fs with CEM56 engines.

ABOVE & OPPOSITE: A Boeing E-3 Sentry with AWACS system

354

TRAINERS & LIGHT STRIKE

At the birth of powered aeroplane flight there were few, if any, restrictive rules to govern the conduct of the intrepid aviators, although the Fédération Aéronautique Internationale (FAI) had been founded in 1905 and became the ruling body over official world performance records. By 1909, however, flying was becoming sufficiently regular that authority had to be established for various activities, and the first 'official' aeroplane meetings were organized to cater for widespread public interest. More importantly, the Aéro Club de France and British Aero Club, formed in 1898 and 1901 respectively (the latter becoming the Royal Aero Club in 1910), began issuing proper Pilot's Certificates, with the first in Britain being awarded to a civilian in March 1910, the 15th to a Royal Navy officer in June and the 17th to a British Army officer that July. Also in March 1910, France certified its first military pilot as its 33rd qualified aviator and the world's first woman pilot as that nation's 36th. A German officer received a flying certificate in 1910, and during February 1911 France awarded its first military flying certificate.

The first aircraft used as trainers were generally two-seat versions of existing 'stick and string' aeroplanes, but already thought had been given to proper means of instruction and Short Brothers, for example, produced its S.32 in 1911 as a purpose-designed trainer with dual controls and was used to instruct members of the British Territorials over that winter. In America, birth-place of powered aeroplane flying, the third and fourth aeroplanes purchased by the Army (Wright Model Bs) were for training, though each had only one set of shared controls, while the U.S. Navy received an early Curtiss type as a dual-control trainer.

After war broke out in 1914, aeroplanes that were no longer suited to first-line duties were often given over to training. However, one of the greatest trainers of all time, the British Avro 504, which had begun the war as a reconnaissance and light bombing biplane, became so successful in its new role from 1915 that it remained in production until 1933, from 1931 providing many pilots with their first taste

LEFT: Cessna A-37 Dragonfly

OPPOSITE: de Havilland D.H.82 Tiger Moth

of instrument 'blind' flying. The equivalent U.S. aircraft was the Curtiss JN 'Jenny', the last examples being retired from the National Guard in 1927.

The RAF's main trainer in 1939 at elementary and reserve flying training schools was the de Havilland Tiger Moth, which was a direct descendant of the original D.H.60 Moth of 1925 appearance. The Moth is perhaps the most important civil trainer of all time, chosen to equip all the flying clubs formed under a British Air Ministry scheme and widely recognized as the aircraft that kick-started the civil flying club movement.

Modern-day basic and advanced training syllabuses are often shared between turboprop- and turbofan-powered types, the former typified by the incredibly successful Brazilian EMBRAER Tucano, while the U.S. forces are currently receiving huge numbers of the Swiss Pilatus PC-9 Mk II built by Raytheon/Beech in the U.S.A. as the T-6A Texan II. But turbofan trainers normally permit a more capable secondary light attack role, with weapon loads in the 1,000–3,000-kg range, some even spawning single-seat combat-dedicated variants.

AVRO 504 (United Kingdom)

Avro 504K

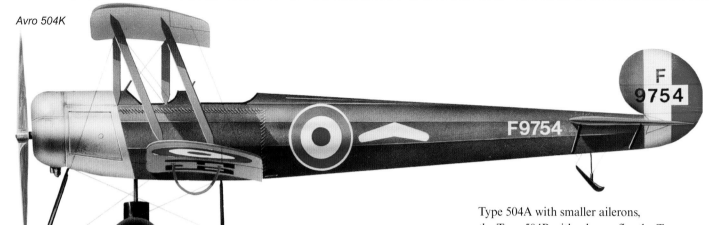

One of the most remarkable aircraft of all time, the Type 504 was developed from the Type 500 basic trainer, and first flew in July 1913 with a 60-kW (80-hp) Gnôme rotary that, in fact, yielded only about 46 kW (62 hp). In the summer of 1913 the British Army and Navy ordered the Type 504 as a general-purpose aeroplane. After a limited amount of front-line service,

which included the successful bombing of the Zeppelin sheds at Friedrichshafen in November 1914, the 504 was relegated to second-line duties, where it found its métier as a trainer.

The main variants were Type 504, the

Type 504A with smaller ailerons, the Type 504B with a larger fin, the Type 504C anti-Zeppelin single-seater, and the Type 504D, all powered by the 60-kW (80-hp) Gnôme Monosoupape rotary engine. Trainer and civil variants were the Type 504E with less wing stagger, the classic Type 504J of 1916 with the same 75-kW (100-hp) Gnôme Monosoupape as the Type 504E, the Type 504K

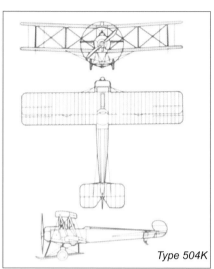

Type 504K

standard trainer with a universal engine mounting able to accommodate a variety of inline, radial and rotary engines, the Type 504L floatplane and the Type 504M cabin transport.

After World War I, many surplus Type 504 models were converted to improved Type 504N standard with a number of structural revisions, revised landing gear that eliminated the central skid of earlier models, and a 134-kW (180-hp) Armstrong Siddeley Lynx IV radial engine. Well over 8,000 Type 504s were built in World War I, and post-war conversions were supplemented by 598 Type 504Ns built between 1925 and 1932.

AVRO 504K

Role: Reconnaissance/trainer
Crew/Accommodation: Two
Power Plant: One 130-hp Clerget air-cooled rotary
Dimensions: Span 10.97 m (36 ft); length 7.75 m (25.42 ft); wing area 30.66 m² (330 sq ft)
Weights: Empty 558 kg (1,231 lb); MTOW 830 kg (1,829 lb)
Performance: Maximum speed 153 km/h (95 mph) at sea level; operational ceiling 5,486 m (18,000 ft); endurance 3 hours
Load: A number of 504s were converted into home defence single-seat fighters with one .303-inch machine gun, plus stowage for hand-released small bombs

Avro 504

OPPOSITE: Avro Type 504R

CURTISS JN 'JENNY' (U.S.A.)

JN-4H 'Jenny'

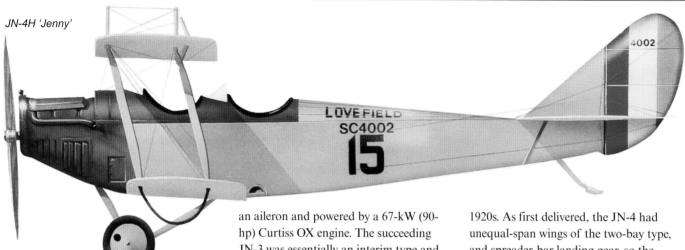

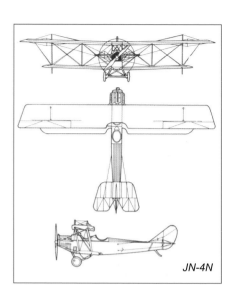

JN-4N

Generally known as the 'Jenny', this celebrated trainer resulted from the Model J. This had a 67-kW (90-hp) Curtiss O inline engine and unequal-span biplane wings with upper-wing ailerons operated by the obsolete Deperdussin-type control system. The contemporary Model N had the 75-kW (100-hp) Curtiss OXX inline and interplane ailerons. Features of both types were included in the JN-2 that appeared in 1915 with equal-span biplane wings each carrying

an aileron and powered by a 67-kW (90-hp) Curtiss OX engine. The succeeding JN-3 was essentially an interim type and had unequal-span wings with ailerons only on the upper surfaces, but these control surfaces were operated by a wheel on the joystick rather than a shoulder yoke. In July 1916 there appeared the definitive JN-4, and this was built in large numbers for useful service well into the

1920s. As first delivered, the JN-4 had unequal-span wings of the two-bay type, and spreader-bar landing gear, so the definitive form of the JN-4 appeared later in the production run.

The JN-4A had a larger tailplane and engine downthrust; the slightly earlier JN-4B introduced the larger tailplane and used the OX-2 engine; the JN-4C was an experimental model of which just

two were produced, the JN-4 Can (generally known as the Canuck) was a development by the Curtiss company's Canadian associate and was a very successful evolution of the JN-3; the JN-4D combined features of the JN-4A and the JN-4 Can to become the nearest there was to a standard variant; the JN-4H was the JH-4D re-engined with the 112-kW (150-hp) Wright-built Hispano-Suiza inline. JHN-4H variants were the JN-4HT, JN-4HB and JN-4HG dual-control trainer, bombing and gunnery trainers. A variant of the JN family produced in smaller but still useful numbers was the JN-6, which evolved via the JN-5 with a stronger aileron structure and was developed in several subvariants.

CURTISS JN-4D
Role: Primary trainer
Crew/Accommodation: Two
Power Plant: One 90-hp Curtiss OX-5 water-cooled inline
Dimensions: Span 13.29 m (43.6 ft); length 8.33 m (27.33 ft); wing area 32.7 m² (352 sq ft)
Weights: Empty 630.5 kg (1,390 lb); MTOW 871 kg (1,920 lb)
Performance: Cruise speed 97 km/h (60 mph) at sea level; operational ceiling 1,981 m (6,500 ft); range 402 km (250 miles)
Load: None

Curtiss JN 'Jenny'

OPPOSITE: A replica of a Curtis JN-4 'Jenny'

de HAVILLAND D.H.82 TIGER MOTH (United Kingdom)

D.H. 82 Tiger Moth

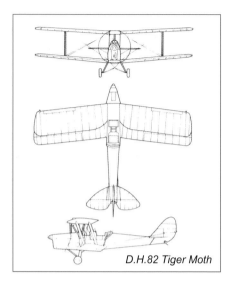

D.H.82 Tiger Moth

The incredible success of its Cirrus-engined D.H.60 Moth, for civil flying clubs (see introduction) and the acceptance of the more powerful Gipsy-engined Gipsy Moth into RAF service as an elementary trainer and communications aircraft, convinced de Havilland that there was a large market for more military trainers. Although the original Moth, and some early versions of the Gipsy Moth (D.H.60G), had wooden structures, in 1929 the company introduced the D.H.60M version with a

metal structure (as for RAF Gipsy Moths) from which it evolved its first all-military Moth version as the D.H.60T Moth Trainer with a strengthened airframe and the 89-kW (120-hp) de Havilland Gipsy II engine. From this latter the company derived the D.H.82 Tiger Moth for the military market with a sturdier airframe for operation at higher weights with equipment such as a camera gun or practice bombs.

Eight pre-production aircraft were built with the same D.H.60T designation as the Moth Trainer, and these also retained the straight lower wing and dihedralled upper wing of the Moth Trainer; stagger was increased as the upper-wing centre section was moved forward to ease movement into and out of the front cockpit. The aircraft were powered by the 89-kW (120-hp) Gipsy III engine in a cowling, the sloping upper line of which improved the pilot's field of

vision, and the lower wing was given dihedral for improved ground clearance.

The definitive form was reached in the D.H.82 prototype that first flew in October 1931 with increased lower-wing dihedral and sweepback. Large-scale production followed, and of the 8,280 aircraft all but a few were of the Tiger Moth Mk II (D.H.82A) variant in which the ridged stringer/fabric rear decking of the Tiger Moth Mk I was replaced by a smooth plywood decking. The D.H.82B was the Queen Bee remotely controlled target drone, and the D.H.82C was a winterized variant built by de Havilland Canada. Surplus military aircraft found a ready civilian market, and the well-loved Tiger Moth is even today flying in fairly large numbers.

OPPOSITE: D.H.82 Tiger Moth

de HAVILLAND D.H.82A TIGER MOTH

Role: Trainer/tourer
Crew/Accommodation: Two
Power Plant: One 130-hp de Havilland Gipsy Major I air-cooled inline
Dimensions: Span 8.94 m (29.3 ft); length 7.3 m (23.95 ft); wing area 22.2 m² (239 sq ft)
Weights: Empty 506 kg (1,115 lb); MTOW 828 kg (1,825 lb)
Performance: Maximum speed 167 km/h (104 mph) at sea level; operational ceiling 4,267 m (14,000 ft); range 483 km (300 miles)
Load: 81.6 kg (180 lb)

D.H.82A Tiger Moth

Model 75/PT-13C

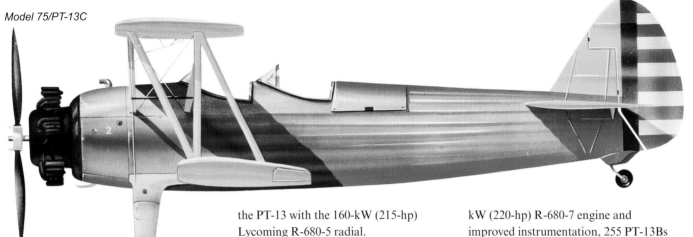

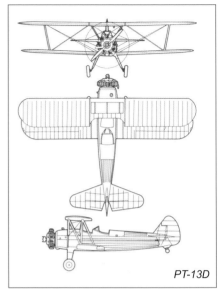

PT-13D

the PT-13 with the 160-kW (215-hp) Lycoming R-680-5 radial.

These 26 aircraft were just the beginning of a major development and production programme. Further evolution led to 92 PT-13As with the 164-kW (220-hp) R-680-7 engine and improved instrumentation, 255 PT-13Bs with the R-680-11 engine, and six PT-13Cs with night-flying instrumentation. A change was then made to the 164-kW Continental R-670-5 radial for the PT-17,

In 1939 Boeing bought Stearman Aircraft, and as a result acquired the excellent Model 75 developed by Stearman from the X-70 first flown in December 1933. The U.S. Navy had taken 61 of the Model 73 production type with the designation NS-1, and development had then led to the Model 75 being accepted by the U.S. Army as

BOEING/STEARMAN PT-17A
Role: Basic trainer
Crew/Accommodation: Two
Power Plant: One 220-hp Continental R-670-5 air-cooled radial
Dimensions: Span 9.8 m (32.16 ft); length 7.32 m (24.02 ft); wing area 27.63 m² (297.4 sq ft)
Weights: Empty 878 kg (1,936 lb); MTOW 1,232 kg (2,717 1b)
Performance: Maximum speed 200 km/h (124 mph) at sea level; operational ceiling 3,414 m (11,200 ft); range 813 km (505 miles)
Load: None

Boeing/Stearman Model 75

of which 3,510 were built in 1940. Specialist versions were the 18 blind-flying PT-17As and three pest-control PT-17Bs. The Navy also operated the Model 75 as the N2S, and this series included 250 N2S-ls with the R-670-14 engine, 125 N2S-2s with the R-680-8 engine, 1,875 N2S-3s with the R-670-4, and 1,051 N2S-4s with the R-670-5 engine. Then came a common Army/Navy model produced as 318 PT-13Ds and 1,450 N2S-5s with the R-680-17 engine. Variants with Jacobs R-755-7 radials were designated PT-18 and, in the blind-flying role, PT-18A.

Some 300 aircraft supplied to Canada were designated PT-27 by the U.S.A. but were called Kaydet in the receiving country. This name is usually given to all Model 75 variants.

NORTH AMERICAN T-6/SNJ TEXAN and FOREBEARS (U.S.A.)

T-6G Texan

This series comprised the Western Alliance's most important trainers of World War II, and production was in the order of 17,000 or more aircraft. The series was pioneered by the NA-16 prototype that flew in April 1935 as an all-metal cantilever low-wing monoplane with two open cockpits, fixed landing gear and the 298-kW (400-hp) Wright R-975 radial. The type was then ordered in a form with a glazed enclosure over the cockpits as the BT-9 and NJ series for the U.S. Army and U.S. Navy respectively. Additional aircraft were produced for export to several countries, including

Canada, where the aircraft was known as the Yale.

This NA-18 version was then developed further with the 447-kW (600-hp) Pratt & Whitney R-1340 radial, equipment comparable with that of contemporary combat aircraft, and

retractable tailwheel landing gear to serve as a combat trainer. This NA-26 variant was first ordered as the AT-6 Texan (initially BC-1) and SNJ series for the U.S. Army and Navy respectively. Production was undertaken in many improved and specialized models up to

the T-6F and SNJ-6. The U.S.A.A.F.'s most numerous models were the AT-6C and AT-6D (2,970 and 4,388) with a revised structure that made fewer demands on strategically important light alloys, while the U.S. Navy's equivalents were the 2,400 SNJ-4s and 1,357 SNJ-5s. The British and their Commonwealth allies also operated the type in comparatively large numbers under the basic designation Harvard, which were delivered from American and licensed Canadian production in variants up to the Harvard Mk 4. From 1949 some 2,086 American aircraft were rebuilt as T-6G multi-role trainers with the R-1340-AN-1 engine, increased fuel capacity, an improved cockpit layout, a steerable tailwheel together with many other modifications.

NORTH AMERICAN T-6D TEXAN (RAF HARVARD)
Role: Advanced trainer
Crew/Accommodation: Two
Power Plant: One 550-hp Pratt & Whitney R-1340-AN1 Wasp air-cooled radial
Dimensions: Span 12.81 m (42.02 ft); length 8.84 m (28.99 ft); wing area 23.57 m² (253.72 sq ft)
Weights: Empty 1,886 kg (4,158 lb): MTOW 2,722 kg (6,000 lb)
Performance: Maximum speed 330 km/h (205 mph) at 1,524 (5,000 ft); operational ceiling 6,553 m (21,500 ft); range 1,207 km (750 miles)
Load: Two .303-inch machine guns

North American T-6

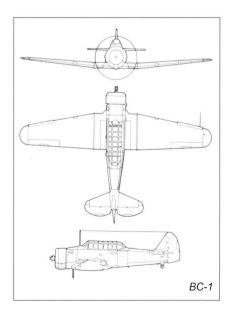

BC-1

MILES MAGISTER (United Kingdom)

Magister Mk I

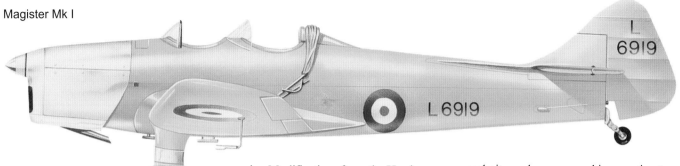

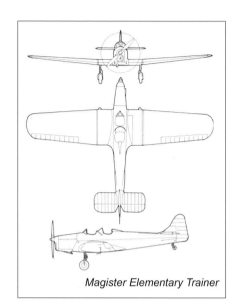

Magister Elementary Trainer

The Magister was the Royal Air Force's most important elementary trainer in the opening stages of World War II, and was also of historical importance as the service's first monoplane trainer. The type was developed to meet a 1936 requirement for a monoplane trainer to complement the monoplane combat aircraft entering Royal Air Force service in this period. It was derived as the M.14 from the Hawk Trainer, of which 25 had been built within the context of the M.2 Hawk series. Modifications from the Hawk Trainer included larger cockpits and blind-flying equipment, the latter including a hood that could be erected over the rear cockpit.

The type was a low-wing monoplane with fixed but nicely faired tailwheel landing gear and open tandem cockpits, and was unusual in reverting to the type of all-wood construction that the RAF had eschewed from the early 1920s. In addition to its monoplane configuration, trailing-edge flaps and full aerobatic capability, the Magister also offered to the pilots who trained on it the advantage of higher overall performance without any significant increase in landing speed. Production began in May 1937, and deliveries of the initial Magister Mk I to the Central Flying School started in October of the same year. The type was generally operated without its main landing gear fairings, and to improve spin recovery the Magister Mk II of 1938 introduced a slightly larger rudder.

Production lasted to 1941 and comprised 1,293 aircraft in the U.K. and another 100 licence-built in Turkey. After the end of World War II, many surplus Magisters were sold on to the civil market, and large numbers of these were adopted by civil flying schools with the designation Hawk Trainer Mk III. The Royal Air Force retired its last Magisters in 1948.

MILES MAGISTER Mk II
Role: Elementary trainer
Crew/Accommodation: Two
Power Plant: One 130-hp de Havilland Gypsy Major air-cooled inline
Dimensions: Span 10.31 m (33.83 ft); length 7.51 m (24.63 ft); wing area 16.35 m² (176 sq ft)
Weights: Empty 583 kg (1,286 lb); MTOW 862 kg (1,900 lb)
Performance: Maximum speed 225 km/h (140 mph) at sea level; operational ceiling 5,029 m (16,500 ft); range 591 km (367 miles)
Load: Up to 109 kg (240 lb) including student pilot

The Miles Magister was a simple yet highly effective trainer

BEECH T-34 MENTOR (U.S.A.)

T-34C Turbo-Mentor

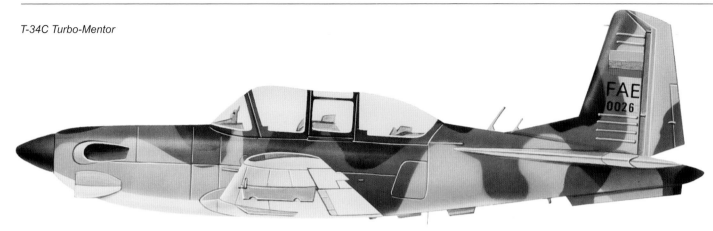

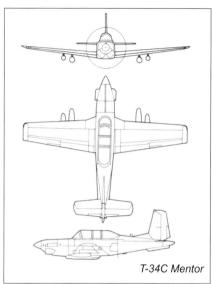

T-34C Mentor

The T-34 resulted from Beech's 1948 decision to develop a trainer derived from the Model 33 Bonanza with a conventional tail and accommodation for the pupil and instructor in tandem. The first example of the Model 45 Mentor flew in December 1948. At this time the U.S. Air Force was looking for a new primary trainer, and in 1950 evaluated three Model 45s under the designation YT-34 with two types of Continental flat-six piston engine. In March 1953 the

Model 45 was selected for U.S.A.F. service, and 450 T-34As were ordered with the 168-kW (225-hp) Continental O-470-13 engine. In June 1954, the U.S. Navy followed this lead with an order for 290 out of an eventual 423 T-34B trainers with the identically rated O-470-4 engine.

The basic soundness of the design is attested by further development of the

airframe in the early 1970s. By this time the turboprop was seen as the better powerplant, offering engine reliability, considerable fuel economies, and the use of turbine engines right through the pupil pilot's training. Two T-34Bs were therefore converted to YT-34C standard with the Pratt & Whitney Canada PT6A-25, and the first of these flew in

September 1973. The engine is provided with a torque limiter that restricts power output to some 56% of the maximum, and this ensures constant performance over a wide range of altitude and temperature conditions.

Successful evaluation led to orders for the T-34C Turbo-Mentor production model with a strengthened airframe. Between November 1977 and April 1984 the U.S. Navy received 334 newly-built T-34Cs, followed by 19 more in 1989-90. For the export market, Beech developed the T-34C-l with four underwing hardpoints for a 544-kg (1,200-lb) warload in the weapon training role, with counter-insurgency and light attack as possible operational tasks. The export civil version without hardpoints became the Turbine Mentor 34C.

BEECH T-34C TURBO-MENTOR
Role: Basic trainer/light strike
Crew/Accommodation: Two
Power Plant: One 550-shp Pratt & Whitney Canada PT6A-25 turboprop (MOO shp in torque-limited form used by the U.S. Navy)
Dimensions: Span 10.16 m (33.33 ft); length 8.75 m (2871 ft); wing area 16.70 m² (179.6 sq ft)
Weights: Empty 1,343 kg (2,960 lb); MTOW 2,495 kg (5,500 lb)
Performance: Maximum speed 396 km/h(246 mph); operational ceiling 9,144 m (30,000 ft); range up to 1,310 km (814 miles)
Load: Up to 544 kg (1,200 lb) of external weapons/fuel for T-34C-1

Beech T-34C

FOUGA CM. 170 MAGISTER (France)

CM. 170 Magister

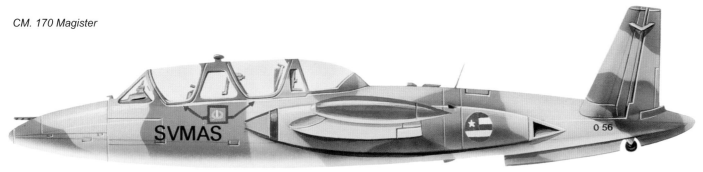

The Magister was designed as the CM. 170 and placed in production by Air Fouga, which later became part of the Potez corporation that was then absorbed in the Aérospatiale group. The CM. 170 was evolved to meet a French Air Force requirement for a purpose-designed jet basic trainer, and in its time was one of the world's most widely used trainers and light attack aircraft. The type's characteristic features are a high cockpit enclosure over the tandem seats, a V-tail, and mid-set wings with the two small turbojets installed in their roots. The type flew in prototype form during July 1952, and in the following year a pre-production batch of 10 aircraft was ordered for evaluation purposes. The French Air Force ordered an initial 95 aircraft in 1954, and the first of these CM. 170-1 aircraft was delivered in February 1956 in a programme that eventually witnessed the delivery of 437 Magisters to the French Air Force.

The CM. 170-1 is exclusively a land-based variant powered by two 400-kg (882-lb) Turboméca Marboré IIA turbojets, and overall production was 916 aircraft including major exports to West Germany and licensed construction in both Finland and Israel. Variants produced in substantially smaller numbers were the CM. 170-2 Super Magister and CM. 175 Zéphyr. The 137 Super Magisters are land-based aircraft powered by two 480-kg (1,058-lb) thrust Marboré VI turbojets, while the 32 Zéphyrs are naval trainers fitted with arrester hooks and powered by Marboré IIA engines. The basic type has a useful light attack capability, and this is improved in the AMIT Fouga, otherwise the Tzukit (Thrush), an Upgraded version developed by Israel Aircraft Industries with Marboré VI engines in a strengthened airframe and fitted with modern avionics.

ABOVE & OPPOSITE: Fouga Magister trainers

CM.170 Magister

FOUGA CM. 170 MAGISTER
Role: Basic/advanced trainer
Crew/Accommodation: Two
Power Plant: Two 440-kgp (880-lb s.t.) Turboméca Maboré I la turbojets
Dimensions: Span 12.15 m (39. 83 ft); length 10.06 m (33 ft); wing area 17.3 m² (186.1 sq ft)
Weights: Empty 2,150 kg (4,740 lb); MTOW 3,200 kg (7,055 lb)
Performance: Maximum speed 700 km/h (435 knots) at sea level; operational ceiling 13,500 m (44,291 ft); range 1,250 km (775 miles)
Load: Two 7.62-mm machine guns

CESSNA T-37 TWEET and A-37 DRAGONFLY (U.S.A.)

A-37B Dragonfly

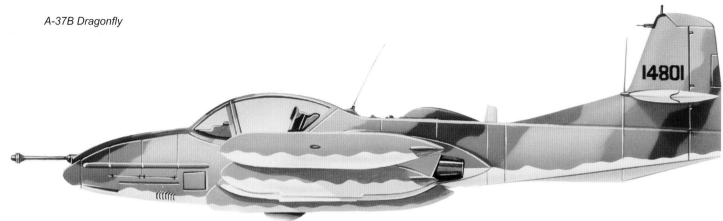

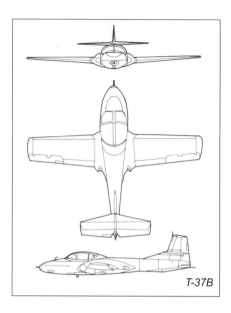

T-37B

In the early 1950s, the U.S. Air Force adopted a programme of all-through training using jet-powered aircraft, and issued a requirement for a new basic trainer with turbojet propulsion as its first purpose-built jet trainer. Several companies responded with design proposals; in 1953 Cessna was declared winner with its Model 318. Two XT-37 prototypes were ordered. The first of these flew in October 1954 with two Turboméca Marboré turbojets licence-built in the United States as 417-kg (920-lb) thrust Continental YJ69-T-9s. The type was ordered into production as the T-37A. Powered by J69-T-9 turbojets, hundreds of these aircraft entered service but only from 1957 as changes were found to be necessary, most notably in the layout of the cockpit.

CESSNA A-37B DRAGONFLY
Role: Light strike
Crew/Accommodation: Two
Power Plant: Two, 1,293-kgp (2,850-lb s.t.)
General Electric J85-GE-17A turbojets
Dimensions: Span 11.71 m (38.42 ft); length
9.69 m (31.83 ft); wing area 17.09 m²
(183.9 sq ft)
Weights: Empty 1,845 kg (4,067 lb); MTOW
6,350 kg (14,000 lb)
Performance: Maximum speed 771 km/h
(479 mph) at 4,724 m (15,500 ft); operational
ceiling 7,620 m (25,000 ft); radius 380 km (236
miles) with 843 kg (1,858 lb) bombload
Load: One 7.62-mm multi-barrel machine gun,
plus up to 2,576 kg (5,680 lb) of bombs or air-to-
ground rockets carried on underwing pylons

Cessna T-37A

These aircraft were followed by examples of the T-37B with 465-kg (1,025-lb) thrust J69-T-25 engines and improved avionics, bringing total production to 985 aircraft. All surviving T-37As were later brought up to T-37B standard. The last trainer was the T-37C, which offered light armament capability on underwing hardpoints, together with the option of wingtip fuel tanks. Production totalled 198 aircraft for delivery in aid packages to eight countries. A special counter-insurgency and light attack version for use in Vietnam was developed as the YAT-37D with 1089-kg (2,400-lb) thrust General Electric J85-GE-5 turbojets. Some 39 of the type were produced as T-37B conversions, and these were evaluated from 1967. Their success with an armament of one 7.62-mm (0.3-in) Minigun multi-barrel machine gun and disposable stores on eight underwing hardpoints led to development of the beefed-up Model 318E, which was ordered into production as the A-37B with 1293-kg (2,850-lb) thrust J85-GE-17A engines, inflight refuelling capability, and the ability to carry a warload of more than 2268 kg (5,000 lb). Many hundreds were built. Tweets are now being replaced in U.S.A.F. service by T-6A Texan IIs.

Cessna T-37 Tweet Birds

371

AERO L-39 ALBATROS and derivatives (Czech Republic)

L-39ZA Albatros

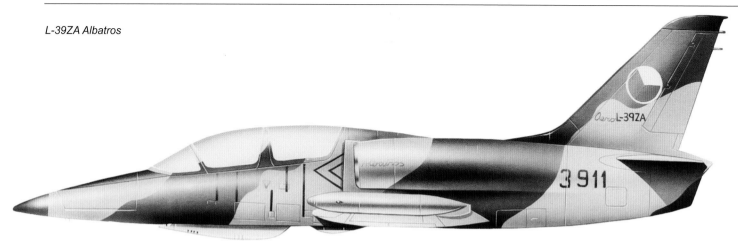

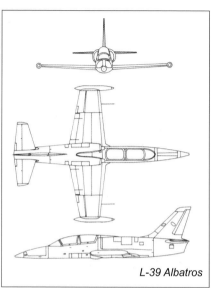

L-39 Albatros

The L-39 is an attractive and effective trainer that was developed to succeed the same company's L-29 Delfin. The first of three prototypes flew in November 1968, and the only major problem was integration of the Soviet turbofan into the Czech airframe. The original L-39C basic training version entered service in 1974 and became the standard jet trainer of most Communist air arms. The unswept flying surfaces curtail outright performance, but in addition to the fuel-economical turbofan engine and height-staggered seating, positive features are the type's tractable handling, reliability, and easy maintenance.

Variants are the L-39C with two underwing hardpoints for up to 284 kg (626 lb) of stores, the L-39ZO weapons trainer with four hardpoints on

The Aero L-39 Albatros has straight flying surfaces and turbofan power

AERO L-39ZA ALBATROS
Role: Light strike/reconnaissance/training
Crew/Accommodation: Two
Power Plant: One 1,720-kgp (3,792-lb s.t.) Ivchenko PROGRESS AI-25TL turbofan
Dimensions: Span 9.46 m (31 ft); length 12.13 m (39.76 ft); wing area 18.80 m² (202.4 sq ft)
Weights: Empty 3,565 kg (7,859 lb); MTOW 5,600 kg (12,346 lb)
Performance: Maximum speed 755 km/h (469 mph); operational ceiling 11,000 m (36,090 ft); range 1,350 km (839 miles) at 4,470 kg all-up weight on internal fuel only
Load: One 23-mm cannon, plus up to 1,290 kg (2,844 lb) of externally underslung ordnance

strengthened wings, the L-39ZA attack/reconnaissance type with four hardpoints and a detachable underfuselage pack containing one 23-mm twin-barrel cannon, the L-39ZA/MP multi-purpose variant with Western avionics and a head-up display (as used by Thailand), and the L-39V target-tug. All versions with four hardpoints can carry a 1,290-kg (2,844-lb) load. Well over 2,200 L-39s have been delivered to date to many countries. The L-39MS became the more powerful and more capable L-59, delivered from 1991, while subsequent developments have been the more advanced L-139 Albatros 2000 (flown 1993) and single/two-seat L-159 ALCA multi-role combat aircraft (flown 1997).

Aero L-39 Albatros

373

BRITISH AEROSPACE HAWK Family (United Kingdom)

Hawk 200

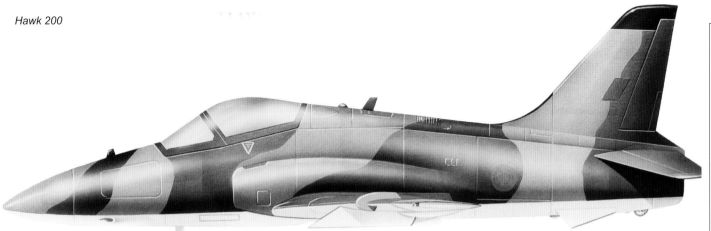

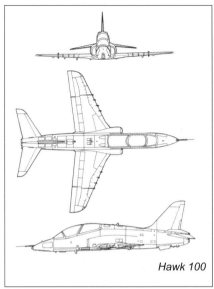

Hawk 100

The Hawk was developed to replace the Hawker Siddeley (Folland) Gnat in the training role, and first flew during August 1974 as the P. 1182 prototype.

The RAF received 176 as Hawk T.Mk1s of which 88 were later converted to permit a secondary air-defence role as Hawk T.Mk 1As with provision for AIM-

9L Sidewinder air-to-air missiles on four rather than two hardpoints under the wings. They use the 2,376-kg (5,240-lb) thrust Adour 151 engine. There have also

been several export models. The Hawk Mk 50 series is based on the T.Mk 1, but with a similarly-rated Adour Mk 851, and the Hawk Mk 60 has a slightly lengthened fuselage and usually the 2,590-kg (5,710-lb) thrust Adour Mk 861

British Aerospace Hawk T1

BRITISH AEROSPACE HAWK 60 Series
Role: Light strike/trainer
Crew/Accommodation: Two
Power Plant: One 2,590-kgp (5,710-lb s.t.) Rolls-Royce Turboméca Adour 861 turbofan
Dimensions: Span 9.4 m (30.83 ft); length 12.42 m (40.75 ft); wing area 16.69 m² (179.64 sq ft)
Weights: Empty 4,012 kg (8,845 lb); MTOW 9,100 kg (20,062 lb)
Performance: Maximum speed 1,037 km/h (560 knots) Mach 0.81 at sea level; operational ceiling 14,000 m (46,000 ft); radius 842 kn (524 miles) with two rocket pods and two drop tanks
Load: Up to 3,000 kg (6,000 lb) of weapons/fuel carried externally

turbofan for improved field performance, acceleration, climb and turn rates, and payload/range. Other and more radically developed variants are the Hawk 100 two-seat dual-role trainer and light ground-attack aircraft, and the Hawk 200 single-seat attack model.

The 100 is based on the Mk 60 but has the 2,600-kg (5,730-lb) thrust Adour Mk 871 and an advanced nav/attack system based on a digital databus and including a head-up display, weapon-aiming computer and radar-warning receiver. Most importantly, it used a new wing with leading-edge droop to enhance manoeuvrability and manual combat flaps, and has the option of FLIR/laser ranging in the extended nose. The 200 is also based on the Mk 60 but has a single-seat cockpit, Adour Mk 871 engine, Mk 100 wings and Mk 100 advanced electronics; it also introduced APG-66H multi-mode radar and provision for state-of-the-art weaponry.

The Hawk's basic design was adapted by McDonnell Douglas (now Boeing) as the T-45 Goshawk carrier-capable trainer for the U.S. Navy. This has a revised cockpit, strengthened landing gear (including long-stroke main units and a twin-wheel nose unit), an arrester hook, ventral finlets, larger tail surfaces, a revised wing, and the 2651-kg (5,845-lb) thrust F405-RR-401 version of the Adour Mk 871 turbofan.

British Aerospace Hawk

RECONNASSANCE & COMMUNICATIONS

In practical terms, aerial warfare has its origins in 1794, when Captain Coutelle of the French Republican Army carried out an aerial reconnaissance from a tethered balloon at Maubeuge in Belgium during the Battle of Fleurus. Another balloonist became the first-ever pilot to be shot down in war when, in 1898, American Sgt. Ivy Baldwin of the Army Signal Corps was brought down (virtually unharmed) by Spanish ground fire during the Battle of Santiago. These two unrelated events, involving balloonists a century apart, were portents of aerial warfare in the 20th century, with the need for reconnaissance being later countered by a requirement to prevent an enemy using that information or gaining a similar advantage.

A Blériot monoplane, accompanied by a Royal Aircraft Factory B.E.2a, made the first RFC reconnaissance flight over German lines during the 1914–18 war on 19 August 1914. Just days later, aerial reconnaissance was instrumental in bringing victory to German forces at the Battle of Tannenberg, when 120,000 Russian soldiers and 500 guns were captured, and from that time to this reconnaissance has been a vital part of tactical and strategic planning, though modern-day commanders can also call upon satellites.

Communications has been a less glamorous military role, yet of

importance in peace and war. Normally undertaken by off-the-shelf light aircraft or small transports, such types have traditionally provided the means for VIPs to be air-lifted on urgent non-regular business, either for connecting bases or flying to other destinations. An advantage of the lightplane has been its ability to operate from unprepared airstrips, and the Fieseler Storch that had

incredible short take-off capability was not only the favoured transport of wartime Generalfeldmarschall Erwin Rommel in North Africa, but a captured example was used by his opponent, Field Marshal Bernard Montgomery.

Examples of important communications work are numerous: one worthy of recounting came during the 1939–45 war when RAF de Havilland

Dominie biplanes co-operated with Air Transport Auxiliary in vital aircraft ferrying work, returning pilots after they had delivered combat aircraft to base. Occasionally, even combat aircraft have found their way to communications units, and it should be remembered that, as one example of many, a Fairey IIIF general-purpose biplane, set aside for such duties, took Lord Londonderry to the 1932 Disarmament Conferences in Geneva. Even fighters have been used by commanders as personal mounts to flit between bases, and in America a Boeing F4B-1A biplane of the early 1930s was used for communications flights by the Assistant Secretary of the U.S. Navy, while in recent times even a Russian Mach 2 Sukhoi Su-27 allegedly became the 'personal' transport of a test pilot.

The Lockheed SR-71 'Blackbird' was an advanced, long range, Mach 3+ strategic reconnaissance aircraft. It was developed from the Lockheed A-12 reconnaissance aircraft in the 1960s by the Lockheed Skunk Works as a black project. Clarence 'Kelly' Johnson was responsible for many of the design's innovative concepts. During reconnaissance missions the SR-71 operated at high speeds and altitudes to allow it to outrace threats; if a surface-to-air missile launch was detected, standard evasive action was simply to accelerate.

BLÉRIOT MONOPLANES (France)

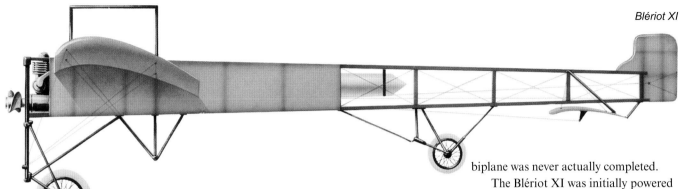

Blériot XI

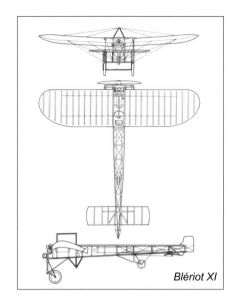

Blériot XI

Blériot XI-2 and -3 two- and three-seat forms. (See introduction for early military missions.)

Louis Blériot was one of the true pioneers of aviation, and secured his place in history during 1909 as the first man to fly a heavier-than-air craft across the English Channel. The machine involved in this epoch-making flight was a Blériot XI with an 18.7-kW (25-hp) Anzani engine, the culmination of a series of monoplanes that had started with the unsuccessful Blériot V of 1906. The V was Blériot's first design after he had ended his association with Gabriel Voisin, and was a canard type that made a few hopping flights, then crashed and was scrapped. Next came the tandem-wing Blériot VI that achieved a few hops

during 1907. The Blériot VII was a modestly successful tractor monoplane, and this layout was used in the fabric-covered Blériot VIII that was later rebuilt as the Blériot BHIbis with flap-type ailerons and Blériot VHIter with pivoting wingtip ailerons. The Blériot XI had paper-covered wings of short span and a fuselage partially covered in fabric, but never flew, while the Blériot X pusher

biplane was never actually completed.

The Blériot XI was initially powered by a 21-kW (28-hp) R.E.P. engine, but its lack of success with this engine led to its modification as the Blériot XI (Mod) with the 18.7-kW (25-hp) Anzani. Blériot's XI (Mod)'s cross-Channel triumph secured a comparative flood of orders for his aircraft, which was steadily upgraded with more powerful engines. The type was also developed for the military as a reconnaissance machine in

BLERIOT XI-2

Role: Reconnaissance/training
Crew/Accommodation: Two
Power Plant: One 80-hp Gnôme air-cooled rotary
Dimensions: Span 10.35 m (33.96 ft); length
 8.4 m (27.56 ft); wing area 19 m² (205 sq ft)
Weights: Empty 335 kg (786 lb); MTOW 585 kg
 (1,290 lb)
Performance: Maximum speed 120 km/h
 (75 mph) at sea level; endurance 3.5 hours
Load: None other than crew

Blériot monoplane

FIESELER Fi 156 STORCH (Germany)

Fi 156C

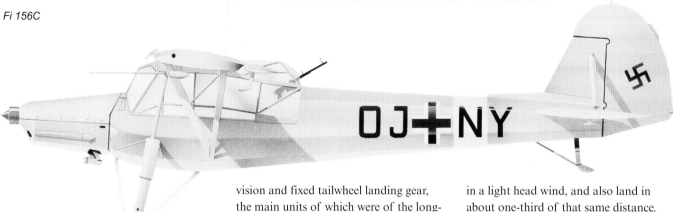

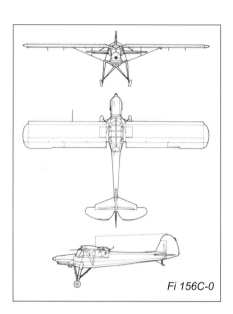

Fi 156C-0

The Fi 156 Storch (Stork) was Germany's most important army co-operation and battlefield reconnaissance aircraft of World War II, and the first of four prototypes flew in the early part of 1936. The Fi 156 was a braced high-wing monoplane with an extensively glazed cockpit offering very good fields of vision and fixed tailwheel landing gear, the main units of which were of the long-stroke type to absorb landing forces at high sink rates. The prototype displayed exceptional STOL capabilities because of its wing, which combined good aerodynamic qualities with the advantages offered by fixed slats and slotted ailerons/flaps over the entire leading and trailing edges respectively. The prototypes showed that the Storch could take off in as little at 60 m (200 ft) in a light head wind, and also land in about one-third of that same distance.

The type was adopted for a wide assortment of army co-operation and associated duties in its Fi 156A-1 initial production form. The civil Fi 156B remained only a project, so the next variant was the military Fi 156C. This had improved radio equipment and a raised rear section of the cabin glazing allowing a 7.92-mm (0.312-in) machine gun to be mounted. Fi 156C variants were the Fi 156C-1 for liaison, two-seat Fi 156C-2 for tactical reconnaissance or casualty evacuation with a litter in the rear cockpit, Fi 156C-3 for light transport, and Fi 156C-5 with a ventral tank for extended range. The last production model was the Fi 156D-1 ambulance powered by an Argus AS 10P engine and with provision for one litter loaded through a larger hatch.

Production totalled about 2,900 aircraft built in Germany and, under German control, Czechoslovakia and France. Mraz and Morane-Saulnier continued production in these two countries after the war.

FIESELER Fi 156 C-1 STORCH
Role: Army co-operation/observation and communications
Crew/Accommodation: Two or one, plus one litter-carried casualty
Power Plant: One 240-hp Argus As 10C air-cooled inline
Dimensions: Span 14.25 m (46.75 ft); length 9.9 m (32.48 ft); wing area 26 m² (279.9 sq ft)
Weights: Empty 930 kg (2,051 lb); MTOW 1,320 kg (2,911 lb)
Performance: Maximum speed 145 km/h (90 mph) at sea level; operational ceiling 4,600 m (15,092 ft); range 385 km (239 miles)
Load: One 7.9-mm machine gun, plus provision to evacuate one litterborne casualty

Fieseler Fi Storch

OPPOSITE: Fieseler Fi 156 Storch

WESTLAND LYSANDER

Lysander Mk III

The Lysander resulted from a 1934 British Air Ministry requirement for a two-seat army co-operation aircraft. Key features of the requirements were good fields of vision and STOL performance, and for this reason the design team opted for an extensively

glazed cockpit supporting the roots of the unusually shaped high-set wing, the outer portions of which were braced by V-struts to the cantilever main legs of the fixed tailwheel landing gear. These legs were also fitted with small stub wings which could carry up to 227 kg (500 lb) of light bombs or other types of stores.

The first of two prototypes flew in June 1936 with the 664-kW (890-hp)

Bristol Mercury XII radial, and after successful trials the type was ordered into production as the Lysander Mk I, of which 169 were built for service from June 1938. Further development of this aircraft resulted in the Lysander Mk II, of which 517 were built with the 675-kW (905-hp) Bristol Perseus XII radial, the Lysander Mk III of which 517 were built

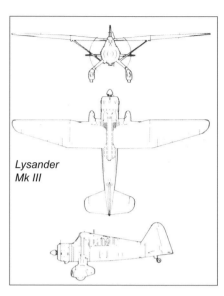

Lysander Mk III

with the 649-kW (870-hp) Mercury XX, and the Lysander Mk IIIA of which 347 were built with the Mercury 30. Early operations in France revealed that the Lysander was too vulnerable for its designed role in the presence of modern fighters and anti-aircraft defences, and though the type saw further limited first-line service in the Middle East and the Far East, most aircraft were relegated to second-line duties such as target towing, air-sea rescue, radar calibration and special agent infiltration and extraction. Some 14 Mk I conversions to Lysander TT.Mk I standard validated the target tug version, and a similar process provided five TT.Mk IIs, 51 T.Mk IIIs and 100 TT.Mk IIIA aircraft.

OPPOSITE: Westland Lysander

WESTLAND LYSANDER Mk III
Role: Communications/tactical reconnaissance
Crew/Accommodation: Two
Power Plant: One 890-hp Bristol Mercury XX air-cooled radial
Dimensions: Span 15.24 m (50.00 ft); length 9.29 m (30.50 ft); wing area 24.15 m² (260.00 sq ft)
Weights: Empty 1,980 kg (4,365 lb): MTOW 2.865 kg (6.318 lb)
Performance: Maximum speed 336 km/h (209 mph) at 1.524 m (5,000 ft): operational ceiling 6.553 m (21.500 ft): range 966 km (600 miles)
Load: Four .303-in machine guns, plus up to 227 kg (500 lb) of bombs

The Westland Lysander had excellent STOL performance

ARADO Ar 234 BLITZ (Germany)

Ar 234B-2 Blitz

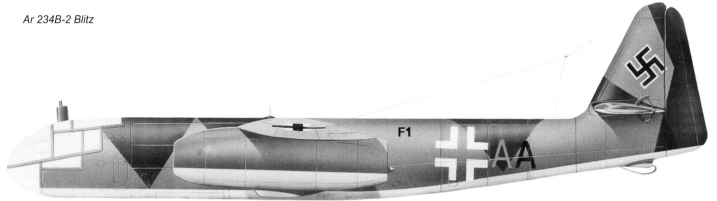

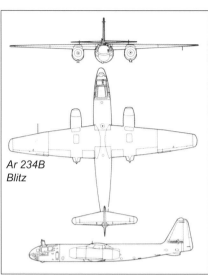

Ar 234B Blitz

The Ar 234 Blitz (Lightning) was the world's first purpose-designed jet reconnaissance aircraft and bomber. As first flown in June 1943, the all-metal Ar 234A had straight flying surfaces, with two Junkers Jumo 004B turbojets in nacelles slung under the shoulder-mounted wings, and a fuselage too slender to accommodate retractable wheeled landing gear. As a result, the first prototypes were designed to take off from a jettisonable trolley and land on retractable skids. Some 18 prototypes

were trialled with twin Jumo 004B or quadruple BMW 003A turbojets. The trolley/skid arrangement proved workable but was hardly effective, so the 20 pre-production aircraft featured a wider fuselage to make possible the installation of retractable tricycle landing gear.

These paved the way for the 210

examples of the Ar 234B production model with two engines but no pressurization or ejector seat; this series included the Ar 234B-1 reconnaissance and Ar 234B-2 bomber variants.

Another 12 prototypes were used to develop the multi-role Ar 234C model, which had four engines, cabin

pressurization and an ejector sea; only 14 of this late-war model were built, and the series included the Ar 234C-1 reconnaissance and Ar 234C-4 multi-role bomber and ground attack variants. The Ar 234C-4 bomber and Ar 234C-2 armed reconnaissance variants remained projects, as did several other variants.

The Ar 234 first entered service in the summer of 1944 in the form of two evaluation prototypes operated by 1 Staffel for reconnaissance, followed that September by Ar 234B-1s going to Sonderkommando Götz. From 24 December, Ar 234B-2 jet bombers went into action, initially with II/KG 76 during the Ardennes offensive. Night operations by KG 76 began on the last night of 1944 against targets in Brussels and Liège.

ARADO Ar 234B-2 BLITZ
Role: High-speed bomber
Crew/Accommodation: One
Power Plant: Two 900-kgp (1,980-lb s.t.) Junkers 004B Orkan turbojets
Dimensions: Span 14.44 m (47.38 ft); length 12.64 m (41.47 ft); wing area 27.3 m² (284.2 sqft)
Weights: Empty 5,200 kg (11,464 lb); MTOW 9,800 kg (21,715 lb)
Performance: Maximum speed 742 km/h (461 mph) at 6,000 m (19,685 ft); operational ceiling 10,000 m (32,810 ft); range 1,556km (967 miles) with 500 kg (1,102 lb)payload
Load: Two rear-firing 20-mm cannon, plus up to 2,000 kg (4,410 lb) of bombs

Arado Ar 234 Blitz

LOCKHEED SR-71 (U.S.A.)

SR-71

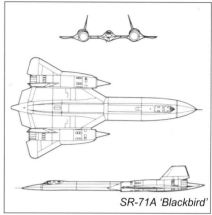

SR-71A 'Blackbird'

Until its first retirement at the end of 1989 and then the planned reactivation of two in the mid 1990s but followed by the announcement of continuing full retirement in April 1998, the SR-71 was the world's fastest and highest-flying 'conventional' aircraft. It was a truly extraordinary machine, designed for the strategic reconnaissance role with a mass of sensors including ASARs-1 (advanced synthetic aperture radar system) or the Itek camera that could scan to the horizon on each side of the flightpath, and two pre-programmable high-resolution cameras.

The 'stealthy' airframe was designed for a crew of two (pilot and systems operator) and minimum drag, and was therefore evolved with a very slender fuselage and thin wings of delta planform blended into the fuselage by large chines that generated additional lift, prevented the pitching down of the nose at higher speeds, and provided additional volume for sensors and fuel. The airframe was built largely of titanium and stainless steel to deal with the high temperatures created by air friction at the SR-71's Mach 3+ cruising speed at heights over 21335 m (70,000 ft). Power was provided by the two special continuous-bleed turbojets which at high speed provided only a small part of the motive power in

LOCKHEED SR-71 A

Role: Long-range high supersonic
  reconnaissance
Crew/Accommodation: Two
Power Plant: Two 14.742-kgp (32.500-lb s.t.)
  Pratt & Whitney J58 turbo-ramjets
Dimensions: Span 16.94 m (55.58 ft); length
  32.74 m (107.41 ft); wing area 149.1m²
  (1,605 sq ft) Weights: Empty 30,618 kg
  (67,500 lb); MTOW 78,020 kg (172,000 1b)
Performance: Cruise speed 3,661 km/h (1,976
  knots) Mach 3.35 at 24,385 m (80,000 ft);
  operational ceiling 25.908 m (85.000 ft); range
  5,230 km (2.822 naut. miles) unrefuelled
Load: Up to around 9,072 kg (20,000 lb) of
  specialized sensors

Lockheed SR-71B trainers

the form of direct jet thrust from the nozzles (18%), the greater part of the power being provided by inlet suction (54%) and thrust from the special outlets at the rear of the multiple-flow nacelles (28%). Nicknamed 'Blackbird' for its special overall colour scheme that helped dissipate heat and absorb enemy radar emissions, the SR-71 was developed via three YF-121-A interceptors which reached only the experimental stage, from 15 A-12 (including one trainer) Mach 3.6 reconnaissance aircraft ordered for the CIA (and, in the case of two A-12 (M)s, as launching platforms for D-21 hypersonic cruise reconnaissance drones) and first flown from Groom Lake in March 1962.

The SR-71A entered service in 1966 and 30 aircraft were built, while training was carried out on a conversion type comprising one SR-7 IB and one similar SR-71C converted from SR-71 standard.

RIGHT & OPPOSITE: The Lockheed SR-71 was known as the 'Blackbird' for its special overall colour scheme

TRANSPORTS

By the time the Great War ended in 1918, aeroplanes had firmly established themselves as vital to any nation possessing fighting forces. Their influence extended not only far beyond the skies, but also to the very deployment and use of traditional land armies and naval ships, as all were within reach of 'spying' and armed aeroplanes.

There was one form of aeroplane, however, that had been largely overlooked due to the nature of warfare on the Western Front and elsewhere –

that of the military transport. Post-war, the RAF found itself much diminished in size but still tasked with new and hitherto untested roles such as policing the vast areas of Iraq under the so-called 'air control' duties, whereby it was hoped that a small number of RAF squadrons could enforce law and order from the air, thus replacing large army garrisons. To the initial four squadrons of de Havilland (Airco) D.H.9As, one of Bristol Fighters and one of Sopwith Snipe fighters were added and from 1922

two squadrons of new Vickers Vernons, the first-ever purpose-built troop-carrying transports. Based on the Vimy bomber but given a rotund fuselage to provide internal accommodation for 12 troops, the newly-built Vernons joined just two squadrons in the Middle East, where their duties were varied; on one day in 1922, the year air control operations in Iraq began, Vernons evacuated sick British troops from Northern Iraq to a Baghdad hospital, while other duties included mail-carrying.

The 22-troop Vickers Victoria began replacing the Vernons from 1926, based on the Virginia bomber, such had been the success of the first troop carriers, and these remained in use for nearly a decade. So with the Vernon began a new venture for the aeroplane, that of military transport.

In the United States a Martin GMB bomber had been completed in 1919 with the fuselage height raised and windows added for carrying ten passengers, and was followed by six so-modified MB-1 bombers for use by the Postal Service. These were later transferred to the U.S. Army Air Corps, thus becoming the first Army aircraft to use the original 'T' for transport designation. Two T-2s followed and were imported Dutch Fokker F-IVs, one later becoming the A-2 ambulance aircraft, while the first aircraft of the new Army 'C' serial designation (for transports) system, introduced in 1925, was the Douglas C-l eight-passenger transport.

By the 1930s the production of new commercial transports provided also military equivalents for the armed forces, with the Luftwaffe taking in huge numbers of Junkers Ju 52/3ms, for

LEFT: Lockheed Martin C-130 Hercules

OPPOSITE: Boeing C-17A Globemaster III

example, and the important wartime Allied C-47 was based on the Douglas DC-3 airliner.

But, once peace had again been restored, military needs for freighting vast numbers of troops or heavy loads of military equipment, such as tanks and guns, meant that giant transports began to appear as specialized military types to meet Cold War demands, a tradition of original design that continues today with the latest Boeing C-17A Globemaster III for the U.S.A.F. Interestingly, the Lockheed Martin C-l30 Hercules that first joined the service in 1956 as a turboprop-powered tactical transport in original C-130A form, continues in production today in latest C-130J form, and is well-set to become the first aeroplane in history to complete over half a century of production by its original company and possibly the first to complete (by 2056) a full century of service!

DOUGLAS DC-4 and C-54 SKYMASTER (U.S.A.)

DC-4

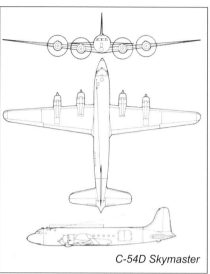

C-54D Skymaster

Even before the DC-3 had flown, Douglas was planning a longer-range air transport with four engines, retractable tricycle landing gear, and greater capacity. The DC-4 (later DC-4E) pressurized prototype first flew in June 1938, but was too advanced for its time and therefore suffered a number of technical problems. The DC-4E's performance and operating economics were also below specification, and the company therefore dropped the type. As a replacement, Douglas turned to the

unpressurized and otherwise simplified DC-4 with a lighter structure, a new high aspect ratio wing, and a tail unit with a single central vertical surface in place of the DC-4E's twin endplate surfaces. The type was committed to production with 1081-kW (1,450-hp) Pratt & Whitney R-2000-2SD1-G Twin Wasp radial engines even before the first example had flown.

With the United States caught up into World War II during December 1941, the type was swept into military service as the C-54 (Army) and R5D (Navy) long-range military transport, and the first aircraft flew during February 1942 in U.S. Army Air Forces markings. The main military versions were the 24 impressed C-54s with R-

2000-3 radials for 26 passengers, the 207 fully militarized C54As and R5D-1s with R-2000-7s for 50 passengers, the 220 C-54Bs and R5D-2s with integral wing tanks, the 380 C-54Ds and R5D-3s with R-2000-1 1s, the 125 C-54E and R5D-4 convertible freight/passenger models with revised fuel tankage, and the 162 C-54G and R5D-5 troop carriers with R-2000-9s.

After military service many of these aircraft found their way on to the civil register and performed excellently in the long-range passenger and freight roles. Two civil models were produced after World War II; total production was 1,122 aircraft.

DOUGLAS DC-4 and C-54 SKYMASTER
Role: Long-range passenger transport
Crew/Accommodation: Four, plus three/four cabin crew, plus up to 86 passengers
Power Plant: Four 1,450-hp Pratt & Whitney R.2000 Twin Wasp air-cooled radials
Dimensions: Span 35.81 m (117.5 ft); length 28.6 m (93.83 ft); wing area 135.35 m² (1,457 sq ft)
Weights: Empty 16,783 kg (37,000 lb); MTOW 33,113 kg (73,000 lb)
Performance: Cruise speed 309 km/h (192 mph) at 3,050 m (10,000 ft); operational ceiling 6,705 m (22,000 ft) ; range 3,220 km (2,000 miles) with 9,979 kg (22,000 lb payload
Load: Up to 14,515 kg (32,500 lb)

Douglas C-54D Skymaster

CURTISS-WRIGHT C-46 COMMANDO (U.S.A.)

C-46A Commando

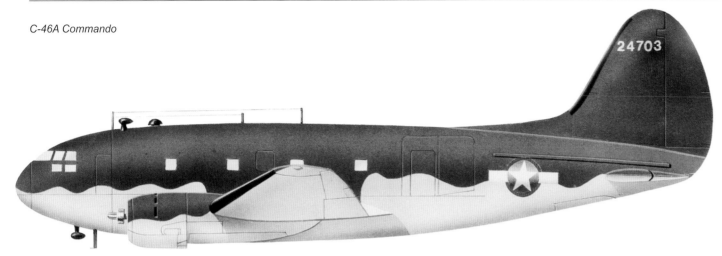

The aircraft that entered widespread production as the C-46 Commando troop and freight transport was conceived as a civil type to pick up where the Douglas DC-3 left off by offering such advantages as longer range, higher cruising speed, cabin pressurization, and a larger payload in the form of 36 passengers carried in a smooth-nosed fuselage of the double-lobe type. The twin-finned CW-20T prototype flew in March 1940 with 1268-kW (1,700-hp) Wright R-2600 radials, but soon afterwards was converted into the CW-20A with a revised tail unit featuring a single vertical surface and flat rather than dihedralled tailplane halves.

Such were the needs of the growing U.S. military establishment, however, that subsequent development was geared to the requirements of the U.S. Army Air Corps (later U.S. Army Air Forces), which evaluated the CW-20A as the C-55 and then ordered the type as the militarized CW-20B. This version became the C-46 with 1491-kW (2,000-hp) Pratt & Whitney R-2800-51 radials and accommodation for 45 troops. Some 25 of the original C-46 troop transports entered service from July 1942 as the U.S.A.A.F.'s largest and heaviest twin-engined aircraft. The series was used almost exclusively in the Pacific theatre during World War II.

There were several variants after the C-46, including 1,493 C-46As as the first definitive model with R-2800-51 engines and a strengthened fuselage floor that could take up to 50 troops or freight loaded through large port-side cargo doors. Later variants, such as the 1,410 C-46D troop and 234 C-46F utility transports, were comparable with the C-46A, apart from minor modifications and adaptations. The type was also used by the United States Navy with the designation R5C, and after the war many ex-military machines were released on to the civil market where some remain to the present.

C-46A Commando

Curtiss-Wright C-46 Commando

CURTISS-WRIGHT C-46A COMMANDO
Role: Long-range transport
Crew/Accommodation: Four, plus up to 50 troops
Power Plant: Two, 2,000-hp Pratt & Whitney R-2800-51 Double Wasp air-cooled radials
Dimensions: Span 32.91 m (108 ft); length 23.26 m (76.33 ft); wing area 126.34 m² (1.360 sq ft)
Weights: Empty 13,608 kg (30,000 lb); MTOW 25,401 kg (56,000 lb)
Performance: Cruise speed 278 km/h (173 mph) at 4,572 m (15,000 ft); operational ceiling 7,468 m (24,500 ft); range 1,93.1 km (1,200 miles) with full payload
Load: Up to 6,804 kg (15,000 lb)

FAIRCHILD C-82 AND C-119 Family (U.S.A.)

C-119C

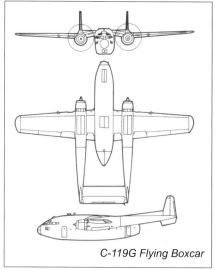

C-119G Flying Boxcar

In 1941, Fairchild began work on its F-78 design to meet a U.S. Army Air Forces' requirement for a military freighter. The XC-82 prototype first flew in September 1944 as a high-wing monoplane with twin booms extending from the engine nacelles angles of the inverted gull wing to support the empennage so that clamshell rear doors could provide access to the central payload nacelle. The payload could comprise 78 troops or 42 paratroops, or 34 litters or freight. The only production version was the C-82A Packet with 1566-kW (2,100-hp) Pratt & Whitney R-2800-34 radials, and delivery of 220 such aircraft was completed.

The basic concept was further developed into the C-119 Flying Boxcar with 1976-kW (2,650-hp) Pratt & Whitney R-4360-4 radial engines and the cockpit relocated into the nose of the nacelle. The XC-82B prototype of 1947 led to production of the C-119B with 2610-kW (3,500-hp) R-4360-20 engines, structural strengthening, and the fuselage widened by 0.36 m (1 ft 2 in) for the carriage of a heavier payload that could include 62 paratroops or freight. The 55 examples of this initial model were followed by 303 C-119Cs with R-4360-20WA engines, dorsal fin extensions, and no tailplane outboard of the vertical tail surfaces, 212 examples of the C-119F

FAIRCHILD C-119C FLYING BOXCAR
Role: Military bulk freight/paratroop transport
Crew/Accommodation: Four, plus up to 42 paratroops
Power Plant: Two 3,500-hp Pratt & Whitney R-4360-20 Wasp Major air-cooled radials
Dimensions: Span 33.32 m (109.25 ft); length 26.37 m (86.5 ft); wing area 134.4 m² (1,447 sq ft) Weights: Empty 18,053 kg (39,800 lb); MTOW 33,566 kg (74,000 lb)
Performance: Maximum speed 452 km/h (281 mph) at 5,486 (18,000 ft); operational ceiling 7,285 m (23,900 ft); range 805 km (500 miles) with maximum load
Load: Up to 8,346 kg (18,400 lb)

C-119C Flying Boxcar

TROOP CARRIER

CQ-581

with ventral fins and other detail modifications, and 480 examples of the C-119G with different propellers and equipment changes. The 26 AC-119G aircraft were gunship conversions of C-

119Gs and were later upgraded to AC-119K standard, the 62 C-119Js were C-119F/G transports revised with a flight-openable door in the rear of the central pod, the five C-119Js were C-

119Gs modified with two 1293-kg (2,850-lb) thrust General Electric J85-GE-17 booster turbojets in underwing nacelles, and the 22 C-119Ls were C-119Gs updated and fitted with new propellers.

Fairchild C-82

391

ANTONOV An-2 and An-3 'COLT' (U.S.S.R.)

An-2 'Colt'

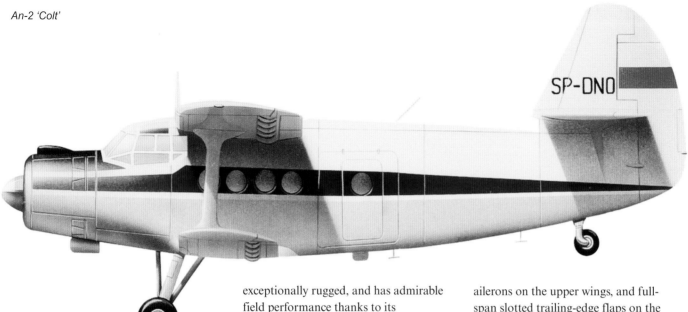

SP-DNO

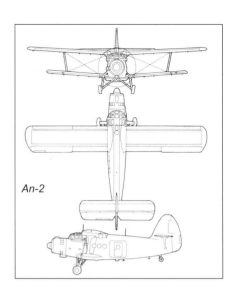

An-2

exceptionally rugged, and has admirable field performance thanks to its combination of automatic leading-edge slats, slotted trailing-edge flaps, drooping ailerons on the upper wings, and full-span slotted trailing-edge flaps on the lower wings. The type entered service with the 746-kW (1,000-hp)ASz-62IR radial, and though designed primarily for agricultural use, it was and still is produced in a number of variants suited to a variety of other roles. Typically, these are for use as transport (12 passengers and two children or 1,240-kg/2,733-lb of freight), float-equipped transport, paradropping, ambulance work, fire-fighting, meteorological

The An-2 first flew in August 1947 with the 567-kW (760-hp) Shvetsov ASh-21 radial engine, and was an anachronism for being a large biplane with I-type interplane struts, fixed but exceptionally robust tailwheel landing gear, and a strut-braced tailplane. The first production An-2s left the original Kiev factory in 1949 as general-purpose aircraft and, after production of 3,167 up to 1962, Dolgoprudnyi became the Russian source of 429 An-2Ms during 1964-65. The type became known to NATO as 'Colt'.

An all-metal but unpressurized type with fabric covering on the tailplane and rear portions of the wings, the An-2 is

The Antonov An-2 is a modern oddity

An-2TD 'COLT' by PZL-Mielec in Poland
Role: Utility transport/agricultural spraying
Crew/Accommodation: Two, plus up to 12 passengers
Power Plant: One 967-hp WSK-Kalisz ASz-62IR air-cooled radial
Dimensions: Span 18.18 m (59.65 ft); length 12.74m (41.8 ft); wing area 71.5 m² (770sq ft)
Weights: Empty 3,445 kg (7,959 lb); MTOW 5,500 kg (112,125 lb)
Performance: Cruise speed 190km/h (118 mph) at 800m (2,625 ft); operational ceiling 4,160 m (13,650 ft); range 1,390 km (863 miles)
Load: Up to 1,500 kg (3,307 lb)

research, geophysical research, photogrametric survey and TV relay.

Well over 16,000 examples of the An-2 have been built, about 10,600 of them in Poland since 1960. This total also includes many hundreds of examples of the licensed Chinese model, the Shijiazhuang Y5, although the original Chinese source was Nanchang (727 built between 1957 and 1968). The An-3 was developed as a turboprop-powered version using a 701-kW (940-shp) Glushenkov TVD-10B to offer 40% more payload.

Antonov An-2

393

LOCKHEED MARTIN C-130 HERCULES (U.S.A.)

L-100-30 Hercules

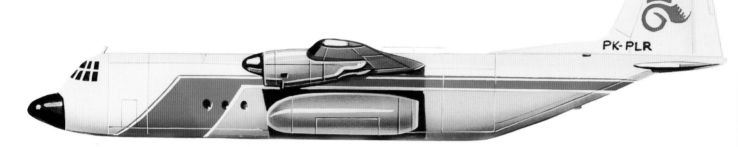

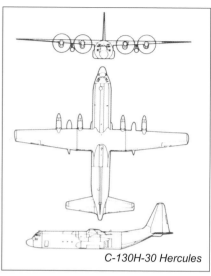

C-130H-30 Hercules

The Hercules is the airlifter against which all other turboprop tactical transports are measured. It was the type that pioneered the modern airlifter layout with a high-set wing, a capacious fuselage with a rectangular-section hold terminating at its rear in an integral ramp/door that allows the straight-in loading/unloading of bulky items under the upswept tail, and multi-wheel landing gear with its main units accommodated in external fairings. No demands are made on hold area and volume, leaving the hold floor and opened ramp at truckbed height to help loading and unloading.

The type was designed in response to a 1951 requirement for STOL transport, and first flew in YC-130 prototype form during August 1954 with 2796-kW (3,750-shp) Allison T56-A-1A turboprops driving three-blade propellers. Over 2,200 aircraft have been delivered and the type remains in both development and production, having been evolved in major variants, from its initial C-130A form to the C-130B with

LOCKHEED C-130H HERCULES

Role: Land-based, rough field-capable tactical transport

Crew/Accommodation: Four crew with up to 92 troops or 74 stretchers

Power Plant: Four 4,508-shp Allison T56-A-15LFE turboprops

Dimensions: Span 40.4 m (132.6 ft); length 29.8 m (97.75 ft); wing area 162.1 m² (1,745 sq ft)

Weights: Empty 34,702 kg (76,505 lb); MTOW 79,380 kg (175,505 lb)

Performance: Maximum cruise speed 621 km/h (335 knots), at 3,658 m (12,000 ft); operational ceiling 10,060 m (33,000 ft); range 3,600 km (2,240 miles) with 18,143 kg (40,000 lb payload

Load: 19,340 kg (42,637 lb)

A U.S. Air Force Lockheed Martin C-130H Hercules

more fuel and a higher maximum weight; the C-130E with 3020-kW (4,050-shp) T56-A7a turboprops driving four-blade propellers, greater internal fuel capacity and provision for external fuel tanks; the C-130H with airframe and system improvements as well as 3362-kW (4,508-shp) T56-A-15 turboprops, and the C-130H-30 with a lengthened fuselage for the accommodation of bulkier payloads.

The latest versions are the C-130J and lengthened C-130J-30, the latter first flown in April 1996 and first joining the RAF's No. 24 Squadron in 1998. The 'J' introduces 3424 kW (4,591-shp) Allison AE 2100D3 turboprops with six-blade composite propellers and an advanced 2-pilot flight deck with multi-function displays and digital avionics, among other changes. There has also been a host of variants for tasks as diverse as Arctic operations, drone and spacecraft recovery, special forces insertion and extraction, airborne command post operations, and communication with submerged submarines. It has also been produced in L-100 civil form that has secured modest sales, with the new L-100J representing a commercial version of the C-130J-30.

The Hercules known as Fat Albert, *the support aircraft for the U.S. Navy Blue Angels demonstration team*

BOEING KC-135 STRATOTANKER (U.S.A.)

KC-135A Stratotanker

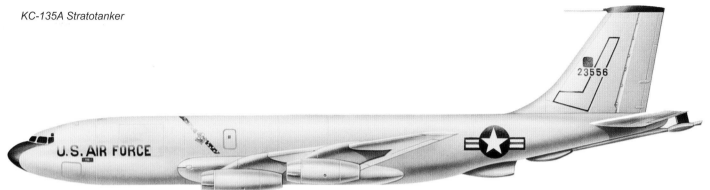

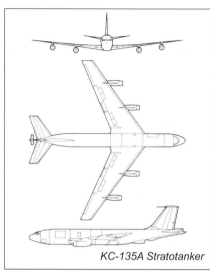

KC-135A Stratotanker

One of the provisions of Boeing's Model 367-80 prototype was for the company's patented 'flying boom' inflight refuelling system, and after this had been proved in trials, the U.S. Air Force announced in August 1954 that it was to procure the KC-135A inflight refuelling tanker based on the 'Dash 80'. The first of these flew in August 1956. Such was the priority allocated to this essential support for the United States' strategic bombers that production built up very rapidly, and eventually 732 KC-135 Stratotankers were produced with 6237-

kg (13,750-lb) thrust Pratt & Whitney J57-P-59W turbojets; later aircraft were built with the taller vertical tail surfaces that were retrofitted to the earlier machines. In addition, 48 Stratolifter long-range transports were completed as 18 turbojet-powered C-135A and 30 C-135B turbofan-powered transports; but as the role was better performed by the Lockheed C-130 Hercules and C-141

StarLifter, the aircraft were later converted into special-purpose machines to complement a number of KC-135As also adapted as EC-135 command post and communication relay platforms, or as RC-135 photographic/electronic reconnaissance platforms.

The type remains so important that most are being upgraded for continued service. A total of 163 KC-135As

operated by the Air Force Reserve and Air National Guard are being improved to KC-135E standard with reskinned wing undersurfaces, new brakes and anti-skid units, and 8165-kg (18,000-lb) thrust Pratt & Whitney JT3D turbofans (complete with their pylons and nacelles and redesignated TF33-PW-102s) plus the tail units from surplus civil Model 707 transports. A similar but more extensive upgrade is being undertaken to improve U.S.A.F. KC-135As to KC-135R standard with better systems, a larger tailplane, greater fuel capacity, and 10000-kg (22,050-lb) thrust CFM International F108-CF-100 turbofans. The KC-135T is similar to the 'R' but could refuel the SR-71 (when in service).

OPPOSITE: Here, a Boeing E-4B advanced national command post is being refuelled from a KC-135 Stratotanker

BOEING KC-135A STRATOTANKER
Role: Military tanker-transport
Crew/Accommodation: Four, including fuel boom operator
Power Plant: Four 6,237-kgp (13,750-lb s.t.) Pratt & Whitney J57P-59W turbojets
Dimensions: Span 39.88 m (130.83 ft); length 41.53 m (136.25 ft); wing area 226.03 m² (2,433 sq ft)
Weights: Empty 44,664 kg (98,466 lb); MTOW 134,718 kg (297,000 lb)
Performance: Cruise speed 888 km/h (552 mph) at 9,144 m (30,000 ft); operational ceiling 15,240 m (50,000 ft); range 1,850 m (1,150 miles) with maximum payload
Load: Up to 54,432 kg (120,000 lb)

An F-16C Fighting Falcon refuelling from a Boeing KC-135R Stratotanker

LOCKHEED MARTIN C-5 GALAXY (U.S.A.)

C-5A Galaxy

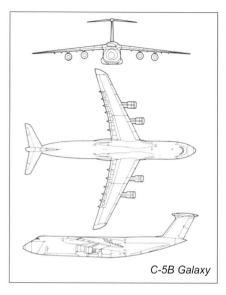

C-5B Galaxy

The Galaxy was produced to meet a U.S. Air Force requirement, ultimately shown to be considerably over-ambitious in its payload/range requirements of the early 1960s, for a long-range strategic airlifter to complement the Lockheed C-141 StarLifter logistic freighter. As such, it was to be capable of operating into and out of tactical airstrips close to the front line, through use of its 28-wheel landing gear that keeps ground pressure to the low figure that makes it possible for the

Galaxy to use even unpaved strips. The C-5A first flew in June 1968, and the type has many similarities to the C-141, though it is very much larger and possesses a lower deck 36.91 m (121 ft 1 in) long and 5.79 m (19 ft 0 in) wide. This hold can accommodate up to 120204-kg (256,000-lb) of freight, and is accessed not only by the standard type of power-operated rear ramp/door arrangement

but also by a visor-type nose that hinges upward and so makes possible straight-through loading and unloading for minimum turn-round time.

Production comprised 81 aircraft with 18597-kg (41,000-lb) thrust General Electric TF39-GE-1 turbofans, and the first operational aircraft were delivered in December 1969 as the first equipment for an eventual four squadrons. Service use

revealed that the wing structure had been made too light in an effort to improve payload/range performance, so the 77 surviving aircraft were rewinged and

LOCKHEED MARTIN C-5 GALAXY
Role: Military long-range, heavy cargo transport
Crew/Accommodation: Five with provision for relief crew and up to 75 troops on upper decks as well as 340 troops on main deck in place of cargo
Power Plant: Four 18,643-kgp (41,100-lb s.t.) General Electric TF-39-GE-1C turbofans
Dimensions: Span 67.89 m (222.75 ft); length 75.54 m (247.83 ft); wing area 576 m² (6,200 sq ft)
Weights: Empty 169,643 kg (374,000 lb); MTOW 348,812 kg (769,000 lb)
Performance: Maximum speed 919 km/h (571 mph) at 7,620 m (25,000 ft); operational ceiling 14,540 m (47,700 ft); range 5,526 km (3,434 miles) with maximum payload
Load: up to 120,200 kg (265,000 lb)

Lockheed Martin C-5 Galaxy

fitted with 19504-kg (43,000-lb) thrust TF39-GE-1C engines to maintain their operational viability. This process also allowed an increase in maximum take-off weight from 348809 kg (768,980 lb) to 379633 kg (837,000 lb), allowing the carriage of a maximum 124740-kg (275,000-lb) payload. Another 50 aircraft were later built to this standard as C-5Bs with improved systems. The first C-5B flew in September 1985 and deliveries took place between January 1986 and February 1989. Two C-5As were also modified for outsized space cargo operations as C-5Cs.

Lockheed Martin C-5 Galaxy

RESEARCH AIRCRAFT

It is strange, but nonetheless true that all aircraft produced during the so-called 'pioneering period' of aeroplane flight were research types. Arguably, the pioneers themselves who went on to establish production companies were among the best of the few, as designers were frequently also the test pilots, and those who survived their own inventions had thereby demonstrated the ability to construct aeroplanes of sufficient strength and competence to keep themselves safe.

When considering research aircraft, it is important to keep firm demarcation between a research type and a prototype, as they are quite different. The most simple demarcation is, perhaps, to understand that the first is built solely to gain knowledge, while the latter is intended to be a direct forerunner of a production model.

Rocket motors have powered many important research aircraft that can be said to have originated with the German Ente powered sailplane which, in 1938, flew for approximately one minute on the power of two slow-burning rocket

motors. Though aeroplane applications for rocket motors were extensively researched, the only operational production aircraft to properly benefit from this form of powerplant has been

ABOVE: The Douglas Skyrocket first flew in 1948

LEFT: The Northrop N-1M research demonstrator was intended to provide data for a large flying-wing transport. It was then the most successful flying-wing aircraft ever tested and eventually accumulated over 200 flights

OPPOSITE: The rocket-powered North American X-15 developed flights of up to seven times the speed of sound, taking its pilot to the edge of space

the German Messerschmitt Me 163 Komet interceptor that entered brief service in 1944/45, although rocket motors were fundamental in providing the necessary thrust for some of the most historically important aircraft every built, including the U.S. Bell X-l that first flew supersonically in 1947. Also, around this time, rocket power and turbojet engines were sometimes brought together in an attempt to merge the benefits of the long-endurance turbojet and the high thrust rocket motor. The Douglas Skyrocket, that first flew in 1948, was one such mixed application, built to investigate sweptback wings, and was the first manned aircraft to exceed twice the speed of sound, while another was the French Sud-Ouest SO 9000 Trident of 1953 appearance that was expected to provide data for a mixed-power interceptor.

Early British and German turbojet engines had been flight-tested on research airframes, and it was during World War II that Germany investigated so many advanced concepts that assisted the victorious Allies in the early post-war period to develop sweptback wings, tail-less aircraft, variable-geometry, ramjet aircraft, delta wings, vertical aeroplane flight, ballistic missiles and more besides. But, while Germany is particularly remembered for its wartime research, it should not be overlooked that during this conflict others too conducted important work for the future, with the U.S.A. making particular strides into the development of flying-wing aircraft which, half a century later, finally came to fruition with the B-2 bomber, while

Britain eventually became the conqueror of practical vertical aeroplane flight, though a great many weird and wonderful aircraft from many countries had earlier tried and failed.

But, perhaps one aircraft above all others encompasses the ideals of research. The rocket-powered North American X-l5 had been ordered in 1955 for manned flight at up to seven times the speed of sound, to investigate heating, control and stability at hypersonic speed and the problems associated with re-entry into the earth's atmosphere, occasionally taking its pilot so high that he became an astronaut. Though, at that time, the first supersonic fighters were only just appearing, it was not an impossible dream for, in 1961, the X-l5 exceeded Mach 6 and some years later almost reached its Mach 7 goal.

WRIGHT FLYER (U.S.A.)

Flyer I

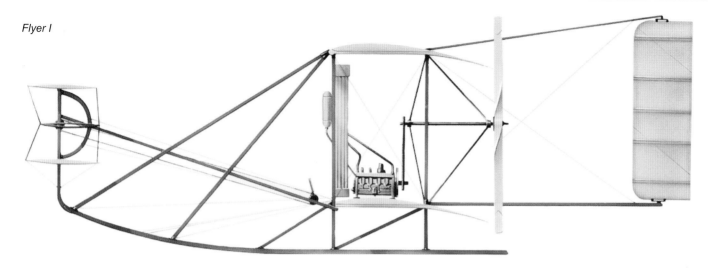

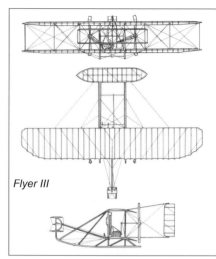

Flyer III

With the Flyer (or Flyer I), Orville Wright made the world's first powered, sustained and controlled flights in a heavier-than-air craft in 1903 at Kill Devil Hills, Kitty Hawk, North Carolina. The machine was a canard biplane powered by a 9-kW (12-hp) Wright engine driving two pusher propellers that turned in opposite directions as the drive chain to one was crossed, and take-off

was effected with the aid of a two-wheel trolley that carried the Flyer on a 18.3-m (60-ft) wooden rail.

On that historic day, 17 December 1903, the Flyer achieved four flights: the

first covered 36.6 m (120 ft) in 12 seconds, and the last achieved 260 m (852 ft) in 59 seconds. The improved Flyer II of 1904 was of the same basic configuration and dimensions as its predecessor, but its

wings had revised camber and the engine was an 11-kW (15-hp) type. Take-off was aided by the use of a trolley that was boosted by a weight that was dropped

WRIGHT FLYER I
Role: Powered flight demonstrator
Crew/Accommodation: One
Power Plant: One 12-hp Wright Brothers' water-
    cooled inline
Dimensions: Span 12.29 m (40.33 ft); length
    6.41 m (21.03 ft): wing area 47.38 m²
    (510 sq ft)
Weights: Empty 256.3 kg (565 lb); MTOW
    340.2 kg (750 lb)
Performance: Cruise speed 48 km/h (30 mph) at
    sea level; operational ceiling 9.14 m (30 ft);
    range 259.7 m (852 ft)
Load: None
*Note: the range quoted here was the longest of
    four flights made by the Wright Brothers on 17
    December 1903*

Replica of a Wright Flyer

from a derrick to pull the tow rope connected to the trolley.

The Flyer II took off about 100 times and achieved some 80 flights as the brothers perfected the task of piloting this inherently unstable aircraft. The flights totalled about 45 minutes in the air, and the longest covered about 4.43 km (2.75 miles) in 5 minutes 4 seconds.

The machine was broken up in 1905, the year in which the brothers produced the world's first really practical aircraft as the Flyer III, with improved controls but with the engine and twin propellers of the Flyer II. This machine made more than 40 flights, and as they were now able to control the type with considerable skill, the emphasis was placed on endurance and range. Many long flights were achieved, the best of them covering some 38.6 km (24 miles) in 38 minutes 3 seconds.

The Wright Flyer demonstrations at Fort Myer, Virginia on 3 September 1908

BELL X-1 (U.S.A.)

Bell X-1A

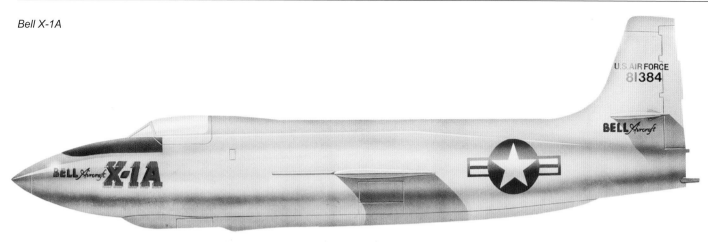

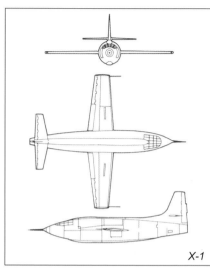

X-1

The X-l has a distinct place in aviation history as the first aircraft to break the 'sound barrier' and achieve supersonic speed in level flight. The origins of the type lay in the February 1945 decision of the U.S. Army Air Forces and National Advisory Committee for Aeronautics for the joint funding of an advanced research aircraft to provide data on kinetic heating at supersonic speeds. Bell had the choice of

turbojet or liquid-propellant rocket power, and opted for the latter in a very purposeful design with an unstepped cockpit, mid-set wings that were unswept but very thin, unswept tail surfaces, and tricycle landing gear, the units of which

all retracted into the circular fuselage. This girth of body provided the capacity for the rocket fuel and oxidizer.

The type was designed for air launch from a converted Boeing B-29 bomber, and the first of three aircraft was

dropped for its first gliding flight in January 1946. The first powered flight followed in December of the same year,

BELL X-1
Role: Trans-sonic research
Crew/Accommodation: One
Power Plant: One 2,721-kgp (6,000-lb s.t.)
   Reaction Motors E6000-C4 (Thiokol XLR-11)
   four-barrel liquid fuel rocket
Dimensions: Span 8.54 m (28,00 ft); length
   9.45 m (31.00 ft); wing area 12.08 m²
   (130.00 sq ft)
Weights: Empty 3,674 kg (8,100 lb); MTOW
   6,078 kg (13,400 lb)
Performance: Maximum speed 1,556 km/h
   (967 mph) Mach 1.46 at 21.379 m (70,140 ft);
   operational ceiling 24,384 m (80,000 ft);
   endurance 2.5 minutes at full power
Load: Nil, other than specific-to-mission test
   equipment

Bell X-1A

and on 14 October 1947 Captain Charles 'Chuck' Yeager achieved history's first supersonic flight with a speed of Mach 1.015 at 12800 m (42,000 ft) altitude. The third X-1 was lost in an accident on the ground, but in total the X-1s flew 156 times.

Three more airframes were ordered for the type's immensely important research programme, and these were delivered as one X-1A with a stepped cockpit and a fuselage lengthened by 1.40 m (4 ft 7 in) for the greater fuel capacity that made possible a maximum speed of Mach 2.435 in December 1953 and an altitude of more than 27430 m (90,000 ft) in June 1954; one X-1B, which was used for thermal research; and one X-1D variant of the X-1B that was lost when it was jettisoned after a pre-launch explosion. The X-1E was the second X-1 that had been modified to have wings of 4% thickness/chord ratio instead of 10%, a distinctive stepped knife-edge canopy and ballistic control rockets; it was flown 26 times.

Front view of the Bell X-1A

405

DOUGLAS D-558-1 SKYSTREAK and D-558-2 SKYROCKET (U.S.A.)

D-558-2 Skyrocket

D-558-2 Skyrocket

In 1945, the U.S. Navy's Bureau of Aeronautics and the National Advisory Committee for Aeronautics issued a joint requirement for a research aircraft able to generate the type of high-subsonic, air-load measurements data that was unobtainable in current wind tunnels. The resulting D-558-1 Skystreak was kept as simple as possible, and was based on a circular-section fuselage and straight flying surfaces. The type was powered by one 1814-kg (4,000-lb) thrust

Allison J35-A-23 turbojet, and the first of three aircraft flew in May 1947; later a 2268-kg (5,000-lb) thrust J35-A-11 engine was fitted. The type secured two world speed records, and also a mass of invaluable data using a pressure recording system with attachments to 400 points on the airframe and strain gauges attached to key positions on the wings and tail unit.

Soon after the Skystreak programme began, the official requirement was altered to also encompass investigation of sweptback wings. To provide higher thrust, a rocket booster was needed and the Skystreak concept was thus modified into a new type with swept flying surfaces. This materialized as the D-588-2 Skyrocket, which not only had the mixed powerplant and swept flying surfaces, but

also a larger-diameter fuselage incorporating a pointed nose as the D-558-1's nose inlet was replaced by two lateral inlets. Three aircraft were again ordered, and the first of these flew in February 1948.

The original flush canopy offered the pilot wholly inadequate fields of vision and was soon replaced by a more conventional raised enclosure. The Skyrocket flight programme proved successful in the extreme before it finished in December 1956, and included such milestones as an altitude of 25370 m (83,235 ft) in August 1953 and the first 'breaking' of the Mach 2 barrier in November 1953 with a speed of Mach 2.005.

DOUGLAS D-558-2 SKYROCKET
Role: Swept-wing research
Crew/Accommodation: One
Power Plant: One 2,721-kgp (6,000-lb s.t.) Reaction Motors XLR-8 rocket plus one 1,360-kgp (3,000-lb s.t.) Westinghouse J34-WE-22 turbojet
Dimensions: Span 7.62 m (25.00 ft); length 13.79 m (45.25 ft); wing area 16.26 m² (175,00 sq ft)
Weights: MTOW 7,161 kg (15,787 lb) from airborne launch
Performance: Maximum speed 2,078 km/h (1,291 mph) Mach 2.005 at 18,900 m (62,000 ft); operational ceiling 25,370 m (83,235 ft)
Load: Nil, other than specific mission test equipment

Douglas D-558-2 Skyrocket

OPPOSITE: A Douglas Skyrocket in flight with an F-86 chase plane

FAIREY DELTA 2 (United Kingdom)

Delta 2

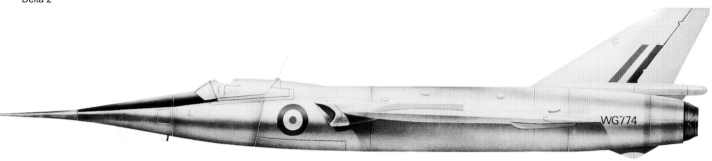

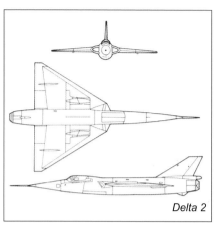

Delta 2

After a number of experiments in 1947 with vertically launched models, which confirmed the basic feasibility of the delta-winged planform, Fairey was asked to consider the possibility of supersonic delta-winged models. The company anticipated that this would eventually lead to a piloted supersonic research aircraft, and started initial work in advance of any officially promulgated requirement. When a requirement was eventually announced for a research aircraft able to investigate

flight and control characteristics at transonic and supersonic speeds, English Electric and Fairey each secured a contract for two prototypes.

The English Electric type was the P. 1, that led finally to the swept-wing Lightning fighter, and the Fairey design was the droop-snoot-nosed Fairey Delta 2. This was designed only as a supersonic

research aircraft, and was based on a pure delta wing and a slender fuselage sized to the Rolls-Royce Avon turbojet. Greater priority was given to the company's Gannet carrierborne antisubmarine warplane, so construction of the first F.D.2 began only in late 1952.

The machine first flew in October 1954, and after a delay occasioned by the

need to repair damage suffered in a forced landing after engine failure, the type went supersonic for the first time in October 1955. The world absolute speed record was then held by the North American F-100A Super Sabre at 1323 km/h (822 mph), and the capabilities of the F.D.2. were revealed when it raised the speed record to 1822 km/h (1,132 mph) in March 1956, the first-ever over-1,000-mph world speed record. The second F.D.2 joined the programme in February 1956, and the two aircraft undertook a mass of varied and most valuable research work. The first F.D.2 was later revised as the BAC 221 with an ogival wing for test before its use on the Concorde supersonic airliner.

FAIREY DELTA 2
Role: Supersonic research
Crew/Accommodation: One
Power Plant: One 4,309-kgp (9,500-lb s.t.) Rolls-Royce Avon RA14R turbojet with reheat, the use of which was limited, but gave 5,386 kgp (11,875 lb s.t.) at 11,580 m (38,000 ft)
Dimensions: Span 8.18 m (26.83 ft); length 15.74 m (51.62 ft); wing area 38.4 m² (360 sq ft)
Weights: Empty 5,000 kg (11,000 lb); MTOW 6,298 kg (13,884 lb)
Performance: Maximum speed 1,846 km/h 1,147 mph; operational ceiling 14,021 m (46,000 ft); range 1,335 km (830 miles) without reheat
Load: Confined to specialized test equipment

The first of the two Fairey Delta 2 research aircraft

OPPOSITE: Fairey Delta 2

NORTH AMERICAN X-15 (U.S.A.)

North American X-15

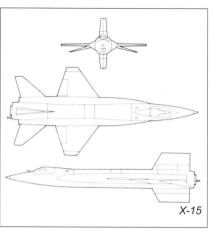

X-15

The X-15 was designed to meet a U.S. Air Force and U.S. Navy requirement for an aircraft able to reach an altitude of 80500 m (264,000 ft) and a speed of Mach 7 after air-launch from a modified Boeing B-52 bomber. Though funded by the two services, the programme was overseen at the technical level by NASA's predecessor, the National Advisory Committee on Aeronautics. In December 1954 a request for proposals was issued to 12 airframe manufacturers, and in February 1955 four companies were invited to tender for

the planned machine's rocket propulsion system. Contracts eventually went to North American for the NA-240 aircraft and Reaction Motors for the XLR99 rocket engine.

The X-15 was made mainly of titanium and stainless steel, with an armoured skin of Inconel X nickel alloy steel to permit extreme temperatures of -300°F to +1,200°F, and comprised a

long cylindrical fuselage with lateral fairings to accommodate control systems and fuel tanks, small thin wings of 5% section, an all-moving tailplane, and wedge-shaped dorsal and ventral fins; control at very high altitudes was by twelve rocket nozzles in the wingtips and nose. The lower fin was jettisoned before landing to provide ground clearance for the retractable twin skids that, with a

nosewheel unit, formed the landing gear. The first of three X-15As was powered by two 3629-kg (8,000-lb) thrust LR11-RM-5 rockets, as the XLR99 was not ready, and made its initial unpowered free flight in June 1959, followed by the first powered flight in September 1959. The second X-15A, also initially with the LR11s, made its first powered flight in November 1960.

The X-15As made 199 flights, including those of the second machine that made very important contributions after being rebuilt as the X-15A-2 with Emersion Electric T-500 ablative material as a heat-resistant surface treatment, a fuselage lengthened by 0.74 m (2 ft 5 in) and external auxiliary fuel tanks. In this form the machine reached 107960 m (354,200 ft) and 7297 km/h (4,534 mph) or Mach 6.72.

OPPOSITE: North American X-15

NORTH AMERICAN X-15A-2
Role: Hypersonic research
Crew/Accommodation: One
Power Plant: One 25.855-kgp (57,000-lb s.t.) Thiokol XLR99-RM-2 rocket motor
Dimensions: Span 6.81 m (22.33 ft); length 15.98 m (52.42 ft); wing area 18.58 m² (200 sq ft)
Weights: Empty 6,804 kg (15,000 lb): MTOW 23,095 kg (50.914 lb) air-launched
Performance: Maximum speed 7,297 km/h (3,937 knots) Mach 6.72 at 31,120 m (102,100 ft); operational ceiling 107,960 m (354,200 ft); radius 443 km (275 miles)
Load: Nil, other than dedicated mission test equipment

The X-15 had great endurance and high speed

TRAINERS, TOURERS & EXECUTIVE AIRCRAFT

An earlier section of this book describes various military trainers, and also details how the de Havilland Moth biplane brought about huge interest in civil flying clubs and private flying after its appearance in 1925. Understanding that inexpensive and economical-to-operate aeroplanes were needed to kick-start club flying had, however, already been recognized and in 1923 the first lightplane competition in Britain had been organized at Lympne in Kent by the Royal Aero Club, with the intention of encouraging construction of extremely light single-seaters. One prize, partly sponsored by the *Daily Mail* newspaper, was for the longest flight on one gallon of petrol by an aeroplane with an engine of 750 cc or less, which in the event was shared by two aircraft managing 141 km (87.5 miles).

The success of the competition was not really matched by the useful worth of the entries, and in 1924 the Royal Aero Club organized a similar competition for two-seaters, with the Air Ministry offering a £3,000 prize. Here, the winning entry was the Beardmore Wee Bee with a 32-hp engine, but this too was not a particularly practical design. Then in 1925 came the Moth, as a scaled-down D.H.51 with a 120-hp engine cut in half to produce 60 hp!

Public interest in lightplanes was greatly heightened by highly-publicized long-distance flights, such as that from London to Karachi made in stages by Stack and Leete in a Moth between November 1926 and January 1927, and from London to Cape Town (South Africa) by Lt. R. Bentley in another Moth in 1927. England to Australia was accomplished in an Avro Avian lightplane in 1928, while a similar aircraft was flown to England from South Africa that same year by Lady Heath, marking the first time the journey had been flown by a woman. In 1930, Amy Johnson became world-famous for flying a Gipsy Moth solo from England to Australia, and many other lightplane flights brought about a new awareness in flying. Of course, a certain gentleman named Charles Lindbergh had played his part in May 1927, when he had flown alone from New York to Paris across the North Atlantic in a single-engined Ryan monoplane named *Spirit of St. Louis*, taking over 33 hours to cover 5810 km (3,610 miles).

For most private pilots, of course, long distance flying meant touring in lightplanes. A great industry grew to satisfy this requirement, many of the aircraft being equally suited to training, while for business companies that needed larger transports to communicate between facilities, highly appointed executive aircraft were eventually evolved and, with the advent of turbine power, purpose-designed executive jets.

LEFT: Raytheon/Beech Bonanza

OPPOSITE: Cessna 182

BELLANCA PACEMAKER (U.S.A.)

CH-300 Pacemaker

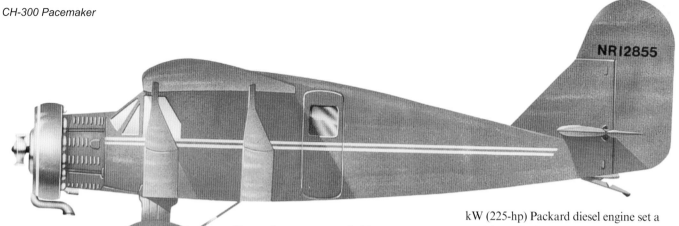

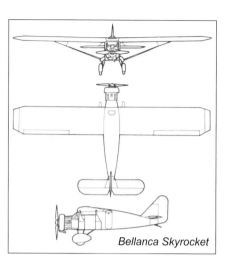

Bellanca Skyrocket

The Pacemaker was a logical development of the CH-300 utility transport, and the first model was the PM-300 Pacemaker Freighter. This was certificated in September 1929, and the cabin was laid out for four passengers and 386 kg (850 lb) of freight in its forward and aft sections respectively; three of the seats could be removed to allow a 714-kg (1,575-lb) freight load. For its time the

Pacemaker was a remarkable transport, for on the power of a single 224-kW (300-hp) Wright J-6 it could carry a payload greater than its own empty weight. The type could be used on wheels, skis or floats, and though not many Pacemaker Freighters were built, some CH-300s were in fact modified to this standard. In May 1931 a Pacemaker Freighter with a 168-

kW (225-hp) Packard diesel engine set a world unrefuelled endurance record of 84 hours 33 minutes.

The basic Pacemaker design was refined during its six-year production life. The Model E Senior Pacemaker of 1932 had a 246-kW (330-hp) Wright engine that was soon replaced by the 313-kW (425-hp) Wright R-975-E2. In concert with a larger wing and spatted landing gear, this offered

improved performance with a payload of six passengers; this model also had chair-pack parachutes that formed part of the upholstery until needed. Another variant was the Senior Pacemaker Series 8, which was a pure freighter that could carry a 907-kg (2,000-lb) payload over a range of 805 km (500 miles) in wheeled configuration, or a 811-kg (1,787-lb) payload over the same range in floatplane configuration. As an alternative to the R-975, Bellanca offered the Pacemaker with the Pratt & Whitney Wasp Junior radial of the same power. While the only known U.S. military Pacemaker was a single JE-1 operated by the U.S. Navy as a nine-seat communications type, the Royal Canadian Air Force used 13 CH-300s in all, the type being operated by the R.C.A.F. between 1929 and 1940.

BELLANCA CH-300 PACEMAKER

Role: Utility transport
Crew/Accommodation: One, plus up to five
  passengers
Power Plant: One 300-hp Wright J-6E Whirlwind
  air-cooled radial
Dimensions: 14.12 m (46.33 ft); length 8.46 m
  (27.75 ft); wing area 25.36 m² (273 sq ft)
Weights: Empty 1,201 kg (2,647 lb); MTOW
  1,952 kg (4,300 lb)
Performance: Maximum speed 230 km/h
  (143 mph) at sea level; operational ceiling
  5,181 m (17,000 ft); radius 2,189 km (1,360
  miles with full fuel)
Load: Up to 408 kg (900 kg)

Bellanca Senior Skyrocket

OPPOSITE: Bellanca Pacemaker

PIPER J-3 CUB and L-4 GRASSHOPPER (U.S.A.)

L-4 Grasshopper

L-4A Grasshopper

In 1929, C. Gilbert Taylor and his brother created the Taylor Brothers Aircraft Corporation, reorganized as the Taylor Aircraft Company in 1931. When the company ran into financial problems, the rights to the Taylor Cub were bought by W.T. Piper Snr, the company's secretary and treasurer. In 1937, Piper bought out the Taylor brothers and renamed the company the Piper Aircraft Corporation in order to continue

PIPER L-4 GRASSHOPPER
Role: Observation/communications
Crew/Accommodation: Two
Power Plant: One 65-hp Continental 0-170-3 air-cooled flat-opposed
Dimensions: Span 10.47 m (32.25 ft); length 6.71 m (22 ft); wing area 16.63 m² (179 sq ft)
Weights: Empty 331 kg (730 lb); MTOW 553 kg (1,220 lb)
Performance: Maximum speed 137 km/h (85 mph) at sea level; operational ceiling 2,835 m (9,300 ft); range 306 km (190 miles)
Load: Up to 86 kg (190 lb)

A Piper L-4E with British markings. This is a military version of the Piper J-3 Cub

production of the Cub, which had first flown in September 1930.

The Cub was a classic braced high-wing monoplane of mixed construction with fabric covering, and could be powered by any of several types of flat-four piston engine. The initial J-3 Cub was powered by the 30-kW (40-hp) Continental A40-4, but production soon switched to the J-3C-50 with the 37-kW (50-hp) A50-4, the suffix to the aircraft's basic designation indicating the make of

engine and its horsepower. Further development produced the Continental-engined J-3C-65 and then variants with Franklin and Lycoming engines as the J-3F-50 and F-65 and the J-3L-50 and L-65, while a radial-engined model was the J-3P-50 with the Lenape Papoose. Some 14,125 Cubs were built in these series for the civil market, and another 5,703 military liaison and observation aircraft expanded this number.

The U.S. Army evaluated several

types of civil lightplane in these roles during 1941, and the four J-3Cs evaluated as YO-59s with the 48-kW (65-hp) Continental O-170-3 paved the way for 140 0-59s and 948 0-59As that were later redesignated L-4 and L-4A in a sequence that ran to L-4J and included training gliders; the U.S. Marine Corps also adopted the type as the NE. Such has been the abiding popularity of the type that it was reinstated in production during 1988 with a number of more

refined features that, however, fail to obscure the essentially simple nature of the basic aircraft.

Piper L-4 Grasshopper

417

FAIRCHILD 24 (U.S.A.)

Model 24R

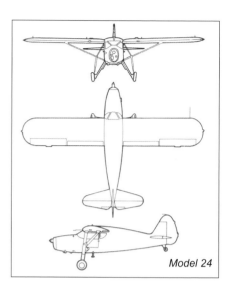
Model 24

HB-ERO

In 1931, Sherman Fairchild bought the American Aviation Corporation's Kreider-Reisner subsidiary, and with this new Fairchild Aircraft Corporation came the rights to a two-seat sport and training aircraft of braced parasol-wing layout. This was marketed as the Fairchild 22 Model C7 that survived slow initial sales to become a commercially successful and popular type. The success of the Model C7A variant persuaded Fairchild to produce a version with enclosed accommodation for two seated side-by-side in a higher fuselage that turned the parasol-wing Model C7A into the high-wing Fairchild 24 Model C8. The type was certificated in April 1932 with the 71-kW (95-hp) A.C.E. Cirrus Hi-Ace inline engine and though only 10 of this variant were produced, the type paved the way for extensive development and production.

The main developments (with approximate production total) were the Model C8A (25) with the 93-kW (125-hp) Warner Scarab radial, the Model C8C (130) with slightly greater size and the 108-kW (145-hp) Warner Super Scarab, the Model C8D (14) with three seats and the 108-kW Ranger 6-390B inline, the Model C8E (50) version of the Model C8C with improved equipment, and the Model C8F (40) version of the Model C8D with improved equipment. The designation then changed to Model 24, and this series ran to some 200 aircraft in four Model 24-G to Model 24-K three/four-seat variants. The final civil models were the two Model 24R (60) and four Model 24W (165) variants with Ranger inline and Warner radial engines. Another 981 inline- and radial-engined aircraft were built to military order as the U.S. Army Air Forces' UC-61 Forwarder, including large numbers supplied to the Royal Air Force with the name Argus. Additional aircraft were impressed for the American forces, the U.S. Navy and U.S. Coast Guard models being the GK and J2K.

Fairchild Model 24

FAIRCHILD MODEL 24W-9
Role: Touring
Crew/Accommodation: One, plus up to three passengers
Power Plant: One 165-hp Warner Super Scarab 175 air-cooled radial
Dimensions: Span 11.07 m (36.33 ft); length 8.79 m (25.85 ft); wing area 17.96 m² (193.30 sq ft)
Weights: Empty 732 kg (1,613 lb); MTOW 1,162 kg (2,562 lb)
Performance: Maximum speed 212 km/h (132 mph) at sea level; operational ceiling 4,267 m (14,000 ft); range 1,028 km (639 miles)
Load: Up to 245 kg (540 lb)

OPPOSITE: Fairchild 24W-40

BÜCKER Bü 131 JUNGMANN and Bü 133 JUNGMEISTER

Bü 133 Jungmeister

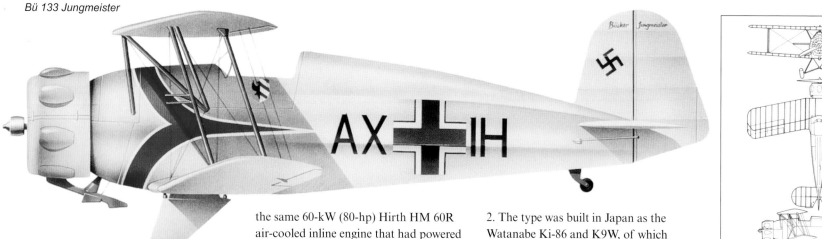

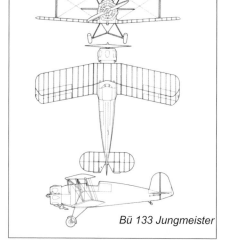

Bü 133 Jungmeister

the same 60-kW (80-hp) Hirth HM 60R air-cooled inline engine that had powered the prototype, while the improved Bü 131B had the 78-kW (105-hp) HM 504A-

2. The type was built in Japan as the Watanabe Ki-86 and K9W, of which more than 1,250 were produced, and was also widely exported by the parent

The Jungmann (Young Man or Youth) was the first product of Bücker Flugzeugbau, and first flew in April 1934 as a compact trainer of the classic single-bay biplane formula with tandem open cockpits in a fabric-covered airframe comprising wooden wings and a steel-tube fuselage and empennage. The type entered production as the Bü 131A with

BÜCKER BÜ 131B JUNGMANN
Role: Trainer
Crew/Accommodation: Two
Power Plant: One 105-hp Hirth HM 504A-2 air-cooled inline
Dimensions: Span 7.4 m (24.28 ft); length 6.62 m (21.72 ft); wing area 13.5 m² (145.3 sq ft)
Weights: Empty 390 kg (860 lb); MTOW 680 kg (1,500 lb)
Performance: Maximum speed 183 km/h (114 mph) at sea level; operational ceiling 3,000 m (9,843 ft); range 650 km (404 miles)
Load: None

Bücker Bü 131 Jungmann

factory. The Bü 131B spanned 7.40 m (24 ft 3.25 in) and had a maximum take-off weight of 680 kg (1,499 lb).

To meet production for its Bü 131, Bücker opened a second factory and here the company's design team evolved for the advanced training role the basically similar Jungmeister (Young Champion).

This had smaller dimensions than the Bü 131, had single-seat accommodation, and was stressed for full aerobatic capability. The first example flew with the 101-kW (135-hp) HM 6 inline engine and revealed excellent performance. The type was ordered in large numbers by the German Air Force, and the major variants were

the Bü 133A with the 101-kW (135-hp) HM 6 inline, the Bü 133B with the 119-kW (160-hp) HM 506 inline and the Bü 133C main production model with the 119-kW Siemens Sh 14 radial.

Bücker Bü 131 Jungmann

421

BEECH 18 (U.S.A.)

Beech C-45G

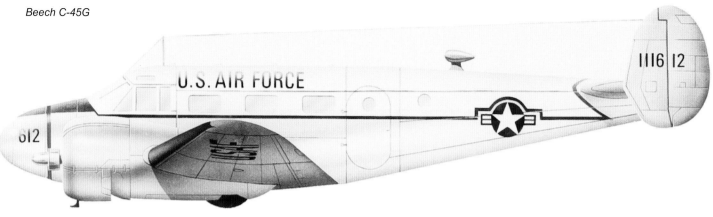

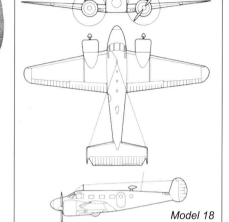

Model 18

In 1935, Beech began the development of an advanced light transport of monoplane layout to supersede its Model 17 biplane transport, whose reverse-staggered wings had earned the soubriquet 'Staggerwing'. The Model 18A was an all-metal type with a semi-monocoque fuselage, cantilever wings, electrically retracted tailwheel landing gear, and endplate vertical tail surfaces. The first example of this celebrated aeroplane flew in January 1937 with two 239-kW (320-hp) Wright R-760-E2 radial engines, and the type then

remained in manufacture for 32 years.

The initial civil models were powered by a number of radial engine types,

reaching an early peak as the Model 18D of 1939, which was powered by two 246-kW (330-hp) Jacobs L-6 engines that

BEECH D18S

Role: Light passenger/executive transport
Crew/Accommodation: Two/one, plus up to seven passengers
Power Plant: Two 450-hp Pratt & Whitney R.985-AN14B Wasp Junior air-cooled radials
Dimensions: Span 14.50 m (47.58 ft); length 10.35 m (33.96 ft); wing area 32.4 m² (349 sq ft)
Weights: Empty 2,558 kg (5,635 lb); MTOW 3,980 kg (8,750 lb)
Performance: Cruise speed 338 km/h (211 mph) at 3,050 m (10,000 ft); operational ceiling 6,250 m (20,500 ft); range 1,200 km (750 miles)
Load: Up to 587 kg (1,295 1b)

The Model 18 was a superlative light transport

combined the Model 18A's economy of operation with higher performance. The American military acquired an interest in the type during 1940, and during World War II the type was produced to the extent of 4,000 or more aircraft in various roles. The staff transport in several variants had the American designations C-45 (army) and JRB (navy), and the British name Expediter. In 1941 Beech introduced the AT-7 Navigator and AT-11 Kansan (or naval SNB) navigation and bombing/gunnery trainers.

After the war improved civil models appeared. From 1953 the Super 18 appeared as the definitive civil model with drag-reducing features, cross-wind landing gear, and a separate flightdeck, and from 1963 retractable tricycle landing gear was an option. Substantial numbers were converted to turboprop power by several specialist companies, these variants including the Volpar Turbo 18 and Turboliner, the Dumod Liner, the PAC Turbo Tradewind, and the Hamilton Westwind.

A Beech H18 fitted with the optional tricycle undercarriage

RAYTHEON/BEECH BONANZA (U.S.A.)

V35B Bonanza

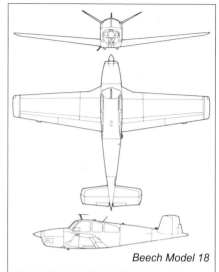

Beech Model 18

Another long-lived Beech design, the four/five-seat Bonanza first flew in December 1945 as the V-tailed Model 35 with the 138-kW (185-hp) Continental E-185-1 piston engine, though later aircraft have the 213-kW (285-hp) Continental I0-520 flat-six engine. The type was an immediate success for, even before the first production Bonanza had been delivered, the company had orders for some 1,500 aircraft, many of them for pilots who had learned to fly with the ever-expanding military forces during World War II. Large-scale production of the Bonanza was undertaken in a number of forms with normally aspirated or turbocharged engines, the use of the latter being indicated by the suffix TC after the model number. From the beginning, the Model 35 had retractable tricycle landing gear, but from 1949 the original castoring nosewheel was replaced by a steerable unit to create the model A35.

In 1959 the company introduced the

BEECH BONANZA

Role: Tourer
Crew/Accommodation: One, plus up to three
  passengers
Power Plant: One 196-hp Continental E185-8 air-
  cooled flat-opposed
Dimensions: Span 10.01 m (32.83 ft); length
  7.67 m (25.16 ft); wing area 16.49 m2
  (177.6 sq ft)
Weights: Empty 715 kg (1,575 lb); MTOW
  1,203 kg (2,650 lb)
Performance: Cruise speed 272 km/h (170 mph)
  at 2,440 m (8,000 ft); operational ceiling
  5,485 m (17,100 ft); range 1,207 km (750 miles)
Load: Up to 373 kg (822 lb)

Beech Model 33 Debonair

Beech 33 Debonair with a conventional tail and lower-powered engine for those worried about the 'gimmickry' of the V-tail. The lower-powered engine dictated that passenger accommodation was reduced from four to three, and in 1967 this variant was taken into the designation mainstream as the Model E33 Bonanza.

The third Bonanza type is the Model 36 Bonanza. This was intoduced in 1968 as a utility six-seater. This is based on the Model V35B with its fuselage lengthened by 0.25 m (10 in), and fitted with the tail unit of the Model 33 as well as the strengthened landing gear of the Model 55 Baron. The fuselage is accessed by double doors so that the type can double as a light freight transport. Many variants were in fact produced.

Beech Bonanza

de HAVILLAND CANADA DHC-1 CHIPMUNK (Canada)

Chipmunk T.Mk 10

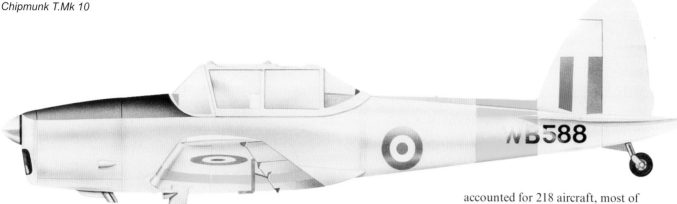

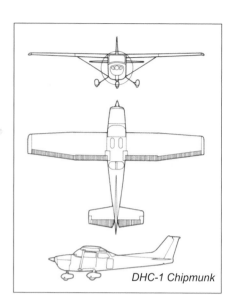

DHC-1 Chipmunk

The DHC-1 Chipmunk was the first aircraft designed by de Havilland's Canadian subsidiary, and was evolved as a successor to the legendary D.H.82 Tiger Moth, of which a special version had been built in Canada. The type was therefore designed as a primary trainer, and despite its low performance and fixed tailwheel landing gear, the DHC-1 was a thoroughly modern type with enclosed tandem accommodation, stressed-skin construction of light alloy, a low-set wing with trailing-edge flaps, and attractive lines highlighted by the typically de Havilland tail unit. The first example flew in May 1946 with a 108-kW (145-hp) de Havilland Gipsy Major 1C inline engine. Production of the Chipmunk in Canada lasted to 1951 and accounted for 218 aircraft, most of which had a bubble canopy.

Aircraft suffixed -1 and -2 were powered by the Gipsy Major 1 and Gipsy Major 10 engines respectively, and the main variants were the semi-aerobatic DHC-1 A and the fully aerobatic DHC-1B in a total of nine subvariants including the Royal Canadian Air Force's DHC-1A-1 and DHC-1B-2-S3 used as the

Chipmunk T.Mk 1 and T.Mk 2 respectively, the latter for refresher training at civil clubs. In its fully aerobatic form, the type also found favour with the Royal Air Force, and this resulted in British manufacture of 1,014 Chipmunks, of which 735 Gipsy Major 8-powered examples went to the RAF as Chipmunk T.Mk 10 *ab initio* trainers for use by all 17 university air squadrons and many RAF Volunteer Reserve flying units.

Aircraft of the Chipmunk T.Mk 20 were produced for the military export market (217 Chipmunk T.Mk 20s with the Gipsy Major 10-2) and for the civil market (28 basically similar Chipmunk T.Mk 21s). Another 60 Chipmunks were built under licence in Portugal by OGMA.

OPPOSITE: De Havilland Chipmunk

de HAVILLAND CANADA DHC-1 CHIPMUNK T.MK 10
Role: Primary trainer
Crew/Accommodation: Two
Power Plant: One 145-hp de Havilland Major 8 air-cooled inline
Dimensions: Span 10.46 m (34.33 ft); length 7.82 m (25.66 ft); wing area 15.98 m² (172.00 sq ft)
Weights: Empty 643 kg (1,417 lb); MTOW 908 kg (2,000 lb)
Performance: Maximum speed 223 km/h (138 mph) at sea level; operational ceiling 4,876 m (16,000 ft); radius 483 km (300 miles)
Load: Nil

DHC-1 Chipmunk

CESSNA 170, 172, 175 and 182 Series (U.S.A.)

Model 172 Skyhawk

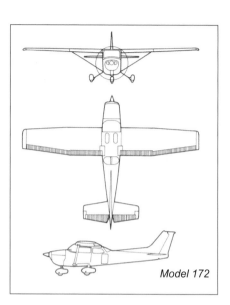

Model 172

This series enjoys the distinction of being the most successful lightplane of all time. The Model 170 first flew in 1948 as the two-seat Model 120 with the 108-kW (145-hp) Continental C-145-2 engine and its fuselage re-engineered to four-seat configuration. Good sales were later boosted by the advent of the Model 170B with improved field performance as a result of the Fowler slotted trailing-edge flaps, a type pioneered in the Cessna range by the Model 305. In 1955, the company introduced the Model 172, which was basically the Model 170B with the original fixed tailwheel landing gear replaced by fixed tricycle landing gear. In 1958, Cessna placed into production the Model 175, which was in essence the Model 172 with a number of refinements (including a free-blown windshield and speed fairings), as well as the more powerful 131-kW (175-hp) GO-300-C geared engine driving a constant-speed propeller. This short-lived variant also appeared in upgraded Model 175A and de luxe Skylark forms.

A comparable de luxe version of the Model 172 was also produced as the Skyhawk, and this was later revised with a swept vertical tail of the type which market research had shown to be desirable as a means of keeping the model's appearance fully up to date. From 1980, a new and slimmer rear fuselage with rear windows was introduced on the Skylark II and Skyhawk II. The Model 182 of 1956 introduced more power in the form of the 172-kW (230-hp) Continental O-470-S engine, and was also produced in upgraded Skylane versions.

Further development of the Models 172 and 182 has produced a host of versions with improved furnishing, better instrumentation, retractable landing gear, and turbocharged engines. The Model 172 has additionally been produced in T-41 Mescalero trainer form.

CESSNA 172 SKYHAWK (T-41 A)

Role: Light touring (and military basic trainer)
Crew/Accommodation: One, plus up to three passengers
Power Plant: One 160-hp Lycoming 0-320 air-cooled flat-opposed
Dimensions: Span 10.92 m (35.83 ft); length 8.20 m (26 ft); wing area 16.16 m² (174 sq ft)
Weights: Empty 636 kg (1,402 lb); MTOW 1,043 kg (2,300 lb)
Performance: Cruise speed 226 km/h (122 knots) at 2,438 m (8,000 ft); operational ceiling 4,328 m (14,200 ft); range 1,065 km (575 naut. miles) with full payload
Load: Up to 299 kg (660 lb)

ABOVE & OPPOSITE: Cessna 172 Skyhawks

PIER CHEROKEE (U.S.A.)

Cherokee 140

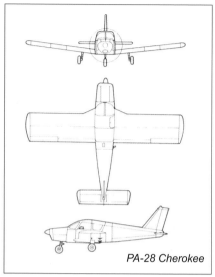

PA-28 Cherokee

First flown in prototype form during January 1960, the four-seat Cherokee and its successors have been a remarkable success story for Piper. This all-metal cantilever low-wing type has gone through a large number of developments and variants with engine horsepower indicated by the numerical suffix appended to the basic designation; thus the initial PA-28-150 with the 112-kW (150-hp) Lycoming O-320 engine and

fixed tricycle landing gear was followed in chronological sequence by the PA-28-160, PA-28-180, PA-28-235, and PA-28-140. An upgraded series introduced in June 1967 with retractable landing gear, a

fuel-injected engine and a constant-speed propeller was the Cherokee Arrow in PA-28-180R and PA-28-200R forms. The first series was then redesignated, the PA-29-140 becoming the Cherokee Flite

Liner and, in de luxe form, the Cherokee Cruiser 2 Plus 2, the PA-28-180 becoming the Cherokee Challenger with a slightly lengthened fuselage and increased-span

PIPER PA 28-161 CHEROKEE WARRIOR II
Role: Tourer
Crew/Accommodation: One, plus up to three passengers
Power Plant: One 150-hp Lycoming 0-320-E3D air-cooled flat-opposed
Dimensions: Span 10.65 m (35 ft); length 7.2 m (23.8 ft); wing area 15.8 m² (170 sq ft)
Weights: Empty 590 kg (1,301 lb); MTOW 1,065 kg (2,325 lb)
Performance: Cruise speed 213 km/h (133 mph) at 2,438 m (8,000 ft); operational ceiling 3,930 m (12,700 ft); range 1,660 km (720 miles) with full payload
Load: Up to 342 kg (775 lb)

Piper Cherokee Archer III

Piper Cherokee

wings, and the PA-28-235 becoming the Cherokee Charger. In 1974 further changes in name were made: the Cherokee 2 Plus 2 became the Cherokee Cruiser, the Cherokee Challenger became the Cherokee Archer, and the Cherokee Charger became the Cherokee Pathfinder.

A new type introduced was the PA-28-151 Cherokee Warrior based on the Cherokee Archer with a new and longer-span wing. The Cherokee Cruiser and Cherokee Pathfinder went out of production in 1977, when the PA-28-236 Dakota was introduced with the longer-span wing and the 175-kW (235-hp) O-540 engine. In 1978 there appeared the PA-28-201T Turbo Dakota that went out of production in 1980 to leave in production aircraft now designated PA-28-161 Warrior II, PA-28-181 Archer II and PA-28RT-201T Turbo Arrow IV.

Starship 1

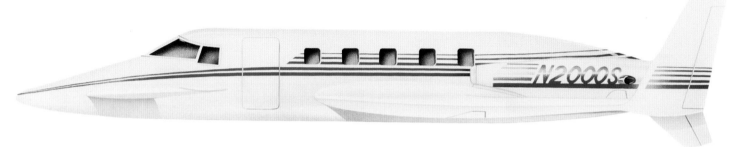

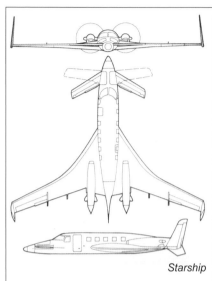

Starship

The Starship marks a radical departure from previous aircraft in the Beech line, being a futuristic canard design with swept flying surfaces and two turboprops located in the rear-mounted wing to drive pusher propellers. The engines are located as close to the rear fuselage as possible to reduce thrust asymmetry problems in the event of an engine failure. The type is also notable for the high percentage of composite materials used in the airframe: this offers an extremely attractive combination of low weight with great strength. The Starship's wings are monocoque structures with composite wingtip stabilizers, and terminate in endplate surfaces that provide directional stability as well as serving as drag-reducing winglets. The foreplanes are of the variable-geometry design that contribute to the Starship's good field performance before being swept back to improve maximum cruise speed.

In overall terms, the Starship reflects the design concepts of the adventurous Burt Rutan, and the type was first flown during August 1983 in the form of an 85 per cent scale version developed by Rutan's Scaled Composites Inc. Full-scale flight trials began in February 1986 with the first of six pre-production Starships. The type received Federal Aviation Administration certification in 1989, with deliveries beginning later in the same year despite the fact that payload/range performance is lower than guaranteed because of unexpected drag and weight problems. A number of fixes are being developed, and it is expected that these shortfalls will be eliminated in the early 1990s.

BEECH STARSHIP 1
Role: Executive transport
Crew/Accommodation: Two, plus up to ten passengers Power Plant: Two 1,100 shp Pratt & Whitney Canada PT6A-67 turboprops
Dimensions: Span 16.46 m (54 ft); length 14.05 m (46.08 ft); wing area 26.09 m2 (280.9 sq ft)
Weights: Empty 4,044 kg (8,916 lb); MTOW 6,350 kg (14,000 lb)
Performance: Cruise speed 652 km/h (405 mph) at 7,620 m (25,000 ft); operational ceiling 12,495 m (41,000 ft); range 2,089 km (1,298 miles) with maximum payload
Load: Up to 1,264 kg (2,884 lb)

Beech Starship

RAYTHEON/BEECH KING AIR and SUPER KING AIR (U.S.A.)

C-12A

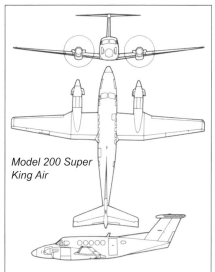

Model 200 Super King Air

The King Air was developed as a turboprop-powered derivative of the Model 65 Queen Air, and first flew in 1963 as the Model 65-80 conversion with two 373-kW (500-shp) Pratt & Whitney Canada PT6A engines. The type entered production as the unpressurized Model 65-90T King Air to meet initial orders from the military for what became the U-21 Ute utility and special mission series, the first examples of which were delivered in 1967. This family was in fact preceded into service by the initial civil version, the pressurized Model A90. The type went through many variants and in 1994 deliveries started of the C90SE, a lower-cost and reduced-specification model of King Air, to accompany the standard 7/8-seat King Air C90B.

Delivered from August 1969, the Model 100 King Air introduced a reduced-span wing based on that of the

BEECH SUPER KING AIR 350
Role: Pressurized executive transport
Crew/Accommodation: Two plus up to 15 passengers
Power Plant: Two 1,050 shp Pratt & Whitney Canada PT6A-60A turboprops
Dimensions: Span 17.65 m (57.92 ft); length 14.22 m (46.66 ft); wing area 28.8 m2 (310 sq ft)
Weights: Empty 4,110 kg (9,062 lb); MTOW 6,804 kg (15,000 lb)
Performance: Maximum speed 583 km/h (363 mph); operational ceiling 10,670 m (35,000 ft); range 3,507 km (2,180 miles) at 10,670 m (35,000 ft)
Load: Up to 1,660 kg (3,600 lb)

Beech King Air

Model 99 Airliner, larger elevator and rudder areas, and a fuselage lengthened for 15 persons (including the pilot) rather than the 10 carried by the Model 90. Powered by 507-kW (680-shp) PT6A-28 turboprops, the Model 100 was followed in 1971 by the improved Model A100 (military U-21F), and from 1975 by the Model B100 with 533-kW (715-shp) Garrett TPE331-6-252B turboprops. In October 1972 the company flew the first Model 200 Super King Air with a T-tail, an increased-span wing, and greater fuel capacity for its more powerful PT6A-41 turboprops.

The type is used by the U.S. military as the C-12 Huron communications and special mission series with a number of engine marks, while civil models include the Model B200 with PT6A-42 engines for improved cruise performance. This can also be delivered in freighter or maritime surveillance configurations, and has itself formed the basis of the RC-12 Guardrail and Guardian Common Sensor intelligence and communications intercept/direction-finding military versions. The Model 350 Super Air King was introduced in 1988, also offered in RC-350 Guardian form.

OPPOSITE: Beech Super King Air 200

RIGHT: Beech King Air B200

CESSNA CITATION (U.S.A.)

Citation I

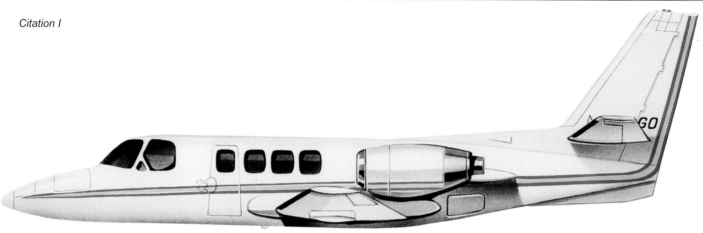

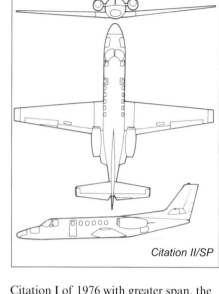

Citation II/SP

With its Citation family, Cessna moved into the market for high-performance 'bizjets' offering its purchasers the combination of performance and fuel economy they wanted for commercial reasons, together with the low noise 'footprint' that avoided the vociferous complaints of the growing environmental lobby. The company's investment in the project was very considerable, and when the prototype, at that time called the Fanjet

500, first flew in September 1969, it became clear that Cessna had a type that offered serious competition to market leaders such as the BAe HS 125, Dassault Falcon 20, and Gates Learjet. The type was typical of Cessna twin-engined aircraft in many features other than its aft-mounted podded engines, and was

renamed Citation shortly after its first flight. Test flights revealed the need for several important modifications before certification could be secured, so this straight-winged type entered service only in 1971 with Pratt & Whitney Canada JT15D-1 turbofans.

Later developments have been the

Citation I of 1976 with greater span, the Citation I/SP for single-pilot operation, the Citation II of 1978 with greater span, a lengthened fuselage and 1134-kg (2,500-lb) thrust JT15D-4 engines, the single-pilot Citation II/SP, the completely revised Citation III of 1982 with swept wings of supercritical section, a lengthened fuselage for two crew and 13 passengers, a T-tail and 1656-kg (3,650-lb) thrust Garrett TFE731-3B-100S turbofans, and the most recent Citation V, which combines the short-field performance of the Citation II with a larger cabin and the speed and cruising altitude of the Citation III.

OPPOSITE: Cessna 550B Citation

CESSNA CITATION S/II (T-47A)
Role: Executive transport and military trainer
Crew/Accommodation: Two, plus up to eight passengers
Power Plant: Two 1,134-kgp (2,500-lb s.t.) Pratt & Whitney JT15D-4B turbofans
Dimensions: Span 15.90 m (52.21 ft); length 14.39 m (47.21 ft); wing area 31.83 m² (342.6 sq ft)
Weights: Empty 3,655 kg (8,059 lb); MTOW 6,849 kg (15,100 lb)
Performance: Cruise speed 746 km/h (403 knots) Mach 0.70 at 10,670 m (35,000 ft); operational ceiling 13,105 m (43,000 ft); range 3,223 km (1,739 naut. miles) with four passengers
Load: Up to 871 kg (1,920 lb)

Cessna Citation V

RACING & SPORTPLANES

Racing has long been accepted as a means of speeding development in aviation in addition to providing public spectacle. The very first international air race was held in Paris, France in September 1906, as a balloon meeting for the Gordon Bennett Trophy. At this time few people in France has any idea that proper powered aeroplane flights had already taken place years earlier in the U.S.A., and so this balloon event was seen as state-of-the-art flying. Therefore, when

in November that same year Alberto Santos-Dumont lifted off the ground in a tail-first biplane for just 220 m (772 ft), many thought this to be the world's first flight by a powered aeroplane.

With flights in the U.S.A. and France, and some progress in Germany and elsewhere, by 1908 it began to look as though Britain was lagging behind in aeroplane development. The *Daily Mail* newspaper, having awarded a cash prize for a model aeroplane competion in 1907

that had been won by the young Alliot Verdon Roe (of later Avro fame), decided to offer further large cash prizes for aviation achievements. In July 1909 a £1,000 prize went to Frenchman Louis Blériot for making the first aeroplane crossing of the English Channel, while that October a similar prize went to J.T.C. Moore-Brabazon as the first Briton to fly a mile in a British aeroplane. Other *Daily Mail* prizes followed which greatly encouraged progress. By then, however, the first international aeroplane meeting in the world had been staged at Reims in France, during August 1909, which only served to show the dominance of French and U.S. types.

Also in France, in 1912, Jacques Schneider had been concerned at the slow rate of progress in developing seaplanes, believing that such craft were best suited to expanding air transportation. In response he established La Coupe d'Aviation Maritime Jacques Schneider, better remembered as the Schneider Trophy Contest, with the first event gaining only seven entries at one race at the April 1913 international Hydro-Aeroplane Meeting in Monaco. Although the start was modest, it later became an event of international prestige, attracting many nationally sponsored teams that fielded purpose-developed and streamlined racers. The final contest was won by Britain in 1931

with the Supermarine S.6B, which soon after became the first-ever aeroplane to exceed 640 km/h (400 mph) and was an early inspiration for the Spitfire fighter.

In America, the first Pulitzer Trophy Race took place in 1920, while many other important races culminated (pre-World War II) in the first trans-World air race in 1934, known as the MacRobertson Race. Flown from England to Australia, it was sponsored by MacRobertson Confectionery of Melbourne to commemorate the centenary of the founding of the State of Victoria.

Aerobatics had begun by error, when pilots entered unintentional spins. It was a fatal manoeuvre until 1912 when a Royal Navy pilot managed to recover his Avro by correct stick and rudder movement. The first loop was performed in Russia in 1913 and the first sustained inverted flight in France the same year. It was just the beginning, and even now new manoeuvres are being devised, such as Pugachev's Cobra performed by a Russian Sukhoi Su-27 jet fighter at Paris in 1989 and the Kulbit or somersault displayed by an Su-37 fighter in 1996, the latter involving rapid deceleration with a 360-degree tight loop.

The Blades: an aerobatic display team of former Red Arrow pilots who fly Extra 300 LPs, one of the leading high-performance aircraft in the world

MACCHI MC.72

MC.72

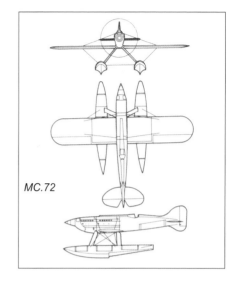

MC.72

The MC.72 was the culmination of a long series of racing floatplanes designed by Mario Castoldi for the Schneider Trophy races and, despite the fact that it never won such a race, the MC.72 was without doubt the finest machine of its type ever produced. The starting point for this family was the M.39, which pioneered the twin-float layout with a low-set wing wire-braced to the floats and the upper part of a slim

fuselage tailored to the frontal area of the inline engine.

The first of six M.39s flew in July 1926 as a trainer with the 447-kW (600-hp) Fiat AS.2 engine, and a racer powered by a 597-kW (800-hp) version of the same engine won the 1926 race; the

type also raised the world speed record to 416.68 km/h (258.875 mph). For the 1927 race, the company produced three examples of the M.52 with slightly smaller dimensions but powered by the 746-kW (1,000-hp) AS.3. Technical problems knocked all three out of the race, but one machine later raised the speed record to 479.29 km/h (297.818

mph) and another was fitted with a smaller wing to become the M.52R that raised the record to 512.776 km/h (318.625 mph).

For the 1929 race, Castoldi designed the M.69 of which three were built with the 1342-kW (1,800-hp) Isotta-Fraschini 2-800 with coolant radiators on the wing surfaces, underside of the nose, sides of the rear fuselage, float legs, and upper sides of the floats! Neither of the entered aircraft finished the race.

The MC.72 was designed for the 1931 race, and was powered by a Fiat AS.6 engine (two 1119-kW/1,500-hp) AS.5 units mounted front to back and driving contra-rotating propellers). Five aircraft were built, but problems prevented any of them from taking part in this last Schneider Trophy race. Two of the machines later set world speed records, the latter at 709.209 km/h (440.683 mph).

MACCHI MC.72
Role: Racing
Crew/Accommodation: One
Power Plant: One 3,100-hp Fiat AS.6 liquid-
cooled inline
Dimensions: Span 9.48 m (31.10 ft); length
8.32 m (27.29 ft) wing area 15.00 m²
(161.46 sq ft)
Weights: Empty 2,500 kg (5,511 lb) MTOW
2,907 kg (6,409 lb)
Performance: Maximum speed 709.209 km/h
(440.681 mph) at 500 m (1,640 ft)
Load: Nil

The Macchi MC.72 drove contra-rotating propeller units

GEE BEE SPORTSTER (U.S.A.)

Sportster R-1

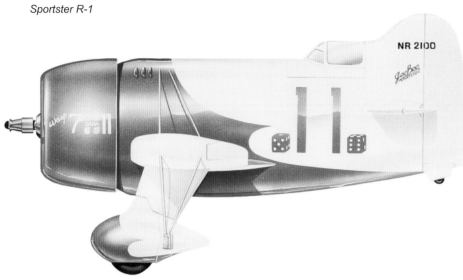

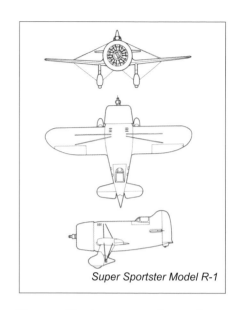

Super Sportster Model R-1

The period between 1925 and 1935 saw the development of many fascinating aircraft specifically for racing, especially in the United States, where the philosophy of cramming maximum engine into minimum airframe approached extraordinary levels. One of the main protagonists of the philosophy was the team of five brothers running Granville Brothers Aircraft. Gee Bee's

first type was the Model 'A' side-by-side two-seater, but the brothers then graduated to a low-cost sporting machine, the Model 'X' Sportster single-seater of 1930, that developed into the

Model 'Y' Senior Sportster two-seater.

A number of racing successes followed, so the brothers decided to produce a pure racer as the Model 'Z' Super Sportster that introduced the distinctive barrel-shaped fuselage tailored to the diameter of its 399-kW (535-hp) Pratt & Whitney Wasp Junior, and featured a diminutive vertical surface that projected only marginally above the enclosed cockpit, a wire-braced low/mid-set monoplane wing, and fixed but nicely faired tailwheel landing gear. The type enjoyed some racing success, but broke up in an attempt on the world air speed record in December 1931.

For the 1932 season there followed two Model 'R' Super Sporters: the Model R-1 with a 597-kW (800-hp) Pratt & Whitney Wasp and the Model R-2 with a 410-kW (550-hp) Wasp Junior. The first flew in August 1932, and won the

Thomson Trophy race as well as setting a landplane record of 476.815 km/h (296.287 mph). Both aircraft were entered for the 1933 Bendix Trophy race, the Model R-1 with a 671-kW (900-hp) Pratt & Whitney Hornet and the Model R-2 with the R-1's original Wasp. The R-1 was later damaged and the R-2 virtually destroyed, but components of both were used to create the Model R-1/R-2.

GEE BEE SUPER SPORTSTER R-1

Role: Racing
Crew/Accommodation: One
Power Plant: One 730-hp Pratt & Whitney Wasp TD3-1 air-cooled radial
Dimensions: Span 7.62 m (25.00 ft); length 5.41 m (17.66 ft); wing area 9.29 m² (100.00 sq ft)
Weights: Empty 835 kg (1,840 lb); MTOW 1,095 kg (2,415 kg)
Performance: Maximum speed 473.82 km/h (294.418 mph) at sea level
Load: Nil

Replica of a Gee Bee Model 'Z' Super Sportster

PERCIVAL P. 6 MEW GULL (United Kingdom)

P.6 Mew Gull

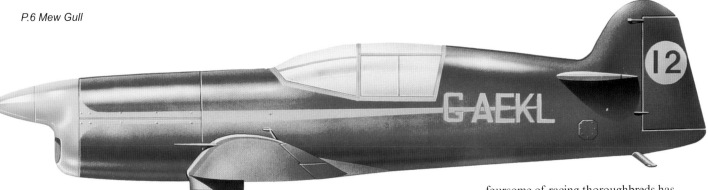

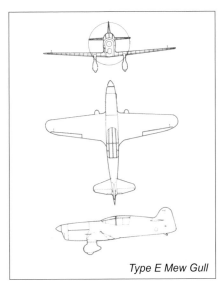

Type E Mew Gull

First flown in March 1934, the P.2 prototype was of angular and somewhat austere appearance that gave little hint of the beautiful P.6 Mew Gull to follow. Altogether, five examples of the P. 6 were to be built, including the converted P.2, and these subsequently dominated the British air racing scene during the three years prior to September 1939 and the outset of World War II. Of exceptionally well-proportioned shape, the P. 6 Mew Gulls were constantly in the headlines, frequently being flown by the aircraft's designer/pilot Captain Edgar Percival in such events as the annually held King's Cup air race. One of this foursome of racing thoroughbreds has had a particularly long and illustrious career, remaining airworthy into the 1990s. Initially built for the South African pilot A. H. Miller and carrying the appropriate ZS-AHM registration, this machine took part in the September 1936 Schlesinger England-South Africa air race, having to retire at Athens as a result of a fuel-feed problem. Shortly thereafter, this machine passed into the hands of

PERCIVAL P.6 MEW GULL
Role: Racer
Crew/Accommodation: One
Power Plant: One 205 hp de Havilland Gipsy Six Series II air-cooled inline
Dimensions: Span
  7.54 m (24.75 ft); length 6.88 m (21.92 ft); wing area 8.18 m2 (88 sq ft)
Weights: Empty 562 kg (1,240 lb); MTOW 1,066 kg (2,350 lb)
Performance: Maximum speed 398 km/h (247 mph) at sea level; range 3,219 km (2,000 miles) with 3,861l (85 Imp gal) tankage Note: figures are for Alex Henshaw's modified G-AEXF as configured for his February 1939, record-breaking England-Cape Town return flight

Percival E2 Mew Gull

Alex Henshaw, receiving the British registration G-AEXF. Initially acquired by the extremely youthful but capable Henshaw, G-AEXF was powered by a DH Gipsy Six I, in which form Henshaw flew it to victory in the 1937 Folkestone air race and the 1937 King's Cup race, from which he retired with contaminated fuel. Prior to the start of the 1938 racing season, Henshaw had his aircraft re-engined with the higher-powered Gipsy Six R, simultaneously fitting a Ratier variable pitch propeller to better utilize the extra 23-kW (30-hp) engine output. In this form, G-AEXF achieved 398.3 kph (247.5 mph) in both the Hatfield-Isle of Man and Manx Air Derby races of 1938. Later that year, by now sporting a new DH propeller, Henshaw romped home to win the King's Cup with a record-setting speed of 380 km/h (236 mph).

de HAVILLAND D.H.88 COMET (United Kingdom)

D.H.88 Comet

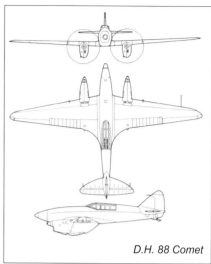

D.H. 88 Comet

The Comet was planned specifically as a competitor for the October 1934 Victorian Centenary Air Race between Mildenhall in England and Melbourne in the Australian state of Victoria. Prize money was donated by Sir MacPherson Robertson, and de Havilland received three orders before the expiry of its February 1934 deadline. The design was very clean by the aerodynamic standards of the day, and based on an all-wood

structure as a low-wing monoplane with two wing-mounted engines. The fuselage accommodated three large fuel tanks in the nose immediately ahead of the two crew members, who were seated in tandem

under a canopy faired into the tail unit by a dorsal decking. The engines were 172-kW (230-hp) de Havilland Gipsy Six R inlines driving two-position propellers which used the air pressure of 240-km/h

(150-mph) speed for the shift from take-off fine pitch to cruising coarse pitch. Other notable features were split trailing-edge flaps and manually retractable main units for the tailwheel landing gear.

The first Comet flew in September 1934, and all three machines had received their required certificates of airworthiness before the start of the race on 20 October. The speed section of the race was won by Grosvenor House in 70 hours 54 minutes, and is now preserved at the Shuttleworth Trust. Black Magic was forced to retire at Baghdad, and G-ACSR finished fourth but then set an out-and-back record of 13.5 days when it came straight back to England with film and mail. Two other Comets were later built, one as a mailplane to French government order and the other for two unsuccessful attempts on the London to Cape Town record.

De HAVILLAND D.H.88 COMET
Role: Long range racing
Crew/Accommodation: Two
Power Plant: Two 230 hp de Havilland Gipsy Six R air-cooled inlines
Dimensions: Span 13.41 m (44.00 ft); length 8.84 m (29.00 ft); wing area 19.74 m2 (212.50 sq ft)
Weights: Empty 1,329 kg (2,930 lb); MTOW 2,517 kg (5,550 lb)
Performance: Maximum speed 381 km/h (237 mph) at sea level; operational ceiling 5,791 m (19,000 ft); range 4,707 km (2,925 miles)
Load: Nil

The D.H.88 Comet was an elegant high-speed monoplane

PITTS SPECIAL (U.S.A.)

S-1 Special

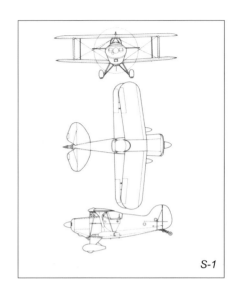

S-1

Designed and built by Curtis Pitts for the celebrated aerobatic display pilot Betty Skelton, the Pitts 190 Special first flew in September 1944 with a 67-kW (90-hp) Continental engine and single-seat accommodation in an open cockpit. The type was of mixed construction, with a covering of fabric over the wooden wings and the steel-tube fuselage and tail unit. The result was a diminutive braced biplane with fixed tailwheel landing gear, and from the very beginning the design revealed exceptional aerobatic capabilities. Pitts then developed the design for homebuilders as the Special Biplane with engines in a range between 48 and 71 kW (65 and 90 hp) and ailerons on the lower wings only.

The type's aerobatic qualities meant that an increasing number were built for competition purposes with airframes stressed to higher levels, ailerons on the upper as well as lower wings, and engines of up to 134 kW (180 hp).

In the mid-1960s Pitts developed a two-seat model, and this first flew in 1967 as the S-2 Special to complement what now became the S-1 Special. The S-2 was somewhat larger than the S-1 and powered by the 134-kW (180 hp) Lycoming O-360-A1A, while aerodynamic refinements made it stable in rough air and also enhanced manoevrability. This model reintroduced factory production with Pitts Aviation Enterprises (later Pitts Aerobatic Company), and definitive models were the S-1S with the 134-kW (180 hp) IO-360-B4A engine, the S-1T with the 149-kW (200-hp) AEIO-360-A1E driving a constant speed propeller, the S-2A with the same engine, and the S-2B with the 194-kW (260-hp) AEIO-540-D4A5.

In 1983 Christen Industries bought Pitts, continuing production of current models and introducing the S-2S single-seat version of the S-2B.

PITTS S-1 SPECIAL
Role: Aerobatic sportsplane
Crew/Accommodation: One
Power Plant: One 180-hp Lycoming 10-360-B4A air-cooled flat-opposed
Dimensions: Span 5.28 m (17.33 ft); length 4.72 m (15.5 ft); wing area 9.15 m² (98.5 sq ft)
Weights: Empty 327 kg (720 lb); MTOW 522 kg (1,150 lb) Performance: Maximum speed 285 km/h (177 mph) at sea level; operational ceiling 6,795 m (22,300 ft); range 507 km (315 miles)
Load: None

Pitts S-2C Special

INDEX

INDEX

ACKNOWLEDGEMENTS

All images in this book are the copyright of Regency House Publishing Limited, other than the following, which were sourced through www.creativecommons.org and www.gnu.org licenses via www.wikimedia.org and www.flickr.com.

Page 436: 100yen, Page 287: Bill Abbot, Page 258: Abdallahh, Page 306: Aero Icarus, Page 283: Akradecki, Page 378: Albrechtsburg1485, Page 157: Allocer, Page 334: Andy from Glasgow, Page 386: Arkansas Shutter Bug, Page 388, 442: Ruth AS, Page 69: Dylan Ashe, Page 105: Peter Astby, Page 318: Barcex, Page 399: Cory Barnes, Page 428, 434: Josh Beasley, Page 422 Martin Bergner, Page 302: Bidgee Page 431: Bob Bixby, Page 415: Derek Blackadder, Page 240: Bledoliki, Page 259, 344: boeingdreamscape, Page 345: Bot (Magnus Manske), Page 210: Brian Burnell, Page 324, 339: BriYYZ, Page 346: Calflier001, Page 249, 261: Phillip Capper, Page 111: George Chernilevesky, Page 330, 340: Contri, Page 310: Guy Coroller, Page 363: Craig Cullum, Page 397: James Dale 10, Page 104: Daniel VDM, Page 8: Darren, Page 245: Dan Davidson, Page 327: Gerald Delafond, Page 323, 333, Andrei Dimotte, Page 201: DJGB, Page 101: Donderwonk, Page 440: El Grato, Page 353, 369: Robert Emerley, Page 398: ep-jhu, Page 412: Mark Evans, Page 419: Fairchildbrad, Page 368 Flavio@Flickr, Page 358: Andy Fogg, Page 365: Böhringer Friedrich, Page 307: Paul Friel, Page 338: Matteo Forni, Page 94, 95, 171, 213: Duch. Seb, Page 199: Marc Evans, Page 237: Europfighter Typhoon Image Library, Page 247: Foucdeg, Page 128: Franiaz, Page 56: Garette, Page 320, 361: Lukasz Golowanow & Maciek Hyps, Page 161 above & below, 383: Jim Gordon, Page 152: Roger Green, Page 409: Greenlane, Page 426: GSL, Page 392: Teijo Hakald, Page 29: Aaron Headley, Page 127: High Contrast, Page 282: Tony Hisgett, Page 423: Spotter Iannuon, Page 432: Michael Perekas, Page 172, 314: Premyslaw Jahr, Page 107: Jochem Jansen, Page 416: JLS Media, Page 246: Patr Kadlec, Page 288: Chad Kainz, Page 429: S. Kaiser, Page 221 KellyV, Page 356: Doo Ho King, Page 319, 336: Pavel Kobersky, Page 132: Konflikty.pl, Page 118: KGyst, Page 33, 52, 59 144 above, 193: Kogo, Page 316: Laangmo, Page 277: Last minute, Pafge 382 Jason Leffowitz, Page 115, 174: Leonid Kruzhkov, Page 31: Vassilii Khachaturov, Page 299: Makaristos, Page 166, 325, 372: Ronnie Macdonald, Page 298: Trevor Macinnis, Page 12: Marco, Page 227: Maarten (supercharged), Page 57 below, 194, 195, 413, 417: Pete Markham, Page 83: Paul Maritz, Page 303: Matze1989, Page 260: Stefan Maurer, Page 2, 3, 5, 51, 58, 168, 169, 225, 375, 376, 384, 385, 387: mashleymorgan, Page 315: Mathieu Marquer, Page 34: Thom May, Page 290: Ad Meskens, Page 265: Michael Miley, Page 41, 61: Ken Mist, Page 305, 311, 328, 332, 337, 347: Dean Morley, Page 292, 293, 317: Dmitry A Mottl. Page 155: Peter Mulligan, Page 304: Ian Multto Page 151 below, 390: Nehrams 2020, Page 167 Nerdamano, Page 178: Richardo Nicola, Page 253: NJRZA, Page 309: SSGT David Nolan, Page 341: Outanxio, Page 301: Paavo, Page 322 Angel Paez, Page 443: Guillaume Paumier, Page 286: Dimitry Pichugin, Page 258: Paava Pihelgas, Page 380 Jean-Guy Pitre, Page 9: Adam Pniak, Page 335: Douchet Quentin, Page 364: H Raab, Page 427: Richardo Reis, Page 436: karen Roe, Page 248: Andrew RT on behalf of Wing Cmdr. Derek Martin, Page 393 David Rubin, Page 381: Donna Rutherford, Page 218, 256: Scott Sanders, Page 110: Shirephantom, Page 203, 228: Sergei Sorokin, Page 57 top, David Steadman, Page 357, 373: Jim Sher, Page 17: Shuttleworth Collection, Page 435: Hugh Simmons, Page 144 Below: Mark Skarratts Page 300: Skistar, Page 185: Lucas Skywalker Page 143: Jane Belinda Smith, Page 400: Ryan Sommer, Page 97, 420, 430: Stahkocher, Page 85, 100, 271: Harranders Svensson, Page 145: Andrew Stawarz, Page 242, 243: Sukhoi, Page 389: Konrad Summers, Page 35: Tataquax, Page 321: Martin Teschner, Page 425: T.M.O.F, Page 102: Jarek Tuszynski, Page 89, 177, 211: Ronald Turner, Page 410: TWM1340, Page 6: TVL1970, Page 266, 284: Hauhu Uet, Page 151 above: Ed Uthman, Page 331: Vince42, Page 114: Walle 83, Page 421: Jens Wiemann, Page 113: Wojsyl, Page 297, 355, : WO ST 01, Page 55: TM Wolf, Page 359, 366: TSRL, Page 184: Year of the Dragon, Page 342: Yummifruitbat, Page 279, 294: Yssy guy, Page 216: Taras Young,

447